HIDES, HEMLOCKS AND ADIRONDACK HISTORY

HIDES, HEMLOCKS AND ADIRONDACK HISTORY

How the Tanning Industry Influenced the Region's Growth

Barbara McMartin

NORTH COUNTRY BOOKS

Utica, NY

Published by North Country Books, Utica, New York, 13501

Library of Congress Cataloguing-in Publication Data

McMartin, Barbara
Hides, Hemlocks and Adirondack History / by Barbara McMartin
p. cm.
Includes bibliographical references (p.) and index.
ISBN 0-932052-99-1 (cloth)
1. Tanners-New York (State)-Adirondack Mountains-History-19th entury. 2. Tanning-Adirondack Mountains-History-19th century. 3. Leather industry and trade-New York (State)-Adirondack Mountains-History-19th century. 4. Tsuga.
I. Title
HD9780.U53A356 1992
338.4'767523'097475-dc20 91-42447
CIP

Printed in the United States of America

Jacket design by Richard Loomis;
jacket and end paper photograph courtesy of the Adirondack Museum

Acknowledgements

Numerous individuals have helped me with this book: town and county historians who have shared their files, people who remembered the tanneries, collectors who found old photographs, and writers who have documented parts of the history. I am indebted to all of them and have listed them in footnotes and in the Bibliography because they provided the true resources for this book. Most notable was the last-minute help I received from Joe Conway, Tim Fitzgerald, and Ted Comstock that enabled me to solve a Lewis County mystery. I wish to thank all those who gave me permission to quote extensively from the various sources listed in the Bibliography.

I was aided immensely by the Baker Library at Harvard Business School, which gave me permission to study and use material from the R. G. Dun Ledgers. Helen Burnham of the Croton Free Library helped me secure microfilms of the U. S. Census of Manufactures so I could study them leisurely. Jerold Pepper of the Adirondack Museum and Barbara Germain of the Johnstown Public Library were most helpful.

Special thanks are due James C. Dawson for help with maps; Jerold Pepper for commenting on the book's organization; E. H. Ketchledge for insight into forest history; Philip G. Terrie, Adirondack historian, for pushing me to explore just how much forest was left; Richard Nason of International Paper Company for checking my discussion of the lumber industry; Clyde Griffen of Vassar College for suggesting ways to strengthen the book and for encouraging me to look at the industry's effects on Adirondack towns and their inhabitants; and Richard Wiles, economic historian from Bard College, who shared his knowledge of the earlier Catskill tanning industry and national trends at the end of the Adirondack era.

Thanks also to my husband, W. Alec Reid for helping prepare the charts and drawings and for carefully reading the text. Paul S. Brady and Carlene Lankton also gave the text a careful reading and offered many suggestions for making the writing clearer and more precise.

Barbara McMartin has a PhD in Mathematics. She grew up in Fulton County on the fringe of the Adirondack Park and has long been fascinated by that county's tanning industry and the wild lands within the Park. She has written thirteen guides for outdoors people, a history of an Adirondack town, booklets explaining various aspects of the Adirondack Park Agency, and numerous articles.

For the past three decades she has devoted herself to Adirondack causes, most recently as chairman of the Committee for the 1992 Adirondack Park Centennial. In this book she combines her interest in wild lands with her thirst for historical knowledge.

Contents

Part II A County-by-County Look at the Tanning Industry

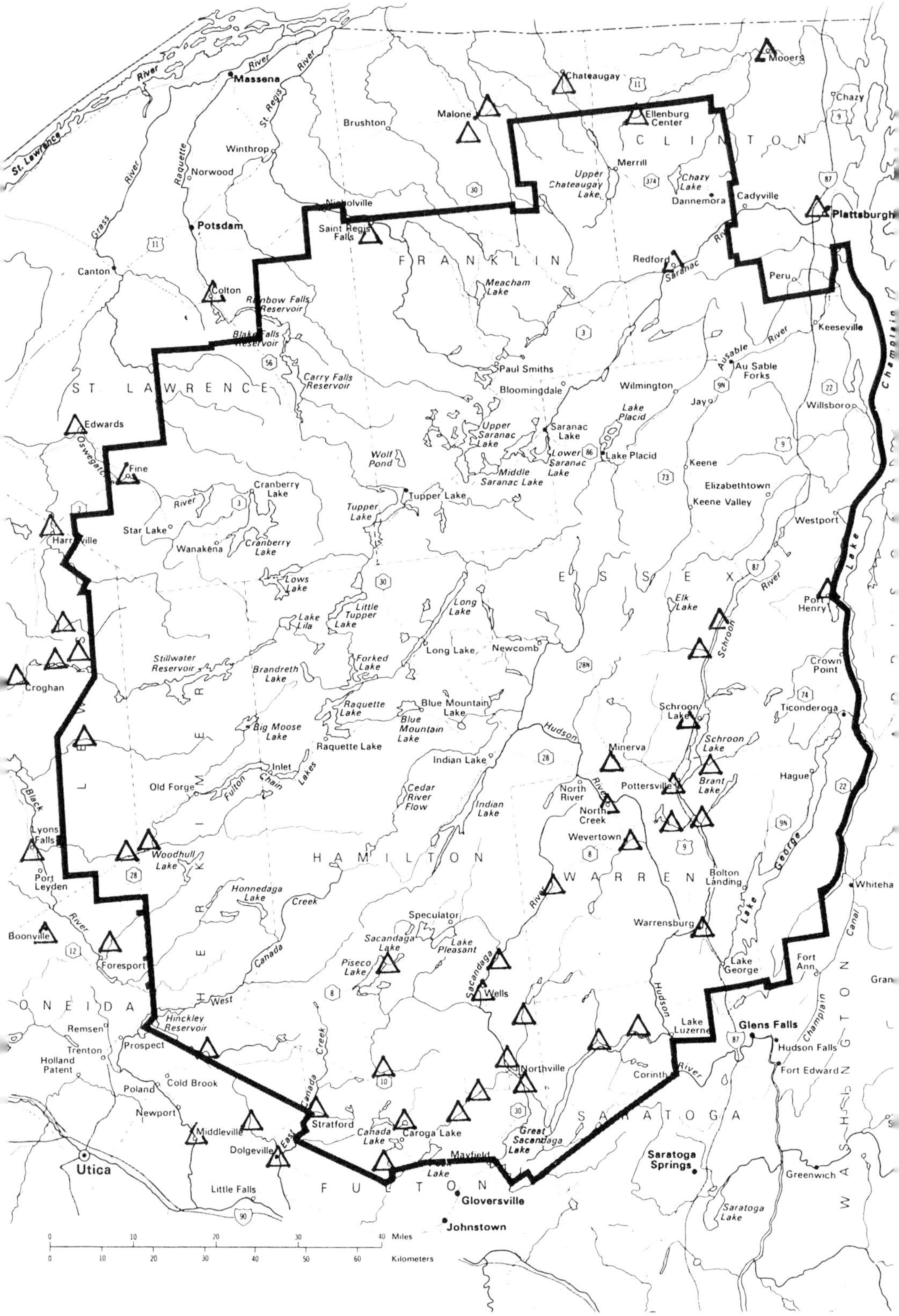
St. Lawrence
River
Massena
River
St. Regis
River
Brushton
Malone
Chateaugay
Mooers
Chazy
Ellenburg Center
CLINTON
Winthrop
Norwood
Raquette
Grass
River
Merrill
Upper Chateaugay Lake
Chazy Lake
Dannemora
Cadyville
Plattsburgh
Nicholville
Saint Regis Falls
Potsdam
Canton
FRANKLIN
Redford
Saranac
River
Peru
Colton
Rainbow Falls Reservoir
Meacham Lake
Blake Falls Reservoir
Keeseville
Ausable
River
Au Sable Forks
Carry Falls Reservoir
Paul Smiths
Bloomingdale
Wilmington
ST. LAWRENCE
Jay
Willsboro
Lake Placid
Edwards
Upper Saranac Lake
Saranac Lake
Oswegatchie
Wolf Pond
Lower Saranac Lake
Lake Placid
Keene
Fine
Middle Saranac Lake
Cranberry Lake
Tupper Lake
Elizabethtown
Keene Valley
River
Tupper Lake
Westport
Star Lake
Harrisville
Wanakena
Cranberry Lake
Lake
ESSEX
River
Lows Lake
Long Lake
Elk Lake
Port Henry
Lake Lila
Little Tupper Lake
Schroon
Long Lake
Newcomb
Crown Point
Stillwater Reservoir
Brandreth Lake
Forked Lake
Croghan
Raquette Lake
Blue Mountain Lake
Schroon Lake
Ticonderoga
Big Moose Lake
Blue Mountain Lake
Hudson
Raquette Lake
Schroon Lake
Inlet
Indian Lake
Minerva
Black
Old Forge
Fulton
Chain
Lakes
Cedar River Flow
North River
Pottersville
Hague
Brant Lake
Indian Lake
North Creek
Lyons Falls
Wevertown
Woodhull Lake
HAMILTON
Bolton Landing
George
Port Leyden
WARREN
Whitehall
Honnedaga Lake
Creek
River
Lake
River
Warrensburg
Canal
Boonville
Speculator
Sacandaga Lake
Lake Pleasant
Foresport
Piseco Lake
Sacandaga
Lake George
Fort Ann
ONEIDA
West
Canada
Wells
Hudson
Remsen
Hinckley Reservoir
Lake Luzerne
Glens Falls
Champlain
Trenton
Prospect
Creek
Hudson Falls
Holland Patent
Northville
Corinth
River
Fort Edward
Cold Brook
Poland
Canada
Newport
Stratford
SARATOGA
Middleville
Canada Lake
Caroga Lake
Great Sacandaga Lake
WASHINGTON
Utica
Dolgeville
East
Mayfield
Saratoga Springs
Lake
Greenwich
FULTON
Gloversville
Little Falls
Johnstown
Saratoga Lake
Lake Champlain
0 10 20 30 40 Miles
0 10 20 30 40 50 60 Kilometers

Illustrations

Photographs and Drawings

Foundation Sketches

Charts

Maps

Foreword

Deep in the Adirondack wilderness are any number of hidden stories, rocks and excavations that tell of long-lost communities. I remember the first time I crossed the bridge above the beautiful Griffin Falls and headed into the second-growth forest of balsam and popple—tall, straight, mature trees that concealed a row of boulders. What appeared to be an old fence is the foundation of a tannery, which was built in the late 1870s. I followed the rock-work; it leads to a second foundation, this one with a cellar with arched windows. After poking about in the rubble of old fire bricks, I found metal pipes, straps, and fittings for the old steam boiler. Later, I even discovered pieces of leather and parts of a bark grinder.

Since that first discovery, I have explored many such sites, wondering at their origins, the people who worked there, and their role in Adirondack history. I began a collection of old photographs, newspaper clippings, diaries, deeds, and reminiscences. I consulted county histories and wrote to town historians to discover what I could. I talked with as many as I could find of the old timers, who have themselves pursued the tannery stories, mostly because their ancestors were a part of that history.

Then, more than a decade ago, I put aside all the pieces of the puzzle in a box, frustrated that all the pieces fit imperfectly. No matter how hard I tried to match the bits gathered from one source with the clues from another, the picture remained fragmented. With the exception of a few articles and local histories, tanning in the Adirondacks has never been documented. The more than one hundred years that have transpired since the heyday of Adirondack hemlock bark tanning has removed reality from living memory; the hand-me-down stories I found were riddled with fancy. I was thwarted at every turn, for not only was no portion of the account without missing pieces, the pieces I found did not fit. Worst of all, the whole just did not add up to the exciting story I knew the fragments concealed.

When I bemoaned this state to Stephen Farrar of Warrensburg (another tannery buff, now deceased, whom I interviewed over a decade ago, when he was in his 90s), he wisely said, "Don't think of it as a cup half empty, but a cup half full." I revised my plans for the book, asking questions that led to a much fuller understanding of the industry as a whole and its relation to the Adirondacks. It became obvious that the details I had uncovered were too much to integrate into a cohesive work. The solution was not to try to weave all the components together into as complete a story as possible, but to divide the book into two parts.

Part I of this book explores the effects of sole-leather tanning on Adirondack forests, the lost communities of the Adirondacks, the economic value of the industry to the region, the lives of a few of those associated with the tanning industry, and the ultimate return of many of the tannery sites to wilderness. It investigates those whose investments made tanning possible in the Adirondacks, and describes how successful were these investments. It examines the changes tanning brought to the Adirondacks and attempts to compare the impact of the tanning industry with that of the logging industry. It does so by summarizing the elements of these topics common to Adirondack tanneries in general. The economics of Adirondack hemlock bark tanning are analyzed in the context of nineteenth century economic patterns. All these aspects are ultimately directed toward discovering why the industry disappeared from the mountains as precipitously as it did.

Then, in a county-by-county analysis of tanneries, chapters in Part II illustrate the themes of Part I with anecdotes from specific tanneries. In this way, the second part of the book, the "what happened," but not the "why it happened," is, on the one hand, a series of appendices that substantiate the statements in Part I and on the other hand it is a richer narrative of the occurrences in each county than has ever before been assembled. Part II is enlivened by comparisons of the relative size of the tanneries in this industry where everything was large and inspired exaggeration.

Originally, this book was conceived as the contents of Part II, a description of the locations of tanneries and tales of how they produced leather in the wilderness. But, as the economic picture of individual tanneries emerged, it became obvious that there were some major patterns governing all of them. These patterns permit Part I to show why and how the tanning industry developed in parts of the Adirondacks, how its growth and prosperity paralleled events in the rest of the nation, and why tanning ultimately disappeared from these mountains.

This division allowed me to include in Part II all the individual stories and the statistical information, as well as the few first-hand accounts available. They are designed to give a sense of place and people through small stories arranged according to their geographical origins. They are organized so that the stories told by the few voices from the past are included as they were written or spoken. It is their sum that illustrates the Adirondack story. I had attempted to weave all these details into a work that breathed the life of long ago and at the same time explored the industry as a whole. That attempt defeated me and frustrated me. I was frustrated that the parts are not all equally rich in detail; some in fact are so sketchy that whole tanneries are lost in the haze of history. The inevitable inconsistencies of the historical record, some markedly stronger than others, make uneven descriptions. But no one tannery could give all the details of the complex story of tanning in the Adirondacks. The short accounts flesh each other out and add up to a rich mosaic. Their inclusion permits a bit of effervescence in the individual stories that reflects the life of long ago. This book is organized like a two-dimensional matrix, and is designed to be read that way. Pick and choose among the stories to illustrate the major Adirondack themes, or read the county-by-county chapters for the details that are of regional interest.

> *That errors have occurred in so great a number of names and dates as are here given is probable; and that names have been omitted which should have been inserted is quite certain. We can only say that we have exercised more than ordinary diligence and care in this difficult and complicated feature of book making. Of such as feel aggrieved in consequence of errors or omissions we beg pardon, and ask the indulgence of the reader.*

I found this paragraph in the preface to the 1872-1873 **Gazetteer and Business Directory of Lewis County**. That H. Child, the author, should be so convinced of his potential errors is prophetic—this book is based on resources just like his, making it impossible to detect and correct the errors of people and place that this book must inevitably contain. I welcome corrections of these particular errors; but do not let these details detract from reading what follows for the larger story of how the tanning industry influenced the development of the Adirondacks.

Barbara McMartin

Part I

A Look at Tanning Throughout the Adirondacks

I

Introduction[1]

Tanning is one of the world's oldest crafts—or arts. Tanning has been carried on since before the time of the Pharaohs, when leather was thought to be as valuable as gold, silver, or ivory. It was used for clothing and footwear in almost every culture; for harnesses, helmets, and shields for warriors in ancient Greece; and for boat fittings on the earliest sailing vessels. Excavations and ruins have yielded pieces of leather that have been preserved for thousands of years.

Tanning is essentially the way of preserving the hides and skins of animals, turning them from something that will rot when wet to something called leather that is pliable, strong even when wet, and virtually waterproof. Many different methods of tanning have been employed over the centuries, but until just over a hundred years ago, almost all leather was made using some vegetable matter as the tanning agent.

Writings from many early cultures describe tanning: oak bark was used by the Hebrews of the Old Testament; the word tan can be traced to the Romans for it derives from the Medieval Latin word "tanare," which in turn derived from the Latin "tannum" meaning oak bark. It was a French chemist in the early nineteenth century who first applied the word "tannin" to the substance common to nuts and bark of many species that affected the tanning process.

In the Middle Ages guilds of tanners and leather workers were established. By the seventeenth century, both England and France had growing tanning centers. The earliest settlers in America did learn different techniques from the Indians for tanning deerskins, such as using the brains of deer as a tanning agent; but as early as 1623, settlers brought with them from

---

[1] Watson, Merril A. *Economics of Cattlehide Leather Tanning*, pp. 1-21. *The introduction to this study is an excellent short history of tanning and forms the basis of this introduction.*

England and Europe the knowledge of tanning with vegetable materials such as oak bark.

For many years, tanning leather for boots and shoes in America was basically a domestic craft carried out by almost every farmer, anyone who raised and slaughtered a cow. As communities grew and occupations became specialized, the local tanner received the hides of his neighbors' freshly slaughtered cows, oxen, or horses. These he laboriously cleaned and tanned in vats sunk in the ground. There were innumerable small, one-man tanneries throughout the early colonies. By 1810, there were 867 tanneries in New York State, twenty percent of the total number of tanneries in the country.[2]

By the nineteenth century, tanning had become such a well-documented craft that numerous books were written about it. Tanning centers concentrated the work as tanneries grew in size. One of the early large complexes was located in the "Swamp" in the area of Manhattan that is beside the East River and now under the Brooklyn Bridge. In New York State, tanning was a vital part of the region's growth and the fifth largest industry in the number of establishments.

Early in the nineteenth century, the country grew rapidly, and the need for shoes and boots kept pace. The need for leather was so great, in fact, that the slaughter of cows for hides outstripped their slaughter for meat. A segment of the economy became devoted to importing and shipping hides from the western United States and from South and Central America, and as Chapter II will show, these regions became the principal source of hides for New York State's tanning industry.

Tanning was dependent on such enormous amounts of tanning materials, the barks of oaks and hemlocks, that the tanneries followed the forests–through Delaware and the Virginias seeking oak, west across Massachusetts and north along the Hudson River seeking hemlock. When these supplies were exhausted, tanneries sprang up in the northern Catskills, and after a few short decades there, they moved south and west through the Catskills an on to Pennsylvania as well as north into the Adirondacks. Finally, toward the end of the nineteenth century, the tanneries moved west across New York and Pennsylvania and on to Michigan and Wisconsin in search of hemlock.

---

[2] United States Census of American Manufactures, 1810

For a brief moment in history, tanning was a very important industry in the Adirondacks. This book will show that tanning had **a value to the local economy at least half the size and scale of logging** and the production of finished lumber. This moment, which began in the eastern and southern Adirondacks just before 1850, reached its zenith in the Adirondacks in the two decades from 1860 to 1880. Tanning declined precipitously in the eastern and southern Adirondack regions after 1880 but continued at a reduced level in the northwestern mountain region until 1890. By 1895, hemlock bark tanning of sole leather was all but a fleeting memory. But, in these four decades, tanning helped shape the pattern of development and expansion in the Adirondacks; and when tanning ceased, many Adirondack communities declined so much that it took seven decades for their populations to begin to recover. Tannery sites spawned small towns in every county, over a dozen in Warren and Essex counties alone, but even in these communities, there is hardly any evidence today that the tanneries had ever been there. And, some of the largest tanneries and their settlements have just faded back into wilderness.

Huge tannery centers were located around the borders of the Adirondacks. They were built where hemlock was abundant and where transportation by railroads, canals, and plank roads was not too distant to bring in the raw hides, which had been shipped across the seas from distant ports. Most tanneries were built on the fringes of what is now the Adirondack Park, but several were located in the heart of the Park's mountain region. By 1870, a few tanneries were built at sites so deep in the wilderness, so far from railheads and navigable waters, that today their locations seem almost impossible as industrial sites. The roads that reached them were dirt tracks, usable only a few months of the year. The desperate need to be close to the source of hemlock forced the tanneries to move deeper and deeper into the wilderness; modes of transportation were influenced by the ruggedness and remoteness of the region. Ultimately, transportation proved to be a limiting factor. Whole regions within the Park never had tanneries and many forests never were harvested for hemlock.

Tanning was dependent on enormous quantities of water and the waste waters, laden with hair, flesh, acids, and spent bark polluted many streams. Contemporary stories and anecdotes will document the way tanneries were tremendous sources of pollution. In the century plus since the last Adirondack hemlock bark tannery closed, nature has erased that pollution as effectively as time has caused the tanneries to fade from memory.

Tanning was never considered a romantic industry as logging was—less romance attached to hauling bark than to shooting logs down rain-swollen rivers, and none at all to the tanneries with their stench and filth. The life of a tannery worker was a back-breaking, twelve-hour day (ten in winter), six days a week, in smelly, drafty, dirty conditions that made the dangers of a sawmill seem a welcome challenge. For most of the workers, the pay was not good.

Hemlock trees were cut and stripped of their bark, and more often than not, their naked trunks just left to rot where they were felled. Tanners cleared the hemlock from huge circles ten to twenty miles in diameter around their tanneries. In those pockets where hemlock happened to be the dominant species, forest destruction was fairly dramatic. When most of the readily accessible hemlock vanished, the demise of the tanning industry was precipitous and spectacular. But the most surprising aspect of what happened to the forests was not how much of the hemlock forest was gone, but how much was left.

For the owners, the financial risks were great, the rewards only rarely commensurate with the risk. A few local tanners prospered, but more failed; bankruptcies were common. Searching for the identities of owners and investors leads to leather brokers and dealers in New York and Boston. Their larger wealth and greater access to money insulated them for a time from the industry's problems, but even these men experienced financial difficulties. Then suddenly, beginning about 1880, more and more tanneries closed, and in a remarkably brief few years, they all disappeared. For years, it has been said that the advent of chemical tanning agents and the loss of bark were responsible for the sudden demise of the tanneries. These are myths which I believed, and helped perpetuate. Neither is true. Chemical tanning agents had no direct effect on the departure of the sole-leather tanneries from the Adirondacks. The failure of the accessible bark supply had a dramatic impact; but, as will be shown, the real reasons for the industry's demise in the Adirondacks were much more complicated. They are rooted in the nation's economy—bank failures and financial panics—and changes in the tanning industry throughout the country that revolutionized the industry and redirected its focus to new sites.

A distinctly Adirondack feature comes from the tanners themselves. Curiously, while some Catskill tanners were men of letters and political influence, giants who left a written record of their activities, this was not the case in the Adirondacks. Here we meet men of mystery, mere footnotes in local history or distant owners whose primary interests lay elsewhere. The few first-hand accounts of tanneries are newspaper articles or reminiscences of workers, not of the men who owned or ran the tanneries. And the record that exists is scarcely enough to breathe life into the story of the countless immigrants, mostly Irish, who toiled in the tanneries and the adjacent woods.

It is surprising how meager are the references to tanneries in most nineteenth and early twentieth century local histories. For most writers, the tanneries were an enigma. Many referred to the local tannery as the "largest in the area," or the "largest in the state." Even local newspaper accounts contain such superlatives. These exaggerations are a humorous leitmotif in all the accounts, but they are much more than local boosterism: they depict a lack of local understanding of the industry as a whole.

Other themes that are common to all the accounts in the second part of this book are "the tannery failed," "the forest failed"; but the stories are much more complex. The failures were sometimes personal ones, sometimes as the result of outside economic pressures, sometimes occurring through natural causes such as fire and flood, and sometimes from the rising cost of bark. Even though the stories fall in patterns, they are all quite different. Those details endow the economic patterns with a richness that is a vital characteristic of the Adirondack story.

Both these themes, the exaggeration and the hints of economic problems, appear in contemporary accounts in short phrases for a reason. Contemporary writers and later historians viewed the local tannery in the same way as the proverbial mouse trying to describe an elephant. They had no idea of the relative size of the industry, the role of the financiers, and the complexities of the financial arrangements associated with Adirondack tanneries. The local manager was remembered, but the real owner was often unknown or known only as a disembodied name. Even local historians have failed to sense the relation between the local managers and the owners; in fact, they often were unaware of the true owners. Descriptions of the industry lack a sense of perspective between the local tannery and the national industry. The naieveté with which the tanning industry was viewed and remembered is a striking theme in the Adirondack story; imparting this missing perspective to the Adirondack tanning industry is the major theme of this book.

A particularly salient element of the Adirondacks is the paradoxical role of size and scale that tanning played in the economy. On the one hand, tanning had an extraordinary effect on the region, building whole towns. Because it was a year-round manufacturing operation, tanning had a greater impact on the growth of the region than did logging. On the other hand, in relation to the tanning industry in the rest of the country, Adirondack tanning played a minor role. Through the examination of figures that quantify tanning in the Adirondacks, this paradox becomes apparent.

The most pronounced effect of tanning on the Adirondacks was what it did for the region's towns and settlements—tanneries spawned whole towns. For many different reasons, some of those towns survived, though their populations shrank. Population levels of 1880 were not attained again in most towns until after the middle of the twentieth century. Few towns were as prosperous through the first half of the twentieth century as they were in 1880. More spectacularly, some of the towns faded into the wilderness, disappearing as completely as if they had never existed. Both kinds of development are important features of the Adirondack story.

The era of Adirondack tanning occurred at a time when the number of tanneries in the United States was rapidly decreasing and when the size of tanneries was significantly increasing. This pattern of consolidation of industry and increasing size of manufacturers typifies the second half of the nineteenth century, not just in the tanning industry, but in almost every industry in the nation. Here the Adirondack story parallels the national pattern.

Between 1840 and 1860, the number of tanneries in the country fell from 8,229 to 5,188 while the value of the product increased threefold. By 1890, the number of tanneries had declined to 1,787. Already, by 1860, 148 of New York State's 863 tanneries (of all kinds) were in or near the Adirondacks.[3] Following the same pattern, the number of tanneries in the Adirondacks as well as the State total decreased through the end of the century. What differentiates the Adirondacks is the fact that the

[3] United States Census of Manufactures

tanneries did not merely decrease in number, they disappeared altogether.

As the numbers shrank, the tanneries grew in size. In 1850, only 14 of the 153 tanneries in the Adirondack region were large complexes; but in 1880, fully 54 of the remaining 112 tanneries were truly large.[4] Some of the tanneries were without question among the largest in the nation at the time. The sheer size of the operations and their rapid demise are important Adirondack characteristics. Part II recovers details of that lost world.

The exploration of these themes richly illustrates the growth of the industry, but it leaves unexplained the causes of the industry's demise.

The existence of the local tannery was vulnerable to all sorts of threats from the terror of fire to the precarious financial nature of the industry and the failure of the local bark supply. However, ultimately, it is the separation between the region and its outside owners and financiers that explains the industry's demise. National trends controlled the industry. The outside entrepreneurs were the ones who bore the weight of the failures; they were the ones who sought to make the industry survive, even if that meant relocating it. Changes in the industry nationally and the consolidation and verticalization of the industry are the underlying reasons the giants of the tanning world concluded that the Adirondacks was no longer the place in to expand their operations. Business decisions that had little relation to the Adirondacks finally drove the industry away so completely that it became obliterated, not even a part of the region's memory.

Paradoxically, improved transportation, new rail lines that pierced not only the heart of the Adirondacks but the wilds of Wisconsin and Michigan, made it possible to bring hemlock bark and extract to tanneries that were built closer to either meat packers or shoe manufacturers. Methods of using chemicals for tanning were being perfected, diminishing the need for bark. At the end of the Adirondack tanning era, the region began to ship bark to distant tanneries. The region no longer enjoyed the economic benefits that derive from manufacturing. The Adirondacks became a supplier of raw materials; and, as this classic story of

---

4 *See the definitions in Chapter V for the way this text quantifies the size and scale of Adirondack tanneries.*

exploitation for raw materials unfolded, the region's economy and population began to shrink.

The lands were here for their forests to be taken; then the lands were abandoned to revert to wilderness. Only one owner had any concern for what was left; the Claflin enterprises created the first planned resort community in the Adirondacks from their tannery lands. No other owner saw that the lands were valuable for uses other than the harvest of logs.

Historically this was a lost story, with few visible signs to point to its existence. Discovering the story and its underlying rationale has been an exciting challenge.

II

The Tanning Process[1]

What Does Tanning Do?

Every nineteenth-century account and many local Adirondack histories dwelt on the peculiarities of the process, often omitting much that was historically interesting, information that is of much greater interest today. Perhaps writers placed emphasis on the process because it seemed so strange and was so poorly understood. Even though tanning texts noted great variations in procedures, all tanning followed certain basic steps.

As noted, tanning is a process that prevents the rotting of hides and skins even when they are wet, making the skins strong, pliable, and waterproof. Animal skins consist of fibers and gelatins that quickly decompose and rot when wet. Tanning alters the gelatins so that they will not putrefy. They are somewhat changed chemically to make them sufficiently pliable to be useful, yet durable, under the types of wear intended. Many, many kinds of hides and skins are tanned, and there are many different tanning processes. Similarly, there are many different uses of leather: clothing, shoes and boots, harnesses, industrial belting, saddles, gloves, and so on.

The Adirondack story is basically about cattle hides that were tanned for soles and uppers for boots and shoes. This book describes both kinds of tanneries, but focuses on those that tanned the heavy hides used for sole leather. Tanning was a

---

[1] This summary is compiled from five sources: Watson, ibid, pp. 2-3; New England Tanners Club, *Leather Facts*, pp. 1-40 and most important of all, the treatise by Charles Thomas Davis, *The Manufacture of Leather*. This book was written in 1885 and sumarizes all the processes and equipment from barking to finishing leather in use in the United States at the time. The fourth source is Campbell Morfit, *The Arts of Tanning, Currying, and Leather Dressing*, 1852, which describes tanning as the Adirondack era began. The fifth source is *Modern American Tanning*, 1902, compiled from articles in **Hide and Leather**, which describes tanning practices at the close of the Adirondack era. .

vegetable process that, in the Adirondacks, used exclusively the bark of hemlocks as the source of tannin. Hemlock bark contains more tannin than other northern trees and it replaced the tannin from oak and chestnut bark that was becoming exhausted in southern states.

Hides were taken from large animals such as oxen, cows, and horses. (The term skins is used by tanners to refer to the skins of smaller animals, goats, sheep, deer, and pigs for instance, which involve different tanning methods and materials). At first, as tanning became a specialized craft, the tanner either slaughtered cows or bought **hides** from neighbors. In the tanning process, the tanner cut the hides in two along the back from neck to tail to make them easier to handle. These halves of tanned hides were called **sides**. In all the statistical references noted in this book, input is given in numbers of hides, output is exactly doubled, for it represents the number of sides.

The tanning of each hide required twelve times its weight in bark, dozens of gallons of water, and a series of labor-intensive operations. The steps in the process, which are described below–beaming, bating, unhairing, plumping, fulling–were all similar to those of today. The only differences today are the synthetic chemicals that replace the vegetable matter–bark–used in the tanning process and the fact that hides do not have to be shipped to the chemical source. With the exception of a few labor-saving devices and better organization and greater efficiency that reduced the time required for tanning, the nineteenth century's operations were remarkably similar to those of early colonial times; they were almost as labor-intensive and only fractionally less time-consuming.

Steps in the Process

If the tannery was close to the source of hides, the tanning process began immediately, with "**green**" hides; but, most often, the tannery was at some distance from the source. After a cow or steer was slaughtered and the hide removed, it was either **dried** or **salted** or sometimes both salted and dried to temporarily halt any rotting. Hides were salted to dry and preserve them. The salted hides were often shipped to tanneries over great distances by boat, so the condition of the hides when they arrived at the tanneries was often not the best.

At the tannery, salted hides were trimmed and sorted, then soaked in water to remove the salt and soften the hides somewhat. Sometimes, hides were suspended from **rockers**, whose agitating action hastened the softening of the hides and their water absorption. After the **soak**, they were sometimes placed in a softening mill—a device that beat or agitated the hides in water. Then they were scraped to remove any flesh, blood, or fatty substances—the **fleshing** process.

Next they were placed in warm rooms to **sweat** in order to loosen the hair, a tricky process that brought the hides to the point of incipient decomposition. Further soaking in a **lime** solution loosened the **hair**, and permitted its removal—the **unhairing** process. **Liming**, which took from four to six days, also caused the hides to swell, making them, the tanner thought, more susceptible to the tanning operation. From time immemorial, lime, which is a fine source of alkali, has been used in the preparation of cattle hides for tanning. The alkali penetrates the hide, opens the hair-follicles so that the animal hair may be removed, and assists in the disposal of the epidermal tissue, which is not useful in the leather. Liming not only removes much useless material, it has a hardening effect, useful in the ultimate production of sole and belt leather.

As part of the unhairing process, hides were usually placed upon a beam—a convex array of boards forming a sort of half-barrel, and **beamed** or scraped with a blunt, curved knife. (A few beam boards and knives survive from the Adirondack era.)[2] During the nineteenth century, mechanical methods of beaming were introduced, but there is no indication that any these of devices were used in Adirondack tanneries. Some tanneries sold the removed or **spent** hair to be used as a binder in plaster or for felt and blankets. Except in one case, there is no indication that hair was shipped out of the Adirondacks for these uses.

The cleaned hides were washed again, then **bated** to remove the lime. Tanning is basically an acidifying process. It is essential to get rid of the alkali, which liming has introduced. This is done by **bating**, a word for soaking in a fairly strong acid solution. Until the nineteenth century the acid solutions were wholly natural in origin: skins were bated by the process of adding dung

2 *The Fulton County, Caroga, and Adirondack museums all have beam boards and knives.*

and animal manure, which, in addition to countering the alkali of lime, restored some of the bulk to the hide that was removed by the lime and allowed a separation of fibers, so that a much softer texture is produced. Those Adirondack tanners who tanned upper leather did bate the hides, but bating with animal wastes was not generally used in the tanning of heavy hides for sole leather. For these hides, the process was referred to as **plumping**[3], which completed the swelling of the cells, distending the pores, and rendered the hides ready to absorb the tannin. Plumping was achieved either by washing the lime away or by reducing the alkali by the addition of an acid solution, of either sulphuric acid or an organic acid such as acetic acid. Carboys of acid were regularly transported to the distant tanneries along with the hides to be tanned.

It was at this stage, or earlier, before they were unhaired, that hides were cut in two lengthwise, creating two **sides** of more manageable size.

At every step in the process, great quantities of water were used; and, by today's standards, the spent water was considerably polluted with flesh, hair, lime, acid, tannin, and spent bark. Tales of pollution are found in the descriptions of Wheelerville and Griffin in Part II.

At each step, note that the tanner had to use his best judgment as to whether the step was completed, and the bating process, the removal of the lime, was considered the "most delicate and critical operation in the whole range of the manufacture of leather," because the tanner could only guess at the amount of lime removed.

Sides, now ready for the tanning process, were thought to contain indestructible fibers and a gelatin that must be made indestructible through the **tanning** process. At the beginning of the process in some operations, sides were suspended on **rockers**, movable frames that could agitate the suspended sides in huge tanks that contained the tanning **liquor**—an infusion of the bark from which the tannin was leached, by a method similar to the way coffee is infused from ground beans. A few Adirondack tanneries were equipped with rockers, but most took the cleaned and unhaired sides directly to the **vats**.

These vats were large rectangular wooden boxes, sunk into the ground, that measured three by eight feet by four feet

---

[3] Davis, ibid, p. 174

deep or larger. Sometimes these vats were filled with alternating layers of ground bark and sides and then filled with water. The water leached the tannin from the ground bark. As tanning proceeded, bark was added to increase the strength of the tanning **liquor.**

The vats were often arranged in vast rows of a hundred or more, either with a channel between the rows or a series of pipes connecting them, through which water and **liquors** could be circulated. Vast numbers of vats were required because of the length of time—upwards of eighteen months in Colonial times, more than six months in the later nineteenth century—that hides had to be soaked in tannin solutions to complete the tanning process. In the most elemental tanneries and in particular in most early Adirondack tanneries, this method of layering sides and ground bark was commonly used. The sides were moved from vat to vat with increasing amounts of bark added to increase the level of acidity. The combination of ground bark and water was also called the "**ooze.**" The sides had to be lifted from one vat to the next to make sure the tanning liquors reached all parts equally, or to advance them into stronger solutions.

Somehow, the tannin was thought to combine with the gelatins in the sides to complete the tanning process. While the heavy sides that were to become sole leather could be left in the tanning vats for as little as six months, usually most heavy Adirondack sides destined to become sole leather spent a much longer time in the vats. Temperature played an important role in the rate of tanning, and cool temperatures meant that most Adirondack sides took longer. Numerous inefficiencies on the part of the tanner also added to the time so that periods of twelve to eighteen months were not uncommon in the Adirondacks. Tanners and experts in tanning methods argued endlessly about the proper amount of time sides were required to remain in the vats with tannin.

In the more "modern" Adirondack tanneries, an alternate method was used. Tannin was leached from the ground bark in **leaches,** huge circular tubs filled with ground bark through which heated water was pumped. This tanning liquor was then circulated through the vats in increasingly acidic solutions.[4]

---

[4] The chapter on Clinton County contains the best contemporary descriptions of the complex workings of a tannery.

Complex systems of pipes and pumps were needed to circulate the tanning liquor.

A very few Adirondack operations used the large leaches to produce **extracts** of tannin for shipment to tanneries far from the source of the bark. Extract operations are discussed in Chapter V.

One figure that remained relatively constant throughout was the amount of bark needed to tan a hide: one cord could tan four to five hides.[5]

After they were deemed tanned, the sides were hung to dry in huge sheds that were often steam heated. Again, the tanner's judgement was critical, for if a side was dried too quickly, it became brittle; too slowly and it began to mold. Humidity in these open drying sheds had to be controlled to ensure the proper rate of drying. During the drying process, organic oils were applied to dry sides; either cod or menhaden oil, or paraffin, was used. Glucose and other sugars were sometimes added to the sides, to give them added weight and stiffness or strength.

Tanning added weight to the dry hides. Measures of quantities of hides or sides were often given in total pounds as well as in numbers of sides. The weight added by the tanning process was referred to as the **gain**, a measure of how successful the tannery was in converting the raw hides to leather.[6] In the 1830s, Gideon Lee said a maximum of 130 to 150 pounds of leather could be obtained from 100 pounds of dry hides.[7] However, a gain of 65% was common in the Catskills.[8]

Dyeing was not usually required because hemlock tanned sides were naturally a rich dark red-brown color, though the dark brown of oak tanning was considered superior in the early

---

[5] Although there is some disagreement on this figure, it is quoted in almost every nineteenth century text. Further, the Adirondack average of sides produced to cords of bark consumed as given in the United States Census of Manufactures confirms this figure.

[6] Gain is one of the consistent factors in comparing a tanner's economic effectiveness; figures relating to gain, either in pounds or in increased monetary value are analyzed in the economic studies of Chapters VI and VII. An average weight of 18½ pounds per side is used to convert figures from pounds to sides and vice-versa.

[7] A few tanners reported output in pounds tanned; most reported output in the number of sides tanned.

[8] Chapter III explores the improvements and simple efficiencies of operation that made resulted in increased gain in the Catskills.

nineteenth century. The bark available apparently changed the fashions of the times.

In the final steps, leather was rolled and beaten to produce a firm and uniform surface. By the middle of the nineteenth century, steam-powered machines had replaced beating the leather with the soles of the tanner's feet or pounding it with hammers. When beating machines and rolling mills were introduced, they did lighten somewhat this aspect of the tanner's backbreaking work; but the machines were dangerous to use and the work of operating them was—and remains even today—arduous as well. (Watching the lunging arm of the mechanical beaters that are still in use in the tanning industry is terrifying.) Rolling mills were quite common in the Adirondacks; mechanical beaters were not.

This book concentrates on **sole leather** tanners, but many Adirondack tanners used hemlock bark in the production of upper leather. The process for tanning **upper leather** was similar to that for sole leather, except that in the final processes the sides were shaved or split to make them thinner. **Splitting** or slicing laterally through the leather permits the outer, grain side to be used for uppers, the inner flesh side for gloves and clothing. The final step in producing upper leather was **currying**—treating the sides with oils to make them soft and pliable.

Smaller Adirondack tanners produced both sole and upper leather; a few concentrated on upper leather and skins other than cattle hides.

Chrome tanning was first described in 1858, but its use was not perfected and patents for it were not issued until 1884. This much-sought method of tanning would ultimately relieve tanners of their dependence on expensive forest operations and of the need to locate tanneries close to forest sources of tannin—and far from sources of hides and markets for leather. Initially, there were so many problems with chrome tanning that it was not used commercially until 1887[9], and then only for thinner, upper leather. Only Middleville among the Adirondack upper leather tanneries used chrome, and it did not do so until 1901. Cattle hides were not tanned with chrome until after 1920 because of the inherent difficulty of using chrome for these heavier hides.

---

[9] Watson, *Economics of Cattlehide Leather Tanning*, p. 9

Chemical tanning with chrome, thus, is not a factor in Adirondack tanning.[10]

Vegetable tanning for shoe and boot leathers remained the best and almost only way for heavy hides and it is used for soles even today, for some of that small proportion of soles not made from synthetic materials.

The sum of all these steps and operations is evidence that tanning was always labor intensive. In a later chapter, a review of the number of workers and their output demonstrates the level of this intensity in the Adirondacks.

For all the modifications in the process introduced in the nineteenth century, the basic steps and processes were the same as those performed by the Colonial tanner before the nineteenth century. The basic difference was that a pole to agitate sides in a vat served the role of rockers in later tanneries, but most of the tools were the same. Beam boards and beaming knives, scrapers, and vats sunk in holes in the Colonial tanner's yard accomplished the same work in early times as in the Adirondack era.

Art, Not Science

Even as the age of science and chemistry in industry was dawning, the tanning process was not only little changed, it was not really understood. Tanning was still an art or craft, handed down from tanner to tanner, described in writing in terms that detailed, but never explained, the process.

As late as 1838, Gideon Lee, a New York tanner whom we will meet in the introduction to the Swamp, wrote in his "Two Lectures on Tanning," delivered before the Eclectic Fraternity of New York, that "The still prevailing idea is (at least, with a large portion of the tanners,) that the tannin merely fills the open pores of the hide, *as mechanically as the mason's mortar fills the interstices of a wall, or as the shoemaker's threads or pegs fill the awl-holes.*"[11] Tanners were just beginning to understand the concept that tanning was a chemical reaction. Lee was the first to note that "the process of the formation of leather, from the moment the

---

[10] Ibid

[11] Emphasis added by Lee. Lee, *Two Lectures on Tanning*, p. 9

prepared hide or skin comes in contact with the ooze (the solution of tanning) until it is perfect leather is a purely chymical [sic] operation. It is the creation of a new substance, by means of chymical union of the pre-existing elementary substances."[12]

Understanding that this was the process, even if the process itself was not understood, did make tanners more aware of the need for care in the various tanning steps. As nineteenth century tanners became aware of the chemical nature of the process, they analyzed the tannin and acid content of different barks. That analysis led to the acceptance of hemlock as a tanning agent, but still the process was not fully understood. It is not surprising that an aura of mystery surrounded the tanning process until after the nineteenth century ended. Even in 1902, a treatise[13] on tanning talked about aspects of the process as if they were more a matter of art and not science; it warned of problems of putrefaction from the heating of piles of sides or of too much lime that removed too much gelatin, but there were still no scientific analyses of what were the right amounts.

That the tanning process was such a mystery is even less surprising when you consider that even today chemists can give no single chemical equation to describe the various kinds of tanning. Because it was not until the end of the nineteenth century that chemists began to study the properties of the tanning process, the Adirondack tanner had no idea of the physical properties of the proteins that made up his hides, or the enzymes that accomplished bating, or the role of acids in softening leather, or even methods to improve the leaching of tannins from bark.

Nineteenth Century Improvements

Studies and experiments in the United States and abroad led tanners to believe that hemlock was as valuable a tanning agent as the more traditional oak, which had been used extensively in Europe and the southern United States. Sir Humphrey Davy, an English scientist and tanner, and others even experi-

[12] Ibid, p. 10
[13] Contributors to **Hide and Leather**, *Modern American Tanning*

mented with the various **tanning agents** to determine which were best and most economical.

Improvements were made in the methods of extracting tannin from bark. Horse-powered mills, similar to those employed in grist mills, were used to grind bark until after 1807, when the first **bark mill** was patented. The inventor was William Tobey of Hudson, New York.[14] Bark ground between stones varied in coarseness and its lack of uniformity was a problem. Too coarse bark did not yield all its tannin; too fine bark was a dust, difficult to wet, and all too flammable. During the 1800s, several water- or steam-powered bark mills were patented, and most resembled huge, cast-iron coffee grinders. Bark was forced against blades or against sharp ridges that lined the insides of the grinders. The number of patents suggest great improvements in bark grinding; but, in fact, the newer models were better only because they had more and more removable parts that could be quickly replaced when the inevitable breakages occurred.

Leather from heavy hides was suitable for soles of boots and shoes, for harnesses and industrial belting, but much too heavy, thick, and rigid for uppers for boots and shoes. Until the nineteenth century, tanned hides were laboriously shaved to produce thinner leather for uppers. The most revolutionary machine in the tanning industry was the **splitter**, introduced in 1809, perfected before the Adirondack era, and widely used in the second half of the nineteenth century. It permitted a hide to be separated in two–the grain or outer side was pliable enough to be used for uppers, and the flesh side was no longer wasted as it could be used for gloves or clothing. Those few Adirondack establishments that tanned uppers ennumerated splitting machines as part of their equipment.

In 1812, William Edwards, a Catskill tanner whom we will meet later, invented a **roller** widely used in the Adirondacks for finishing sole leather and patented an arrangement for leaches and vats.[15] In all, Edwards conceived technological developments in the 1830s that significantly reduced the cost of tanning.[16]

The invention of a **barkometer**, a simply calibrated, sealed and weighted glass tube that measured the specific gravity of the ooze greatly assisted the tanner in assessing the strength or acid-

---

[14] Ellsworth, p. 150
[15] Ibid, p. 140
[16] Ibid, p. 147

ity of the tanning liquors, but treatises of the times lament the unreliability of these devices.

Steam was a tool in nineteenth century tanneries. Steam-powered finishing machines were introduced for **beating** dry hides to help soften them and for **rolling** tanned sides. Applications of heat and steam radically changed the speed at which tanning was accomplished. The steam was generated by wood-fired boilers; later developments pemitted the burning of spent bark to fire the boilers. Tanners devised elaborate systems of gravity-fed pumps and pipes that were installed to circulate water and steam. After 1835, steam was used extensively in most of the country's large tanneries; it quickly became an important source of power in Adirondack tanneries, though it was not used in the earliest ones built there in the late 1840s.

The rest of the machines, mostly wooden, which were patented as improvements in the tanning process, were very simple hand-powered devices that aided the workers in the back-breaking labors of moving the sides from place to place. There was little that was revolutionary. The processes remained the same. In fact the Industrial Revolution seems to have only slightly affected the tanning industry when compared with the revolutions brought about in such industries as weaving and sewing and the manufacturing of machine tools.

An amazing number of problems confronted the tanner, and his inability to analyze the problems scientifically left him ill-equipped to find solutions. The best methods were learned by experience.

Morfit, in his comments on the industry written in 1852 to supplement a treatise on tanning that he translated from the French, describes many problems of the tanning process. It is interesting to compare the problems of 1852 with those described in a treatise on "Modern American Tanning" written in 1902. In the latter, the same terms are used to describe the same kinds of problems and to offer remarkably similar solutions as offered by Morfit a half century earlier. They both bemoan the problems of soaking and washing, putrefaction, dirt and holes in sides, excess heating in piles of hides before unhairing, the ravages of too warm weather, and the loss of gelatin through excess liming.[17]

*Overleaf: Sketches from **Harper's Weekly**, 1890, "A Day in a Tannery"*

[17] *Modern American Tanning*, pp. 64-65

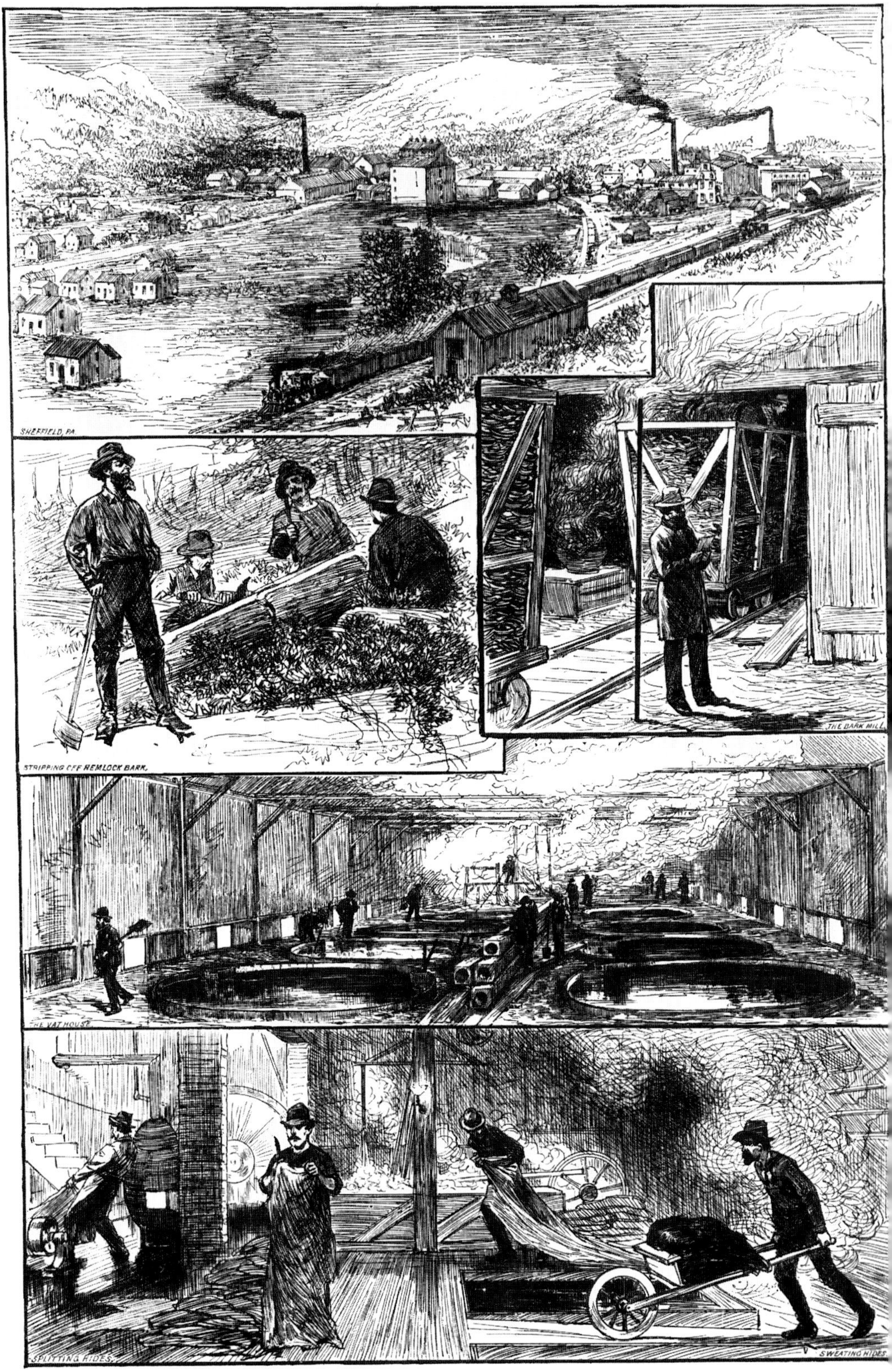
SHEFFIELD, PA.
STRIPPING OFF HEMLOCK BARK.
THE BARK MILL
THE VAT HOUSE
SPLITTING HIDES.
SWEATING HIDES

Fleshing Hides.

Washing Tanned Hides.

Vat House.

Finishing Leather.

Because this is an industry for which the Industrial Revolution had a curiously minor technological impact, the unscientific and only slightly mechanized state of operations prevailed all through the period in which the craft of tanning was so important in the Adirondacks.

Economies were achieved by simple labor-saving devices and by careful attention to the quality of the leather and the temperatures of the process, which permitted a significant shortening of the process. By the end of the Catskill era, tanners had reduced the time to tan a hide from eighteen to six months. While it is true that tanning methods were significantly improved during the nineteenth century, the improvements were not accomplished as much by inventions as by efficiencies and improved organization, by building larger tanneries, dividing the different kinds of labor among different classes of workers, and by designing better factory layouts so the hides could be handled more expeditiously. The philosophy of the industrial era called for the separation of a job into many tasks, steps to make each worker more efficient, and steps to enlarge operations so that a division of labor was possible. This philosophy that was so important to the Industrial Revolution was articulated by Adam Smith. His concepts were essential to the theories of Zadock Pratt of the Catskills who wrote at length on their application to the tanning industry. How this philosophy was exemplified in the work of this Catskill tanner is summarized later. Pratt's work was important because he envisioned and drew designs for the sort of tanneries that were built in the Adirondacks. They accomplished greater efficiencies in the operations through improved controls over the processes. However, the greatest period of development of tanning machinery and process did not occur until the last decades of the nineteenth century, after the Adirondack era, when inventions finally did make basic changes in the process of tanning sole leather.

The numerous variables in the tanning process and the fact that they were imperfectly understood made it impossible to completely standardize the operation. One of the most variable elements was the raw material itself and this stemmed from the source of the hides and the distances over which they traveled to reach the State's tanneries. It is here that the Industrial Revolution did have a significant impact on the tanning industry, for tanning could only grow when the industry could follow the sources of bark further into the woods and when raw materials could be brought from far away. As we see next, it was the improvements in transportation—railroads, steamboats, and canals—that made possible the expansion of tanning. This aspect of the Industrial Revolution, combined with the availability of hemlock bark, directly accounts for the spread of tanning into the Adirondacks.

Nineteenth Century Steps in the Tanning Process

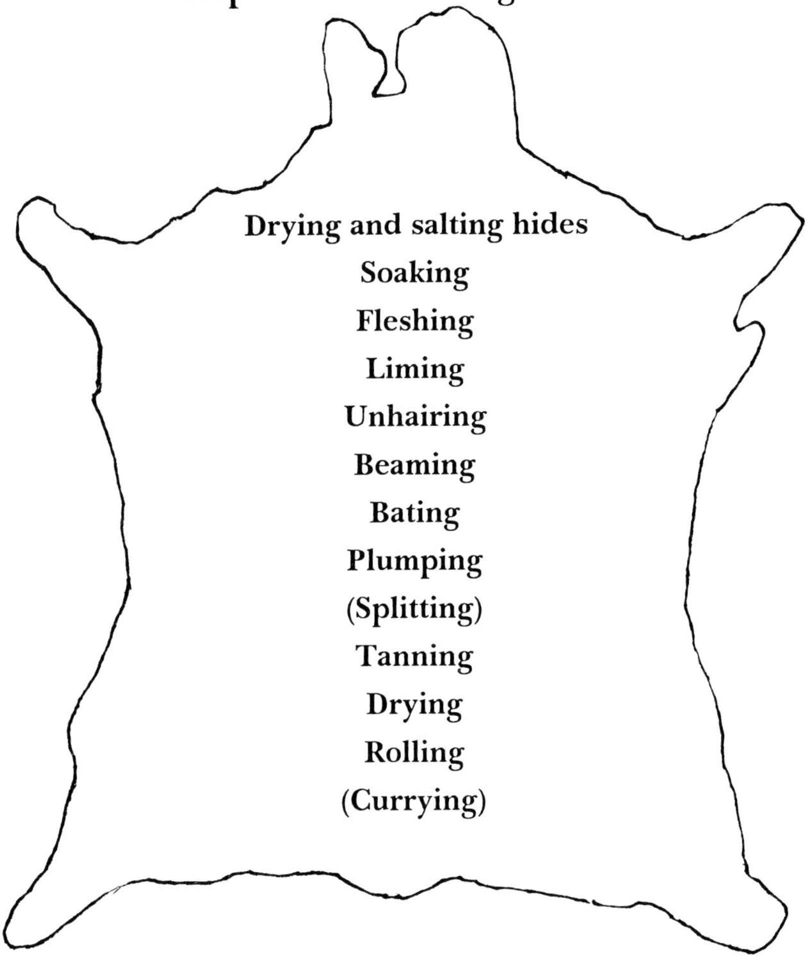

III

Tanning in New York State Before the Expansion Into the Adirondacks

Sources of Hides

Local farmers supplied small Colonial tanneries, but as tanneries grew to achieve the economies of size and specialization, local supplies became inadequate. As early as 1700, hides imported from Central and South America reached the growing tannery centers along the east coast. Shipments of oak bark, and later hemlock bark, were also sent to these centers from not-too-distant forests.

With the growth of cities in the early nineteenth century and the doubling of the country's population every two decades, tanners could scarcely keep up with the growing need for leather for boots and shoes. As early as the 1830s, cattle were driven from western and mid-western states to large slaughter houses that not only produced meat for the cities, but hides for the tanners. By 1830, the growing country had a network of canals and that aided that shipment. Hides were shipped by boat from California and the Rio Grande Valley to ports on the east coast; but ports in Central and South America shipped even greater numbers of hides. By 1850, 70% of all the hides tanned in the United States were shipped from Central and South America, from such places as the pampas of Brazil and Argentina and the Orinoco plains. Different types of hides bore the names of the geographical origins—Buenos Ayres [sic], Cartagena,

Montevideo, San Juan, Orinoco, Chagras, and Matamoras.[1] The hides shipped to Catskill tanneries were almost 100% imported, a pattern that continued when tanning reached the Adirondacks.

These hides were almost all salted and dried or just salted to preserve them for the long trips to eastern seaboard ports. Water still affected poorly salted hides. Hides were often packed with flesh and dirt that caused parts of them to rot. Some hides had holes caused by ticks and other insects common to more tropical regions. Pity the poor tanner who not only had to judge the quality of the hides he received by their place of origin, but by the misfortunes that caused them to deteriorate in shipment.

The Swamp

In New York City, the area where tanning was concentrated moved several times in the eighteenth century. Americans did not make sole leather until the end of that century and continued to import it, mainly from England. Tanning was not separated from the manufacture of shoes and boots until after the Revolution, circa 1780. About 1790, New York City's tanners moved again to cluster in an area known as the Swamp, then the northern border of the city. The area around Ferry, Beekman, Jacob, Gold, Frankfort, and Pearl streets contained many tanneries, but far from being a place isolated because of smells, the Swamp quickly changed the emphasis of its business.[2] Water for tanning was in short supply and the area was too distant from sources of oak and hemlock bark for the tanneries to continue in New York City. The tanners became merchants, importing hides, supplying them to tanneries that sprang up in the Catskills and Pennsylvania and the Adirondacks, and then selling the finished leather for a fee.

The leather merchants built fancy homes as well as trading halls in the Swamp, the name by which the area continued to be known. The tanners expanded their sphere of interest beyond trading and soon many prominent men lived and had stores and

---

[1] Each of these sources of hides was mentioned in the United States Census of Manufactures for various Adirondack tanneries.

[2] Norcross, Frank. W. *A History of the New York Swamp*, p.3

offices in the Swamp. Many made fortunes and they became the city's politicians and philanthropists. For a century, the Swamp, along with Massachusetts' boot and shoe manufacturers, controlled the country's tanning industry.

The men of the Swamp were called the "Kings of the Tanning Trade."[3] Tanners formed the "Swamp Clique,"[4] a split of the Bucktail Party. The first public reading room in New York City was opened in the Swamp. Swamp tanners joined to form the Eclectic Fraternity for the "purpose of mutually aiding each other in mental cultivation."[5] Gideon Lee, the tanner who presented his important treatise on tanning (discussed above) at meetings of the Eclectic Fraternity, also served as Mayor of New York City in 1833-4. The leather brokerage house founded by Lee was prominent in New York City for a hundred years.[6]

While its early members were merchants on a small scale and more closely related to the oak tanners of Philadelphia and Baltimore, men from the Swamp financed the first hemlock tanning in the Catskills at Hunter in 1810. That sparked the expansion into the Catskills and eventually the move south and west into Pennyslvania and north into the Adirondacks. As we shall see in some of the individual accounts, Swamp tanners provided the capital for constructing and expanding tanneries as well as arranging shipment of green hides and selling finished leather. The leather merchants started their clerks or relatives in business with loans of ten to a hundred thousand dollars. "These 'special partners' got 7% interest for their investments, besides a share of the profits."[7]

Throughout the nineteenth century, men from the Swamp served as brokers of hides and finished leather, supplying the former, marketing the latter. The contracts (indentures) between the Burhans Tannery of Warrensburg and a merchant from the Swamp indicate the way such agreements were arranged. Fraser, Major and Company of New York City acquired an interest in two Warren County tanneries, Pottersville and Mill Brook, and one Essex County tannery, Olmstedville. In these instances, it appears that the New York City firm acted as receiver for

---

[3] Ibid, p. 1
[4] Ibid, p. 10
[5] Ibid, pp. 67-68
[6] Ibid, p. 51-59
[7] Ibid, p. 66

tanneries that were bankrupt. A significant number of the tanneries in Lewis, Herkimer, and Oneida counties were built or financed by men with roots in the Swamp: H. D. H. Snyder, John VanWoert, and Thomas E. Proctor illustrate this connection.[8] These Adirondack connections to the Swamp are explored in Chapter VII and in Part II.

Men from the Swamp founded family dynasties with interests in tanning throughout the east. (It was said that the more children in a family, the more tanneries the family business could control.)[9] Family holdings in Pennsylvania and New York State were enormous; it is amazing how small a part their Adirondack holdings contributed to their wealth. The Adirondack tanneries were the pawns in a giant chess game; the kings from the Swamp and those with roots in Boston's shoe and boot factories, who will be introduced later, maneuvered the local pawns for their own benefit. These giants of the industry finally joined forces to survive economically, while, at the same time, they obliterated the surviving pawns as they moved their holdings west to Michigan and Wisconsin.

Pursuing the Hemlock Forests

The choice of tanning agent depended on availability. The bark of the quebracho, a South American tree, was used in the southwestern United States and oak and chestnut were commonly used in the southeast. Oak was the tanning agent of choice in the eighteenth century. Because of the difficulties of obtaining oak, New York City tanners began in the second half of the eighteenth century to experiment with hemlock bark as a tanning agent. Although it gave leather a distinctive reddish tinge, unlike the rich, dark brown of oak-tanned leather, its effectiveness as a tanning agent and its availability made its use dominant in the City, but by the end of the eighteenth century local supplies were exhausted. Bark was harvested from hemlock that graced the hills along the Hudson River and shipped by boat to the Swamp. But shortly tanneries were built in Hudson

[8] Ibid, p. 183
[9] Ibid, p. 109

and other river towns, as tanners realized the economies of bringing the hides to the source not only of the bark, but to the streams and rivers, which supplied the needed water.

Not only were sources of hemlock in southern New York State exhausted early in the nineteenth century, but so were those near the coast of Massachusetts, which had supplied the leather for the huge shoe factories that were established along the eastern coastline in the early nineteenth century.

As tanneries were built farther north along both the Hudson and Mohawk rivers, the supply of hemlock accessible to those rivers was soon exhausted. Tanning moved deep into the Catskill region after 1816 and several large tanneries were built along its hemlock-shrouded valleys.

The move into the heart of the Catskills was given impetus by the War of 1812; just as half a century later, the move into the Adirondacks was spurred on by the needs of Civil War armies. The move to the Catskills was accompanied by a change in the size and construction of the tanneries themselves. Before 1816, New York State law did not allow the formation of a corporation for the purpose of tanning, except by special permit. Colonel William Edwards, originally a tanner in Massachusetts, discovered the vast stands of hemlock growing in the Schoharie Valley in the north-central Catskills. With his son, he lobbied to change New York's law. As a result of his efforts, tannery corporations were to be permitted, but only in Greene and Delaware counties, and not in Ulster and Sullivan because already they were perceived as a threat to forests and a destroyer of surrounding land values.[10]

Colonel Edwards acquired 2,500 acres of rich hemlock stands in 1816 in what became Hunter on the Schoharie Creek. The capital for the company, the New York Tannery, came from traders from the Swamp, who continued to supply hides and to broker the leather produced. As manager of the company, Edwards supervised the building of a 300-foot long tannery building, one that was later extended to 500 feet. He was the inventor of a roller for sole leather that sole leather tanners used throughout the nineteenth century.

Within two decades after Edwards arrived, tanneries were built on almost every stream and river in the northern Catskills. And, among Catskill tanneries, the one devised by Zadock Pratt

---

[10] Ellsworth, ibid, pp. 66-67

became the archetype for later expansion of tanneries into the Adirondacks.

Zadock Pratt and the Catskills

In the company of those who built huge tannery complexes in the Catskills, Zadock Pratt was pre-eminent; he was a member of Congress, an architect, and a theorist as well as a tanner. The design for his tannery represents the state of the art in the period just before the Adirondack era. It was built far from the good transportation offered by the Hudson River, deep in the Schoharie Valley beside slopes dense with hemlock. He completed his tannery in 1824 and kept meticulous records about it, which are summarized in a letter written in 1860. This letter is reproduced as an appendix, so the reader can compare it with contemporary descriptions of some of the giant tanneries of the Adirondacks, such as those in Fulton and Clinton counties, for surely his tannery was a model for many of them. Pratt's influence appears to have been so great that his treatise is a very accurate description of the way tanneries were built and run in the Adirondacks. It is also worth comparing the records he kept for his tannery's operations and expenses with such Adirondack tanneries as the Wheeler-Claflin enterprise, for which similar statistics exist.

Pratt was very innovative, though perhaps less so than Edwards. Pratt designed the huge tannery built of wood that was the forerunner for almost all the tanneries built elsewhere in the second half of the century. He advocated efficiencies in operations and his designs accommodated these efficiencies. He devised wooden machines that greatly aided the tanner in transporting sides from one operation to the next. He wrote extensively on the benefits of having one huge tannery. His greatest contribution was his writings and promotion of his ideas. However, he did not introduce any new machines or chemical techniques. An analysis of Pratt's improvements shows they were essentially those of size of the operation and of careful attention to such details as the conditions of hides and the temperatures at which the tanning processes were allowed to take place. It remained a time-consuming, labor- and capital-intensive industry.

These larger tanneries, such as Pratt's, quickly exhausted the source of hemlock in surrounding forests. In 1850, tanning was the fifth largest industry in the country in the number of establishments[11] and the need for tanning materials continued to grow, but the supply of Catskill bark was nearly depleted. By 1850 a few tanneries had already been built in the eastern Adirondacks, and the quest for Adirondack hemlock had begun. With remarkable rapidity, tanneries sprang up everywhere on the fringes of the Adirondacks, some of them among the largest in the state. The depletion of Catskill hemlock, coupled with the beginning of the Civil War, gave the impetus for the explosion of tanneries to the south and west and to the north. The Adirondacks, after 1840, was poised to be a part of that explosion.

[11] Watson, ibid, p. 9

IV

The Adirondack Region

Defining the Adirondack Region

This book extends the Adirondack region beyond the present boundaries of the Blue Line, the line that delineates the Adirondack Park. It does so by including the tanneries that drew bark from within the Adirondack Park region, as it is now defined. The book attempts to record all the major tanneries in Warren, Essex, Clinton, Fulton, Hamilton and Lewis counties. It enumerates the tanneries in St. Lawrence, Franklin, and Jefferson counties, but focuses on only a few in those counties that lie within or close to today's Blue Line. The tanneries in the portions of Oneida, Saratoga, and Herkimer counties closest to the Park are detailed, but no attempt has been made to enumerate those tanneries in the southern part of those counties, the regions closest to the Mohawk river that were settled and cleared for farming before 1850. Many county histories mention early Colonial tanners, but this information relies on second-hand sources and is not presented in a systematic way.

In this study area, there were roughly 153 tanneries in 1850, of which fourteen can be termed in some way large manufacturers of sole leather. The number of tanneries in the same region was 148 in 1860, but the number of large tanneries had tripled to forty-three. The total number of tanneries in the study area shrank to about 116 in 1870, when thirty-eight can be considered large operations. The total number of tanneries was almost the same in 1880 (112), but fifty-four of them, almost 50%, were large manufacturers of leather, which figure in some way in our statistical analyses. Note that some totals and averages are given for the north country as a whole; some are for specific subregions. Some figures describe the large sole leather manufacturers only; other include both sole and upper leather manufacturers, where separating the two is not possible. Note that eighty to ninety percent of tanning in the Adirondacks was of heavy sole leather. Limiting some statistical analyses to those dealing with sole leather allows many comparisons in all four Census decades that would be impossible otherwise.

The Census for the State of New York for 1855, 1865, and 1875 is used in order to compare lumber and tanning operations. Because these records are not broken down into townships, a different study area has to be defined. For this comparison the study area includes all parts of the twelve counties mentioned.

Methods for Examining The Adirondack Region

The United States Census of Manufactures

To give structure to the many different and highly variable accounts of the tanneries obtained from local records and histories, this book relies quite heavily on the United States Census of Manufactures, particularly for the years 1850, 1860, 1870, and 1880. This creates as many problems as it solves. The entries are often illegible; the spelling of names is wildly inconsistent; different names are attached to the same tannery in the Census and in local reports, making it sometimes impossible to properly assign the statistical information; not all tanneries gave all the categorized information.

Outweighing these problems is the way the Census is used in this account. The information is ordered according to county and town. The number of employees, the number of sides produced, their cost and value as finished leather, and the amount of bark used are all objectively reported. Capital investment figures as given may be subjective and it may not be appropriate to treat the reports as absolute figures for an individual tannery, but they do offer ways of comparing the various tanneries. From the figures we can compare the size of the operations and form a rough picture of the total amount of tanning in different sub-regions at different times.

Combining these statistical comparisons with measurements of the physical size of the tanneries obtained from contemporary accounts gives an even fuller picture of the relative importance of individual tanneries. And, although the precise totals may be suspect, they certainly do back up the story of the great impact of the tanning industry on the Adirondack region.

To obtain the Census information, I created a form with headings corresponding to each Census category. I filled in this form from the Census microfilms for every tannery in the defined region in the four Census decades, 1850 through 1880. Thus, I had available a file that contained all the Census information and the references in this book are to the information laboriously copied onto that file.

The R. G. Dun and Co. Ledgers

To flesh out contemporary accounts of failures, bankruptcies, and changing owners, the R. G. Dun and Co. Ledgers proved invaluable. They underscore the volatility of the tanning industry in the nation and particularly in the Adirondacks. However, these ledgers are even more valuable in another way: they report the existence of silent partners, outside investors, even relatives in Boston or New York, who were the real financiers of the Adirondack tanning industry. Local people often knew only the resident managers; local histories and deeds often failed to report outside connections, and if they did, they offered no indication of the size and scope of the business of the outside owner or financier. The R. G. Dun and Co. ledgers are a rich resource for answering the question, "Who really financed and built the Adirondack tanneries?"

Local lawyers or businessmen were hired to submit short reports on people in their towns. This information was compiled into ledgers in cryptic notes, which often contained encoded information about the amount of money it was safe to lend the individuals. The R. G. Dun and Co. ledgers generally corroborate information on capital investments as given in the Census. However, in none of the thirty reports on Adirondack tanneries that experienced difficulties did the authors predict future failures. It has been noted that R. G. Dun and Co. failed to predict the depression of 1873.[1] In a few instances, the ledgers do indicate the

[1] Norris, James D. *The Development of Credit Reporting in the Nineteenth Century*, p. 92

cause of on-going failures (litigation, problems in settling estates, losses in unrelated areas by owners). Although some local operations may have been inefficient, most of the time problems encountered by the tanneries were related to financial troubles of the era rather than to specific local weaknesses in the industry.

For all the value of the ledgers in sorting out complex ownership patterns, the ledgers do not directly reveal any answers to the questions, why were so many Adirondack tanneries failing and, more importantly, why did they leave the Adirondacks entirely?

None of the ledgers tells whether or not a local tannery was being run efficiently or whether the manager was a talented tanner. All that the ledgers report are whether or not the owner or manager was a good credit risk. Several reports mention that a tanner purchased green hides at an elevated price; none of the studied reports mentions the rising cost of hauling hemlock bark or the reported failure of the bark supply that was noted on so many Census entries in the late 70s and the 80s. In this respect, the R. G. Dun and Co. reports were disappointing. Did their failure to report problems with raw materials indicate there were none, or were the reporters unaware of the importance of the bark supply to the financial health of the tanneries? The Census and local accounts all emphasize the failure of the bark supply. Were reports of failures of the bark supply not as important to the demise of the tanneries as other aspects of the economic climate?

Generalizations from the ledgers yield insights into the pattern of local failures. It is only in observing the parallels between Adirondack tannery failures and national business cycles that answers begin to emerge, for there is a very close relationship between the health of Adirondack tanneries and the national economic scene, up through the early 1880s. The divergence in the second half of the 1880s indicates the influence other factors. The failure of the accessible bark supply is one factor. It is only through weaving together all three sources—local accounts, Census data, and anecdotes from the records of the R. G. Dun and Co. Ledgers—that the fate of the Adirondack tanning industry is explained.

V

Characteristics of Adirondack Tanning

Transportation

Before exploring the advent of tanning in the Adirondacks, let us take a brief look at the modes of transportation that made it possible.

Certainly steamships and ports were important in bringing hides from distant lands, but delivering them to the remote mountain regions where hemlock abounded required varied modes of transportation. The Hudson and Mohawk rivers served as transportation corridors when hemlock was first depleted near the coast; the canals and the steamboat were essential. The Erie Canal, completed in 1825, opened lands in western New York along its route and spurred tanning there long before the Adirondack era. The Champlain Canal, which reached Whitehall in 1823, made possible the expansion of tanneries to the north, which was also enhanced by the parallel expansion of the Delaware and Hudson Railroad, to Saratoga in 1833 and Whitehall in 1848. It is curious to note, however, that the rapid expansion of tanneries into remote regions of Warren County preceded, for the most part, the further extensions of the railroad. Tanneries were dependent initially on the construction of plank roads to Warrensburg and on to the north and west. The Delaware and Hudson Railroad routes through Saratoga and Warrensburg and on to North Creek followed the tanneries by nearly two decades.

The Black River Canal brought industry to the northwestern part of the Adirondack region. Though proposals for this canal were made at the time the Erie Canal was being completed, construction from Rome to High Falls was not completed until

1855, delaying the spread of large tanneries until well after that date. In fact, the tanneries followed the Black River and Utica Railroad, which reached Boonville by 1855, but did not reach Lowville until 1867, Carthage until 1871, and Clayton until 1873.

The Fonda, Johnstown, and Gloversville Railroad, which was extended to Northville in 1870, played a part in the development of the tanning industry in the southern Adirondacks, but even here, several larger tanneries were built before the railroad was completed.

The Mohawk and Malone Railroad, later known as the Adirondack Division of the New York Central Railroad, was essential to the growth of the north central Adirondacks and to the logging that occurred there, but that line was not completed until 1891 and 1892, too late to serve the tanneries, which for the most part were closing. Only one or two tanneries in Franklin County seem to have benefited from this line.

The railroads and canals do not completely explain the spreading pattern of tannery building. The large Adirondack tanneries came first to Warren County and shortly after to Lewis County, but only a few of the largest tanneries were built at sites adjacent to the railroads. The histories of individual tanneries will illustrate that as important as the railroads and canals were, most of the Adirondack tanneries depended ultimately on the simplest modes of transportation—horse and wagon, driven by the inveterate teamster over very rough roads.

Just as quickly as the canals or railroads got within striking distance of the distant forests, plank roads or dirt tracks were built from the canal ports or railheads to interior valleys. The roads were essential for hauling heavy loads of hides, carboys of acids, and the finished leather. The plank road from Warrensburg to Chestertown was vital to the expansion into interior Warren County. Plank roads north from the Erie Canal served tanneries in Fulton County.

Planks for roads were sawn from hemlock; this is one of the few nineteenth century uses for hemlock. The cost of building a plank road in Fulton County was given as $7 a rod.[1] Some towns advanced funds to build roads to encourage new tanneries. (The Oregon Tannery in Johnsburg illustrates this.)

---

[1] In the sections dealing with economic analyses, it will be shown that the cost of building plank roads was quite substantial in comparison to the cost of land.

Building a plank road near Pine Lake, Fulton County, courtesy of Bruce Busch.

At least one tannery (Sornberger in Fulton County) closed because the town would not build a needed bridge.

Tanneries in Essex County, at Jerden Falls in Lewis County, and at Griffin and Piseco in Hamilton County, for instance, survived without benefit of a plank road. Rough dirt tracks, muddy in wet weather, rolled and sometimes iced in winter, dusty and rutted in summer, were all that led to these and other remote tanneries.

This dependence on plank and dirt roads further explains the limits on the way tanneries spread north and west from Warrensburg, north from the Mohawk Valley, or east from the Black River Valley. A one-day haul of about twenty miles was about all a team could manage. Teams could make three round-trips a week, bringing in shipments of dry hides one day, carrying out finished leather the next. Almost all the Adirondack tanneries were within this one-day distance from railheads or canal ports. The few exceptions, in northern Warren and southern Essex counties, for instance, where the one-way hauls required two-day trips, were demonstrably marginally profitable; distance from the railheads appears to be the principal reason for this. In spite of this, a few of the largest tanneries, those built fairly late in the tanning era, such as at Oregon, Griffin, and Fine, were located at the end of such long dirt roads. The Rudeston Tannery in Hamilton County was built a four-day's trip away from a railroad.

Hemlock Forests

Through the 1800s, hemlock bark gradually became the most widely used source of tannin, until by 1879 three times more hemlock was used for tanning in the United States than oak and chestnut combined. In spite of early nineteenth century questions about the desirability of hemlock as a tanning agent, all of the Catskill tanneries used hemlock. Before mid-century, hemlock was definitely preferred, but the Catskill stands were all gone and the Adirondack's forests beckoned.[2]

Adirondack forests were scarcely touched by the woodsman's axe before 1800, a fact that continues to amaze, given the country's westward expansion. The ruggedness of the mountain region and its isolation account for this. As a result, at mid-century, the forests were almost pristine and the forest cover was as it had evolved since the last ice age. The difficult mountain terrain explains why, even by 1850, logging was restricted to a few river valleys and the fringes of the mountainous dome. By 1870, loggers had pushed their search for pine, spruce, and balsam into many of the areas where tanneries were built, but even then, the forests were relatively little disturbed. When tanneries were built in the heart of the Adirondacks, their sites were often cleared from deep wilderness stands.

Many of the forests of the Adirondack Park, those that have been part of the Forest Preserve for a century or more, are remarkably similar to those that enticed the first loggers and tanners. The species are the same, only the proportions differ. In some places, even the diameters of second-growth trees are approaching those of a virgin forest.

Adirondack forests were about forty percent hard woods: sugar maple, yellow birch, and beech, with scatterings of black cherry and the white birch and popple that pioneered the few forest openings created by fire and windfall. Hardwoods were

[2] Watson, *The Economics of Cattlehide Tanning*, p. 20

dominant in the lower elevations, in the dryer slopes with rich soil.

The fifty-eight percent that was soft wood comprised white pine, spruce, balsam-fir, cedar, and hemlock. The balsam was a pioneering species, with older stands more prevalent on higher elevations. Cedar preferred the edges of more northern ponds and streams. Red spruce dominated the mountain tops and flat, wet, swampy areas; black spruce was restricted to shorelines in the north and to a few mountain summits. Pine preferred sandy, well-drained soil and pioneered after fires and windfall and wherever the soil had been disturbed enough to expose the underlying mineral soils, thus permitting pine to become established.[3]

Hemlock, *Tsuga canadensis*, made up as much as fifteen percent of the total forests. They occurred as scattered specimens interspersed among hardwoods where there was sufficient moisture. More spectacularly, they occurred in magnificent stands with no other species present. These were found along sheltered mountain valleys and on the more moist northern slopes. Hemlock require much moisture, but they are shallow rooted—characteristics that restrict the places they can grow. In a mature forest, you will occasionally find a thin, upturned root mass, a dozen or fifteen feet in diameter. This dislodged root mass has a sculptured beauty that is a fitting footstone for the fallen hemlock giants.

Hemlock trees cannot survive if their roots dry out. They usually start under the shade of other trees and grow very slowly, forcing their way during a period of a century or more into the crown cover overhead. The very denseness of hemlock stands preserves the required moisture and keeps out most plants of the lower and middle stories. Ferns proliferate beneath them only where sunlight penetrates their shading canopy.

Today, hemlock in the Adirondacks are commonly found with diameters of three or four feet, and heights over sixty feet; but diameters of over five feet and heights approaching one

---

[3] Fox, William F. *The Adirondack Black Spruce.* From calculations based on Fox's reports of stands in Essex County and around Nehasane and Cranberry lakes after the railroad was completed in 1891, when the pine had basically been harvested, the forests contained softwoods, 58%, of which spruce was 27%, hemlock - 15%, balsam - 3%, white cedar - 11%, and white pine - 2%, of the total; and hardwoods, 42%, of which birch was 16%, maple - 11%, Beech - 11%, and white birch - 2%.

hundred feet were common in the virgin forests. Specimens approaching these dimensions are found in several Adirondack stands, among them Pine Orchard east of Wells. Hemlock are a long-lived species, attaining a maximum age of 600 years.[4] Their majestic form and habit of growing in stands with little beneath imparts a sense of scale and proportion exceeded only by isolated pines. Their broad sweeping branches, like dancers' expressive arms, reach out with graceful elegance. Their tiny needles, green above and white below, make their branches seem like silvery lace silhouetted against the sky.

For all its beauty, the eastern hemlock was little prized for its wood. It splinters, is of poor quality, and has knots that chipped a woodsman's axe. It was used for railroad ties and road planking, and recently it has been used for pulp for paper. It was sometimes used to build the tannery buildings and many of the workers' homes, but logs were rarely shipped to distant markets and often left in the woods to rot.[5] (Hemlock was always used in the Catskills at the tannery sites, primarily because there was relatively much less other desirable timber in those mountains than there was in the Adirondacks.)

Hemlock was desirable primarily for its bark, but that trait was enough to doom the accessible Adirondack stands.

---

[4] Harlow and Harrar, *Dendrology*. New York: McGraw Hill, 1958

[5] This may be another Adirondack myth. Richard Nason, of Fynch, Pruyn and Co., wrote that company records show that 8.2 million of the 10 million board feet cut in 1867 was hemlock. It is not clear what it was used for; even Nason, whose avocation is that of Finch, Pruyn's historian, is puzzled by this fact. It may be an isolated instance, or it may indicate that greater amounts of hemlock were harvested than traditionally assumed.

Fox, ibid, reported that in 1893 "the total product of all the mills, which obtained their stocks of logs from Adironack forests was 355,050,520 board feet of which nearly one-fifth was hemlock and over two-thirds was spruce."

Hemlock was also used for lath to support plaster, but no other large-scale uses have been identified. It has proved impossible to compute what proportion of the hemlock felled was actually used as lumber and how much was felled for bark alone. What is clear is that photographs of hemlock logs left in the woods are common, as are the remains even today of the larger fallen giants.

Barking Operations

Like barking operations in the Catskills, those in the Adirondacks began in the spring with rising sap that loosened the bark. In the Adirondacks this could be well into May. Hemlock trees were felled and the bark was scored or ringed with an axe into four foot lengths, usually only as far up the tree as the first limbs.

Bark peelers, spuds, were used to loosen the lengths, usually in strips a foot or so wide. (The lowest ring of four-foot lengths was peeled before the tree was felled.) Most often, after the bark was peeled from the trees, the trees were left in the woods to rot.[6] This practice is suggested in the photograph printed on the flyleaf.

The peculiar odor of hemlock sap in spring and its characteristic stickiness led barkers to refer to it as "slime." Very quickly it covered their clothes, leaving them stiff enough to stand alone, and it imparted a distinctive odor that marked the tanbarker as pungently as the smell of rotting flesh marked the men in the beam house.[7]

In the Adirondacks, barking could continue well into summer, as long as the sap was running. The bark was loosely piled near where it was cut, but carefully placed so the rough outer bark was exposed to the elements–tanners had learned that hemlock bark quickly lost a part of its tannin to leaching by rain and snow. These stacks, any number of which can still be found in the forests today, ranged in size from half a cord to about two cords.

In late fall or early winter, with the first snows, bark was **ranked**: horse-drawn small sleds, ranking sleds[8], were used to pull these piles into ranks of barks, piles close to roads or skidways. Often, the bark was stacked in eight-foot wide, square ended piles so that they could be quickly measured.

Teams, drawing huge wagons when the weather was fair, but more commonly huge sleds when the ground was deeply

---

[6] Stories by bark peelers recounted in Part II tell of leaving the logs in the woods.

[7] Haring, A. A. *The Catskills*, p. 102

[8] At least two such sleds exist, one in Caroga and one in the Adirondack Museum. They measure 3 feet by 8 feet and could be pulled over fairly rough terrain by one horse.

Piling bark on top a bark shed, Beaver Falls, courtesy of Lewis S. VanArnum

frozen, transferred these ranks to the tanneries. Here, at some sites, the bark was sometimes weighed as an alternative to measuring, (a photograph shows a sled on a scale at Beaver Falls). Weighing was not a common practice and created such problems as how to estimate the weight of the snow and ice brought in with the bark. A dispute involving the weight of snow in bark delivered to the St. Regis Tannery in Franklin County has been documented.

More often bark was measured by volume in terms of cords. On arrival at the tannery, the bark was stacked in long sheds, rough bark side out. These sheds were not buildings, but solid constructions of bark, tapered on top to form a sloping roof. Photographs of the sheds show them resembling long loaves of bread. The sheds were eight feet wide, twelve feet tall. The sheds were long and narrow because wider sheds were found to trap moisture in the cold north woods and bark in the interior would begin to rot. Pictures graphically show the number and length of these bark sheds surrounding Adirondack tanneries.

Calculating roughly, each four-foot length of shed contained three full cords of bark. Most sheds were over 300 feet long, but the average Adirondack tannery had any number of such sheds. It would take but 4,000 cords to stretch in these long sheds for a distance of a mile. Extrapolating from the sums given in the Census (41,000 cords harvested in 1850, 107,000 in 1860, 117,000 in 1870, and 158,000 in 1880), the eleven counties in this survey[9], which either had tanneries in or pulled bark from the Adirondack region, consumed at least 4,380,000 cords of hemlock bark during the latter part of the nineteenth century. This amounts to bark sheds over 1,100 miles in length! Little wonder that notes in the Census record and local accounts all state that the bark was gone.

How Much Bark and How Much Land Were Needed?

Barking operations in the Adirondacks were not basically different from those of Colonial times-only the scale and the rapaciousness of the harvest distinguished the former. Back in Colonial times, when bark cost about $3.00 to $4.50 a cord, and with the tanning process requiring upwards of a year and a half, few tanners turned out more than a dozen tanned sides a day and the few cords of bark consumed could be harvested nearby. Adirondack tanneries, designed for mass production of leather, consumed much greater amounts.

In the dense Catskill stands, harvests of upwards of fifteen cords of bark per acre were reported, but in most Adirondack areas, only four to six cords per acre were available.[10] One Clinton County tannery reported that five trees had to be felled to harvest a cord of bark; and 12,000 to 13,000 trees, covering 1,000 acres, were harvested in a year to provide bark, 2,500 cords, to tan 8,500 hides, or 17,000 sides. That is only 2.5 cords to the acre. In 1885, as the Adirondack era drew to a close, the Forest

---

9 Oneida County is not included in this figure.

10 Coffin, Nathaniel Wheeler. *The Forest Arcadia.* Coffin reported that in 1864 an acre of Adirondack forest could produce 5 cords of bark. He valued an acre of forest as containing "30 cords of merchantable wood, one spar of 128 cubic feet, five cords of hemlock bark, 2280 feet board measure of pine lumber, 13,680 feet board measure of spruce, hemlock &c, 6840 feet maple, birch, &c, and the mean net value, per acre to be $201." Multiplying that figure by the 6,000,000 acres in the Park produces a sum of $1.2 billion dollars, an astronomical figure for the time and more than enough to explain the rush to harvest the north country.

Commission reported that Essex, Fulton, and Warren counties could produce but four cords per acre average, while Herkimer, St. Lawrence, and Oneida still had the potential for six cords per acre. These numbers are far higher than individual tanneries were reporting. An agreement for bark in Hamilton and Warren counties around 1880 promised all the bark on 43,000 acres, but stipulated that if that was not enough to harvest the needed 50,000 cords, the hemlock could be harvested from additional acreage.

All this points to the fact that enormous acreages were needed to supply the larger tanneries. As we shall see, many of the larger Adirondack tanneries consumed as much as 6000 cords of bark in a season. Assuming the actual rate of production that was given in 1885 at two and a quarter cords per acre, such a tannery would require over fifty thousand acres to sustain twenty years of production. With this level of harvest, a ten-mile radius would yield but 40,000 cords or enough for seven years.

Assuming that one cord of bark could tan four or five hides, these figures for available bark determine the amount of land a tannery needed. To sustain production for a tannery capable of producing 30,000 sides a year, over a period of twenty years, 30,000 acres was barely enough. Lee Claflin and Son in Fulton County, Lyman Lyon in Lewis County, and Stephen Griffin all controlled more than 30,000 acres. The Forest Commission Report for 1895 said that a few tanneries had controlled upwards of 75,000 acres.

A typical large tannery in Warren County could produce 30,000 sides a year, so the fact that they lasted for twenty or more years is understandable. Some of Lewis County's tanneries could tan over 70,000 sides a year; little wonder that these tanneries were relatively short-lived. Such anecdotes as using twenty or thirty teams to pull in loads of bark daily from six to eleven miles away are staggering. Greater one-way distances were simply not possible, so circles with a diameter of twenty miles or so around a tannery defined the forests needed to sustain the tannery and the regions over which bark was harvested.

The map on the facing page depicts circles of ten-mile radius around tannery sites, showing the probable extent of barking operations. Overlapping circles indicate tanneries competing for bark. They undoubtedly had to reach somewhat further into the interior of the Adirondacks.

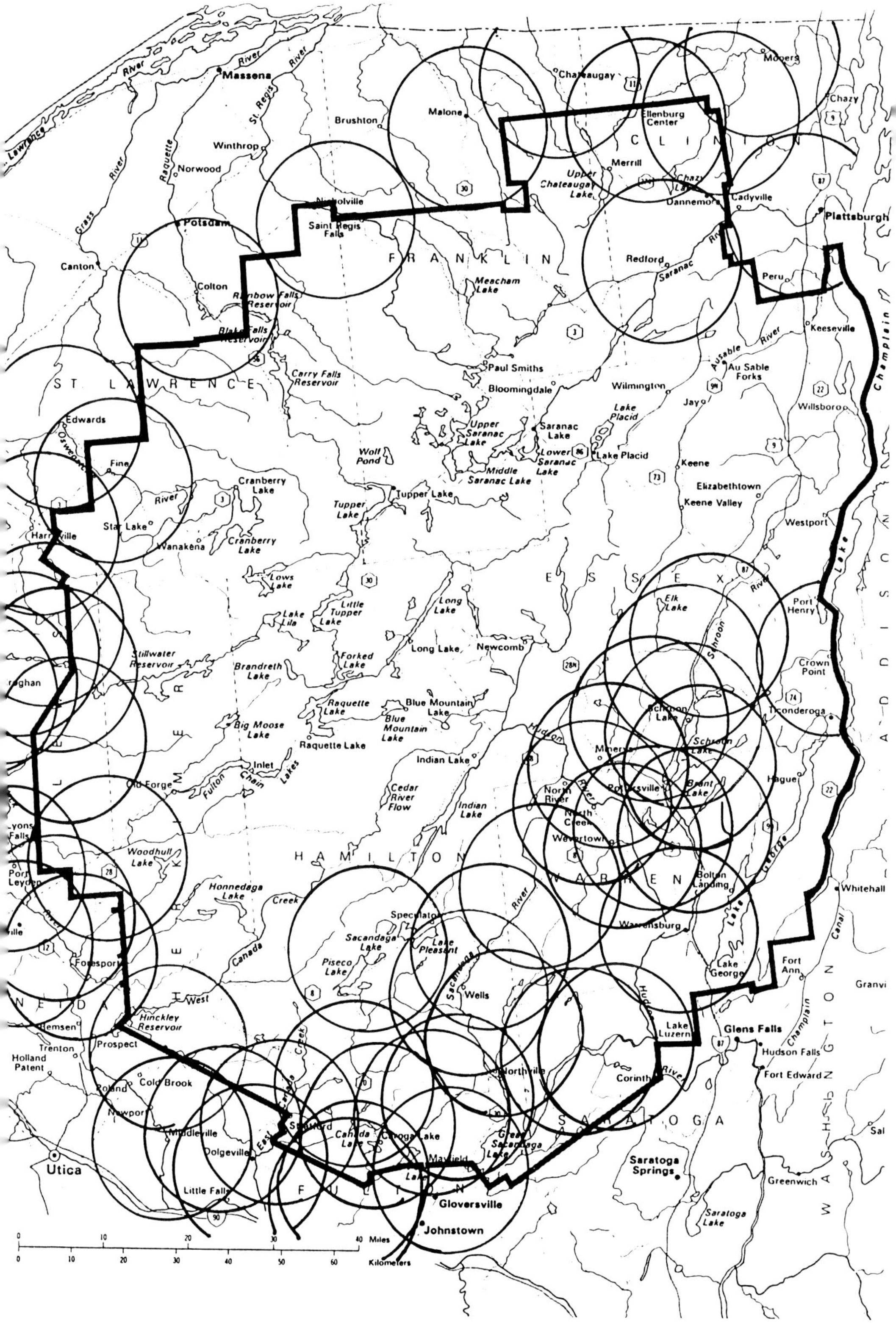
Massena
St. Regis River
Raquette River
Grass River
Brushton
Malone
Chateaugay
Moores
Chazy
Ellenburg Center
C L I N T O N
Winthrop
Norwood
Merrill
Upper Chateaugay Lake
Chazy Lake
Dannemora
Cadyville
Plattsburgh
Nicholville
Saint Regis Falls
Potsdam
Canton
F R A N K L I N
Redford
Saranac River
Peru
Colton
Rainbow Falls Reservoir
Blake Falls Reservoir
Meacham Lake
Keeseville
Ausable River
Au Sable Forks
Carry Falls Reservoir
Paul Smiths
Bloomingdale
Wilmington
Jay
Willsboro
S T. L A W R E N C E
Edwards
Oswegatchie
Fine
Upper Saranac Lake
Saranac Lake
Lake Placid
Lower Saranac Lake
Middle Saranac Lake
Wolf Pond
Keene
Elizabethtown
Keene Valley
Cranberry Lake
Star Lake
Wanakena
Harrisville
Tupper Lake
Westport
Lake Champlain
Lows Lake
E S S E X
Elk Lake
Port Henry
Long Lake
Little Tupper Lake
Lake Lila
Newcomb
Stillwater Reservoir
Brandreth Lake
Forked Lake
Crown Point
Croghan
Raquette Lake
Blue Mountain Lake
Big Moose Lake
Ticonderoga
Schroon Lake
Schroon River
Minerva
Indian Lake
Inlet
Fulton Chain Lakes
Old Forge
Hudson
Cedar River Flow
North River
Pottersville
Brant Lake
Hague
North Creek
Lyons Falls
Warrensburg
Weavertown
Woodhull Lake
H A M I L T O N
W A R R E N
Bolton Landing
Port Leyden
Whitehall
Honnedaga Lake
Lake George
Speculator
Sacandaga Lake
Lake Pleasant
Piseco Lake
Forestport
Wells
Fort Ann
Canada Creek
West
Granville
Hinckley Reservoir
Remsen
Lake Luzerne
Glens Falls
Trenton
Prospect
Hudson Falls
Holland Patent
Fort Edward
Cold Brook
Poland
Northville
Corinth
Newport
S A R A T O G A
Middleville
Stratford
Canada Lake
Caroga Lake
Great Sacandaga Lake
Dolgeville
Mayfield
Utica
Saratoga Springs
Little Falls
F U L T O N
Gloversville
Johnstown
Greenwich
Saratoga Lake
W A S H I N G T O N
A D D I S O N
Champlain Canal
Miles
Kilometers

Accessible Bark

Consider the geographical limits of the areas where Adirondack tanneries could be located, given the constraints of transportation, and combine these limits with the circles in which the harvest of bark was possible and profitable, and you have a map that describes the extent of tanning's influence. This compels the definition **accessible bark** to describe the bark within practical reach of tannery operations. When reading the accounts that say that the bark was all gone or the bark supply was exhausted, substitute this notion of accessible bark and a true picture emerges. This permits the observation that the bark, the accessible bark, was truly gone, when the evidence suggests that there remained significant Adirondack stands of hemlock. The slopes of Giant, the low lands to the northeast of Ampersand, and the interior of the Adirondack League Club are all lands where wonderful stands of hemlock survived into the twentieth century. They were too far away to harvest. In the first third of the twentieth century, loggers' claims that there was too much hemlock were true of the untouched and previously unreachable lands; and this does not contradict the tanner's claim that the bark, the accessible bark, was gone from critical areas close to tanneries, particularly in Warren County.

On the other hand, vast amounts of bark were left. It really was a myth to say that the bark was gone, even though there were local failures in the supply. How much bark was left? Assuming that 4.4 million cords of hemlock bark were harvested with a yield of four cords per acre, then 1.1 million acres would have been cut. A worst case average would be two cords per acre, in which case a little more than 2 million acres would have been harvested for their hemlock. This means that at most a third of the Adirondack Park was cut for hemlock bark.

The accompanying Park map, drawn with circles of radius ten miles surrounding the large sole-leather tanneries, shows just how much of the Park was probably left untouched. Even if, as toward the end of the era, some bark was shipped to distant tanneries, the Adirondack bark supply was nowhere near exhausted. Local failures and exhaustion of the accessible bark supply were affecting tanneries, but much hemlock bark remained. All this confirms that the second myth giving the reasons for the demise of Adirondack tanneries has been dispelled.

Teamster hauling bark, courtesy of Lester St. John Thomas

Teamsters

The teamsters who drove the sleds and wagons of bark were a rugged lot, whose day was long, often beginning at 4:00 in the morning. They drove out for ten miles or more, returning after dark, all for 75¢ a day. The Warren County chapter contains a first-hand account of the ranking process and the role of the teamsters by a woodsman who remembered the Horicon Tannery.

The teamsters who transported hides and finished leather were an equally rugged lot. Because so few of the Adirondack tanneries were built at railheads or near navigable streams, they depended on teams to draw the salted hides from railheads and to return the tanned sides to them. Teams brought in carboys of acid for bating and huge barrels of oil for the finishing processes. The life of a teamster driving between railheads at North Creek and distant tanneries over muddy or frozen tracks was as hard as hauling bark from the woods. In winter, their teams not only had to draw these loads on sleds, they first had to break through the snow and roll the roads. The excerpts, reproduced in Part II, from the diary of David Dodge, who was a teamster for the Oregon Tannery in Warren County, demonstrate just how hard a teamster's life was, especially in the blizzard winter of 1888.

Tannery Complexes

Among the more fascinating aspects of trying to reconstruct what Adirondack tanneries were actually like is a quirk in contemporary accounts of them. Most writers and historians, with few exceptions, were interested in the tanning process. Only a handful recorded physical aspects of tannery locations, but by combining the few newspaper accounts, the dozen or so photographs, and some archeological insights, these pieces add up to a rich picture of the tannery sites.

When I first began researching this book, there were a few people left whose relatives had worked in the Adirondack tanneries. There were even a few who had seen the old tanneries. But most tanneries existed only in the memories of a few Adirondackers, and there was one thing common to their recollections—each claimed that theirs was the largest tannery in the mountains. Even the press of the time exaggerated the size of local tanneries and their relative importance. At first I questioned all such claims, until I realized that they all had merit. The Adirondack sole-leather tanneries were all big; the way in which the descriptions were embellished is one of the most enduring charms of the Adirondack story. This was building, capital investment, development, and manufacturing on a scale that seems awesome in the context of its wilderness setting.

There was a standard for big—the capacity to tan 30,000 sides a year was fairly common. This size had been a standard in the Catskills. A notable few Adirondack tanneries were significantly larger, just as Pratt's and Edwards' tanneries in the Catskill were larger. Generally the older ones in the eastern Adirondacks were of the standard 30,000-side capacity; the giants were mostly in the western region, where there were tanneries with a capacity of up to 70,000 sides per year.

Tanneries built in the second half of the nineteenth century were built along one of two distinctive plans. Several chapters describing specific tanneries have maps, plans, and measurements to show the individual layouts. The components were similar; only the scheme of the plans was different.

Each tannery contained a **beam house** where the fleshing and unhairing processes took place. The **leach or vat house** contained rows of vats, often a hundred vats in a line, with four rows occupying the long narrow buildings, of which the largest in the Adirondacks measured nearly 500 feet in length, though many measured 400 feet or more. (The largest eastern tannery, built at the close of the nineteenth century near the New York-Pennsylvania border measured 1,200 feet in length.) Most Adirondack tanneries had some water power, but almost every one had a **steam house** for power as well as heat. **Drying sheds, finishing rooms**, and an **office** completed the tannery layout.

Tanneries under One Roof

Of the two basic tannery plans, the single building, which contained under one roof rooms or attached structures designed for each operation, was the most common. The single-building tanneries resemble the model devised by Zadock Pratt in the Catskills and many of the early Warren County tanneries follow this model. These were large buildings with up to three stories. They provided for relatively efficient operations, but they had one glaring drawback, that makes it difficult to understand why all but a handful of Adirondack tanneries followed this layout. Seven of the eight sketches of tannery foundations illustrated in Part II follow this dominant design.

Tannery Fires

Because the furnaces for the steam boilers were in the main building, these buildings were prone to fire. In addition, the main buildings also housed the bark grinders, which produced a flammable dust that was an even greater source of fire. Newspaper articles indicate numerous fires over the years, and the existing records are only a sample.

Almost all of those that burned seemed to have housed all the operations under one roof. Records of fires exist for the Glen, Starbuckville, and Alpine (Minerva-Olmstedville) tanneries. Stories of the destruction caused by tannery fires are in accounts of Oregon and North Creek in Warren County, the Moore Tannery in Redford, and the Sawyer Tannery in Ellenburgh. One tannery in Wells, owned by the Shaws, burned twice as did one in Lewis County owned by the Botchfords. The record for fires is held by the Webster Tannery of Malone, which burned "for the sixth and final time in 1893."

Tanneries with Separate Buildings

The largest tannery complexes, in particular those built after 1860 and those erected in the western Adirondacks, followed the plan of separate buildings on a huge cleared site. The site plan and photographs from the tannery at Wheelerville in Fulton County graphically illustrate the sprawl of this type of tannery complex. With four sheds over 400 feet in length and a half dozen other separate buildings, including the beam house and the steam house, the tannery covered an area of twenty acres.

Pictures of Griffin and Wheelerville show the extent of the tannery complexes, but in every such photograph, no matter how large the buildings, the most impressive sight is of the bark sheds. Individual sheds, not buildings, but the solid bark structures, were several hundred feet in length; row after row of bark sheds surround the tanneries. For the larger tanneries, these sheds contained six to seven thousand cords; their total length stretched for a mile and a quarter to a mile and a half, dwarfing the tanneries themselves. Little wonder that to supply this much bark, each of the larger tanneries pulled in bark from a circle as large as twenty miles in diameter.

Auxiliary Buildings

Because each tannery was built in the deep woods far from centers of population, small, self-contained settlements accompanied each site. The owner or head tanner's house was often the most impressive building. Individual worker's houses were small, crude wooden buildings. Most workers lived in workers' boarding houses, which were large and plain, but usually a small improvement on the camps occupied by loggers. Every complex had a company store, the only ready source of both food and clothes. (The Wheeler-Claflin Company Store is the best documented, because a complete inventory for the store with prices for individual items is extant. The inventory is summarized in the Fulton County Chapter to illustrate the costs a tannery worker encountered.) Horse barns for the teams stood nearby. Some settlements were so large that schools were built; churches quickly followed. To accommodate itinerant salesmen and visiting owners, hotels of sorts were added, and the inevitable saloon appeared.

Every tannery site had a blacksmith shop, a carpenter shop, and a harness shop. Sawmills were built near most tanneries; some were small, just big enough to supply the lumber for the tannery buildings; many were very large, independent operations.

Tannery Towns and Settlement Patterns

Such tannery complexes formed the nuclei of many Adirondack settlements. Most settlements began long before rail and plank road transportation reached their locations, so the settlements were not built as a result of good transportation. Nor were they built by loggers. Logging was initially not dependent on rail transportation, but on highways offered by navigable rivers, which could float logs downstream to mills, but were too rapid and seasonal to permit shipments upstream. However, the rivers did permit the shipment out of the region of most logs. Only small saw mills were built initially at remote sites. Many of the logging crews were seasonal workers, who traveled from peripheral towns to camps in the interior; but these camps did not surround themselves with the infrastructure of a small town as the tanneries did.

With the exception of potato farming in northern counties, farming at elevations about 1,200 feet in the Adirondacks was never successful on a large scale. So settlements for the most part were not spawned by agricultural communities either.

It was only the establishment of a fixed industry, one that settled in place for a period of years, that created so many Adirondack towns. Iron mining and smelting created a few towns on the eastern boundary of the region. Tanning created many more.

Shortly after each tannery was built, a school and a post office were added to the tannery complex. Magazines and books arrived; newspapers brought news of the outside world and reported local fires and the trips of important investors to the tannery sites. The account of Jerden Falls, one of the most isolated tannery sites in the Park, describes these ties with the outside world.

In 1885, Warren County Historian H. P. Smith observed that "It is a noteworthy fact that Wevertown, North Creek, and Creek Center in Stony Creek date the origin of their existence as villages immediately subsequent to the erection of the tanneries that now keep them alive."[11]

Horicon, too, in Warren County as well as Schroon Lake, Minerva, and North Hudson in Essex County all trace their roots to their tanneries. Across the Park, it was noted that "the little hamlet of Fine was awakened from slumber by the welcoming music of hammer and saw, in evidence that work had started on the tannery. It was the first worthwhile industry within the town limits."[12] Such development echoed again and again: at Newkirks and Wheelerville in Fulton County, at Hope, Hope Falls, Wells and later at Griffin in Hamilton County. Greig, Jerden Falls, Moose River Settlement, and Gray in the western Adirondacks all began as tannery settlements.

The tanneries brought much more than the complex of buildings associated with their operations. They brought hotels for transients, roads, and even telegraph lines—the permanent infrastructure associated with towns. The description of the individual tanneries given in Part II illustrates how their arrival generated the surrounding communities. The maps reproduced in Part II, depicting the layout of many of the tannery towns, emphasizes the relationship between the tanneries and the communities that grew around them.

As further testimony to the importance of the tanneries to the existence of these settlements, most reached a peak population in the 1880s and began to shrink as the tanneries left. Even logging was not sufficient to sustain more than a few of the remote towns, some of which took until the 1950s to recover their former population levels, and some of which disappeared altogether.

---

[11] Smith, p. 554

[12] St. Lawrence County historical records.

Power

All early tanneries were located beside rivers and streams, not just for the water required for the tanning operation, but for water to power bark grinders and rollers for finishing sole leather. A few early Adirondack tanneries reported using horses to grind bark. However, even with plentiful water, the bulk of the Adirondack sole-leather tanneries used steam in addition to water, sometimes just for heat, but as time went on, more and more for power. Many tanneries listed the number of cords of wood consumed in the Census accounts—a rule of thumb indicates that they burned roughly a third to a half as many cords of wood as the cords of bark consumed and at a far lower cost per cord.

Water wheels of twenty-five horsepower were common early, while steam-powered engines ranged up to sixty-five horsepower.

Toward the end of the era, many tanneries were burning spent bark (bark from which the tannin had been leached in the tanning process). The account of the Moore Tannery at Redford tells how a novel and newly-patented method of burning wet bark was used.

Machinery and Innovations

Rolling mills and bark grinders seem to have been employed in almost all Adirondack sole leather tanneries, though the Census record is not complete. Advances in building the bark grinders had not proceeded far enough to solve problems of unevenness of grind, so leaching was not efficient. Further the unevenness of grind resulted in a fine-powdered dust, which was highly flammable and, as noted, one of the greatest causes of fires in tanneries. As late as 1902, writers noted the inefficiencies of existing bark grinders.[13]

By 1870, the larger tanneries note the use of hide mills, machines that beat and helped soften dry hides as they were being soaked and prepared for the tanning process.

---

[13] Contributors to **Hide and Leather**, *Modern American Tanning*, pp. 64-65

A number of tanneries report having barkometers. The later tanneries all report leaches in addition to the vats. A few reported pumps, one or two listed elevators—presumably mechanical means for lifting sides. One or two reported rockers-mechanical means of agitating the hides in a tannin solution. Even before the Civil War, grinders and rollers were quite common. A number of Census reports indicate that Adirondack tanneries had these machines.[14]

Three processes were not mechanized at all during the Adirondack era: unhairing, fleshing, and scouring. (Scouring means rubbing heavy hides with stones or brushes to stretch them; this process was usually applied to leathers that were to be curried for uppers.)[15] The greatest period of tanning machinery development, the last thirty years of the nineteenth century,[16] came too late for most new machines to reach the Adirondacks.

While it appears that no Adirondack tanner invented new machines or processes that were adopted elsewhere, there were at least three Adirondack innovations employed in the late 1870s. The Sawyer Tannery in Ellenburgh had gravity fed pumps and pipes to circulate water and liquor. Sawyer installed a pump based on the principle of the Archimedean screw to solve problems of particles of bark fouling ordinary pumps. At the tannery at Griffin in Hamilton County, vats were lined with clay, a process that does not seem to have been widely recommended in tanning literature in 1902[17]. C. T. Davis in his important 1885 treatise on **The Manufacture of Leather**, describes an innovation suggested by H. J. Botchford of Port Leyden. It would distill "sour" liquors so the acetic and other volatile acids could be recovered in pure form, freed of other substances of the liquors. "The distillage thus resulting ... is again used as a liquid in which the plumping of the hides may be very expeditiously and satisfactorily accomplished."[18]

---

[14] No figures are given for the numbers of tanneries using the different machines because the number of tanneries reporting the machinery is statistically too small to quantify meaningfully.

[15] Ellsworth, ibid, p. 173

[16] Watson, ibid. p. 10

[17] *Modern American Tanning*, ibid, p. 26

[18] Davis, ibid, p. 174

Categorizing Tannery Sizes By the Number of Workers

When tanning first came to the Adirondacks, it did so with individual farmers who tanned local slaughter hides. This was the same process as in Colonial times. A few such tanneries with one or two, occasionally three employees, usually family affairs, persisted throughout the nineteenth century in the Adirondacks, though their number gradually declined. They tanned a variety of hides and skins, from cattle to skunks. To categorize tanneries, we will refer to this type as a **Colonial** tannery.

To further give some order to the wide variety of sizes of tanneries that tanned imported, dry, or foreign hides, we will generally use a measure of size that reflects the Adirondack penchant for exaggeration. Those tanneries with 4 to 9 employees are called **small**; those with 10 to 19 employees are called **large**; those with 20 to 29 employees are said to be **larger**; and those with more than 30 employees are said to be among the **largest.** This bit of whimsy is based on real numbers, those from local records, and those from the United States Census of Manufactures. The accompanying chart details the numbers of tanneries in each category in each of the four Census years. The tanneries in this instance did not produce exclusively sole leather, but sometimes upper leather or a mixture of upper and sole leather.

Extracts

In addition to using hemlock bark for tanning, at least three Adirondack tanneries prepared extracts of tannin for shipment, this in spite of the weight and difficulty of shipping liquids over great distances. "The 1880 Census recognized only three tanning agents—oak bark, hemlock bark, and sumac. During the next ten years, however, there was a rapid development in the leaching of tanning extract,"[19] and by 1890, nationally, 5.6% of tanning agents was in extract form. The active tanning agent constitutes only about 10 per cent of the weight of

[19] Watson, ibid, p. 10

NUMBER OF TANNERIES SURVEYED AND THEIR RELATIVE SIZE IN RELATION TO EMPLOYEES

COUNTY	TOTAL SURVEYED	COLONIAL under 4 employees	SMALL 4 to 9 employees	LARGE 10 to 19 employees	LARGER 20 to 29 employees	LARGEST over 30 employees	
1850							
Clinton	29	27	2				
Essex	6	6					
Franklin	5	5					
Fulton	17	10	3	2	2		
Hamilton	2		1		1		
Herkimer	18	10	6	1		1	
Jefferson	22	18	3	1			
Lewis	4	3	1				
Oneida	4	2	1	1			only NE county
St.Lawrence	21	20	1				
Saratoga	14	11	2			1	
Warren	11	6	1	1	1	2	
Totals	153	118	21	6	4	4	
1860							
Clinton	13	9	4				
Essex	5	3			2		
Franklin	6	3	3				
Fulton	19	10	2	6	1		
Hamilton	4		1	1	1	1	
Herkimer	19	3	10	2		4	
Jefferson	26	16	5	4	1		
Lewis	9	4	3	1		1	
Oneida	4	1		1	1	1	only NE county
St.Lawrence	19	13	4	1	1		
Saratoga	10	4	2	2	1	1	
Warren	14	4	1	4	3	2	
Totals	148	70	35	22	11	10	
1870							
Clinton	Clinton missing						
Essex	8	4	2	2			
Franklin	8	5	2	1			
Fulton	13	3	2	6	2		
Hamilton	4			1	2	1	
Herkimer	10	7	2		1		
Jefferson	13	7	4	2	2		
Lewis	14	5		1	2	5	
Oneida	6		1	2	3	1	only NE county
St.Lawrence	21	11	7			1	
Saratoga	7	2	2	4	1	2	
Warren	12	1	1		3	3	
Totals	116	45	23	19	16	13	
1880							
Clinton	7		1	2	4		
Essex	4	2	1		1		
Franklin	9	1	3	1	1	3	2 with more than 100
Fulton	9	4	2		1	2	
Hamilton	10		5	1	1	3	2 mostly skins
Herkimer	7		5			2	part skin mills
Jefferson	11	2	3	4	1	1	
Lewis	13	1	3	2	3	4	
Oneida	7	1	3	1	1	1	only NE county
St.Lawrence	21	10	7	2		2	
Saratoga	5	1	2			2	
Warren	9		1	3	3	2	
Totals	112	22	36	16	16	22	

the bark, so this step made it more economical to transport tanning extract to tanneries than to locate a tannery near the forest. "There was a conflicting influence here, however, because if extracts were to be shipped, they required an additional process so that it remained easier to extract tannin from the bark at the tannery."[20]

In spite of the fact that this 1880 introduction came almost too late to influence production in the Adirondacks, there not only were extract mills in the Adirondacks, but some of them may have been in operation before 1880. Catlin and Hunt produced extracts at Griffin.[21] F. Shaw and Co. was known to have three extract operations, and one may have been the Silver Lake Tannery, which shipped extract for a brief period after 1882.[22] Lewis Cranford and Company produced extracts at Chases Lake in Lewis County in 1871.[23] An extract mill was said to be situated on the road to Lake Pleasant in Hamilton County, two and a half miles from Piseco, and extract from this mill was taken to tanneries at Wells.[24]

Because the weight of bark required to tan a hide was twelve times the weight of the green hide, it had been logical to locate tanneries close to the source of bark. In addition to the extra steps required, the weight of the barrels of tannic acid seem to bring questionable economies, especially when the liquor had to be shipped over the great distances between most Adirondack tanneries and the railheads. Only the Chases Lake extract operation was near a railroad; the others were more than a day's team ride away. In spite of the great distances, extract mills not only appeared in the Adirondacks near the close of the tanning era there, they appeared before the process was widely accepted elsewhere.

---

20 ibid, p. 10

21 New York, Vol. 110, p. 474, R. G. Dun Collection, Baker Library, Harvard Graduate School of Business Administration.

22 Mass. Vol. 18. p. 197, R. G. Dun Collection, ibid.

23 Hough, *History of Lewis County*, p. 547

24 Aber and King, *History of Hamilton County*, p. 154

Pollution

All of the tanneries were built near sources of water, which was used in every step of the tanning process; the large tanneries used 250 gallons of water for each hide tanned.[25] Hides were washed to free them of salt, and the salt water was washed down the nearby stream. Pieces of flesh and tissues were washed away. After the hides were sweated and the hair was removed, the hair, too, was washed into the stream. Lime had to be washed out, and flushed down the stream. Spent liquor and spent suspensions of tannin in water had to be flushed away as well. As the individual accounts demonstrate, the streams and rivers became incredibly polluted. Tanbark pollution was noted at the resort hotel, which was just downstream from the Wheeler-Claflin Tannery.

In the Catskills, where stands of pure hemlock were much more prevalent than in the Adirondacks, the rape of the forests and the scenes of destruction etched by piles of trunks and branches drew much comment, but the comments were based on aesthetics and concerns for declining property values as well as concerns about pollution. In the 1870s and throughout the 1880s in the Adirondacks, scenes of forest destruction appeared to elicit little more than the addition of the phrase "and the destruction of the tanbarkers" to the comments about the general destruction of the forests by the loggers. The Adirondacks had no accounts of reduced land values near the tanneries as there were in the Catskills—surely because the land around the tanneries in the Adirondacks was considered valuable at that time only to support the tanneries and produce bark and lumber.

---

[25] Watson, p. 20

VI

Tanners and Leather Brokers

Patterns of Ownership

The individual descriptions of the tanneries given county by county in Part II illustrate the various economic situations that governed tannery ownership. There were three basic types: local owners of individual tanneries, local entrepreneurs with more than one tannery, and outside firms that owned local tanneries. By far the greatest number of tanneries were owned by outside firms.

The simplest arrangements usually involved the Colonial tanneries, owned by individuals or families. Such ownership was often fairly stable, and such tanneries were often passed from father to son.

Similarly, family ownership distinguishes most small tanneries, those with four through nine employees, but there were significant exceptions to their stability. Not only did these tanneries change hands but they were subject to bankruptcies.

A few of the larger tanneries were also family affairs, with resident owners who sometimes passed their tanneries from father to son. A few were remarkably stable, with the tanneries spanning upwards of four decades, but most changed hands with remarkable frequency and quite often had a period of embarrassment[1] or went into receivership.

The second basic type of ownership involved an individual or a family, residents in the area, who acquired several nearby tanneries. There were very few individuals who were entrepreneurs of this sort. Milton Sawyer in Warren County is the

[1] The term "embarrassment" is used in the R. G. Dun and Co. ledgers to indicate financial problems.

owner of this type with the most tanneries. He expanded into Essex County and at one time had interests in nine tanneries, but his financial record is marked by a number of reversals. The Burhans of Warrensburg likewise expanded to the north, but theirs is a story of noteworthy success. And the Botchfords of Lewis County appear even more exceptional in their financial dealings, even though their success was short-lived.

A third type of ownership pattern comes from the monied leather brokers of the Swamp or the shoe manufacturers of Boston. Tanning arrived in the Adirondacks at a time when individual businesses everywhere were growing in size and complexity. In the 1850s, the shoe and boot industry in Massachusetts was becoming organized into efficient factories.[2] Tanners from the Swamp were undoubtedly influenced by the efficiencies of such a large well-ordered complex as that of Gideon Lee. These men, a few of whom became residents of the north country, are particularly evident in the western Adirondacks, where several families held interests in more than one tannery: the Rice brothers and H. D. H. Snyder, Jr. Many, however, were absentee owners, such as William and Lee Claflin of Boston, shoe and boot manufacturers from out-of-state who desired to control the cost of raw materials through controlling the tanning process.

Most of the owners of the larger tanneries also held large tracts of land to ensure supplies of bark for their tanneries. The Claflins' ownership of two-thirds of the Town of Caroga and the Lyons' ownership of a large part of John Brown's Tract illustrate these mega businesses.

The Adirondacks has several other examples of ownership by brokers from the Swamp: the Garners in Luzerne are an example of a New York tannery owner who expanded into the Adirondacks. Jacob VanWoert of Lewis County was an owner with roots in the Swamp who settled upstate. Thomas E. Proctor, also originally from the Swamp had at least three tanneries in the western part of the region. Thorne, Watson and Co., one of the largest houses in the Swamp, figures in deals to place hides in tanneries across the Adirondacks and both Jonathan Thorne and John Watson were the silent partners in many upstate tanneries.

Several New York City tanners took over failing tanneries to protect their investments; among them was Fraser, Major and Company. Rice, Emery and Company was an outside company,

---

[2] Hazard, *The Origin of Boot and Shoe Industry in Massachusetts Before 1875*, p. 108

which built a huge tannery in the Adirondacks. In the eastern Adirondacks, all but one of those companies taken in receivership were closed before the end of the Adirondack era. Several tanneries, most of them in the western Adirondacks, survived to be incorporated into the United States Leather Company. And one company, which acquired many large Adirondack tanneries, failed spectacularly.

F. Shaw and Company, the Shaw Brothers firm of Massachusetts, acquired several tanneries in northern New York State and in Maine in the early 1880s, including the Oregon Tannery in Hamilton County and the St. Regis Tannery in Franklin County. They made their move into the Park rather late in the tanning era, and by then they had acquired so many tanneries that the Shaw Brothers firm owed upwards of four million dollars when it declared bankruptcy in the late 1880s.

Individuals and firms, which illustrate these different patterns of ownership and had the greatest impact on the Adirondacks, are described in greater detail at the end of this chapter and their relationships to particular tanneries in the different towns are described in even greater detail in the county-by-county analysis of Part II.

The men who built the larger tanneries and lived near them were often men of financial substance. Their homes were often the most imposing private buildings located near the tanneries. Some, like Lyman R. Lyons of Lyons Falls, had other interests around which they built their fortunes. Several were bankers: Linus B. Barnes, owner of the Wevertown Tannery, was given a charter for the Warren County Bank of Johnsburg in 1845. That bank closed when the tannery was sold in 1859. Col. B. P Burhans of Warrensburg was the first president of the Old Brown Bank. (Typical of Adirondack tannery exaggeration, both banks were locally said to be the oldest in Warren County.)

As the number of tanneries shrank and their sizes grew, ownership was reduced to a few men or companies with larger holdings. But even these larger businesses were threatened by the wild swings in the price of green hides and by panics in the financial markets. This concentration of tannery ownership prevailed; and by 1892 mergers were building the United States Leather Company, which went on to control upwards of ninety percent of the production of sole-leather in the United States.

The United States Leather Company

The descriptions of individual tanneries are rife with stories or indications of bankruptcies and receiverships. These stories and the downturn in the industry in the late 1870s and 1880s, explored in later economic analyses, indicate just how perilous the tanning business was financially. The price of leather fluctuated widely throughout the nineteenth century. It advanced from 18 to 50 cents a pound in the Civil War years of 1862 to 1865; it dropped drastically in the late 1870s. Cycles of boom and bust wiped out personal fortunes. By the 1880s, competition and overproduction made tanning even more risky. Finally, in 1893, a grand partnership, formed by the largest tanners in the east, was incorporated into the United States Leather Company, creating a virtual monopoly.

The formation of a large corporation was precisely what was happening in almost every major American business—oil, railroads, logging, for example—in the last decades of the nineteenth century. It was a logical result of trying to find ways of dealing with the increased production of the era, the falling prices, and the volatility of business.

The incorporators of the United States Leather Company were tanning merchants and owners with roots in the Swamp and in Boston. Sixty sole-leather tanners with 110 of the largest tanneries in the east joined in the new corporation[3]. The corporation initially controlled sixty percent of the country's sole-leather production and at the time it was formed was the largest corporation in the United States.[4] Several of the incorporators had tanneries in the Adirondack region: N. W. Rice and Company of Boston listed among its four tanneries the huge one at Fine. Thomas E. Proctor and Company of Boston had tanneries on the Oswegatchie and at Wilna as well as on the southern tier of New York State and in Pennsylvania. Lee and Company of New York City owned tanneries at Croghan and Cedar Run; J. V. VanWoert & Company also of New York City was at Greig and Union; Bullard and Company of New York City was at Star, Belfort, and Castorland.

---

[3] Watson, ibid, p. 27; Watson's figures for the size of the corporation differ from the totals given by Norcross.

[4] Norcross, *A History of the New York Swamp*, pp. 183-188; presumably "largest" here is in terms of capital investment.

By 1895, the capital stock of the conglomerate was given as $128,000,000; but the United States Leather Company never had sufficient working capital to take advantage of the swings in the price of hides. A general business depression prevailed for the first six years of the company's existence. The corporation was reorganized in 1904, but long before that time, sole-leather tanning in the Adirondacks had ceased.[5]

As soon as the company was formed, it immediately dismantled some of its north country holdings and bought others in Wisconsin and the west, where the corporation continued tanning sole leather mostly with hemlock. The remaining Adirondack tanneries were dismantled within a few years of the formation of the huge corporation. In spite of significant investments elsewhere, the corporation built no new tanneries in the Adirondacks.

The Adirondacks never entered into the modern phase of tanning, which was reorganized as a vertical business where companies controlled the packers, who were the sources of hides, the tanners, and the factories that produced the leather products. One such firm, Endicott Johnson, was capitalized at over three million dollars in 1901 and in 1939 still controlled over 12% of the country's leather production.

Was the reason the United States Leather Company never expanded in the Adirondacks the precarious business climate, or the failure of the accessible bark supply, or the remoteness of the remaining Adirondack hemlock bark from meat packers and shoe manufacturers? Economic analyses of Chapters VI and VII will begin to answer these questions.

Parenthetically, the American Hide and Leather Company, similarly formed by tanners of upper leather, never attained the size of the United States Leather Company. Only one company with a tannery near the Adirondacks was listed as an incorporator of that group: Hall, Haight, and Company of New York City and Boston built an upper-leather tannery in the Town of Wilton at Ballston Spa, a relatively addition to north-country industry.[6]

---

5 Watson, ibid, p. 29

6 Norcross, ibid, p. 189

Adirondack Firms and Their Styles

Shifting ownerships caused by economic changes are only part of the problem of unraveling clues to various tanneries and of correlating Census information with tanneries identified in deeds and local histories. Some tanneries are listed as belonging to the managers and not the owners. Shifting partnerships and name changes were caused by death or the addition of sons or other relatives to the firms. Sometimes new investors became listed as partners and the partnerships only lasted for a year or two.

As a result, almost every tannery business underwent some change of name or "**style**," in the vernacular of the day. The changed styles not only caused confusion in attempts to sort out who owned which tannery, the numerous styles appear to indicate far more tanneries than there actually were; and it is inevitable that the discussions of particular tanneries includes erroneous associations of records, in spite of the care taken to straighten out the chains of ownership.

Among the more amusing of the styles given family tanneries was what happened to the name of one firm after the death of Thomas Fraser, the founder. His less well-known, surviving brother restyled the firm, Thomas Fraser's Brother and Company.[7]

Turnovers in the ownership of some tanneries seemed to occur almost every year. If this book had included all the turnovers of all the tanneries mentioned in the county-by-county descriptions, not only would there be an interminable list, but the amount of research in deeds and other records would have been overwhelming. The book relies on the research of others, particularly that of Aber and King in Hamilton County and John Hastings in Warren County to spin out a few of the lists of changing owners and managers. Reading them will give the reader a flavor for the rapid turnovers. Note that in these cases there is an attempt to correlate Census information and records from the R. G. Dun and Co. with the records derived from deeds, but even this proved such a difficult task that the result remains, at times, confusing.

---

[7] Norcross, ibid, Norcross's account of the name change may be apocryphal because the Census uses the style Thomas Fraser and Brother, Company, before Thomas's death.

Adirondack Tanners and Tanning Companies

Two aspects of Adirondack tanners and tanning companies stand out: One is that every tannery owner in the north country, with one glaring exception, had a connection with a leather broker or shoe manufacturer in New York City or Boston. The exception was a tanner who seems to have suffered repeated reversals of fortune. The second aspect is that the outside connections—the silent partners, the suppliers of hides, the investors, or the relatives in brokerage houses—were not known locally in the Adirondacks. These mysterious figures wielded tremendous power in the Adirondacks and in many ways shaped its early development. Repeated references in the R. G. Dun and Co. Ledgers indicate that little or nothing was known locally about such men.

The following roster of Adirondack tanners contains both residents, known locally, and outside firms, whose principles remained enigmas in the tannery settlements. The list is not intended to be complete—that would be an impossible task, running into many hundreds of names. This is a list of the more important and unusual tanners, those about whom something is now known. The list will serve as a guide when reading the various county histories, for many tanners had interests in more than one county. These vignettes serve as a summary of Part II's more detailed descriptions of the various tannery operations.

More importantly, the examples gives anecdotal evidence of the vicissitudes of the tanning industry. They introduce the entrepreneurs who created the Adirondack tanning industry and demonstrate that, with few exceptions, the giants of the field were connected to Boston or New York. The examples show that the force behind the building of Adirondack tanneries and hence most settlements came from investors who wished to exploit the region for their personal gain. Analysis of the financial strength and weaknesses of the New York and Boston investors is a fascinating part of the story. Among the local entrepreneurs, only a few were successful, and among those who failed were men with stories as fateful as the outside entrepreneurs.

William Shaw and Son, Fayette Shaw and Company, or Shaw Brothers was the style of a giant tanning company, which included Fayette's brothers and nephews from Boston. It appeared on the Adirondack scene around 1880, buying up tanneries that were already doing poorly. They acquired interests in the tanneries at Oregon (1880) and Wevertown (1883) in Warren County, Rudeston (1881) (Silver Lake or Piseco)[8], Arietta (1882), and Wells (1880 or 1881) in Hamilton County, St. Regis (1879) in Franklin County, the St. Lawrence Tannery (1879), and Wheelerville (1883) in Fulton County. Two of the Fayette Shaw and Company tanneries burned and one was rebuilt by different owners. The brothers' bankruptcy closed the rest around 1883; a few continued under receivership; and only the St. Lawrence Tannery survived for any length of time, and that under new ownership. The Charles Shaw tanneries fared a little better: Wevertown was closed in 1886 after a fire but Oregon remained in operation until 1892.

Rumors in the Adirondacks exaggerated their bankruptcy to eleven million dollars. It was actually less, but the magnitude and drama of their failure exceed its monetary value. When the firm's parent, William Shaw and Sons, opened a Boston office in 1866, it already had another office in Montreal; tanneries in Detroit, Michigan; Plymouth and Dexter in Maine; Roseboro, Waterloo, and West Farnham in Canada, and in Massachusetts. These were said by R. G. Dun and Co. to include the largest tanneries in the United States. The corporation was valued at $1.8 million in 1873 and was considered profitable. Their immense business shipped leather to Europe.

The company suffered in the years 1875 and 1876 with the falling market. In 1877 the firm, styled Fayette Shaw and Bros. (Buckley and William) had a reputation for tanning its own hides at "a less price than any other in country."[9] The family firm had the "secret of tanning-full operation." [10]

In 1879, in spite of some losses, the firm was estimated to be worth $2.7 million with holdings that included five large tanneries and 300,000 acres of timberland in Maine. That year, at the beginning of the firm's expansion into the Adirondacks, the company was importing hides at a rate of 60,000 a month and achieving an estimated gain of 5 to 10 cents a pound, for a yearly profit approaching half-a-million dollars. It continued adding upwards of a million in capital in the next two years.

---

[8] The Rudeston Tannery went by all three of these names at different times.

[9] Mass., Vol 77, p. 294, R. G. Dun and Co.

[10] Mass, Vol 77, p. 375, R. G. Dun and Co.

In 1882, the firm reported assets that included $750,000 in tanneries and related buildings, $225,000 in extract mills and related buildings, steamers, wharves, 150,000 cords of bark worth $600,000, hides worth $600,000, $60,000 worth of goods in eight stores, shingles, leather in eight tanneries worth $1.1 million, machinery, 1.5 million acres of timberland, and so on, for a total net worth of $6.722 million and liabilities of $1.722 million. The Boston house was reported to have annual sales of $6 million, and all assets were clear except the Boston store. Shortly after this report was made, the father William Shaw, died at age eighty-five.

For the next year, the company continued to report substantial assets, but apparently it had a considerable debt due to loans. For some reason, the firm, in July of 1883, suddenly went into bankruptcy and the assets were assigned to a trustee. An audit showed debts totalling $7.5 million as against assets of $5.2 million. The failure of the Shaw firm brought down two other tanners, W. E. Plummer and John F. Mills, who had interests in two of the New York tanneries. "F. Shaw ran away to Canada soon after the assignment was made to avoid arrest."[11]

A committee of creditors was formed to sort out the liabilities. They reduced the original estimate by assuming a value of only 50% of the capital value of the tanneries. Several proposals were made to pay off the indebtedness. For nearly a year, no agreement was made to settle claims against the company.[12] A settlement with the creditors was finally made in May of 1885 at 30% and C. W. Clement "now holds the property as trustee for a syndicate which furnished over a million dollars to make the settlement. ... By terms of the Clements trust deed, he is to sell the ppty [sic] for the benefit of the syndicate within 2 years. ... The tanneries are being run on hides furnished by others. ... Running is in the hands of Fayette, Brackley, and Thaxter Shaw, who receive a salary for their services. ... He [Clement] is selling off the ppty as opportunity occurs. Clement is also in the shoe bus. on his own account as a manufacturer, he was involved in the Shaw failure and compromised at 30 per cent."[13] Final set-

---

[11] Mass. Vol. 18, p. 197, R. G. Dun and Co.

[12] Mass. Vol 18, p. 197. R. G. Dun and Co. *The entire page in the ledger is devoted to the unexplained failure of F. Shaw and Brothers.*

[13] Mass. Vol. 18, p. 88, R. G. Dun and Co.

tlement with the creditors was not arranged until 1887, and even then some of the timber land was seized by the creditors.[14]

This cautionary tale is typical of the problems encountered by even the largest and most respected tanning firms in New York and Boston. For none of the others are records of problems so complete and most of the large firms did not suffer the magnitude of failure as did the Shaws. However, there is evidence that Thomas E. Proctor, and others with reputable firms, did face difficult times in the 1880s; the fact that 75% of the sole-leather tanning industry joined to form the United States Leather Company indicates how widespread the industry's problems were.[15] Paradoxically, even the collapse of the Shaws' firm did not put the brothers out of the tanning business-the brothers were able to relocate in Michigan.[16]

The tanneries at Wevertown and Oregon were owned by Charles Shaw, son of Charles O. Shaw of Dexter, Maine. This Shaw was considered successful, "notwithstanding the shock given other Shaws and leathermen in 1883."[17] Because the Oregon Tannery continued under Charles' ownership, his business must have been somehow insulated from the affairs of Fayette Shaw and Co.

Milton Sawyer was the Adirondack's most active home-grown entrepreneur, but he suffered the vagaries of the business. His lack of personal business success, while not as dramatic as that of the Shaws, marked him as the most significant of the local failures, even though he appears at times to have been quite successful and was able to invest in or build as many as nine Adirondack tanneries.[18] He had interests in five Warren County tanneries, Pottersville in 1845, Sawyer and Mead, North Creek in 1852; Chestertown in 1856; in partnership in the Bowman Tannery at Stony Creek in 1856, and Warrensburg in 1870, and three (possibly four) in Essex County–Hoffman, Schroon Lake, The Branch, and the ephemeral Excelsior-Schroon. Both Hoff-

[14] Mass. Vol. 18, p. 88, R. G. Dun and Co.

[15] There is some confusion about how much of the industry was controlled by the United States Leather Company. Figures range from 75% to 90%. The corporation may have started with the lower figure, but apparently grew so the control was close to 90%.

[16] Watson, ibid. p. 29

[17] New York, Vol. 610, p. 401, R. G. Dun and Co.

[18] See the Warren and Essex County chapters for details of his holdings.

man and the Schroon tanneries in Essex County date back to 1856. R. G. Dun and Co.'s Warren County reporter noted that only the Stony Creek and "maybe" Chester made something in 1857, "but the others were losing concerns." It was reported that there was "some competition as to purchase of timber lands," and all but the two tanneries purchased bark considerably and at high prices. Then came the crash of 1857 and Sawyer used the "means of Sawyer and Bondman (Bowman) against the others and finally sold out Stony Creek to Bondman and received his pay cash down." Sawyer and Mead were reported as having made nothing since 1856 and their tannery at North Creek was idle most of the time in 1857, with considerable bark on hand and "no credit" was advised.[19]

Sawyer's financial reputation improved through the years of the Civil War and after the war he was recognized as a "good businessman making money (in tanning), also in clothing business." In the next few years it was noted that he still had three or four working tanneries, lots of real estate, and a good reputation.[20] He had three sons, Joseph, Charles, and George working in his tanneries at various times.[21]

In 1872, Sawyer's Warren County interests were reported to be "hard pressed - claims has sufficient to pay his debts - that tanning business has not been a success for past 3 years." Before the end of the year, he had gone to Schroon Lake.[22] The R. G. Dun and Co. records indicate that he had two tanneries in the Schroon Lake area in 1872 and one that had "burned last winter." That year he was said to have been running only the larger tannery at North Hudson,[23] but as the Essex County story indicates, Sawyer lost the tanneries in which he still had interest before the end of the decade. His Essex County holdings failed in 1873, with assets of 5,000 acres of timber land, 17,500 cords of bark and tanneries worth $30,000. Some of his holdings were assigned to a trustee in 1874, and by April of 1875, he was out of

---

[19] New York, Vol. 609, p. 69, R. G. Dun and Co.

[20] New York, Vol. 609, p. 69, R. G. Dun and Co.

[21] Letter from Janet Appleyard, Milton Sawyer's great-granddaughter, Jan. 29, 1980.

[22] New York, Vol. 609, P. 68, R. G. Dun and Co.

[23] New York, vol. 93, p. 223, R. G. Dun and Co.

business.[24] He was still hanging on, trying to sell his Schroon Lake Tannery in 1879, but eventually even that effort failed.[25]

Sawyer's story is instructive, for not only did his tanneries suffer in relation to reversals in the nation's economy, his "embarrassments" were more severe than those of the larger outside firms. In addition to losing all his tannery ventures in the two counties, he apparently was responsible for the beginning of Charles H. Faxon's problems in 1858 (see below). For three decades, Milton Sawyer had interests in more tanneries than any other individual in the Adirondacks. (Only F. Shaw and Co. of Boston had interests in a greater number of Adirondack tanneries.) Sawyer expanded well beyond the Burhans family, but he was never worth as much as any of the Burhans. Was it the fact that he had no relatives or silent partners in a brokerage in New York City that left him at the mercy of the ups and downs of the period's business cycles?

Even though he had none of the essential family connections in New York, he did have a brother, Aaron, who built the Ellenburgh Tannery, which as the firm of W. and E. Sawyer, owned by Aaron's sons, became one of the largest in that county.[26]

Charles H. Faxon of Chestertown was one of the kings of the logging industry and a leading industrialist in the region. It has always been assumed locally that his long-running tannery was stable, but R. G. Dun and Co. records indicate otherwise at least for the years after 1856 when Milton Sawyer became a partner. The crash of 1857 was especially devastating to Sawyer, and in 1858, R. G. Dun and Co. reported, "it is supposed that Sawyer will have to suspend, in which case, if Sawyer should fail, Faxon and Bros. would suspend also."[27] This may just be what happened, for the tannery continued to lose. In spite of the fact that local records and deeds indicate Faxon and his son continued as owners of the Chestertown Tannery, R. G. Dun and Co. records indicate that Sawyer and Faxon was sold to Hull and Knapp in 1865. Whatever happened, in 1868 Faxon's tanneries (sic, plu-

---

[24] New York, Vol. 609, p. 109, R. G. Dun and Co.

[25] Letters from Joseph Sawyer to his brother, September 13, and October 10, 1879.

[26] Hurd, *History of Franklin and Clinton County*, p. 321

[27] New York, Vol. 609, p. 27, R. G. Dun and Co.

ral?) were described as "not paying too well now."[28] Faxon's Chestertown Tannery burned with full insurance, and was rebuilt in 1870. It is presumed that without Sawyer, Faxon finally succeeded in the tanning industry, and as the Warren County Chapter indicates, he was able to expand his real estate and other ventures and his logging company so that he was later called one of the kings of the industry.

The Burhans family had interests in three tanneries in Warren and Essex counties. Col. B. P. Burhans' Warrensburg Tannery was among the longer running sole-leather operations in the Adirondacks. In a partnership with Thomas S. Gray, that dated back to 1836, the men expanded the tannery until in 1855 Burhans was reported to be worth, $400,000, Gray $100,000.[29] Burhans, in partnership with his son a decade later, was reputed to be worth upwards of a million, and he was still worth a million when he died in 1875.[30] In addition to the tannery, Burhans owned stores and real estate and founded a bank.

His brother, E. W. Burhans, with Charles W. Osborne, built an Essex County tannery at North Hudson. His son, Frederick O. Burhans, had a large tannery at Horicon, in partnership with Gray. This tannery burned in 1856 with a loss according to R. G. Dun and Co. of $60 to $70 thousand; the loss was insured and the owners quickly rebuilt and recovered their reputation as the safest firm in the vicinity. Gray sold out to the other partners (B. P. Burhans and his son Frederick) in 1860.

The detailed look at Burhans' interests in the Warren County Chapter shows how clever he was at negotiating contracts for green hides. At first glance, it appears that the Burhans family were one of the few local people who made a success of the tannery business without outside connections, but even this was not true. No one knows how much he gained from his connection with the New York leather brokerage firm of Gray and Isham, which was succeeded by Isham and Gallop; but William B. Isham was B. P. Burhans son-in-law, proving once again that family connections helped ensure success in the tanning indus-

---

[28] ibid

[29] New York, Vol. 609, p. 269, R. G. Dun and Co.

[30] New York, Vol. 609, p. 269, R. G. Dun and Co.

try. (Isham was also Vice-president of Union Bank in New York City.)[31]

Jonathan Reed ran the North Creek Tannery and in 1879 he built the tannery at Oregon. According to one account, he leased the Oregon Tannery to a party which was supposed to have furnished dollars to build the tannery. Reed sued the parties, got a judgement, then sold the tannery to Billings and Eton.[32] Reed had acted as agent for Billings and Eton of Boston, and the suit involved these Boston leathermen. Reed struggled for a year or two, and was reported to be worth little or nothing because of the suit. He won a judgement against the Boston firm, but they took the case to the Court of Appeals, and although it was settled in Reed's favor, the tannery was sold to Charles Shaw. When last reported in 1886, Reed was running a boarding house.

Fraser, Major and Company from the Swamp took over two tanneries in Warren County, Pottersville and Adirondack on Mill Brook near Schroon Lake, and one in Essex County, Alpine at Minerva-Olmstedville. All three take-overs appear to have occurred when the tanneries were experiencing difficulties. The Essex County tannery was acquired in 1858, after the panic of 1857, the Mill Brook Tannery in 1860, and the Pottersville Tannery in 1865. The Pottersville Tannery's insolvency stemmed from the 1857 panic as well, and it was taken over in 1859 by Joseph Hallagan, a tanner from Oneida County. In 1865 Joseph Hallagan and Co. was reported as not having been losing too much[33], but obviously enough to spark the sale to Fraser, Major and Co.

Thomas Fraser, Brother and Company was a prominent firm in the Swamp. Thomas Fraser came to New York from Scotland in 1825 and married a daughter of a shoe dealer from the Swamp. He tanned upper leather in Ulster County and on repeal of Great Britain's duty on leather in 1844, Fraser sent the first shipment of United States upper leather to Europe. Fraser had agents in St. Louis and he procured the first hide agreements in the country's western Indian territories. Thomas had two brothers: James, who died in 1897, and Andrew, who died in

---

[31] New York, Vol. 609, p. 269 and Vol. 610, p. 243, R. G. Dun and Co.
[32] New York, Vol. 609, p. 298, R. G. Dun and Co.
[33] New York, Vol. 609, p. 29, R. G. Dun and Co.

1856. Thomas died in 1863 and when he died, James changed the firm's name or 'style' to Thomas Fraser's Brother and Company. In 1865 the firm of Fraser, Major and Company was formed with partners listed as James Fraser, William Kevan Major (Thomas' nephew), and two of Thomas' sons. This firm tanned sole leather until 1893 but did not join the United States Leather Company.[34]

The New York parent company, located on Ferry Street in the Swamp, was rated as the "best in the street"[35] in 1848 by R. G. Dun and Co. The company was said to operate at a profit through 1856, attracting new investors and Jonathan Thorne as a special partner in this period. In 1857, the company "lost some money during the panic, but not enough to affect credit," and was then said to be worth a half million.[36] The company continued to receive the best credit ratings in the Swamp and conducted a large commission business in addition to its hide and leather business. Thorne's $30,000 investment "has been suffered to accumulate til it has reached $240,000. He now goes out and the firm pays him $5,000 a month til whole is paid."[37]

In 1865, when Wm. H. Fraser became a partner in the firm, the remaining brother and Fraser were rated to be of average ability. In 1871, the partners in the firm were worth collectively one million.[38] The firm remained strong and earned such accolades as "strong house," "highly respectable," "large conservative business" from 1874 through 1888.[39]

It is no wonder the company was able to rescue the floundering Adirondack tanneries and keep them profitable. While the firm had many other holdings, it can only be surmised that its Adirondack holdings contributed to the firm's success.[40]

The Moore family of Clinton County had tanneries in Plattsburgh and Redford, none of them among the largest, but certainly among the best documented. Their tanneries were

---

[34] Norcross, ibid, p. 186

[35] New York, Vol. 189, p. 218, R. G. Dun and Co.

[36] Ibid

[37] New York, Vol. 189, p. 300D, R. G. Dun and Co,

[38] New York, Vol. 189, p. 287, R. G. Dun and Co.

[39] New York, Vol. 440, p. 633, 700 R, 700 A/2, R. G. Dun and Co.

[40] *R. G. Dun and Co. ledgers refer to the company as Thomas Fraser Bros. and Co. before the death of Thomas. This is another indication that the delightful story told by Swamp historian Frank Norcross about the origin of the firm's style may be fanciful.*

moderately successful, but again not without outside assistance. One of the three Moore brothers had a firm in Boston that supplied the Clinton County tanneries. In fact, according to R. G. Dun and Co., the Clinton County firm of A. M. Moore and Co., which looked after the tanning, was practically the same as the P. D. Moore Co. of Boston, which looked after the leather.[41]

W. and E. Sawyer Tannery Similarly, Clinton County's other large sole-leather tanner, the firm of W. and E. Sawyer, was actually a part of a Boston firm with the same name. In the 1860s this firm had started as Sawyer and Moore, with Perly D. Moore of Boston as partner. W. and E. Sawyer's Boston connection was strong enough to keep the Ellenburgh Tannery profitable under the direction of brother William right up to 1890, when the tannery closed, claiming it was losing money.[42]

Lee Claflin and Son (William) was a Boston firm which typifies absentee ownership and investment by a large shoe manufacturer. Their tannery at Wheelerville (Caroga) in Fulton County is also very well-documented by contemporary sources (see the Fulton County Chapter). The Claflins were visionaries who began designing the Adirondacks' first planned resort. The Claflins were among the first shoe manufacturers to attempt to secure a steady and uniformly priced supply of sole leather through the acquisition of a tannery. Their first tannery was at Beckett, Mass. Their Caroga tannery appears to be the only tannery in New York State controlled by the company, which poured considerable capital into land and the building of not only the tannery, but a large lumber mill and a hotel. According to Fulton County recorders, the parent Boston firm had an estimated net worth of $500,000 to a million in 1873, but this had declined to no more than $300,000 in 1879.[43] This decline was reflected in a loss of land in Fulton County because of a failure to pay real estate taxes in 1881. The Wheelerville Tannery was sold in 1882 to F. Shaw and Company and that sale sealed the tannery's fate.

The parent firm's decline in net worth was also recorded in the Massachusetts records of R. G. Dun and Co., from up-

---

[41] New York, Vol. 53, p. 440, R. G. Dun and Co.

[42] New York, Vol. 52, p. 60 and Vol. 53, pp. 427, 523, and 606, R. G. Dun and Co.

[43] New York, Vol 99, p. 117 and Vol. 99, p. 280, R. G. Dun and Co.

wards of two million in 1872 to $200,000 in 1878.[44] As with other tanners, it was reported in 1886 that the Claflin firm was "not likely to be making a great deal of money at present."[45]

Thorne, Watson and Co. was one of the largest and most reputable of the Swamp's leather brokerage houses. The company was founded in 1802 by Israel Corse, and became Jonathan Thorne and Co. in 1834. Jonathan Thorne was Corse's son-in-law, while John Watson was Zadock Pratt's brother-in-law,[46] again proving the value of family connections. Restyled Thorne, Watson, Corse and Co. in 1843, the firm broke up in 1852 and continued as Thorne, Watson and Co. In 1855, that firm was said to be the richest house in the Swamp.[47] Jonathan Thorne died in 1884 at the age of 84, a rich man with a farm in Dutchess County where he raised fancy breeds of cattle.[48]

As early as 1838, the company was issuing contracts for green hides in Warren County. (See section on Burhans of Warrensburg, Warren County Chapter.) Jonathan Thorne was a special partner in Fraser, Major and Company, which owned two Warren County tanneries and one in Essex County. Thorne issued contracts for hides with several Lewis County tanneries. Thorne built the huge Manheim Tannery, which is described in the Herkimer County Chapter.

Thomas E. Proctor of Boston controlled many tanneries in New York and Pennsylvania, among them three in the north country: Gray in Herkimer County, Forestport in Oneida County, and Wilna in Jefferson County. His Boston firm was reported as doing up to a million dollars a year in business in 1872.[49] He served as leather broker for the Jerden Falls Tannery run by the Rice brothers. A daughter of one of the Rice brothers remembers "the pleasant relations with his agent, Mr. Dubois, who visited the tanneries at certain intervals and was always a

---

[44] Mass., Vol. 69, p. 599QQ and p. A/92, R. G. Dun and Co..
[45] Mass., Vol 69, p. A/137, R. G. Dun and Co.
[46] Norcross, ibid, pp. 40-50
[47] New York, Vol. 189, p. 237, R. G. Dun and Co.
[48] Norcross, pp. 45-50
[49] Mass. Vol. 67, p. 216 A/70, R. G. Dun and Co.

welcome guest. Mr. Proctor came himself once to see the tannery, but we were not at ease with him."[50]

Perhaps because his Adirondack tanneries engaged in tanning on such a large scale, they were able to operate with a very small profit margin. But as the profits shrank and the business at the end of the 1880s became more precarious, Proctor was one of the movers behind the formation of the United States Leather Corporation. All Proctor's tanneries were folded into that giant corporation when it was formed in 1893 and Proctor became its first president.

Lyman R. Lyon was a Lewis County businessman. In 1866, he was in business with Snyder Bros. in different locations and was said to be worth a quarter of a million. In 1868, R. G. Dun and Co. said that former estimates of his worth were too low and listed his value at a half million.[51] In 1868, he was also said to have interests in tanneries as Lyon and Botchford, (see discussion of Botchford below). This firm received green materials from Thorne, Watson and Co. and Lee and Co. of New York.

Snyder's failure (see below), unrelated to the tannery industry, meant that the Lyon and Snyder Tannery supposedly lost $150,000 in 1868. Whatever the extent of Lyman R. Lyon's tannery interests, they came to a halt with his death in the summer of 1869, when he and H. D. H. Snyder, Jr. not only owned the tannery in Port Leyden but were building a second tannery at Moose River Settlement. The Lyon and Snyder (possibly H. D. H.'s brother Augustus B. Snyder) Tannery in Grieg was run for a short time by Chester Lyon, Lyman's son and heir. It was sold in 1871 to Jacob VanWoert. Lyman R. Lyon's estate left one-quarter of his property, estimated to be worth $100,000, to his son Chester. Apparently Chester ran the Port Leyden Tannery for a brief time and possibly even the Moose River Tannery[52], losing heavily in 1870, and acquiring judgments of $60,000 to $80,000.[53] Shortly thereafter, the Botchfords (see below) took title to the tannery and 20,000 acres of timberland, estimated as

---

[50] Hough, *A Tannery at Jordan Falls*, p. 9, paper in the Lewis County Historical Society collection.
[51] New York, Vol. 147, p. 103, R. G. Dun and Co.
[52] New York, Vol. 147, p. 182, R. G. Dun and Co.
[53] New York, Vol. 147, p. 198, R. G. Dun and Co.

being worth $150,000. Chester left the area taking a job with a railroad.

H. D. H. Snyder, Jr. got his start in the tanning business because of his father's Swamp connections: The father was a partner of William Creighton Lee, son of Gideon Lee.[54] The father had a tannery in Ephratah in Fulton County in 1860, which may have been managed by the son. Snyder Jr., at age 28 in 1861, had moved to Lewis County, and was "married and a little wild" but running a store in Lewis County. In 1863 his father loaned him $12,800 to buy out his brother's interest in a tannery and the store. By the next year he was known as a "speculative genius" and by 1866 his tannery business was said to be worth upwards of $75,000.[55] Later, in partnership with Lyman R. Lyon, he began construction of the "Mammoth" tannery at Moose River Settlement, which was actually big enough to be a candidate for the Adirondack's largest.[56] He also built iron smelters and was one of the Black River Valley's leading industrialists; but his financial problems caused by the failure of his iron smelters and by the death of his partner drove him from the tannery business and from his home in Port Leyden before the mid 1870s.[57]

The Botchford brothers (Henry J. and George M.), with their father, had three large Lewis County tanneries: on Otter Creek, on the Moose River, and on the Oswegatchie. The aggregate value of production from these three tanneries ranks them as the north country's most successful tanners. However, they started with what is obviously the key to success—connections to a substantial Boston leather broker, the Charles W. Hersey Co. In 1872, the Botchfords attempted to take over the tannery at Moose River Settlement, formerly owned by Lyon and Snyder, but occupied that year by Todd and Kennedy.

Apparently the Todd and Kennedy Tannery and lands were sold to or taken over by Thorne, Watson and Co. of New York on foreclosure of $44,000, and the Botchfords were able to acquire half interest. In 1874, it was noted that Henry lived in Boston and that the Botchford firms were run by firms in New

---

[54] Norcross, ibid, p. 59
[55] New York, Vol. 147, p. 92, R. G. Dun and Co.
[56] See Lewis County chapter for details of this Mammoth Tannery.
[57] Conway, *Port Leyden*, p. 34

York "who control everything." H. J. Botchford and Co. was said to be a part of the firm of Low Hersey and Co. of Boston.[58] The Botchford's were also said to have bought 10,000 acres for $80,000, with a $40,000 mortgage in 1874.[59]

In 1875, it was observed that the Port Leyden Tannery remained with the Lyon estate, but was leased by Botchford, backed up with Boston money. That tannery burned and was never rebuilt or again operated by the Botchfords. The family did have a second tannery, one owned by their father in Harrisville, near the border of Lewis and Jefferson counties, which they ran for several years.

The third tannery run by the family was on Otter Creek. The firm of Lyon and Botchford at Moose River (presumably the Lyon estate still had an interest) suspended business in 1878, with "all hands discharged," though their "tannery at Alter (sic, really Otter) Creek is yet in operation, but it is unclear how long they will continue-they are losing." [60]The Botchfords did not fail, however, but continued with George M. managing the Otter (Creek) Lake Tannery (also know as Grieg or Glensdale) and Henry J. at the Moose River Tannery, but always in the background there was Charles Hersey of Boston, apparently because he held controlling interest in the Lyon estate.[61] In 1880, the Botchford's Moose River Tannery had the largest production value of any area tannery, $300,000. Because that tannery burned in 1883, the year of depression, the Botchfords apparently lost control of all of their tannery interests to the Hersey Company.

Jacob VanWoert also had connections to the Swamp. His Greig Steam Tannery, acquired in 1870 from the Lyon estate, was among Lewis County's and the north country's largest. In 1870 he acquired the Brantingham Tannery on Fish Creek and in 1871 he bought a large quantity of land in Lewis County. While his father (Jacob V.) was a leather merchant in New York City,[62] Jacob was said to be rich in his own right. He ran the two

---

58 New York, Vol. 147, p. 153, R. G. Dun and Co.

59 If this figure, given in New York, Vol. 147, p. 253, R. G. Dun and Co. is correct, it is the highest recorded figure for timberlands discovered for this period.

60 New York, Vol. 147, pp. 263, R. G. Dun and Co.

61 New York, Vol. 147, p. 253, R. G. Dun and Co.

62 Norcross, ibid, p. 179-180

large tanneries, which may have been originally financed by his father, and in 1875 took over his father's New York City business. The tanneries were still being run successfully in 1880.

The LeFevre family ran a large tannery under the style J. and G. Le Fevre in Northville in Fulton County from 1858 through 1865. The business experienced difficulties in early 1858, and "lost money along with other traders," because "they filled up their tannery when hides were high."[63] Later that year they were said to have been doing "as well as other tanners all of whom have lost by the price of leather last fall."[64] There are no indications why the tannery closed in 1865, but from then on the family concentrated on their Beaver Falls Tannery in Lewis County, which the Census indicates was never very profitable. In spite of its low level of profitability, it was one of the north country's longest running–from 1856 to 1894. Details of this tannery's operation under the ownership of a son, Martin, are given in the Lewis County Chapter.

The Rice family of Lewis County had tanneries at Croghan and Jerden Falls, the latter one of the most remote sites for a tannery in the western Adirondacks. The story of life in this wild place is recounted by a daughter of one of the Rice brothers in the Lewis County chapter. In spite of the Jerden Falls Tannery's great distance from a railhead, that tannery appears to have been profitable, although its owners, too, sold out to New York brokers. The Rice family appears to have had support from their uncle, Loring Andrews, a Swamp merchant, who invested in the tanneries and supplied them with green hides. The Rice brothers sold out to Bullard and Company during the disastrous decline of 1883, but they do not appear to have suffered reversals of fortune.

Rice, Emery and Company or N. W. Rice and Company of Boston also came to the area late in the tanning era and had interests in tanneries at Edwards and Fine in St. Lawrence County and at Griffin in Hamilton County. The company owned a tannery in Chautauqua and in addition to the tanneries, the parent firm was involved in importing hides. The parent company's

---

[63] New York, Vol. 99, p. 53, R. G. Dun and Co.

[64] New York, Vol. 99, p. 53, R. G. Dun and Co.

business record parallels the ups and downs of the era, improving in 1879, declining in 1881, shrinking in 1886.[65] Their Edwards Tannery was closed before 1880, but the other tanneries were incorporated into the United States Leather Company by the successor N. W. Rice and Co. in 1893.

S. R. Spaulding and Son of Boston built the St. Regis Tannery in Franklin County in 1865 and acquired and expanded the St. Lawrence Tannery in Colton in 1868. In 1869, the Spaulding company bought the Lower Tannery in Wells, Hamilton County. The latter suffered several reversals and changes of ownership and was sold before the end of the decade. The senior Spaulding died in 1875 and his son under the style E. G. Spaulding and Company continued operating the three New York tanneries. Edward G. Spaulding ran into significant problems in 1876 and was said to have considerable real estate but owe a great deal in 1877. That year, R. G. Dun reported that the tannery at Colton had a "serious interruption in business about two years ago-have not recovered." [66]Shortly the business failed and was sold to the Shaw Bros. firm of Boston.

The Brownell family of several sons in several generations were involved in logging and tanning in the Adirondacks throughout the second half of the nineteenth century. They owned two tanneries in Hope in Hamilton County and one in Mayfield in addition to several saw mills. R. G. Dun's Fulton County reporter[67] did not have the same faith in the family's business as the Hamilton County reporter did, but from 1870 on their firm was "considered good in every respect."[68] It held a large amount of real estate and timber lands in addition to the tanneries. Under the style Lewis Brownell and Bros. (John, Robert, and Ira Jr.) the firm remained prosperous through 1880. In 1881, the Brownell tanneries in Hamilton County were tanning hides on commission. Although the tanneries ceased operation in the next decade, the family's logging interests continued to be profitable. The family is remarkable in that it still has logging operations and lumber mills in the same area; in fact, it may

---

65 Mass. Vol. 77, pp. 141, 167, 166, 416 and 445, R. G. Dun and Co..

66 New York, Vol. 553, p. 579, R. G. Dun and Co.

67 New York, Vol. 99, p. 180. R. G. Dun and Co.

68 New York, Vol. 100, p. 240, R. G. Dun and Co.

be the only family in the north country connected with nineteenth century sole-leather tanning still engaged in logging there.

Stephen Griffin, 2nd has always been a mystery. He is remembered as being associated with several Adirondack tanneries, but mostly because he gave his name to the archtypical Adirondack ghost settlement. Even though he did have interests in at least one tannery, little that substantiates his reputation as a tanner has been documented. Primarily, it appears that he arranged for the harvest of bark on his and other land holdings. The information on Griffin detailed in the Hamilton County chapter finally straightens out his land holdings and connections to several tanneries, subjects that have been a mystery for years.

VII

Costs of Adirondack Hemlock Bark Tanning

The most impressive aspect of the figures given for tanning costs is the size of the numbers involved. Huge amounts of money were required and seem astronomical compared with other costs for the times. Even in today's terms, the numbers are large. After analyzing various costs, we will attempt to put them in perspective so we can show the relative importance of tanning to other Adirondack industries and so we can compare Adirondack tanning with tanning in the rest of the State and in the whole country.

It is difficult to give comparable figures for the value of money, though wages do give an indication. Better yet, the items listed for sale in a typical company store, the one in Wheelerville, Fulton County, give an indication of relative costs.

The Costs of Hides

The price of hides fluctuated wildly, undoubtedly determined in part by the quality of the raw material. The ability of a tannery owner or broker to exact a good price and a good contract, while not precisely demonstrated in any of the statistics, certainly seems to be an important factor in the profitability of the tannery operations.

Hides were obtained from merchants and brokers in Boston and New York City. These dealers had contracts that typically obliged the tanners to pay a 5% fee for the purchase of the hides. The dealer also received 4% of the sale price of the finished leather, plus an additional guarantee of 2% of the value of the raw material.[1]

Most Adirondack tanners never really owned the hides; the only property held was the **gain**,[2] the difference between the value of the finished leather and the value of the raw hides. The dollar value of the gain is one important measure of a tanner's financial success. (Gain, as noted earlier, is also a term applied to the increase in weight of finished leather over raw hides and as such also measured the tanner's success as a craftsman.) Financial gain did not reflect the many other elements, wages, the costs of other raw materials such as bark, interest on hides, interest on capital investment, and insurance, that determine financial success. We will later define another measure of a tanner's financial success that considers some of these elements, but in this section the relation of costs to gain is a very important way of determining the effect of those costs on a tanner's ultimate financial success.

There is no question but that the price of hides rose significantly in the second half of the nineteenth century. The average cost of the 476,000 hides acquired by the 128 north country tanneries in 1850 in the study area[3] was $2.20 a hide. In 1860, the average was a dollar more, and yet another dollar more in 1870, almost doubling the cost of two decades earlier. The costs declined slightly in the next decade to about $3.40 per hide, while the price of leather dropped dramatically.

These figures undoubtedly only tell part of the problem of fluctuating supplies and costs. Until the Civil War, the supply of hides was relatively predictable, for cattle were raised primarily for their hides and the bulk of those used for sole leather were imported. After the Civil War and after the completion of a rail network throughout the United States, long-distance shipment of cattle and meat within the country became possible. The industry became less dependent on foreign hides. As this happened, hides became mere by-product and the supply and costs became unpredictable. "When hides became simply a by-product of meat

---

[1] Norcross, ibid, p. 57

[2] Norcross, ibid, p. 59

[3] These figures were computed from a subset of the Census data. Tanneries were included in the subset only if there were sufficient data to make the computation.

packing, the supply lost all relation to demand and a gambling influence was injected into the industry."[4]

The Costs of Adirondack Land

There are no general figures for the cost of land. Lee Claflin and Son were known to have paid almost $4 an acre in 1865 for some of the virgin land in Fulton and southern Hamilton counties. Throughout the 1870s, figures of $2 an acre are common. R. G. Dun and Co. Ledgers indicate that the Botchfords of Lewis County paid $8 an acre for a 10,000-acre tract in 1874.[5] This is the highest amount noted in the area and it seems exceptionally high in light of the fact that Lyman R. Lyon paid $12,500 for 95,000 acres of the John Brown's Tract in 1850.[6]

Stephen Griffin paid just over $7,000 for 10,000 acres in Hamilton County in 1880. The 12,500 acres that make up Santanoni Preserve were purchased for $1 an acre in 1883. But, land on which both timber and bark had been harvested was almost worthless after 1885; witness the amount of land acquired by the State for delinquent taxes (Lee Claflin and Son of Wheelerville forfeited lands in this way as did many others.) The value of land continued to decline at the end of the century. The 1895 sale by Hersey and Company of lands surrounding the site of the Moose River Tannery may even have been high at 75¢ an acre.

Since most land with stands of hemlock could be acquired for $2 an acre in the 1860s and 1870s, the amount of land, 30,000 to 50,000 acres, needed to support an average large tannery for twenty years, required capital investments of upwards of $100,000.

Even if no precise average figures for the cost of land exist for the period in question, one fact stands out: an acre of land had less value than an imported, dry hide! In 1850, hides and acres of land were comparable in value, but by 1860, a hide was worth double the value of an acre of land; and in 1870, a hide was worth slightly more than an acre of land.

---

4 Watson, ibid, page 11

5 New York, Vol. 147, p. 253, R:. G. Dun and Co.

6 Brown. *John Brown's Tract.* p.322

Workers and Wages

Tannery workers in the Adirondacks were predominantly French Canadians and Irish. Details of the families at Griffin illustrate the preponderance of Irish and French Canadians and the way they intermarried. Stories that accompany the description of the tannery at Minerva-Olmstedville show how Irish immigrants were attracted to the tanneries. Agents met the boats in New York City to induce the Irish immigrants to travel to the north country: men for the tanneries and the woods, women for the boarding houses.

Many of the early town records list a heavy majority of men. Single men could travel to the wilds in search of work, albeit work that paid almost too poorly to support a family. The one exception to the fact that tanning was exclusively a man's business was a woman teamster for the Horicon Tannery. Her story is most eloquently told by a man who knew the tannery when he was a boy (the story accompanies the account of the Horicon Tannery). A few women were listed as workers in various tanneries, but probably only as bookkeepers.

The average monthly wage in 1850 was $19.95 for a twelve-hour work day in summer (ten-hour in winter) and a week that was six and sometimes six-and-a-half days long.

The wages increased slightly in the next decade to an average of $23.62. In 1870, the Census changed its method of reporting, giving yearly wage totals rather than monthly totals. The calculated average monthly wage, $37.09, compares favorably with the stated average daily wage of a bit more than a dollar. The average wage for 1880 appears to be slightly lower. The chapter on the Wheeler-Claflin Tannery in the southern Adirondacks summarizes the wage patterns of this typical large tannery, based on the information given in the company's wage book, which has been preserved in private ownership. Wages there in the mid-1870s ranged from 75¢ a day for menial labor, to $2.00 for the more skilled work, but only a few master tanners achieved that level.

How did these rates compare with wages nationally? During the two decades from 1870 to 1890, wages nationally rose only slightly, less than 10%. Adirondack tannery wages were also remarkably constant in this period. But, while the Adirondack worker gained no more than the average worker in dollars, his

TOTAL NUMBER OF WORKERS IN SURVEY TANNERIES
FOCUSING ON SOLE AND UPPER LEATHER

COUNTY	1850	1860	1870	1880
Clinton	30	29	missing	77
Essex	8	62	50	37
Franklin	7	18	42	105
Fulton	95	136	145	116 *
Hamilton	21	72	94	100
Herkimer	75	199	60	177
Jefferson	63	135	84	124
Lewis	10	65	316	366
Oneida				200
St.Lawrence	42	80	109	111
Saratoga	67	102	126	164
Warren	119	184	259	177
Totals	537	1082	1285	1754

* *In 1870 there were 186 additional workers in skin mills, more than 200 additional in 1880.*

These are not absolute numbers, since not all tanneries surveyed reported the number of workers. The numbers should be interpreted as showing trends, only.

buying power, like that of the rest of the nation's workers, improved significantly.

Nationally, prices fell dramatically in this period as a result of mechanization and advances in productivity. This decrease meant that a worker's buying power increased sharply, from 10 to 20% in the decade of the 70s, 25% more in the 80s. Even so, it has been observed that in spite of the increases, the average industrial worker with a family "had a small chance of living properly."[7] Little wonder that most workers in the north were single men.

The Census indicates that some tanneries kept busy twelve months a year; but many did not, operating as few as four months out of the year. Shutdowns were common, the Census reports about 10% of the tanneries were "at rest" in every given Census year. Resulting layoffs led to instability for the workers and enormous fluctuations in the number of workers employed. The maximum number of workers at a given tannery was often two or more times the average.

---

[7] Garraty, *The New Commonwealth*, p. 130

The descriptions of the LaDue Tannery at Gray in the Herkimer County Chapter and the St. Lawrence Tannery at Colton demonstrate how all workers' accounts were credited to the company store. From that account it is easy to conclude that workers lived a hand-to-mouth existence, almost indentured to the company store.

All this seems to suggest a picture of exploitation of labor, about what would be expected in the age of sweat shops and before the time of labor unions.

Woods work was always seasonal, with few woodsmen employed for more than half the year. To give perspective to the wages, lumberjacks in Township 34 (Blue Mountain) earned between $25 and $30 a month, plus room and board. River drivers made $1.75 a day at the end of the century. It has been estimated that loggers averaged between 75¢ and $1 a day for general work in the woods.[8] A few reports indicate that a woodsman on a logging crew could sometimes earn $2 a day, but his work was limited to less than half the year. Only the most skilled workers in a tannery earned as much. Tannery workers were at the low end of the economic stratum; there were obviously enough workers, their numbers fueled by immigrants, to allow the tannery owner to keep the wages low.

Comparing Adirondack tannery workers with those in other industries indicates that in 1890, for instance, textile workers earned about $350 a year, comparable to the average tannery worker. Only boys and laborers earned significantly less. Workers in the steel industry earned an average of $450 a year, about what the more skilled tannery worker earned. Even the master tanners at the top of the scale could not earn as much ($700) as the average brewery worker.[9]

When the tanneries closed, most workers moved on. A few were given land in lieu of wages. Anecdotes in the Hamilton County Chapter tell how this happened in Wevertown to relatives of workers in Griffin. But, for most, when the work was over, there were no other sources of employment. Almost every town in the Adirondacks shrank by over 50% after 1880, as both the tanning and lumbering industries declined.

Wages were a remarkably small part of the cost of tanning, as was the case with most industries of the time. (Labor costs

---

[8] From Finch, Pruyn records compiled by Richard Nason

[9] Average worker's salaries are quoted from Garraty, ibid, pp. 130-131

have become significant only in the last half century.) Total annual wages pale when compared to capital investment or the value of the finished products. However, those relationships changed over the years. Wages rose slightly in the period, but the relationship between wages and gain increased markedly, a further indication of the way tannery profits were squeezed after 1870. For instance, in 1850, total wages were just over 10% of the value of the finished leather, about 25% of the gain; in 1860, the best year, total wages were only 5% to 7% of the value of the finished product and only about 10% of the gain; in 1870, total wages crept up to 8% to 12% of the value of the finished leather but represented between 25% and 35% of the gain; in 1880, wages were only a slightly higher percentage of the value of the finished leather, but they represented from 30% to 50% of the value of the gain, all this without significant rises in the level of wages.

The Costs of Bark

While many economic components affected the profitability of Adirondack hemlock bark tanning, none was more apparently the cause of the demise of the industry than the cost of harvesting bark. The total cost of a cord of bark represented the cost of harvesting the bark, hauling it in from distant forests, and stacking it. That cost, therefore, included the cost of labor to perform these operations. But labor costs rose nowhere as rapidly as did the costs of bark, indicating the increasing distances over which bark had to be hauled.

In the 1850s, Adirondack bark averaged $2.17 a cord to harvest, well below the figures in Colonial times and the costs experienced in the Catskills in the 1840s when the Catskill era was coming to an end. An 1852 contract called for the W. and K. Evans Company to cut, peel, and deliver bark to the Olmsted and Cornish Tannery (Minerva-Olmstedville) for $1.62½ per cord.

A decade later, bark was still quite inexpensive, averaging $2.67 a cord, though the costs in Warren and Fulton counties had risen to just over $3.00 a cord. By 1870, the cost of bark throughout the Adirondacks has risen to $5.58 a cord and some locations were reporting shortages, although two counties reported bark costs well below the average: Franklin County reported $3.88 a cord, and Lewis $4.72 a cord. By the early 1880s, places in Warren, Essex, and Fulton counties were closing for want of bark and even the available bark in the western Adirondacks, which lasted for just a few years longer, brought about $6.00 a cord.

The accompanying chart summarizes the rising cost of bark in the Adirondacks. The chart could almost be represented by the increasing radii of the circles that described the areas from which bark was hauled.

Year	Average cost[10] of a cord of bark
1850	$2.17
1860	$2.67
1870	$5.58
1880	$6.00

Bark costs were often roughly equal to a tannery's total annual wage. It can be argued that because bark costs were actually the costs of men and teams of horses, nearly as many men must have been employed in the woods to harvest bark as were employed inside the tanneries. The few indications of the size of barking crews certainly substantiates this.

Since wages were relatively constant in this period, the near trebling of the cost of bark points up the great distances over which bark had to be hauled to existing tanneries and confirms the disapperance of accessible bark.

The Costs of Borrowing Money

When a large New York or Boston firm sent hides to be tanned at one of its own tanneries, that firm alone was responsible for purchasing the hides. Some large firms could finance

[10] These figures were computed from the Census records for all of the region's tanneries that reported such costs in the four Census years. No chart has been prepared to show variations in the costs in different counties because most of the statistical samples are too small to be meaningful.

their own purchases; most had to issue notes for this. Firms with good ratings were able to obtain loans ("sell paper" in the vernacular of the day) as low as 3%. This ranged up to 7% during the 1870s and 1880s. Because these firms often produced leather for their own shoe and boot factories or because they acted as their own brokers in the sale of finished leather, there was but the one interest charge.

Independent tanners, however, faced two interest charges: a 5% charge when they obtained hides and a 4% commission when the leather was sold. This would seem to indicate that being an independent tanner was difficult and risky, and it was. Almost every tannery that started out being independently owned, sooner or later ended up being owned by one of the large leather brokerage houses or shoe and boot manufacturers in New York City or Boston. The one independent tanner, Milton Sawyer in Warren and Essex counties, was unique; and he paid a high price for his independence for most of his tanneries had difficulties. Investigations reveal either silent partners in New York or Boston or a relative in one of those places in almost every other firm.

Some tanneries took hides and tanned them on commission for a fee, so much per pound of gain. This was not the usual Adirondack practice, but it became more common in the 1880s. Still, only a few instances of this practice in the Adirondacks have been documented.

Not only did the tanner have to finance the acquisition of green hides and pay commissions on their sale, he had to finance the building of tanneries and the purchase of timber land to supply bark. Consider that a tanner had to borrow capital to build a tannery (see below for more on the size of the capital investment): a loan of upwards of $100,000 would be needed for the larger tanneries. Financing the acquisition of timber land might require $50,000 to $100,000 more. Consider also that he had to finance the acquisition of $100,000 worth of green hides, for example; and that he had to process these green hides in his tannery for up to eighteen months. Then, if he had also to pay a commission on the sale of the finished leather, it is quickly obvious that interest charges could wipe out all profits or the margin of profitability as it is later defined in this book. You have to marvel at those who did manage to make money from tanning but you can also begin to understand why almost all of those who did were owned by silent partners or had financial backing from relatives in leather brokerage houses in New York and Boston.

The Value of Finished Leather

Even for the space of a given year, individual tanneries reported wide variations in the price of a finished hide; this variation probably had much to do with quality, but the market did change rapidly.

The average value[11] of a side is given in the figure below:

Year	Value	Number of tanneries in sample
1850	$2.76	8
1860	$3.44	24
1870	$4.23	34
1880	$3.59	43

The decline in the decade between 1870 and 1880 is a further indication of the way the profits of Adirondack tanners were squeezed.

No significant variations between the value of sides produced in the different counties can be detected for the first three Census decades, but in 1880, Lewis and Fulton county hides were worth more than the average, Essex, Hamilton, and Clinton county hides less.

The approximate total value of the output of Adirondack sole-leather tanneries was over $726,000 in 1850 in the twelve large tanneries; over $2,614,000 in 1860 for the twenty-nine large tanneries that were analyzed; over $5,085,000 for the forty-six totaled in 1870; and $5,721,000 for the total production of the sixty-two large sole leather tanneries tabulated in 1880. Note that even though the number of large tanneries (in terms of workers) had increased in 1880 over 1870 by nearly 40%, the to-

[11] Computed from a selection of sole-leather manufacturers. Tanneries were included in the subset only when there was enough data in the Census report to permit the cost to be calculated, but the subset represents almost all of the sole-leather tanneries.

COUNTY BY COUNTY VALUE OF PRODUCTION
LARGEST SOLE LEATHER MANUFACTURERS ONLY

COUNTY	1850	1860	1870	1880
Clinton		$22,500		$185,500
Essex			$256,000	$65,250
Franklin			$255,450	$505,000
Fulton	$103,500	$237,400	$455,300	$425,000
Hamilton		$312,800	$501,000	$447,180
Herkimer	$185,396	$578,000	$120,000	$145,000
Jefferson	$20,000	$165,000	$382,500	$393,000
Lewis		$214,000	$1,471,250	$1,526,500
Oneida				$360,000
St.Lawrence		$80,000	$254,600	$296,000
Saratoga	$142,080	$91,123	$316,000	$593,000
Warren	$275,880	$914,500	$1,073,410	$780,000
Totals	$726,856	$2,615,323	$5,085,510	$5,721,430

tal value of the sides produced by the tanneries increased by less than 14%. This seems to indicate overbuilding and an increase in capacity beyond what made economic sense.

The above chart gives approximate totals by county.

The High Cost of Capital Investment

In the first half of the nineteenth century , it was said that "every owner of a thousand or ten thousand acre tract of hemlock land could build a tannery, get a few skilled workmen from Massachusetts, find a Swamp merchant who would stake him to hides,"[12] and set himself up as a tanner. The one thing omitted from this description was the cost of building the tannery itself.

Consider that one of the typical large tannery complexes reportedly cost $50,000 and that it cost $100,000 to $300,000 to build the largest complexes. This was because a vat shed could cover upwards of 30,000 square feet; a complex could have six or eight buildings and required such machinery as steam boilers, grinders, pipes, and rolling equipment. Add to this the fact that the investment usually included the company store and houses as well and often the surrounding woodlands with their stands of

[12] Norcross, ibid, p. 64

bark. There have been suggestions that the capital investment figures given in the Census are inflated, and it is difficult to judge how much they are inflated. Still, they do give a rough picture of how much money was invested in the north country.

From $10,000 to $125,000 was spent to build an individual tannery before 1850, but most of those we consider large cost around $40,000 at that time.[13] Costs stated in the 1860 Census are roughly comparable to those in the 1850 Census report. In 1870, capital investment in an average large tannery remained about the same, but the cost of building the few new, larger complexes in the years just prior to 1870 rose significantly: In Lewis County, figures of $240,000 and $300,000 were given for capital investment, Jefferson County had two tanneries that cost over $100,000 to build, Fulton County had one that cost over $150,000 to build, and Warren County had one valued at over $100,000. These figures represent both the increase in size of the newly constructed tanneries and the increasing costs of building. The average capital investment reported in 1880 varied only slightly from the 1870 figure; but there were only five reporting more than $100,000, one each in Saratoga, Warren, Franklin, and Hamilton counties and three in Lewis County. Typical of the reporting was the largest tannery in Fulton County, whose stated capital investment, reported at $150,000 in 1870, declined to $50,000 in 1880. It is not clear whether decreases of this type reflect an amortizing of capital investments over a period of years, or actual decline in value.

It really is hard to analyze the costs of tannery investments, for much more than the tannery buildings was involved. Sawmills had to be built, roads had to be pushed into the wilderness, houses and schools were needed. It is not clear whether the Census figures for investment in a tannery include any of these peripheral but essential expenses.

Summing up the capital investment of the dozen largest tanneries[14] in five counties in 1850, the Census figures total just over $400,000. Thirty-five tanneries in nine counties were said to be capitalized at $1,265,000 in 1860. The reported total for

---

[13] Richard Wiles believes that the figures for capital investment during the first half of the nineteenth century are suspect and perhaps not comparable with the figures for the second half of the century.

[14] Large is here determined both by number of employees and size of capital investment.

forty-four tanneries in ten counties in 1870 almost doubled to nearly $2,500,000[15]. And, reflecting the general economic decline that occurred prior to 1880, the 1880 Census reported a decline in total capital investment to $2,300,000 for the sixty-two large sole-leather tanneries.

When the tannery sold or came upon hard times after two decades, the stated capital investment declined sometimes to only twenty percent of the original. The buildings were worthless when the bark on the surrounding forests was gone. The costs of these capital investments and interest on them had to be recovered over an incredibly brief period. In their waning years, most tanneries probably afforded the owners slim profits, if any profits at all. It is hard to see how any great profits were made, even without the wild fluctuations in the costs of raw materials and the price of finished leather, except by those who began in the 1860s and sold out or moved on within little more than a decade.

The costs of building increased throughout the period. Those who built the few largest tanneries that opened in the late 1870s and through the 1880s, faced costs of building that were larger than would be expected from the increases due to size alone. This observation is based on reports of capital investment in Lewis County, which rose significantly through the period, faster than the size of the complexes themselves.

All told, an enormous amount of money was invested in the north country, for the figures cited represent only the sole-leather manufacturers, those with ten or more employees. The number of small tanneries, especially in the earlier years analyzed, was double that of the larger ones; the number of large tanneries devoted to upper leather in later years increased to nearly twenty percent of the total. Capital investments for these tanneries would not double the stated totals, but they would add a significant proportion to them. While it is difficult to give a true figure for the capital investments brought to the north country by tanning, it is fair to say that a tremendous amount of money was invested there in the second half of the nineteenth century and that a great deal of it went to construct the infrastructure of future villages and settlements. The next chapter will assess the relative importance of these investments.

---

[15] This figure is comparable to the totals for the slightly different area that can be derived from the 1865 New York Census.

VIII

Economics of Adirondack Hemlock Bark Tanning

How Profitable Were the Tanneries?

Profits are even more difficult to quantify than some of the expenses, especially as the Census does not give all the data needed, including such important figures as the cost of borrowing money. But no matter how you look at the profit figures, it appears that the profits at first seemed enormous, even when compared with the huge sums given for investments and operating expenses. No wonder so many rushed to invest in the Adirondack region. But while the profits for the late 1860s and early 1870s were substantial, inexorably they began to fall. Profits were down everywhere in the 1880s, and still new investors appeared—most simply taking over a failing enterprise, but a few buying up or taking over existing, marginally profitable tanneries, gambling that profits might still be there. However, most tanneries closed in the 1880s, the few that were left closed in the next decade or so.

Why did the tanneries leave the north country so abruptly after 1880? Every local historian has noted that there were two reasons: the failure of the bark supply and the introduction of chemical tanning agents. Since chemical tanning agents were not widely adopted for sole-leather tanning until after 1920 and since we have focused on manufacturers of sole leather, that part of the double answer is at least wrong. Further, although the accessible bark supply was nearing exhaustion at existing tanneries, hemlock stands were untouched in well over half of the Adirondacks.

What were the other reasons why it was no longer economical to produce leather in northern New York? Was the widespread decline in tanning profits in any way responsible for the end of the Adirondack era? Or was it a combination of economic problems and the dramatic failure of local bark supplies that explains the industry's demise? And, what is the answer to the most important question, "Why were there no further investments in tanneries in the Adirondacks after the 1880s?"

Certainly swings in the costs of hides, the values of finished leather, and the price of bark are relevant. Certainly, as the stories of individual tanneries indicate, there were a number of changes of ownership, bankruptcies, or the frequent takeovers by "assignees," who became owners of floundering businesses. All these point to the financially perilous nature of the tanning industry.

A statistical analysis, based on the United States Census of Manufactures, shows that all were becoming less profitable at an equal rate, independent, apparently, of the available bark supply. What the abrupt failure of the bark supply accomplished was the precipitous closing of tanneries that had already fallen on hard times, and to describe that we will have to look more closely at the profits of individual tanneries and at regional profits.

In the process of creating a statistical norm for the various Census years, it is logical to sum and compare the figures for gain and because figures for financial gain are given for national totals, we can use this figure to analyze just how significant the Adirondack tanneries were in the national picture.

But more information is needed. I will create a model that assesses broader components of a tannery's profitability. The reader may wish to use this figure to check the information given for particular tanneries in order to determine how they varied from the State-wide, or in some instances, county-wide averages.

Figures for very small tanneries are omitted even though some tanned only sole leather. Their costs vary even more wildly than the larger ones, so the statistical base is limited for the most part to the larger (capable of processing over 20,000 hides) tanneries.

The following is an attempt to analyze what little numerical information is available from a significant number of firms in order to determine if there are patterns. To perform the statistical analysis, the basic problem inherent in the Census—the changes in the method of reporting—must be overcome. In addition, there are a number of illegible or missing entries. Some tanneries lumped information on upper and sole leather in a way that could not be separated. The method of analysis I have chosen eliminates these variations in the Census and permits comparisons over all four Census decades. The sample of the sole-only tanners, susceptible to this analysis, is not large. However, it is adequate to determine for each Census year the figures and totals we have already examined, items 1 through 6 below[1], and use them to compute not only gain but one new numerical tool:

1 - The average cost of a cord of bark
2 - The average cost of a raw hide
3 - The average cost of a finished side of sole leather
4 - Total capital investment
5 - Wages
6 - Value of finished leather
7 - Gain—the difference between the value of the finished leather and the cost of the raw hides
8 - **A tannery's margin of profitability**: this is defined to be the percentage given by the equation: Let M be the margin of profitability; let V be the total value of production; let C be the major costs, defined to be the cost of annual wages and raw materials (bark and hides).

$$\text{Then } M = 100 \times (V - C) \div V$$

Other costs of wood, debt service on the large capital investments, debt service on loans to acquire raw hides, insurance, and so on, are not included in the formula because there is not enough information on them to deal with them separately. However, the percentage does give us a measure of profitability against which all the tanneries can be compared and which is quite telling over the decades in question. Further, this percentage indicates what proportion of the revenue was available for debt service, other expenses, and the all-important potential profit.

Because computing this measure of profitability permits a comparison over the full four decade years of the Census and a comparison of the general economic picture in the different

[1] *Figures given for items 1 through 6, on which the computations for gain and profitability are based, are slightly different from those given for the larger survey set to obtain the study region averages computed previously; but the differences are very small and statistically unimportant.*

counties, the results are quite graphic in the way they demonstrate the industry's decline. A few tanners, essentially the financial brokers from New York or Boston who owned several tanneries, were able to sustain their businesses with consistently lower profitability figures because of their large volume. But even these larger businesses met with difficult times in the 1880s, and they either went bankrupt, like the Shaws, or worked to create the United States Leather Corporation conglomerate, like Thomas E. Proctor. Empirical evidence indicates that if the profitability figure for individual tanneries fell below 15%, they were in trouble and changes in ownership followed.[2] For larger businesses, 10% was acceptable, but only for a time.

In 1850, sufficient samples are available only for Herkimer, Fulton, Warren, Saratoga, and Jefferson counties and little variations by county are noted. The average cost of raw hides was $2.85. The average cost of a cord of bark was $2.83. The lowest figures were in Fulton County and $3.00 was a common price elsewhere. The value of a side of leather was $2.60. This is not quite the Colonial standard often quoted as tanning doubling the value of the hide. In fact, as the century progressed, the value of a side of leather gets farther and farther from this norm. Remember that a side is half a hide, so tanning was often viewed as cutting a hide in half and making the value of a tanned half equal to the value of the original whole.[3]

The average profitability for 1850 was 24.4%, for a sample of eleven tanneries, the only figures available. Total gain for these same tanneries was reported at over $300,000.

In 1860, bark was comparably priced and consistently low, with an average of $2.79 a cord, although figures of $3.00 and $3.50 were common. Of the five lowest prices, three were in Warren County. The average cost of a hide was $4.23, computed from a base of 22 samples. The highest cost was $5.00 reported in Lewis County, reflecting growing transportation costs. The average value of a tanned side of sole leather was $3.57. The average profitability figure was 24.9% for the region, and 28% for

---

[2] *There is one glaring exception to this observation: the LeFevre Tannery in Beaver Falls consistently had some of the lowest profitability figures computed. Maybe the family just made a comfortable living from this long-running tannery, without gambling wildly to expand. Maybe they were exceptionally prudent and cautious.*

[3] Earlier, many Colonial tanners would tan a hide for a local farmer, give the farmer one side at no charge, and sell the other side to a shoe or boot maker.

Warren County, where even though individual tanneries ranged from 15% to 45%, most clustered around the average figure. Thirty-one tanneries reported a total gain of $1,177,900.

There were more samples in 1870 and a few more in 1880 reflecting the construction of large tanneries devoted to tanning sole leather. In 1870, the average cost of a cord of bark jumped to $5.20 computed from twenty-eight samples. Since wages did not similarly jump, the cost appears to reflect the distances over which bark was hauled. Most tanneries reported paying $5.00 for a cord, some paid $6.00. The county differences begin to show: Warren County's bark averaged $5.80 a cord, Lewis County's $4.64 (quite a difference!)

The average cost of a hide in 1870 was $5.00, and although it was slightly higher in Fulton County, there were no real variations in the costs between the counties. Nor were there any real county-driven differences between the average value, $4.24, of a side of finished sole leather. However, the profitability figures show marked county differences. The average for the region was 20.6%, almost 4% less than 1860. Even more telling was the fact that the average was only 15.8% in Warren County, while it was 25% in Lewis County. If you throw out one Lewis County figure (Beaver Falls) where the tannery seemed to be having singular problems, the county average is 27%.

For 1880, the Census lumped together the costs of bark and hides, so only the profitability figure and the value of a side of leather can be computed. That year, the average side brought $3.60, a figure considerably below that of a decade earlier, indicating that there was fierce competition and that the tanner was being squeezed for profits; although figures such as $4.27 for Lewis County and above $6.00 for Warren are noted.

The profitability figure, from forty-five tanneries, dropped spectacularly to 14.8% for 1880. Warren County's figure of 15% computed from a sample of eight tanneries is slightly lower than Lewis County's 18.3%. Only Hamilton County, with but four tanneries to analyze[4], seemed to be profitable with a figure of 27%.

[4] *One page is missing from the 1880 Census for Hamilton County.*

STATISTICAL COMPARISON OF TANNING AND LOGGING INDUSTRIES

Source: New York Census of 1865

SUMMARY OF NEW YORK CENSUS OF 1865 FOR TANNING

COUNTY	NUMBER OF TANNERIES	NUMBER OF EMPLOYEES	EMPLOYEES PER TANNERY	CAPITAL	ANNUAL WAGES	CORDS OF HEMLOCK	COST PER CORD	TOTAL COST OF HEMLOCK	COST OF RAW MATERIALS	VALUE OF PRODUCT	GAIN	GAIN AS A PERCENT OF CAPITAL
CLINTON	14	61	4.4	$123,931	$27,895	2,968	$5.83	$17,303	$144,666	$259,418	$86,857	70.1%
ESSEX	10	51	5.1	$43,200	$27,104	4,455	$4.65	$20,716	$34,767	$210,766	$148,895	344.7%
FRANKLIN	9	31	3.4	$55,400	$14,424	2,637	$4.17	$10,996	$85,511	$148,657	$48,722	87.9%
FULTON	18	111	6.2	$139,600	$44,370	11,980	$5.12	$61,338	$225,063	$406,718	$137,285	98.3%
HAMILTON	5	51	10.2	$37,650	$9,900	4,290	$3.90	$16,731	$151,496	$306,232	$144,836	384.7%
HERKIMER	16	157	9.8	$296,300	$43,985	14,445	$6.20	$89,559	$491,301	$901,877	$366,591	123.7%
JEFFERSON	24	131	5.5	$322,700	$55,229	7,852	$5.08	$39,888	$274,606	$419,915	$90,080	27.9%
LEWIS	17	199	11.7	$259,200	$74,770	27,445	$4.50	$123,503	$389,551	$1,073,281	$608,960	234.9%
ONEIDA	29	242	8.3	$547,400	$100,417	23,020	$5.70	$131,214	$518,964	$1,088,531	$469,150	85.7%
ST.LAWRENCE	23	94	4.1	$267,800	$35,349	7,465	$4.27	$31,876	$251,500	$256,127	($30,722)	-11.5%
SARATOGA	16	111	6.9	$205,800	$40,352	9,168	$5.42	$49,691	$284,450	$463,600	$138,798	67.4%
WARREN	16	224	14.0	$400,500	$81,885	25,401	$4.75	$120,655	$465,717	$1,775,971	$1,228,369	306.7%
NO. COUNTRY TOTALS	197	1463	7.4	$2,699,481	$555,680	$141,126	$4.97 AVG. COST	$713,470	$3,317,592	$7,311,093	$3,437,821	127.4%
STATE TOTALS	795	5802	7.3	$10,386,639	$2,253,662	$385,435			$13,762,484	$24,971,708	$8,955,562	86.2%
NO. COUNTRY PER CENT OF STATE	24.8%	25.2%		26.0%	24.7%	36.6%			24.1%	29.3%	38.4%	

STATISTICAL COMPARISON OF TANNING AND LOGGING INDUSTRIES

Source: New York Census of 1865

SUMMARY OF NEW YORK CENSUS OF 1865 FOR LOGGING

COUNTY	NUMBER OF ESTAB.	NUMBER OF EMPLOYEES	EMPLOYEES PER ESTAB.	CAPITAL	ANNUAL WAGES	COST OF RAW MATERIALS	VALUE OF PRODUCT	GAIN	GAIN AS A PERCENT OF CAPITAL
CLINTON	59	571	9.7	$517,950	$132,787	$232,791	$620,513	$254,935	49.2%
ESSEX	35	113	3.2	$38,350	$28,615	$44,234	$97,433	$24,584	64.1%
FRANKLIN	53	150	2.8	$121,600	$34,074	$52,250	$121,628	$35,304	29.0%
FULTON	84	167	2.0	$107,650	$31,783	$61,988	$156,154	$62,383	57.9%
HAMILTON	13	14	1.1	$8,300	$2,680	$8,725	$18,350	$6,945	83.7%
HERKIMER	83	155	1.9	$147,625	$35,601	$100,689	$141,761	$5,471	3.7%
JEFFERSON	90	164	1.8	$137,475	$26,862	$45,133	$98,337	$26,342	19.2%
LEWIS	105	273	2.6	$183,970	$49,475	$77,675	$230,582	$103,432	56.2%
ONEIDA	167	444	2.7	$328,025	$74,867	$135,311	$314,326	$104,148	31.8%
ST.LAWRENCE	97	312	3.2	$394,750	$50,445	$154,982	$332,917	$127,490	32.3%
SARATOGA	69	371	5.4	$283,550	$154,690	$193,370	$355,350	$7,290	2.6%
WARREN	56	163	2.9	$205,650	$37,624	$159,958	$304,875	$107,293	52.2%
NO. COUNTRY TOTALS	911	2897	3.2	$2,474,895	$659,503	$1,267,106	$2,792,226	$865,617	35.0%

The accompanying chart summarizes capital investment, gain, and profitability for all those sole-leather tanneries where sufficient Census data were reported to make the computations.[5]

These figures prompt the conclusion that the market was bad everywhere, tanners were suffering rising costs and declining market values. The tanner's profitability was decreasing, and the rate of decrease was greatest in the eastern Adirondacks where the tanning industry had been established the longest. The wave of tannery closures of the early 1880s was most pronounced where tanning had been going on the longest but was spread across the whole region. The failure of the harvestable bark supply remains an important factor in explaining the closing of individual tanneries but does not explain why no new tanneries were built.

The country had suffered a recession in 1878 and while none of the 1880 economic figures for tanning in the north country were good, they were on a par with the economics of tanning throughout New York and Pennsylvania. The figures explain the declining profits in tanning, but they do not entirely account for what happened in the early 1880s—the closing of all but a handful of the largest tanneries.

The Relative Importance of Adirondack Tanneries

Comparison of New York's Economy With the Nation's Economy

In 1850, tanning was the fifth largest industry in the United States, after lumber, flour, boots and shoes, and blacksmithing. Capital investment in sole-leather tanneries in 1850 in the Adirondack region we have defined amounted to little more than 1.7% of the capital investment in all tanneries nationally,

[5] The average profitability is computed from all the tanneries reporting. Note that the chart shows the size of the statistical samples, which, because of the vagaries of the reporting, is unfortunately very small. However, I believe it remains large enough to give valid comparisons.

and only 7% of the capital invested in all of New York State's tanneries. In 1860, the region's share of capital in New York was over 11%, and its share of national investment capital was just over 3%.

The region's investment in sole-leather manufacture represented just over 15% of the value of the State's production in both 1870 and 1880. In 1870 thc region represented 4% of the nation's total capital investment; in 1880, the region's proportion had shrunk to 3%.

Looking at a slightly different set of base numbers, the total number of tannery workers in the region, not just those in the large sole-leather manufacturers, we find that the region's workers constitute 2.2% of all workers nationally in 1850, 4% in both 1860 and 1870, and 4.4% in 1880. In the same intervals, the proportions of all the northern region's tannery workers to the State totals were 10.3% in 1850, 17% in 1860, 18% in 1870, and 24.6% in 1880.

The value of production in this group amounted to 6.5% of the State's production in 1850, 10.7% in 1860, 15% in 1870, and 20.7% in 1880.

The north country's gain from sole-leather manufacturing amounted to 1.8% of the nation's total in 1850, 5.9% in 1860, 6% in 1870, and only 3% in 1880.

The figures, which compare the region's production in numbers of sides of sole leather with the State's totals, show the north country in an even more favorable light. In 1870, the area we have defined as the Adirondack region accounted for nearly 25% of the State's production; in 1880, the proportion rose to 33%.

In addition to showing the relation between the tanning industry in the Adirondacks and in the rest of the State, these figures suggest that sole-leather production was less expensive in capital investment and employed relatively fewer workers than in the rest of the State.

A corroborating set of figures can be drawn from the Census for the State of New York for 1865, the only year of that Census when such computations are possible. Remember that the study regions, for the way the two Census reports (State and Federal) are used, are different. The 1865 State information includes all the settled areas of Saratoga, Herkimer, and Oneida counties, but it raises the region's proportion of the State's values only slightly. The totals in the accompanying chart show that in

1865, 24.8% of the State's tanneries were located in the region defined by all of the twelve counties. They represented 26% of the capital investment in the entire State. They employed 25.2% of the State's tannery workers, paying them 24.7% of the total State tannery wages. However, these same tanneries consumed 36.6% of the total bark consumed State-wide. They converted 24.1% of the value of raw hides in the State into 29.3% of the total production value of leather. The region's gain represented a whopping 38% of the financial gain derived from tanning State-wide. No wonder so many investors were drawn to the north country in ensuing years.

However, no matter what way the relative value of the components of the north country's economy are assessed, by workers, wages, capital investment, value of production, or gain, tanning is seen to represent a very small proportion of the nation's figures for the same components. Throughout most of this period, New York's leather production trailed behind that of Pennsylvania and just ahead of that of Massachusetts.

With one exception, the figures show that the north country's workers and capital investment were less than 20% of State totals for the critical 1860-1880 period, and that, at best, for a brief period, the total production accounted for between a quarter and a third of the State's total.

For all the interest in regional tanneries, their impact on growth and settlement and their accompanying stress to the forests, these comparative figures show that Adirondack hemlock bark tanning had only a minor importance on a State-wide level, and it was almost insignificant when compared to the output of the national industry, which had begun its move west.

Importance of Tanning To the Growth of Settlements Within the Adirondacks

Next, we try to assess the impact of tanning on the Adirondack economy. This is not an easy task. It is like the proverbial comparison of apples and oranges. Logging and milling lumber, milling flour, mining iron ore and separating it, all of which occurred in the north country region, are industries whose products are based on the raw materials of the region. The product of tanning is based on a raw material that is shipped to the region; the product is only loosely based on the native raw material—hemlock bark.

As has been shown, tanning's capital investments were not great when compared with State-wide totals, but they had an extraordinary impact on the wilderness. The capital that produced the tanneries built whole towns: Wevertown, Chestertown, Olmstedville and Minerva, Wheelerville, Griffin, North Hudson, Adirondack, Schroon Lake, Hope, Wells, Jerden Falls, and Moose River Settlement to name a few. Admittedly, some of these towns were built both by the lumbering industry and by tanning, but tanning put more into the local economy in generating larger, self-contained settlements. The towns near the river corridors used to float logs undoubtedly realized some growth from logging, but their physical growth came basically from tanning; Warrensburg, Horicon, and North Creek exemplify this. Iron mining was localized in Essex and Clinton counties, where whole towns sprang up around the mines, while the surrounding forests were cleared to produce charcoal, which was used in the smelting process. But there remains a long list of whole towns whose infrastructure—stores, homes, hotels, schools, post offices, telegraphs, roads, and water supplies—can be traced to the tanning industry. The tanneries were magnets for growth. So, just how do you assess the relative importance of tanning in the towns which also supported the logging industry?

A Comparison of Tanning with Logging and Lumbering in the Adirondacks

Since it makes no sense to compare the value of the leather produced with the value of the output of a region's sawmills, consider how gain might be used to generate such a comparison. Gain, the difference between the value of finished products, i.e. leather, and the cost of the raw hides, is a figure that must cover not just the owner's profits, but the wages he must pay, the costs of bark and other raw materials, and the funds available to service the debts related to capital investment. In that light, much of the gain, except the profits taken out by absentee owners, represents what remains in the local area. Hence, it provides a comparison with the value of produced lumber products. Even so, the value of the lumber produced in a region may be inflated; it represents what the market will bear, not just the costs of land and mills and wages.

The year 1872 was the peak for shipment of logs down the Hudson River. Many, but not all, of those logs were taken to mills in southern Warren County, most of which were outside the present boundaries of the Adirondack Park. In 1870, the value of both the lumber produced by the county's mills and the charcoal works was $651,285.[6] That year, Warren County's gain from tanning was $432,698. Tanning thus had two-thirds as much economic impact on the county as did the lumber mills.

In 1870, 135 million board feet of logs came down the Hudson River to the Big Boom at Glens Falls. Its value was approximately $1.6 million[7], but because many of those logs were sawn downstream from Warren County, they added little value to the upriver economy. The direct Warren County comparison of the value of lumber and the gain from tanning is thus undoubtedly a better indication of the value to the region of logging and tanning.

Using the larger study area of the 1865 Census, a comparison of gain from tanning with the value of lumber produced can be made in all the counties as the accompanying chart indicates. The total gain from tanning was over $3.4 million, significantly higher than the value of the lumber products, which was just under $2.8 million. In particular, the gain from tanning was higher that the value of the sawn lumber in Essex, Hamilton, Herkimer, Jefferson, and Oneida counties.

The tanneries employed 1,463 workers who had wages of $555,680; the lumber mills employed 2,897 workers with wages of $659,503. In other words, the tanneries were bringing almost 85% as much in wages to the north country as were the lumber mills.[8]

---

6 Calculated from the 1870 Census. I am not sure whether this is the best figure to use for the comparison.

7 Calculated by Finch, Pruyn operations manager and historian, Richard Nason.

8 This computes to a yearly wage of $380 for tannery workers, $228 for lumber workers. The wage rates were really closer and the large difference is explained by the

A principal use of wood is in paper making, but in 1865, all but Saratoga County made an insignificant amount of paper. The shipment of pulp for paper did not become significant until the 1890s.

The total cost of raw material to the lumber mills as given in the 1865 New York State Census, a figure that essentially represents monies paid to local workers—loggers, river drivers, and teamsters—as well as whatever was required for acquiring land or timber rights, was $1,267,106. That year the tanneries spent approximately $715,630[9] to harvest the bark consumed; i.e. the cost of the woods operations of the tanneries (barking) were about 55% of the cost of the woods operations of the lumber mills, the logging itself. This figure compares favorably with computations based on the relation of trees felled for bark to trees felled for logging.[10]

It is unfortunate that computations comparing tanneries and the lumber mills in the following decade cannot be made (the Census does not give the needed raw data). Even the computations and their assessment for 1865 are not absolute, because the figures are only loosely comparable. However, they do corroborate a theory I have had for years: tanning, in the brief era of its existence, was as important in the Adirondack region as the lumber industry was in the same period. It accounted for a significant part of the region's dynamic growth during this heyday period of 1860 to 1880 and was a major force in the building of communities. Even if the figures given are exaggerated and not quite comparable, the tanning industry can no longer be seen as the step-sibling of the Adirondack's celebrated logging and lumbering industry.

---

fact that the lumber workers' jobs were seasonal. Tanbarkers' jobs were also seasonal, but tanners were not.

[9] Both figures are computed from data in the 1865 Census

[10] To make this comparison, the following equivalences were used; 8 market logs (a 13-foot log) yielded 1000 feet of lumber and 1 cord of bark. Three logs per tree and an average of 18 logs per acre yielded 2¼ cords of bark.

SUMMARY OF PROFITABILITY AND GAIN COUNTY BY COUNTY

COUNTY	NUMBER REPORTING	TOTAL CAPITAL	NUMBER REPORTING PROFITABILITY *	AVERAGE PROFITABILITY REPORTED *	NUMBER REPORTING GAIN	TOTAL GAIN
1850						
Clinton						
Essex						
Franklin						
Fulton	2	$15,800	2	32.50%	2	$55,500
Hamilton						
Herkimer	2	$171,500	2	28.00%	2	$81,156
Jefferson	1	$16,000	1	18.70%	1	$6,625
Lewis						
Oneida						
St.Lawrence						
Saratoga	2	$60,000	2	19.00%	2	$50,620
Warren	5	$143,000	4	23.75%	4	$108,860
Totals	12	$406,300	11	24.40%	11	$302,761
1860						
Clinton	1	$30,000	1	27.00%	1	$10,000
Essex						
Franklin						
Fulton	7	$207,900	2	24.00%	5	$83,500
Hamilton	3	$62,000	3	15.85%	3	$98,800
Herkimer	5	$368,000	4	29.60%	5	$439,000
Jefferson	4	$79,800	4	25.00%	4	$64,100
Lewis	4	$95,000	0		3	$74,000
Oneida						
St.Lawrence	1	$20,000	0		1	$20,000
Saratoga	2	$55,000	0		1	$35,000
Warren	9	$347,500	8	28.00%	8	$353,500
Totals	36	$1,265,200	22	24.90%	31	$1,177,900
1870						
Clinton						
Essex	3	$101,340	3	17.00%	3	$77,660
Franklin	5	$50,000	4	22.70%	5	$105,250
Fulton	7	$233,000	6	16.90%	6	$149,258
Hamilton	4	$161,500	4	17.80%	4	$211,000
Herkimer	1	$50,000	1	20.00%	1	$57,500
Jefferson	4	$382,788	3	28.60%	4	$341,987
Lewis	10	$801,000	8	25.00%	9	$657,550
Oneida						
St.Lawrence	2	$113,000	2	23.60%	2	$122,600
Saratoga	2	$150,000	2	27.00%	2	$175,200
Warren	10	$450,500	8	15.80%	10	$432,698
Totals	48	$2,493,128	41	20.60%	46	$2,330,703
1880						
Clinton	2	$58,000	2	10.75%	2	$18,000
Essex	4	$20,500	3		0	$14,350
Franklin	4	$195,000	3	14.00%	4	$140,750
Fulton	9	$108,540	2	20.00%	9	$83,523
Hamilton	4	$132,000	4	27.00%	4	$144,030
Herkimer	3	$128,000	1	12.00%	2	$30,000
Jefferson	2	$19,000	2	18.40%	2	$114,321
Lewis	13	$631,400	10	18.30%	13	$862,439
Oneida	6	$202,800	6	18.00%	6	$86,186
St.Lawrence	2	$117,200	2	29.50%	2	$95,000
Saratoga	3	$230,000	3	14.40%	2	$160,000
Warren	8	$470,000	7	15.00%	8	$180,084
Totals	60	$2,312,440	45	14.80%	54	$1,928,683

** This represents the number of sole leather tanneries where census data permit the calculations of profitability and gain.*

The Adirondack Economy
As a Reflection of the National Scene

The economic picture of the tanning industry in the Adirondacks was certainly one of turmoil and great instability. The enormous distances over which raw materials traveled, the vast capital investments and the tremendous cost of borrowing money, the dependence on a raw material–bark, which could be obtained only from undeveloped areas, the inordinate length of time required to produce leather, and the fluctuating price of finished leather all contributed to this instability. But, were there other factors?

It is instructive to compare the economic situation in the Adirondack region with that of the rest of the country, to see if the instability of the tanning industry there paralleled trends across the country, and to see if national trends had a causal effect on local successes or failures.

Large-scale tanning began in the Adirondacks around 1850 at a time of relative prosperity in the country. The country was swept by a financial panic in 1857 and that panic is definitely reflected in the Adirondacks: a number of tanneries in Warren County experienced changes in ownership and a few bankruptcies around 1857. Stephen Griffin (1st) experienced reverses so severe his son Stephen Griffin 2nd assumed what remained of his holdings. Milton Sawyer, who went on to experience many reversals of fortune, apparently lost his interest in the Bowman Tannery in Stony Creek as a result of the 1857 panic. Sawyer was also involved with Charles H. Faxon in the Chestertown Tannery; Faxon and Sawyer both lost heavily there in 1857 but Faxon was able to recover. That year marks the end of the Newkirks Tannery in Fulton County. Newkirk had been a very substantial businessman and State assemblyman. His failure was so complete he apparently left the area. The LeFevre family who had a tannery in Northville also suffered in the panic of 1857 and ultimately relocated to Lewis County.

The nation's economy picked up with the advent of the Civil War. The army's needs for shoes and boots stimulated the tanning industry, which, in the Adirondacks, experienced a very profitable period, so much so that a number of large tanneries were built or enlarged, many just as the war was ending. Among them were the large Wheeler-Claflin Tannery in Fulton County and the Lyon and Snyder Moose River Tannery in Lewis County. This was a time of prosperity, with only a minor contraction in 1869-70, followed by a boom in the early 1870s.

Nationally, the decades of the 1870s and 1880s were "revolutionary and perplexing."[11] After 1873, it seemed as if a great depression was in progress, with glutted markets, continuously falling prices, increased business failures, and an overall fluctuating pace of economic activity. Most of this is attributable to the impact of the industrial revolution and the maturing of businesses. Productivity levels were greatly enhanced by the industrial revolution, but production levels were at first difficult to control. Parts of the economy continued to grow, but the rate of growth was most erratic. The entire era from 1873 to 1897 was marked by falling prices and the "hardship that deflation works on debtors" created a feeling of depression.[12]

The depression and financial panic of 1873, which was caused by the failure of a large banking firm which had employed unsound banking practices when it issued bonds to build the Northern and Pacific Railroad,[13] was pronounced and reflected in problems in several Adirondack tanneries. The depression of the 1870s was the longest cyclical economic contraction in American history.[14] While the country was experiencing a period of negligible industrial growth from 1873 to 1878, there is only anecdotal evidence of problems in the Adirondack tanneries in this interval. It may be that the truncated picture of the prosperity of Adirondack tanneries obtained by analyzing only the Census at the end of the decade gives an incomplete picture, for tanneries in general seem to have returned to a measure of profitability by 1880.

After 1878, the nation's economy improved so much that it experienced a boom that lasted until 1883, although the 1880 Census shows a narrowing of the profit margin of all Adirondack tanneries over the previous decade. The nation may still have had great confidence in the tanning industry; F. Shaw and Company's continued expansion in the Adirondacks after 1880 can only be explained by this confidence, not by a real knowledge of what was happening on the Adirondack scene to the tanneries it

---

[11] Fels, *American Business Cycles*, p. 62

[12] Ibid

[13] Fels, p. 99

[14] Fels, p. 83

acquired. Investment capital still poured into the Adirondacks in this period, although many Warren and Essex county tanneries were experiencing problems by this time. The tanner remained optimistic in his search for profits. However, according to the 1880 Census, profits at Adirondack tanneries were much smaller than a decade earlier. Reduced profits almost appear to be more pronounced in the larger firms, like those of Thomas E. Proctor, which had survived with already very small margins.

The boom that ended in 1883 was followed nationally by a brief slump from late 1883 to 1885 or 1886, again more of a leveling than an actual downturn, but a period nevertheless punctuated in 1884 by another bank panic. Throughout this period profits in many national industries declined. Again Adirondack tanneries experienced a parallel time of difficulty, but this time more pronounced than nationally. The year of 1883 was marked by a cluster of other failures, closings, or takeovers by leather merchants: among them were the Poor tanneries in Day, Saratoga County; the Moore tanneries in Clinton County; Wheelerville in Fulton County. Three of Lewis County's largest tannery holdings were taken over or sold to Boston firms that year: those of the Rice brothers, the Botchfords, and Jacob VanWoert. Fully two-thirds of those tanneries in business at the beginning of the decade of the 80s closed around 1883. The Shaw Bros. bankruptcy in 1883 was the most dramatic, but every tannery suffered and it appears that the tanning industry was suffering more than most other industries at this time.

About 1880, the economy of the Adirondack hemlock bark tanning industry began to veer away from national trends, and by mid-1886, this divergent course was dramatically evident. Nationally, the contraction of 1883 to 1885 was followed by a weak revival that continued from 1886 until 1891. This upswing was not constant, but the business climate was quite positive from 1888 to 1891. In 1891, a recession began in which the number of business failures rose and peaked in 1893 when there was another bank panic.

The financial problems of 1883 affected Adirondack tanneries more than businesses elsewhere. Here something else was going on, for tannery after tannery was closing. The bark, the accessible bark, was running out; the tanneries' cost of harvesting it was becoming prohibitive, and the Adirondack region was no longer an attractive place for new tannery investments.

What Local Conditions Could Have Caused The Disparity in Economic Trends?

The New York State Forest Preserve was established in 1885; these public lands, on which no trees could be cut, initially comprised a little less than ten percent of the six million acres that now make up the Adirondack Park. In the next few years, the State acquired land, most of which had been heavily cut over, through defaults on taxes; but no other purchases of significant tracts to add to the Forest Preserve were made until after the tanning era had ended. Subtracting the area that had been cut for bark and the area where trees could no longer be cut from the total acreage of the Park, at least half of those six million acres was still available to the tanner. Initially, the creation of the Forest Preserve seems to have had a relatively minor effect on the bark supply.

Philip G. Terrie, Adirondack historian, has theorized that the very threat of the Forest Preserve in the years preceding 1885 was enough to frighten potential investors. All the lands within the Blue Line that delineated the Adirondack Park in 1892 were supposed to be State lands or candidates for acquisition. Terrie feels that the threat that all these lands would be removed from possible harvest was real, but he has not found one written statement expressing those fears.

Edwin H. Ketchledge has speculated that the cost of building roads connected to the new railroads, which were penetrating lands that had never been harvested, put off investors. Certainly roads would have either had to overcome extreme grades as in the eastern portion of the new Park, or they would have had to be built up so they could traverse the sodden and boggy ground in the western portions.

Whatever caused the tanner to lose confidence in the region, it was not for lack of bark. The map accompanying the 1891 Forest Commission Report shows lands on which no timber (presumably with the exception of pine) had been cut. Two observations are obvious: The uncut lands parallel exactly the areas not covered by circles around the tanneries that depict the limits of harvestable bark. There is a remarkable congruence between the uncut lands of the 1891 map and the map on page 49. Second, the estimate that in 1891, at least half of the modern Park area had not been cut for hemlock is conservative.

However, the failure of the accessible bark supply was duly noted in the Forest Commission's "First Annual Report to the Legislature" of 1885. The failure was said to account for the reduction in the number of tanneries that had been noted by the Commission. "Some drew no bark last winter ... and plan to wind up this spring."[15]

The Commission observed that the tanneries each owned from 1,000 to 75,000 acres of timber land and frequently controlled the bark on large additional acreages. With their supplies gone, the Commission anticipated the end of hemlock bark tanning within a few years. The following chart details what the Commission found in its 1885 study:

COUNTY BY COUNTY BARKING OPERATIONS

COUNTY	NUMBER OF TANNERIES	CORDS OF BARK *	NUMBER OF TREES FELLED	ACRES CUT OVER
Essex	2	5,000	15,000	4,000
Fulton	2	6,500	19,500	5,200
Hamilton	5	15,000	45,000	7,500
Herkimer	5	5,000	15,000	2,500
Lewis	3	21,000	63,000	10,500
Oneida	1	4,000	12,000	2,000
St. Lawrence	1	4,500	10,000	2,250
Warren	6	15,000	45,000	12,000
Totals	25	76,000	224,500	45,950

Source: New York State Forest Commission's
First Annual Report to the Legislature, 1885

* *Total consumed during past year (ie. 1884)*

The forests of Herkimer, Lewis, Oneida, and St. Lawrence counties were producing but two cords of bark per acre; Essex, Fulton, and Warren counties had no more than 1.25 cords of bark per acre available. The accessible land had been cut over.

By the late 1880s and early 1890s, the bark accessible to Adirondack tanners was exhausted; in the county chapters, story after story confirms the difficulties of harvesting bark. Almost all existing tanneries were affected by the shortage, but the fact that so much hemlock remained indicates that the loss of accessible

[15] Forest Commission, *First Annual Report to the Legislature*

bark alone does not account for the rapid demise of the Adirondack hemlock bark tanning industry that occurred during the 1880s.

Many stories describe the piles of bark still stacked in tanyards when tanneries closed. There is much evidence that in their haste to close, the tanners moved out so quickly that they even left behind piles of bark in the forests.[16] Loss of accessible bark doomed individual tanneries, but does not account for the failure to build new tanneries.

The completion of the Adirondack Division Railroad in 1891 and 1892 did not entice new investments. Only one individual, Frank A. Cutting, took advantage of the railroads, and he did it by exporting bark from St. Lawrence, Lewis, and Franklin counties by rail until 1926. Bark remained desirable until then and was exported from the Adirondacks right up to the moment the chrome process for sole leather was perfected. Even then, after 1926, vast stands of hemlock remained in the Park.

The improving national economic climate of 1894 and 1895 did nothing for the Adirondacks. There was money to build new tanneries elsewhere; but it was no longer deemed wise to spend that money in the Adirondacks.

The Economic Decisions that Doomed The Adirondack Tanning Industry

The explanation of the industry's demise lies partly in the turmoil that the tanning industry was experiencing nationally. The economic climate for tanning in general had become so fractured that the Adirondack region was no longer an attractive place for the industry to locate; but it is not possible to point to any one change that caused the industry's demise in the north country.

Nationally, the rate of business failures was 6.4% per thousand in 1871, 14.2% in 1876, 6.3% in 1880, and 12.1% in 1884.

---

[16] *I have heard of many such piles and I was taken to see one pile of red hemlock bark covered with moss. It is in the woods near Spy Lake and bark from it would probably have been destined for the Rudeston (Piseco) Tannery.*

These are modest numbers compared to the fate of Adirondack tanneries, which seemed to undergo repeated reversals. Here, where fortunes were made, more seem to have been lost, and all tanneries, with few exceptions, experienced at least some financial difficulty: at best premature closures and changes of ownership, at worst failures and bankruptcies. From the littany of repeated business turnovers recounted in Part II, we can surmise that very few tannery operations avoided "embarrassment" or other financial difficulties.

In the 1880s, many tanneries closed; a number were taken over by Boston or New York firms. Many closures in the 1880s involved assignment of assets to trustees or complete liquidation.

Profits were squeezed, but the most striking aspect of this was the fact that wages in the troubled industry became an ever increasing proportion of the production value, even though tannery wages were not increasing. This occurred at a time when increased mechanization was reducing the labor portion of the cost of production in most other industries. Many industries were mechanizing; tanning was not—muscles and time still did most of the work.

Throughout this period, industrial turmoil in the rest of the country resulted in the growth of large corporations. Verticalization of industry, the combining of dependent operations, was occurring in every field of business throughout the United States. It was thought to be the means of survival for the tanners. Businessmen were forming large conglomerates for mere survival and tanners did likewise. This consolidation took the form of corporations which combined meat packers or shoe manufacturers with tanning operations. Each segment of the industry was working to control prices. The two conglomerate corporations, United States Leather Co. and American Hide and Leather Co., were but one aspect of this. In 1896, Endicott Johnson "concluded that the difference in price between raw hides and finished leather was too heavy a burden for shoe manufacturers,"[17] and the company entered the tanning business, ultimately building the largest tannery in the United States. Meat packers, oversupplied with hides and faced with a market that was oversupplied with leather, contracted to have their stocks tanned at a fixed price to hold until the price of leather recovered. The

[17] Watson, ibid, p. 12

packers even bought stands of forests in the upper mid-west to secure a supply of bark.

The formation, in 1893, of the United States Leather Corporation did nothing to improve tanning in the Adirondacks; in fact, the corporation was the coup de grâce for the Adirondack's dying industry. The absentee owners very quickly realized that the industry's existing Adirondack real estate—timber lands and tanneries—was no longer considered as valuable as they were originally thought to be.

The mega-corporation closed the remaining Adirondack tanneries that had been folded into it in 1893 and relocated their movable assets elsewhere. Almost everyone moved on: those that were just barely hanging on like Proctor and those that had failed like the Shaws. No one considered investing in new tanneries in more remote parts of the Adirondacks where bark supplies still existed and where good transportation was being developed to serve the logging industry.

Gradually, tanneries were built closer to the mid-west, but the move was not to one precise geographical area, but to diverse sites from Broome County in the southern tier of New York to the Ohio Valley and on to Michigan and Wisconsin. The only consistent pattern of movement in the industry was away from the Adirondacks.

The industry was no longer dependent on foreign hides. The country, which depended so heavily on the import of hides at mid-century, was, by the 1890s, producing almost fifty percent of the hides that were tanned.

With the advent of chrome, upper-leather tanneries returned to Brooklyn and New Jersey, but the location of the new sole-leather manufacturers, which continued to use hemlock bark processes until 1926, seems to have been dictated more by the proximity to source of the hides or the end-use of the leather, than to the bark. In fact bark was shipped from the east to supplement mid-western supplies.

Here the railroads had a contrary impact. Initially, most tanneries were located within a day's haul from a railhead, not right beside the railroads; with few exceptions, the railroad came to those that were later found at trackside. And, when the railroads finally did penetrate the wild lands, with the north country's vast, remaining stands of hemlocks, the tanneries did not follow. Instead, the region began to ship its precious bark to distant places.

The region went from a manufacturing area to one that supplied raw materials, permitting others to reap the profits of converting the bark and hides to leather. (This parallels the experience of the lumber industry, which shipped out logs and rough timber in far greater amounts than it ever shipped wood products.)

When the railroads finally reached untouched lands, the area was considered too remote for industry, but not too far for the shipment of bark. It is strange that for decades hides had been brought to the source of the bark; but the advent of cheaper transportation via rail made it possible to bring the bark to the tanner. Bark from Canada joined bark from the Adirondacks to be shipped west to supplement the raw materials needed to tan the fourteen million hides that were processed annually in the country in the late 1890s.

Even at the turn of the century, when stocks of hemlock and oak were being depleted elsewhere, the Adirondacks still had bark. It is curious that at this time the industry began importing quebracho from Mexico to supplement the supplies of bark, but there is no indication that, even at this time, Adirondack stands of hemlock were depleted.

If there had not been so much turmoil in the tanning industry in the years preceding 1893, it is tempting to speculate that investment capital might have been available to expand transportation routes and build sole-leather tanneries deeper in the heart of the Adirondacks. Then the region might have witnessed a harvest of hemlock comparable to the harvest of spruce and balsam, which was fueled at the turn of the century by improved transportation and the appetites of the pulp and paper industry. Then, too, the industry's appetite for hemlock bark might have brought about a complete failure of the supply throughout the Adirondacks. But, even this seems an unlikely prospect, for the industry itself had outgrown its need to be in the Park.

Life Span of Major Tanneries

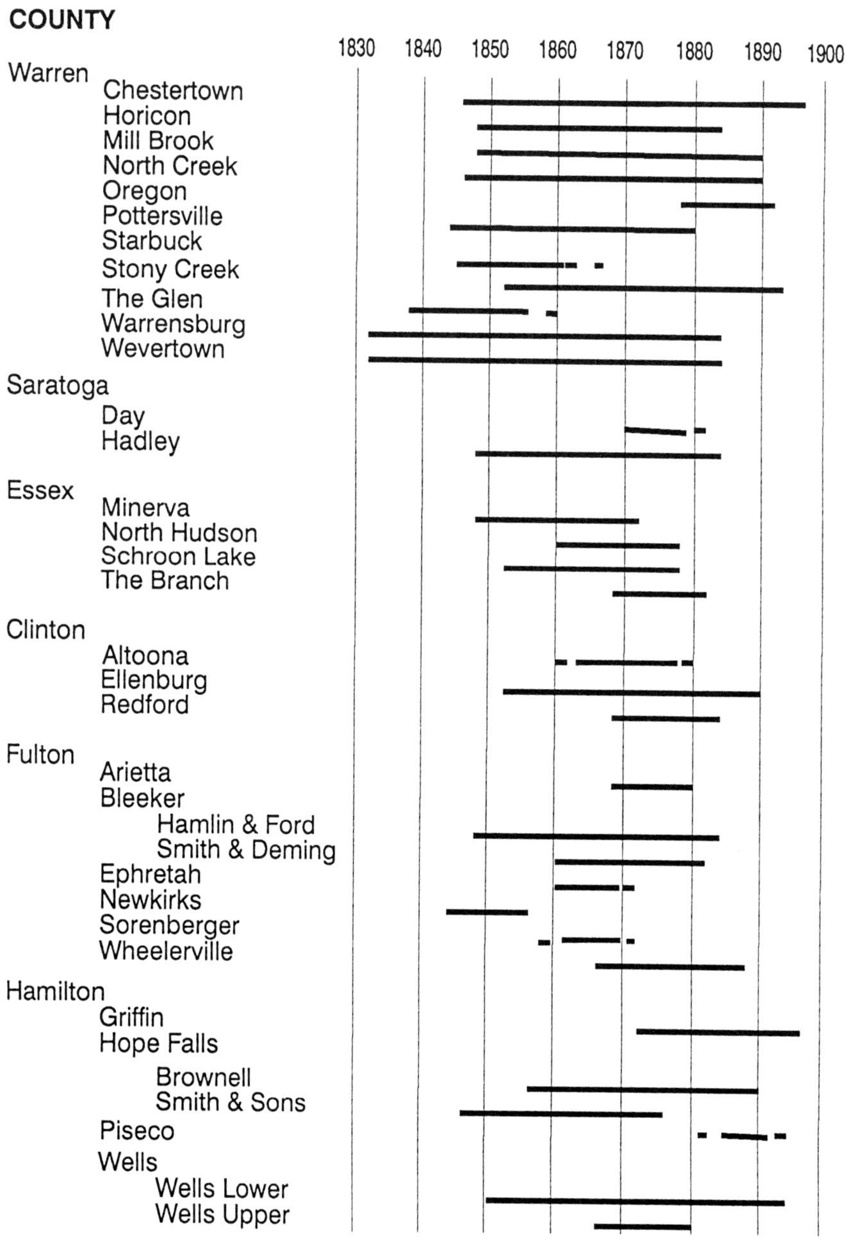

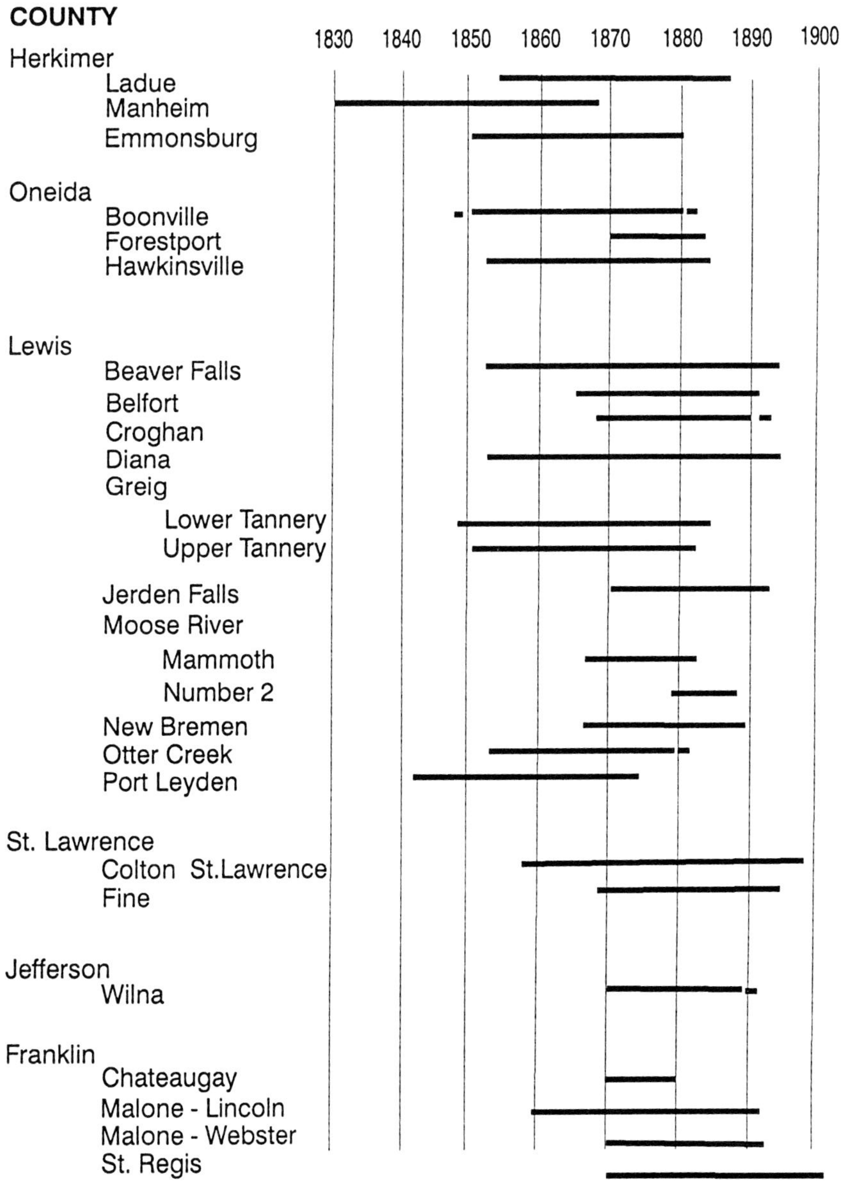

The tanneries shown are those for which beginning and end dates are known or can be approximated (dashed lines).

The End of the Adirondack Era

As the industry died, almost a quarter of the villages and hamlets spawned by the tanneries ceased to exist altogether. Moose River Settlement with its two large tanneries, one of which was truly the largest in the Adirondacks, fulfilled the prophesy of the **Boonville Herald**[18]: "Should this industry leave Moose River, the busy little village would vanish into nothingness and dwindle to nothing more than a stopping place between the railroad and the Adirondacks." The hamlets of Arietta, Griffin, Jerden Falls, and Oregon became ghost towns. The towns that survived did so with much smaller populations, which did not begin to recover until after World War II.

Just as the industry was dying, the State began assembling the Forest Preserve. Often included were the tracts that the tanneries were abandoning, tracts from which all the harvestable hemlock had been taken. Also included were the sites of the abandoned settlements that once covered great bare patches, which had been carved from the wilderness just two decades earlier.

As the forests recovered, the settlements and the tannery foundations became concealed by emerging forests. Now, as the description of Griffin reveals, only the keen eye or errant foot can discover these hidden remains. The end of the story of Adirondack hemlock bark tanning is the re-emergence of the forests that today cloak our wilderness. In lands that have become part of the Forest Preserve, the hemlock is back!

Part II not only traces the beginnings of many of the tanneries, it contains descriptions of buildings that remain as well as the ruins left in the wilderness so the reader can experience the marvels of the age that built so many Adirondack towns.

---

[18] **Boonville Herald**, January 19, 1888

Part II

A County by County Look at the Tanning Industry

X

Warren County

It is little wonder that large-scale, hemlock bark tanning of sole leather made some of its earliest appearances in the Adirondack region in Warren County. Good transportation accounts for the expansion of tanning into the region, and that expansion in turn explains the growth of many of the outlying villages and towns. The Hudson and Schroon rivers offered excellent routes for transporting logs; and the logging industry also sparked the growth of the county's economy. Although the value of exported logs exceeded the value of the locally harvested bark, tanning was the principal reason many of the county's towns were built. The pattern of the county's development is probably best explained by the location of its waterways and the transportation system that made even remote regions accessible.

The Champlain Canal reached Whitehall in 1823; the Feeder Canal connected Fort Edward to Glens Falls in 1832. From that time on, Glens Falls became the center of the shipment of hides and lumber. Plank roads led out from Glens Falls; the road to Lake George was completed in 1848, to Warrensburg in 1849, and the Warrensburg and Chester Plank Road and Turnpike was completed in 1850.

There was a parallel expansion of the railroads. The Mohawk and Hudson Railroad[1] reached Saratoga from Albany in 1833; it was extended to Whitehall in 1848, Luzerne in 1865, Stony Creek in 1869, and North Creek in 1871[2]. As the canals, and later the railroads, were built, tanneries could be located deeper and deeper in the wilderness.

Not only did this network of transportation spark the development of saw mills and tanneries along its routes, the later arrival of the railroads explains in part why the communities that grew up around the mills and tanneries, located at railheads,

---

[1] This division of the Delaware and Hudson Railroad went by several names, including Adirondack Railroad.

[2] Brown, *History of Warren County*, p. 55;
Lamb, *The Lake Champlain and Lake George Valleys, Vol II*, p. 476.

persisted in a way that was not typical of more remote tannery-generated settlements.

Warrensburg saw the county's first tannery as early as 1810. By 1839, there were already sixteen tanneries in Warren County; most were still one-man operations associated with local farming, but four were larger, harbingers of the wave of building to come. Tanneries in Warrensburg, Wevertown, The Glen, and Starbuckville could receive hides from distant places shipped through the Champlain and the Feeder canals, although long hauls on poor dirt tracks did connect the tanneries to the head of the Feeder Canal. Then, the new plank roads made transport even easier. Suddenly, between 1848 and 1853 six large tanneries were built: Horicon, Chestertown, Mill Brook, North Creek, Stony Creek, and Pottersville. Glens Falls, at the head of the Feeder Canal had become an important center for the transshipment of hides and leather. Two more tanneries were built in the county after the arrival of the railroads: at Luzerne and Oregon.

The hemlock stands of northern Warren County and Essex County must have been so enticing to investors that they built their large tanneries deep in the forests at sites served only by plank roads or rough dirt tracks. The ten large tanneries built before 1867 survived for nearly two decades without benefit of a railroad. Most had been built with a capacity of about 30,000 sides per year, large for the time, but small in comparison with later western Adirondack tanneries.

Fewer than 200 men were listed as tanners as late as 1855, an indication that none of Warren County's tanneries were as large as those built later in other Adirondack counties. While the real growth in tanning started even before 1850, the greatest activity in the industry occurred in the decades between 1860 and 1880. By 1865, the county was shipping $1,750,000 in hides.

Warren County supplied a minimum of 800,000 cords of bark in the half century from 1840 to 1890, and the underlying reason given for the closing of all but two of the county's dozen large establishments before 1890 was the high cost and scarcity of bark. Even though bark was brought in from Essex County to the north, it is nevertheless amazing that the county's supply of bark lasted as long as it did. Even more amazing, is that when the last tanneries closed, there were still piles of valuable bark stored beside the tanneries. As Warren County's tanneries ceased operations, the remaining bark was shipped to tanneries near the

Pennyslvatia border that were still in business. H. G. Mason[3] remembered one shipment of bark, perhaps the last such, about 1906. Fourteen teamsters stopped in front of his barn on Ridge Road in Glens Falls as they were drawing loads of bark from Hogtown to be shipped via rail to distant tanneries.

Warren County's tanners experienced the same financial upheavals as those in other counties and the economic climate brought about numerous bankruptcies, changes of ownership, and closings. But the failure of the accessible bark supply had a greater effect on the industry here than in any other Adirondack county. In fact, were it not for the evidence of the remaining hemlock stands elsewhere and the correlation between tannery problems and the national economic scene, it would be logical to claim that Warren County's tanneries disappeared for want of bark. A look at the level of prosperity of individual tanneries will demonstrate that it was the combination of the failure of the bark supply and the economic pressures from outside that brought about the demise of the industry in Warren County.

All but two of Warren County's tanneries closed before the end of the decade of the 80s. Even though, as elsewhere, sole-leather tanning was gone before the turn of the century, the era of Warren County's sole-leather tanneries exceeded that of any other Adirondack county.

Colonial Tanneries

Before 1848, Warren County had several of the Colonial tanneries–one or two-man operations, common in farming communities throughout America in earlier times. Census records for 1850 show that the Town of Queensbury had two such, owned by David Champlain and E. Parsons, and 1860 records one Queensbury tannery, Carpenter and Seymour. These tanneries served Warren County's farmers and even when large tanneries were built, none of the larger ones were located in the southern part of the county because most of the land along the Hudson had already been cleared for farmland.

---

3 Mason, Howard C. *Backward Glances*, Vol I. Privately printed.

A small tannery near Lake George was built about 1804; George Alden ran it until his death in 1826. A tannery occupied that site until 1864, but it was never substantially enlarged.[4]

Early Warren County Sole-Leather Tanneries

Fire cut short the life of two of the very early larger tanneries built in the county to tan hides brought from distant sources. The one at The Glen, recorded in the Census as Cheney and Smith, was built in 1838. It burned, was rebuilt, and then abandoned "with loss to all concerned."[5] The reason the site was abandoned is unclear. While it was not a large tannery (nine workers), it did produce 18,000 sides of leather worth $48,650 in 1850, and a like amount in 1855, when the owners were listed as Griffin and Van Sote.[6] (This is the first tannery with which the north country's mystery tanner, Stephen Griffin, is known to have been associated. There will be more about him in the Hamilton County chapter.)

The second early tannery that burned was built by Isaac Starbuck in 1845 at the settlement on the Schroon River near the outlet of Brant Lake that became Starbuckville. With his brothers, Edward and George, the family also had a sawmill that produced boards and planks and later a shoe factory. The Starbuck Tannery produced $50,000 worth of sole leather in 1850. When the tannery burned, sometime before 1867, it was not replaced.

---

[4] Hastings, *Hemlock and Hides*, p. 18
[5] Farrar, Stephen, *Tanneries in Warren County*
[6] Hastings, ibid, pp. 17-18

Warrensburg

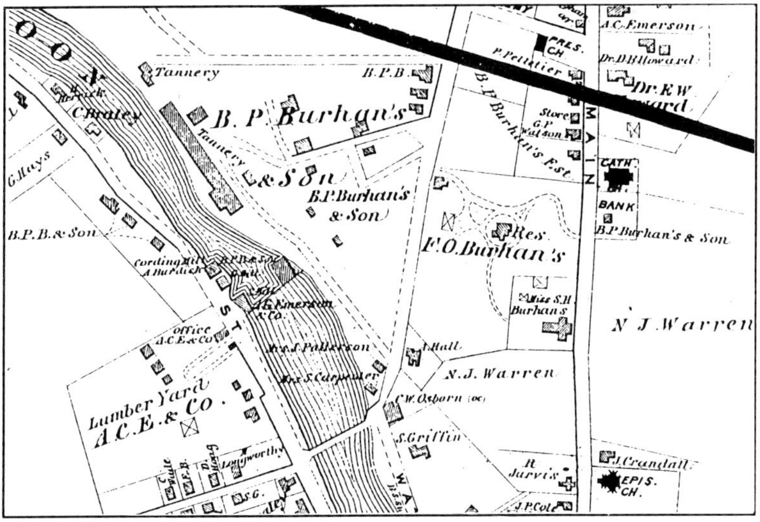

From the 1876 Atlas, Courtesy of the Adirondack Museum

Burhans and Gray

All that is known of Warren County's first tannery is a reference in 1810 to one owned in Warrensburg[7] by Kitchell Bishop. There is no record of it except an 1860 mention of possible remains on the Schroon River above the present dam.

Warrensburg's largest tannery and the first of the county's large tanneries was built in 1831 by H. S. Osborn. In 1834, the tannery along with other "Valuable Property" in Athol, Johnsburg, and Luzerne, which Osborn had purchased but only partially paid for, was offered for sale at public auction by Myron Osborn. H. J. Quackenbush acquired the H. S. Osborn & Co. Tannery, which was located on the banks of the Schroon River. Thomas S. Gray bought into the tannery the next year and Benjamin P. Burhans replaced Quackenbush as a partner in 1836.[8]

The record of the tannery owned by Burhans and Gray is significant in that there exist two indentures between them and Jonathan Thorne of the Swamp in New York City. These documents reproduced in part below, show how agreements to

---

[7] Usually spelled Warrensburgh in early documents, the shortened version is used in this book.

[8] Hastings, John. T., ibid, p. 11

Panorama of the Warrensburg Tannery on left, courtesy Stephen Farrar

obtain hides and sell tanned sole leather were arranged. Their ability to negotiate an agreement that was much more rewarding for Burhans and Gray than one initially offered may account for the tannery's prosperity.

Col. Burhans was born near Rensselaerville in 1796 and was employed at several leather firms until 1826. (The family name was originally Burhaus, but at some point, the letter u was turned upside down.) Burhans started with a tannery in the Catskills, which was supplied with hides from dealers in the Swamp.[9]

When Col. Burhans entered the business, the Warrensburg Tannery became Burhans & Gray. In 1850, the property was valued at $40,000 and tanned 411,000 pounds of hides (approximately 20,500 hides) valued at $45,000, producing 720,000 pounds of sole leather, valued at $87,000, and consuming 2,500 cords of bark in the process.[10]

In 1854, his son Fred O. Burhans became associated with the firm and the name was changed to Burhans, Gray & Co. In 1860, Col. Burhans bought out Gray's interests and renamed the company B. P. Burhans and Son, the name by which the tannery was known until it closed in 1885.

---

[9] Except as noted, information on Burhans was gathered by Stephen Farrar.

[10] 1850 Census, Warren County

Note the bark sheds below the Mansion in the right half of the picture.

Apparently, there was an interruption in the operation of the tannery, for the 1860 census notes that the company had been in production for only a month, and the capital investment and number of workers are much lower than the figures given in 1850.

In 1848, Col. Burhans built the Horicon Tannery (see Horicon), which Thomas Gray later took over. Burhans and Gray were also partners in a Warrensburg store.

The Colonel, as Burhans was always known, had a "splendid physique, upwards of six feet in height."[11] He had a large stone mansion on the hill built for his son (the builder was the grandfather of Stewart Farrar, who provided much of this information). Gray had also built a house on the hill above Warrensburg; it was originally called the Elms (later the Pillars). This house was bought by Burhans and he was living in it at the time the stone mansion was being built for his son. Burhans was the first president of Old Brown Bank, the oldest bank in Warren County. Burhans was also a "notable visitor to the Swamp" where according to the Swamp historian, Frank W. Norcross, "two votaries of the muses of the Swamp dedicated a poem [to

[11] Norcross, *A History of the New York Swamp*, p. 151

Burhans' partner Gray] entitled 'Gray's Elegy in a Country Tanyard'."[12]

The tannery appears to have been quite profitable in this period. Burhans ability to negotiate contracts must have helped, but so did, undoubtedly, his personal ties. As early as 1860, Burhans had a family connection with the Swamp in New York City–his son-in-law, William B. Isham, partner in the leather store of Gray and Isham and later executor of Burhans' estate.

The census for 1870 lists expenses of $15,000 for wages, $95,787 for 16,720 hides, $21,804 for 3,634 cords of bark, and $460 for oil. The 32,340 sides of sole leather produced brought $160,740, or a profit of over $27,000.

Col. Burhans died July 16, 1875 and the company continued under the direction of his heirs. His estate was said to be worth over a million dollars.[13] In 1880, twenty-six workers had an annual wage of $8,877 and 22,326 sides worth $71,500 were tanned. The profits were less than $10,000.

The **Warrensburg News** reported several times on the delivery of bark to the tannery: 103 loads of bark were delivered by January 19, 1878. The cost of bark, $6.00 a cord in 1870 may have affected the decrease in production noted in the 1880 census, in spite of the fact that the tannery had added a large 60 horsepower turbine.

Whether or not the decline in profits contributed to the closing of the tannery, it was noted locally in 1885 that the closing was for lack of bark.

Other Warrensburg Tanneries

Joseph Crandall operated a tannery and made shoes and boots in Warrensburg in 1860. The 1870 Census lists two other tanneries, one operated by Milton Sawyer, who figured in three other Warren County tanneries and three in Essex County. His Warrensburg tannery was not very large, since it produced only $27,500 worth of sole leather in 1870. The Census record is too illegible to determine more about this tannery. The other Warrensburg tannery listed in the 1870 Census was said to be owned by W. (M?) Sawyer. If the faint writing of the 1870 Census can be believed, the latter had a production valued at $200,000.[14]

---

[12] ibid

[13] New York, Vol. 609, p. 269, R. G. Dun and Co.

[14] This information points up the difficulty of using the Census. With managers and others often listed as the owners, it is difficult to assign Census information to the

Contracts for Green Hides

Two indentures, the second reproduced in its entirety below, indicate the terms by which Burhans and Gray obtained hides from a broker in New York City. A June 15, 1838 agreement was signed between Jonathan Thorne and Benjamin P. Burhans and Thomas S. Gray. It was vague as to the number of hides "in Hair" to be supplied by the New York hide and leather merchant, while the second agreement was more specific. In this first agreement, the merchant only agreed to sell the tanned leather at auction and pay Burhans and Gray only what was left after deducting the value of the skins with interest, any advances, and a six and a half percent commission. The July 28 indenture improves on the agreement by specifying the number of hides (three to five thousand) and by giving Burhans and Gray six cents per pound on credit of ninety days for the tanning. The merchant would not only receive his commission on the sale of the leather, but a five percent commission on the purchase of the hides.

According to the first agreement, the value of the hides was to be "estimated and rated as the parties thereto shall mutually agree upon from time to time as they may want (so long as shall be mutually agreeable and convenient for the party of the first part to furnish)." Further, in the initial indenture, Thorne only agreed to "receive the Leather so manufactured and sell the same by Auction or Otherwise and after deducting the above value of the Hide or Skins and Expenses paid thereon, with Interest on the Same, together with any expenses he may have to pay in the receipt of the Leather, as well as any advances he may have made and Six and a half percent Commission."[15]

The July document implies a sharing of the risk and is much more advantageous to the Warrensburg tannery. This demonstrates a good business sense that may explain what made Burhans so successful in Warrensburg.

---

correct tannery. With a lot of sleuthing, most Census data used in this book has been correctly assigned, some is given as a best guess, but a few mysteries remain. This is one of them. In this case, all the known tanneries correlate with the Census, so this information really does not relate to any known tannery.

[15] Indenture, copied from the collection of Lewis Waddell

Indenture[16]

This Indenture made and entered into this Twenty Eight day of July in the year of our Lord One Thousand Eight hundred and Thirty Seven - Between Jonathan Thorne Hide and Leather merchant of the City of New York of the first part - and Benjamin P. Burhan and Thomas S. Gray of Warrensburgh Warren County all in the State of New York. Composing the firm of Burhan & Gray Tannery of the second part - Witnesseth that for and in consideration of the Covenants and agreements herein Contained and of one dollar in hand paid by the Party of the first part the receipt whereof is hereby acknowledged. The parties of the second part agree to receive Three Thousand to Five Thousand Hides or more this year from the party of the first part if convenient for him to furnish, and Tann the Same at Warrensburgh Warren County and State aforesaid as soon as practicable after the receipt of said Hides in a good workmanlike manner and return all the leather so manufactured to the Party of the first part at New York City, for which they are to be allowed Six cents per Pound for so Tanning on a credit of Ninety days from the time of the inspection of the Leather in New York, And the party of the first part is to be allowed Five percent advance on the gross amount for purchasing said Hide, and Six and one Half percent Commission and guarantee on the gross amount of the sale of said Leather when returned. The Hides to be furnished on joint account and delivered on the wharf in the City of New York and the leather to be received there and the Party of the Second Part to take the Hides from the said wharf and deliver the Leather at the same place at their own expense for which they are to be paid as above and the Profit or Loss accruing from above Contract to be equally divided and borne by the parties hereto after paying for said Hides and advances thereon and Interests, and Commissions on July of Leather as well as Tannage &c. And the party of the second part still further agrees that they will have and keep Hide & Leather made from the same fully insured against Loss or damage by Fire while in their possession, and the party of the first part also stipulates to take the same precaution with the Leather when received by him. It is further agreed and understood between the parties to these present that all of the Hide and Leather that may be in the possession of the parties of the second part by virtue of this Contract shall be and remain the property of the party of the first part and that all the interest the parties of the second part have in said Hides and Leather is as heretofore expressed in this Contract, when ascertained by the party of the first part.

It is also stipulated and agreed that a settlement shall take place between the parties to this present at least once a year during the continuance of this Contract.

To the faithfull performance of the several parts of this Contract, the parties to the same find themselves their Heirs, Executors, Admin-

---

16 ibid

istrators and signs firmly by these present to each other in the final sum of Twenty Thousand Dollars.

In witness whereof we have hereunto set our hands and seals the day and year first written.

Witness Present
Jonathan Thorne

Wevertown Tannery

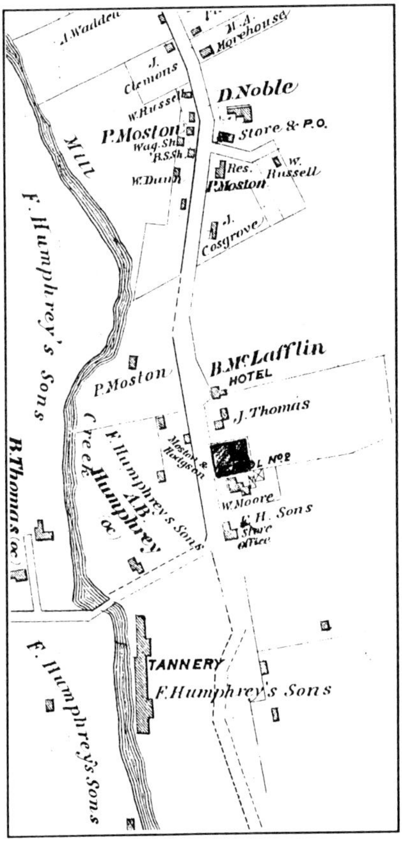

From the 1876 Atlas, courtesy of the Adirondack Museum

Certainly the opening of the Champlain-Glens Falls Feeder Canal in 1832 sparked the spread of tanneries into the interior of Warren County and the building at such remote locations as Wevertown. However, it is difficult to imagine how hides and leather were transported between the end of the canal and this site for the eighteen years it was in operation before the plank road was built. The Wevertown Tannery was chronologically the second large sole-leather tannery built in Warren County, following the tannery in Warrensburg by only a year.

Charles O. Shaw figures as owner of several Warren County tanneries at the time of their demise; and the Wevertown Tannery on Beaver Brook, later Mill Creek, was one of them. Like other tanneries, it had a number of owners and a series of name changes. The tannery was built by William Watson and James Wasson of Blandford, Massachusetts, on land purchased from Robert Gilchrist in June of 1832.[17] Linus B. Barnes joined them as a partner. In 1842, Watson and Wasson were described as extensive leather dealers, of good habit, and said "to be rich."[18] At about that time, the tannery took the name of Linus B. Barnes, when Watson and Wasson sold out to him. The company became Thomas and Barnes when Jarret Thomas became a partner in 1849. The firm of Thomas and Barnes, with twenty-two employees, tanned 26,000 sides worth $55,280 in 1850.[19] The 1860 Census indicates production rose to 32,000 sides worth $112,000.

The company became insolvent in 1860 or 61[20] and was sold to F. Humphrey and Sons, leather merchants from Albany. For a time they prospered. In 1870 they produced 30,000 sides of sole leather, some 245 tons, worth $138,000. The Census indicates their costs were only about half that sum, but the 2,500 cords of bark consumed cost $15,625, or over $6. a cord. The figures for 1880 are quite different, for although the value of the leather produced, $134,000, was comparable, costs were way up: 20,000 hides cost $100,000, double the cost of a decade earlier. In fact there could have been little profit. Financial difficulties must have escalated because the tannery was forced into receivership in 1883[21], and the assignee, George Stedman, sold all the Humphrey interests, tannery, store, houses, and 3247 cords of bark for $15,250 to Augustus Sherman of Glens Falls on August 22, 1883. Sherman was an agent for Charles O. Shaw, whose company ran the tannery for two more years, until the tannery burned in 1885. After the fire, the Shaw operations moved to Oregon in western Warren County.

The tannery building was 45 by 400 feet long and three stories high, with a "very large and high smokestack on the boilers."[22] The west end housed the water wheel and boilers; the vats were housed in the eastern three-quarters of the first floor, fleshing rooms were above, and a drying loft occupied the third floor. About 500 feet downstream from the main tannery building at a second dam on the creek, a building 30 by 122 feet

---

[17] Research by Lewis Waddell; Murphy, *The Wevertown Tannery*
[18] New York, Vol. 609. p. 71, R. G. Dun and Co.
[19] 1850 Census, Warren County
[20] New York, Vol. 609, p. 69, R. G. Dun and Co.
[21] New York, Vol. 609, p. 62, R. G. Dun and Co.
[22] Letter from Lewis Waddell

housed the rolling mill, which was run by water power from the dam.[23]

David Noble, who ran the company store from 1833 to 1843, kept an account book while he was also agent for the tannery. On October 1, 1838, he wrote a note to remind himself "tell Watson about California hides, see what cost, bad shape."[24]

The tannery complex included a harness shop, a school house, the tannery scale, a windowless beam house, a sweat pit, and eight to ten houses, as well as the company store. Some of the tannery houses are still standing, others are marked only by cellar holes. James A. Murphy, who researched this tannery for the local historical society, noted that it was interesting that the houses here were far enough apart so that the owners could have a garden and keep cattle, unlike the houses in North Creek and Chestertown, where the workers' houses stood close together in tight rows.

Linus B. Barnes was granted a charter for the Warren County Bank of Johnsburg in December of 1845. The bank closed in November of 1859 just before Barnes sold the tannery to Humphrey.

A footnote to the tannery: The large and beautiful weathervane from the top of the tannery was put on top of the saw mill that succeeded the tannery. It is currently in the Adirondack Museum at Blue Mountain Lake.

Horicon Tannery

The Horicon Tannery, known as the Pitt or Pit, stood on the east side of the Schroon River, just north of its confluence with the outlet of Brant Lake. The 400-foot long stone structure was built in 1848 by Col. B. P. Burhans and Thomas Gray of Warrensburg.[25] The large tannery was destroyed by fire in 1856. R. G. Dun and Co. noted that the owners were Gray and Frederic O. Burhans, son of Col. B. P., and that their loss, estimated at $60,000 to $70,000 was insured and the tannery was rebuilt. Gray bought out Burhans' interest in 1862 for $15,000.

---

[23] ibid

[24] Murphy, ibid

[25] Hastings, ibid, p. 13

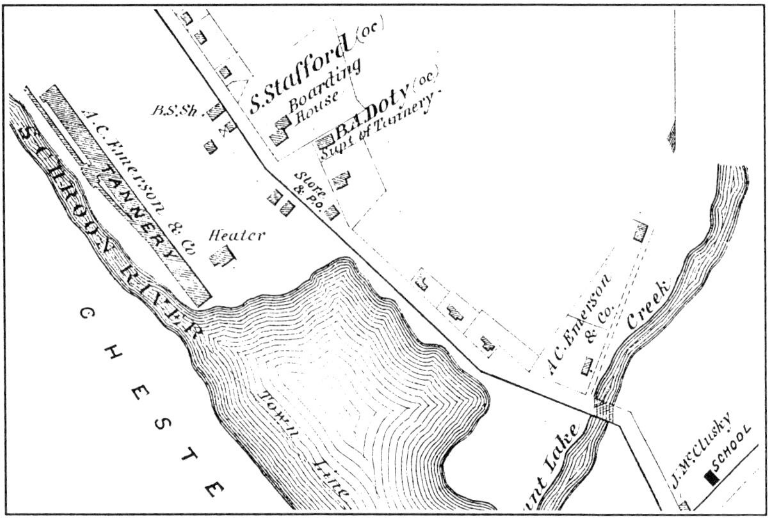

From the 1876 Atlas, Courtesy of the Adirondack Museum

The building, with a wooden upper story, was struck by lightning in 1864 and again rebuilt. Gray sold his interest in the tannery in 1867, and in the next few years, his personal wealth was estimated at upwards of $400,000.[26]

Local history has it that one Philo Pitkin traded his mill and house at South Schroon for half interest in the property with A. C. Emerson. Records show Isaac Starbuck and Albert C. Emerson purchased the tannery in 1867. In 1870, the tannery went by the name of A. C. Emerson & Co., with partners Emerson and Isaac, Edward, and George Starbuck, whose own tannery had burned; and Isaac Woodward. They were reported to be "considerably extended" the very next year, and the Starbuck interests were sold to George Harvey of Saratoga Springs.[27]

Said to be capitalized at $50,000 in 1850, the tannery employed forty men that year, with $12,500 in wages. It consumed 3,000 cords of bark at $2.00 a cord and produced sole leather worth $41,900. In 1860, the capitalization was said to be $90,000. Thirty workers with $18,000 yearly wages produced sixty thousand sides worth $245,000. The 3,000 cords of bark used cost $9,000 and with green hides costing $140,000, the owners realized a fair profit. The successor company, A. C. Emerson, did not

[26] New York, Vol. 609, p. 58, R. G. Dun and Co.
[27] New York, Vol. 609, p. 59, R. G. Dun and Co.

fare as well. In 1870, the production slumped to a value of $100,000 and still further in 1880. The tannery closed in 1884.

Horicon's population peaked at just over 1,600 in 1880 and dropped with the closing of the tannery, staying at about half its peak number until after 1950 when the area began to grow again.

The Tavern, Ranking, and Teamsters

James Truman Hayes of North Argyle was born at South Horicon on May 4, 1865. He was a lumberjack for twenty-five years, starting when he was but thirteen years old. In 1940 he reminisced about the old Horicon Tannery and his recollections became an article in the **Glens Falls Post Star and Times** in 1941. That article omitted a few choice comments that appear in a similar interview also dictated by Hayes. The latter version is in the Adirondack Museum and the spicy comments, omitted from the newspaper article, are included below.

The old Horicon Tannery was built, as near as I can recollect, in 1840. It was the largest one in the state.[28] *It was 400 feet long, 20 feet high, had a capacity of 30,000 hides a year. It was located about three and one-half miles southwest of Brant Lake, and one mile north of the Pit, now South Horicon. The Schroon River ran on the south side of the Tannery.*

More about this Tannery later on, but first I wish to say something about the men that worked in and about the Tannery and the men that helped furnish the hemlock bark that was used to tan the hides into leather. Among the men that worked inside were the Murphys, Kennovans, Donovans, McCarthys and McCluskeys. The fathers and mothers of these men were all born in Ireland. One Owen boy was scalded to death when he slipped and fell into a vat of hot liquor that was being used to tan the hides in.

Tavern in the Cellar

There was a man who went by the name of Pat O'Hara who kept a grog shop about a quarter of a mile from the Tannery. The boys called his place the "Hole-in-the-Wall." The place was located in the cellar,

---

[28] Hayes statements on the relative size of the tannery are typical; everyone said his tannery was the biggest. His memory may also exaggerate the size and depth of the vats, but not by much. With the exception of one paragraph (here omitted) where Hayes described fleshing and unhairing as processes that occurred after tanning, all other apsects of his account appear likely.

or if your prefer, in a dim lighted basement. Pat was born in Ireland, and the map of it was written on his face. He was a short stocky man, shrewd and calculating, and was always after the money. This was the place, the "Hole-in-the-Wall" where the Irish who worked in the Tannery met evenings, and many a hard earned dollar went over Pat's Bar, and many a fight took place in the "Hole-in-the-Wall." I can tell you how the men looked after the fight by quoting a line or two from a song called "Paddys Wake." It ran something like this -

Eyes were gouged out
Ears and noses were bit off
Teeth were knocked out
And there was but one whole nose
left in the whole party -
That belonged to the teakettle.

Popular Meeting Place

There was a tavern just across the road from Pat's "Hole-in-the-Wall," which was owned and run by Homer Davis. It was a large tavern and was where lumberjacks, who peeled the hemlock bark that kept the tannery going, would meet and get rid of some of their money - or perhaps all of it. Homer always had plenty of whiskey as well as gambling tables. Several of the lumberjacks would be found there Saturdays or Sundays. I suppose they met to plan how they were going to get rid of Old John Barleycorn and judging from the way some of the men looked when they left, Old John must have put up a hard fight.

Among those who frequented Davis' place were Jim Kelly, a good fellow; Tim Hull, a big chopper; Wash Baker, who was never happy unless he was fighting; George Middleton, who liked to gamble; Sant Wilcox, and Alf Wilcox. All of these men were soldiers in the Civil War. Others were Ham Birch and Bill Birch, and last but not least, Dan Vaughn. Dan was a born poet and given two or three hours he would produce a string of good poetry a mile long.

About all the difference there was between the men of the West and the men of the Town of Horicon was that the men in the West fought with guns and knives. The men in Horicon fought with their fists, feet and bottles - and occasionally a billiard cue.

Hauling the Bark

In getting the bark from the woods to the tannery the men peeled the bark from the trees and piled it in one-half to two-cord stacks. These piles were scattered all through the woods. The trees that the bark had been taken from were cut up into logs 13 feet, six inches long. The logs were hauled and piled in skidways, which were located on the roads through the woods.

The bark that was scattered through the woods had to be 'ranked' out, as it was called, on to the roads where the skidways were for the men to haul to the tannery. My father-in-law, L. D. Tripp, and I had a job one fall of 'ranking' out two or three thousand cords of hemlock bark onto the log roads. We had to pile the bark up in good snug piles, and in some of these piles there would be two or three cords, and in some eight or ten, and in some 30 or 40 cords. We made a 'wood-shod' sled to draw the bark on. This sled was eight feet long and about three feet wide, and one horse drew it. We could 'rank' out about 10 to 15 cords a day, and had the bark all out on the roads before the snow came.

When the snow arrived 15 or 20 teams drew the bark to the tannery in Horicon. They drew it from several different places, some of it being hauled as far as 20 miles. Among those who hauled were Ed Brown, who weighted about 200 pounds and I don't believe there was a man in the Town of Horicon who could have licked him in a fist fight. And then there was Ben Wood a fine man with whom I worked a great many days. I never saw him in a bar room or saw him take a drink. He was one of the best teamsters that ever sat on a load of logs or bark. He saved my life once when I was a boy of 16, at the risk of his own life.

Woman at the Reins

Another who hauled bark was Emeline Brace. She had a family of five children and no one to help her take care of them. Did she go out on relief? No Sir! Not Em! What did she do? She hauled bark all winter - several winters in fact. She owned a team of black horses, and I have seen her more than once drive up to the old Horicon Tannery, sitting on top of a large load of bark, three or four cords. The first winter she hauled bark she had a baby boy who was about 15 months old. She had no one to leave the baby with so she made a wooden box just big enough to hold the baby. In the bottom of this box she placed straw and on top of that a large feather pillow. On this she put the baby and covered him with blankets. She made a wooden cover for the box with hinges on it, and this shut down tight. She bored two or three small holes in the side of the box hear the top so the baby would have fresh air. In the morning when she was ready to start for the woods after a load of bark, long before daylight, with the thermometer perhaps 30 below zero, she would put the box with the baby in it on the sled and away she would go the length of Brant Lake, through the woods, across Lake Pharo and then on, still further, a distance of some 15 miles.

Now this same baby boy became a man and went by the name of Dick Brace. I worked with him two or three years in the lumber woods. When Dick was past middle age he moved to Gloversville and became a merchant and was elected as a Member of the Assembly and went to Albany where he served two or three years.

Most all of the old lumberjacks that I have told you about started out in life just about as hard as Dick Brace. People who read this after I am gone will not be able to conceive what these men who hauled hemlock bark to the old Horicon Tannery went thru.

They were compelled to get up around four in the morning, get a team ready, do other chores, and be ready to start by five.

Early Morning Start

Starting out when it was 30 to 40 below zero wasn't much fun. The men would usually get in the woods where the bark was about 9 or 10 AM, and it would usually take about an hour and a half to get a load of bark on the sleds. Nearly half an hour before the bark was on the sleds the teamster would put some grass in the horses' nose bags and hang it on the horses' heads so that by the time the bark was loaded the horses would be through eating. With the bark on the sleds the teamster took three or four thick slices of bread out of his overcoat pockets, and with each slice of bread he had a large slice of fat pork, sometime fried and sometimes raw. He stood besides his horses and ate his bread and meat, sometimes it was frozen so hard it was difficult to eat.

The teamster was then ready to start for the tannery, perhaps 15 miles away. Sitting on top of a big load of bark, as large as a big load of hay, was not a very hot place to roost, not when it was 30 below zero and you were riding on the ice on Brant Lake, and the wind was blowing the snow thick and hard, so that you could hardly see your horses. The men would usually get to the tannery about four in the afternoon, although sometimes it would be later. Then they would have to unload their bark and then go home, sometimes a distance of three or four miles.

Arriving home, he would put his team in the stable, take off the harness and put it on a peg, which was often driven into a log. Many of the stables were built out of logs, as well as many houses. His team had to be blanketed, and the manger filled with hay, and then he could go on to the house, whistling or perhaps singing "Come all ye brave shanty boys and listen to my song."

The tannery was located in a small hamlet made up mostly of Irish who worked in the tannery. There was a store and post office that was kept by Orin Burge, and a fine man he was and a fine Christian gentleman. There was also a boarding house owned and run by Lemuel Stafford, who was also justice of the peace.

Bark Piled High

The tannery was the largest one in the State of New York. As a boy of 10 or 11 years, in 1875, I was there once or twice a week. In the winter there were load after load of hemlock bark being hauled into the yard, where there was eight or ten thousand cords of bark piled, some of them 20 rods long and some 12 feet high. There was always a man to pile the bark good and tight, with the rough side up.

Now I mustn't forget Old Sam, the horse. Sam commenced work in the yard when he was three years old. He worked every day, except Sundays, for 30 years, dying at the ripe old age of 33 years. I have watched Old Sam many times when I was a boy, when I went after the mail. As I look back over 60 years I can still see Old Sam hitched to a cart, with a big load of bark on it, going toward the tannery all alone. He would pull the lead up to the building where the big grinder was located, that ground the bark fine as meal. Arriving at the building, Sam would turn halfway around and back up some 20 feet to the big grinder, then one of the men would release a lever and the back end of the body of the truck would tip down and the bark would slide out onto the floor. Then Old Sam would turn the cart halfway around, back up to the bark pile, to be loaded up all over again. No one had to speak a word to Old Sam. He knew his business. He was never out of the bark yard after he was three years old, and died one day when he was drawing a load of bark. If the Lord didn't make a place for such faithful old horses, He sure made a mistake.

The Tanning Process

(I can't tell accurately the length of the tannery but to my boyish eyes it didn't seem to have any end.) You went in the east end of the Tannery and could see the whole length of the building. It surely seemed a long ways, and there was a board walk running through the center the entire length of the building. This walk was about three feet wide, and on each side were vats, which as I remember, were about eight feet wide and 10 feet long. There were a great number of these vats, and each one was about eight feet deep. Into these vats went several bushels of tan bark. Fresh tan bark had to be added from time to time, and then the vats were filled about half full of water. This made a strong liquor after standing two or three days. There were hot water

pipes running through the vats which kept the liquor scalding hot. Into this hot liquor the raw hides were placed, a hundred or so at a time. They were left about six weeks, and by that time they would be tanned. The hides had been purchased in the West and were shipped in carloads to Riverside Station, and then hauled from there to the tannery, a distance of 12 miles. They were drawn by horses.

After the hides were tanned, men with iron hooks would pull them out of the vats and throw them over large poles to dry. No one except an experienced man could pull hide out of a vat and throw it over one of these poles that was as high as a man's head. If you were to stand and watch one of these Irishmen pull one of those wet heavy hides out of this hot liquor you would say that there was nothing to it. But let someone try it who did not know how. He wouldn't be able to throw a hide over the pole in half an hour and I dare say he would give up trying. Yet the men who were doing the work would throw one over every three or four minutes. The hides were left hanging to dry two or three days.

The old Horicon Tannery was burned down many years ago, but in its day it gave work to a great many men.

Chestertown Tanneries

Milton Sawyer became a partner in the Chestertown tannery, known locally and in some records as the South Chester Tannery, seven years after it was built. The tannery, originally known as Robertson, Faxon & Co. was constructed in 1849 by Robertson with Charles H. Faxon and James Crandall. In 1856, when Sawyer became a partner, replacing Crandall, the firm became Sawyer, Faxon, & Co.[29] Faxon assumed Robertson's interest in 1860 and Sawyer's in 1865. Sawyer, who figures in accounts of eight other Warren and Essex county tanneries, nearly brought the business down with his financial difficulties following the panic of 1857. Sawyer sold out his interest in the firm and R. G. Dun and Co. records indicate that the tannery continued to lose money through 1861 and that there was an intervening owner in that period.[30]

---

29 Hasting, ibid, p. 15

30 New York, Vol. 609, p. 27, R. G. Dun and Co.

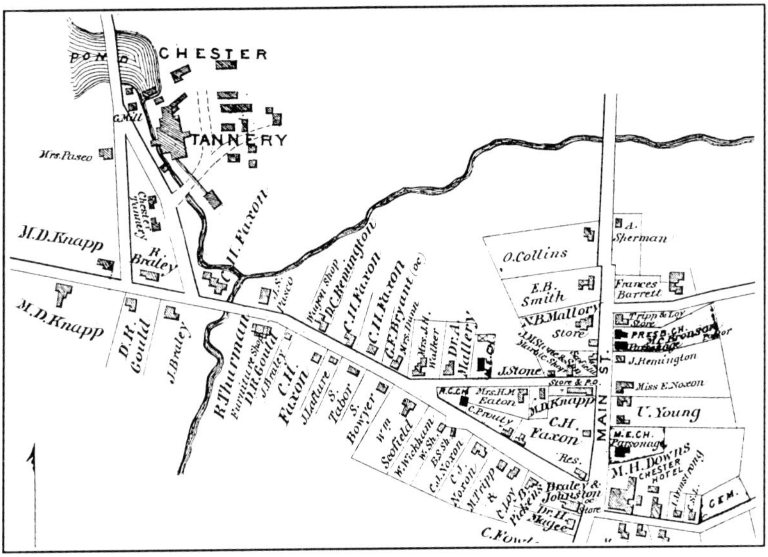

From the 1876 Atlas, Courtesy of the Adirondack Museum

Somehow, Faxon regained control of the tannery and ran the business until he was joined by his son, William H., in 1882. Faxon's business talents must have been outside the tannery, for in 1868, it was not doing too well. The tannery burned in 1869 and because it was insured for $20,000, it was promptly rebuilt.[31] The C. H. Faxon & Co. tannery continued until 1893, when it was sold to United States Leather Company. It closed altogether in 1898. This makes it not only the longest running sole-leather tannery in Warren County, but the longest running in the Adirondacks.

Faxon was said to be Chestertown's "leading industrialist," having also a grist mill capable of milling 30,000 bushels of wheat in 1885. Faxon owned and improved the Chester Water Works. William F. Fox, chronicler of the State's lumber industry, lists Faxon in his chapter "Captains of Industry";[32] he was the only giant of the tanning industry accorded this dual honor. According to local historian, Caroline Fish, Faxon was one of the original incorporators of the United States Leather Co.

---

[31] R. G. Dun records New York,Vol. 609, p. 27, indicate that Faxon had two tanneries in 1870. What the other might be has not been discovered.

[32] Fox, *History of the Lumber Industry*, p. 74

Chestertown Tannery, courtesy Charles H. Appleyard

Deeds indicate the tannery property was acquired in stages and several parcels were acquired from J. W. Leggett, who had a saw mill. Planks from this saw mill were used in the building of area roads, especially the vital links that permitted the building of tanneries in North Creek and Oregon.[33]

In 1849 Leggett sold Mead and Alva Palmer land around the flume on Chester Creek with the right to draw water from Leggett's Pond. In 1873, Faxon acquired the pond behind the dam, known today as Faxon's Pond, and the stream that flowed into it.

From a relatively small production, 125,250 pounds (approximately 6,250 hides) worth $17,000 in 1850, the company expanded to employ 30 men in 1860 and produced 36,000 sides worth $111,000. The real property value doubled between 1860 and 1870 to $100,000, indicating the acquisition of two bark mills, two hide mills, and two rolling mills. The 1870 production of 30,000 sides worth $120,000 appears fairly profitable, in spite of the fact that the 3,000 cords of bark cost $6.00 per cord.

[33] Letter from Caroline Fish

The area of Chestertown on joint highway, NY 8 and 9, was once called "Dublin," for the row of houses on both sides of the road where many of the tannery workers lived. The census for 1850 lists seven tanners, all but one born in Ireland. James Braley, blacksmith, provided iron work and spikes for the mill dam at the site of the Chestertown Tannery. The grist mill, on the opposite side of the dam, was run by his brother, Reese Braley. The miller's wife, Eliza Dowling, who came to this country from Londonderry, kept a boarding house for tannery workers.

Friends Lake Tannery

William Mundy operated a tannery at Friends Lake in 1870 and 1880, moving there from a site near Loon Lake where water proved insufficient.[34] This may have been known as the North Tannery, but local records seem to confuse that name. It is unclear whether the name North Tannery should apply to this tannery or the one at Pottersville, both of which were recorded under the Census as Chester tanneries. The Census for 1850 and 1860 list a small tannery, owned by Mead and Palmer, and that may have been the predecessor of the Mundy tannery. Even in 1880, Mundy's output remained small, less than $800 worth of leather.

[34] Hastings, ibid, p. 18

Pottersville Tannery

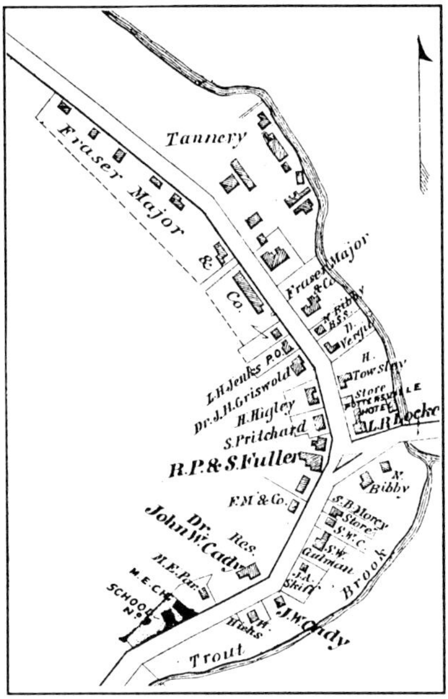

From the 1876 Atlas, Courtesy of the Adirondack Museum

The Pottersville Tannery was built in 1845 on the banks of Trout Brook by Milton Sawyer, Warren and Essex counties' ubiquitous entrepreneur. He was helped by his brother Aaron, who went on to build the Ellenburg Tannery in Clinton County.[35] The litany of owners and the succession of name changes is typical: On April 4, 1853, Sawyer sold the tannery to Homer and Francis Fenn and James H. Young. The following year, Lewis Munger joined the firm. Fenn and Munger was transferred to Frederick and George Fenn, then to Joseph Hallagan, Thomas Fraser, James Fraser, and William Major.

Fenn and Munger were owners of the tannery at Olmstedville, Essex County,[36] which experienced problems at the same time, selling out also to Fraser, Major and Company of New York, a firm that had supplied them with hides. Hallagan sold his half interest to Fraser, Major and Company in 1865.[37] For details on the latter firm, see Chapter VII.

The 1860 Census recorded the tannery's statistics under the name J. Hallagan & Co., which was said to employ nearly 30 men and produced 32,000 sides of sole leather worth $108,800. The 1870 production was given as 20,556 sides worth $81,170. Fraser, Major and Company, from New York City, ran the tannery for a dozen years before it was sold to Cyrus F. Kipp. The one Chester entry for 1880 that could apply to this tannery gives the owner as W. R. Stout Brothers, who tanned 24,000 sides worth $96,000 with 18 employees. He may have leased the tan-

---

35 Hurd, *History of Clinton and Franklin Counties*, p. 321
36 Watson, *History of Essex County*, p. 476
37 Hastings, p. 13, from Warren County deeds

nery that year. The Census notes that bark was taken from Essex as well as Warren County. Kipp eventually turned the building into a cider mill and the structure burned in 1882, with the fire remaining in piles of tanbark for eighteen months.[38]

Mill Brook Tannery

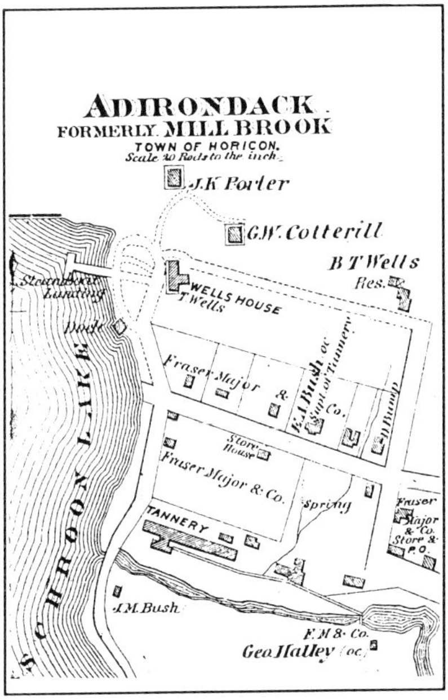

From the 1876 Atlas, Courtesy of the Adirondack Museum

Fraser, Major and Company were also the last owners of record of the Mill Brook Tannery, which was built in 1849 by Benjamin T. Wells. The next year, J. Russell joined Wells as partner, and bought out Wells' interest in 1853. Russell sold to E. A. Bush in 1855, of Bush and Metcalf.[39] Fraser, Major & Co. bought the tannery in 1860 and E. A. Bush ran it for them until about 1885.The 1860 Census indicates that Bush and Flick were owners of the tannery as assignees of Bush and Metcalf. Its production, 30,000 sides worth $142,500, places it among the larger tanneries, although in 1860, it employed only fifteen workers.

According to Warren County History, the tannery burned in 1864 and was rebuilt. Bush and Metcalf's production in 1870 was reduced to 20,000 sides worth $80,000.

Mill Brook Tannery, sometimes called Adirondack Tannery, spawned the community of Adirondack on the shores of Schroon Lake. Its workers lived in Gregoryville, about four miles inland from the lake in what is now the Pharaoh Lake Wilderness. Along with the Horicon tanneries, it pulled bark from what

---

38 Smith, *History of Warren County*, p. 547
39 Hastings, ibid, p. 18

is now the Pharaoh Lake Wilderness, an area with particularly rich pockets of hemlock, but apparently not enough accessible hemlock to sustain production. In 1860, the 1,800 cords of bark consumed cost only $5,000 to harvest; in 1870, 2,500 cords cost $14,000, more than double the cost of a decade earlier.

In 1880, Fraser, Major and Company produced $120,000 worth of both hides and skins, but their costs were rising. No figure is given in the census for the cost of bark, but there is the note that the 4000 cords of bark consumed came from Warren and Essex counties, the latter involving transportation over a significant distance. The tannery closed sometime after 1881.[40]

North Creek Tannery

The extent of the mid-century expansion of tanneries into the far reaches of Warren County long before the advent of the railroad is typified by the building of the North Creek Tannery, which was in operation at the time of the 1850 Census.[41]

Originally known as Sawyer and Mead after its builders, Milton Sawyer and Wheeler Mead, it was capitalized at $25,000 and the main building was 350 feet long. In 1850 North Creek produced 24,000 sides of sole leather valued at $90,000 from $54,000 worth of hides. The process consumed 2,500 cords of bark worth $3.00 a cord. The sixteen workers averaged an aggregate of $384 per month. As labor intensive as the process was, the costs of labor only roughly equaled the cost of bark. If the Census had listed transportation costs and other elements of the tannery's overhead, it would be possible to judge costs more realistically. Still, the indicated profits of close to $20,000, with costs about $70,000 are great enough to explain the continued rapid building of new tanneries in Warren County at mid-century. The problems of tracing tannery ownership are exemplified in what happened to the North Creek Tannery in the next two decades. Neither Sawyer nor Mead are named as owners in the 1860 Census. Milton Sawyer bought Mead's interests in 1866, and his firm indicated a slightly decreased production in 1870.

---

[40] Smith, ibid, p. 600

[41] Smith gives its construction as 1852, but in light of the Census report, that date is suspect.

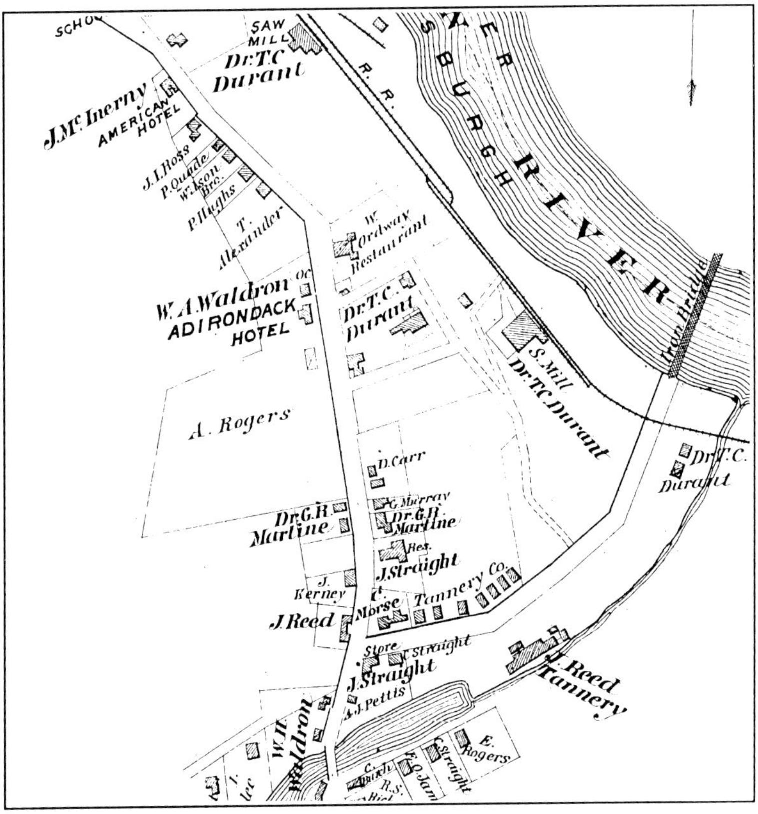

From the 1876 Atlas, courtesy of the Adirondack Museum

Deeds for the property indicate Sawyer took Joseph Russell as partner in 1872. A William Healy is associated with the tannery in the next few years, for he is listed as seller to John Reed in 1875. Reed was successful enough at North Creek to branch out -- in 1879 he built the Oregon Tannery, although his problems with suits involving that tannery seem to have brought him close to financial ruin. It is not clear whether a Boston firm provided the capital for building the Oregon Tannery, but Reed was certainly dependent on Boston money for acquisition of green hides at both tanneries. Reed was presumed to be an agent for Billings and Eton and made purchases in that Boston firm's name. Whatever the reason for the law suit against Boston leathermen, the suit was initially settled in Reed's favor. Two years later he was said to be worth "little or nothing" personally and in 1883 it was noted that "his solvency depends on lawsuit which is now in the court of appeals."[42] Reed apparently struggled on until 1886, when the North Creek Tannery was sold; Reed ended up running a boarding house instead of a tannery.

Certainly the completion of the Adirondack Railroad as far as North Creek in 1871 helped both the North Creek and Oregon tanneries. In 1880, Reed tanned $72,000 worth of sides; but currying these, and possibly the sides from Oregon, added $30,000 to the value of his production.

The North Creek Tannery, with most of its operations in one building, burned in June of 1890. A note in the Warren County News of June 12, 1890, states that "Our tannery is fast working out the stock of leather in the yards. Considerable damage was done to the top layers by the fire. There are some 10,000 sides yet to come out and finish, then the North Creek Tannery will be a thing of the past." An 1891 map shows no buildings on the site, but a 1908 photo depicts a saw mill, which had been erected there.

Stony Creek

According to local history, Stony Creek, originally Creek Center, sprang to life with the building of its tannery by J. P. Bowman in 1852. It was not closed until 1904, making it the longest continuous tanning operation in Warren County, though not in the entire Adirondack region; and, from 1887 on, it no longer tanned sole leather.

Bowman, a Vermonter, worked for Col. Burhans first in Saugerties, Ulster County, then in Warrensburg. For a few years he ran a sole-leather tannery in Cuttingsville, Vermont, then moved to Stony Creek in 1852 to complete the building of the tannery.[43]

In 1857, Milton Sawyer was a partner in this tannery[44], though no local records confirm this fact. He was reported to have sold his interests after the crash of 1857. Bowman accumulated a sizeable fortune before selling the tannery in 1887 to E. M. Garner, Jr. of Luzerne.

---

42 New York, Vol 609, p. 112, R. G. Dun and Co.

43 **Warrensburgh News**, September 24, 1891, obituary

44 New York, Vol. 609, p. 69, R. G. Dun and Co.

Stony Creek Tannery in the foreground, with bark shed between the tannery and the church, courtesy of Janet Whipple.

Garner was the son of the owner of the tannery in Luzerne and converted the Bowman Tannery from the production of sole leather to sheepskins for book bindings, the same operation as at the Garner Tannery in Luzerne.

Like all the early Warren County tanneries, this one preceded the Adirondack Railroad. Hides had to be hauled all the way from Saratoga and teams always went in pairs so they could be doubled up on the Cornish Hills -- it was thirty miles from the railhead, a two-day trip each way. Bowman's tannery was quite substantial; it was enlarged several times before 1869, when the railroad reached Stony Creek, though its production decreased gradually over the years: 32,000 sides in 1860, 28,000 in 1870, and 19,000 in 1880. At the same time, the costs of hides rose from $3.00, to $6.43, to $7.47, with a parallel decrease in profits.

The **Warrensburgh News** lamented the closing of the tannery in 1894, "What a pity some factory or business enterprise of some description could not be started up here so men and women, too, might earn an honest living."[45] The tannery was torn down in 1921. Typical of the Adirondack tannery towns that survived, Stony Creek temporarily withered when the tannery left. The population maximum reached in 1890 was not attained again until 1950.

---

[45] **Warrensburgh News**, May 3, 1894

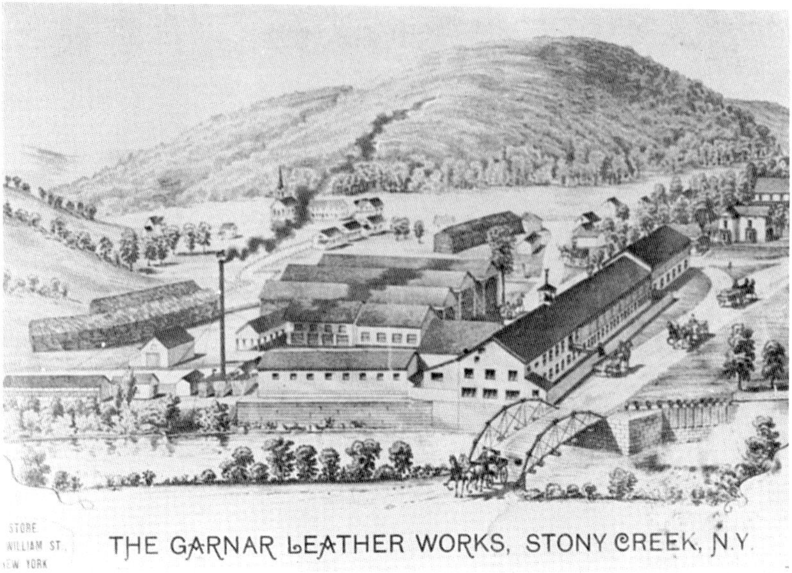

Courtesy of Janet Whipple

Luzerne Leather Works

Known formally as the Garner Leather Works of Luzerne, this tannery does not properly belong in this book because it did not produce hemlock-bark tanned sole leather. Throughout its long existence, it produced leather from sheepskins, which was primarily used as book covers. The tannery is included, nevertheless, because it was an Adirondack tannery and consumed hemlock bark.

The Delaware and Hudson Railroad from Saratoga Springs to Luzerne was completed in 1865 and two years later the tannery was built. It was bought out in 1868 by Thomas Garner & Co. of New York. The Garner family owned and operated the tannery until it closed in 1909—a unique record given the number of turnovers of ownership experienced by the sole-leather tanneries. Thomas, who had a tannery in Brooklyn, was joined in the venture by his brother Edward, who was just returning from the Gold Rush in Australia. Edward managed the Luzerne Tannery, expanding it in the 1880s to employ fifty to seventy men. His son, Ned, Edward Jr., took over the management of the tannery in 1887, and ran it and the former Bowman

Tannery in Stony Creek, which the firm had acquired. The Luzerne mill closed in 1909.[46]

Garner Leather Works had a 20-acre field near the mill that was full of bark piles and consumed some 2,000 cords at a cost of $4 to $5 a cord. The Thomas Garner Leather Company of New York had an even larger sheep-leather tannery in Malone. Thomas continued to run the business in New York until his death in 1898, but the Thomas Garner Leather Company continued in business until 1950.

When the Luzerne Tannery closed, 625 cords of bark were left in the yards. Records of this tannery come from two sources, Lester St. John Thomas, Luzerne historian, and Ira Gray, who wrote me that he drove the last stages, pulled by a team owned by Amasa Woodward, from Luzerne to Saratoga. The stages carried the left-over bark to be shipped to a company in Pennsylvania. The stages he drove were piled with five to six thousand pounds of the still valuable bark.

Oregon Tannery

The last of the large Warren County tanneries, the one at Oregon on the banks of the East Branch of the Sacandaga River, presents a triply fascinating story. The community at Johnsburg apparently raised the funds to build a road to the tannery site, an early example of local government attracting business. A teamster, who brought hides to Oregon from the railhead at North Creek, kept a diary that gives the only extant first hand account of the life of a teamster (see following chapter).

The events that transpired at the tannery site after the tannery burned are more intriguing than the typical tannery's fate. Compounding the difficulty of piecing together what happened at Oregon is the fact that Stephen Griffin of the Griffin Tannery was remembered to have been associated with the Oregon Tannery as well. His association was a loose one at best; he did contract to provide the Oregon Tannery with bark. He may have been a part of the original sale of the land because the deed for the property was registered in Hamilton County, not Warren

---

46 Thomas, *Timber Tannery and Tourists*, pp. 60-61

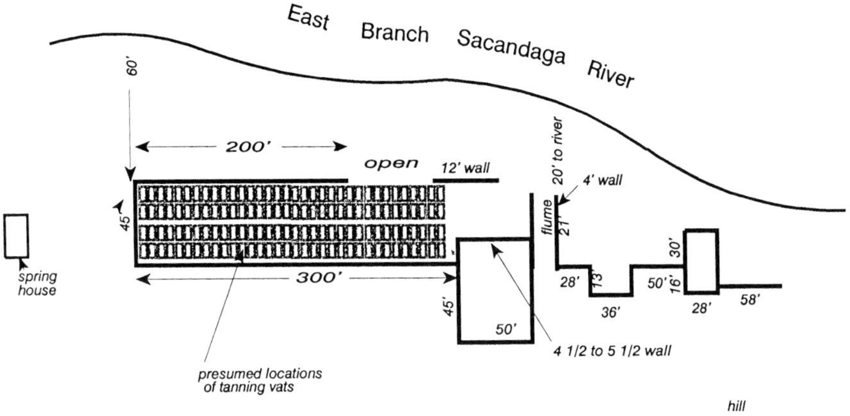

Oregon Tannery
Oregon, New York

County where the tannery was located. (See the chapter on the Griffin Tannery in Hamilton County.)

The Oregon Tannery was built at the 400-acre site of the Smith farm, which was sold by Zenas Van Dusen to the firm of McConnell and Gardner. John Reed acted as agent for that sale and supervised the tannery's construction. On May 12, 1877, the Town of Johnsburg agreed to build a road to the tannery from Sodom.

From the record of the Town Board of Johnsburg:

Whereas John Reed of North Creek in the Town of Johnsburg or other parties contemplate the erection of a Tannery on the Sacandaga River at or near the Shephard Smith farm.

Therefore it is hereby resolved by the inhabitants of the Town of Johnsburg at a special town meeting called according to the law held at the house of John Lyons at North Creek in said town on the 12th day of May 1877 that if said Reed or any other parties shall erect on the Sacandaga River at any point within the Town of Johnsburg then the supervisor and town clerk of said town are hereby authorized to ishue (sic) upon credit of said Town of Johnsburg Bonds or give notes to amount of one thousand dollars payable to the order of Rob. Waddell having interest of 7% payable February 4, 1878 and said money shall be exfunded on the road from the Stone School House in Sodom to Shepherd Smiths on the Sacandaga River. All of the money to be expended under supervision of Samuel Eldridge and John Reed. All of the Labor to be performed by day labor.

Road construction camp, Oregon, Black Mountain in the distance, courtesy of William R. Waddell.

The **Warrensburgh News** of January 30, 1878, reported that "John Reed has moved to Oregon in the west part of town to personally take charge of the large tannery he is building there." The 400-acre site was assessed at $600 in 1877, and then re-assessed for $7,000 in 1878 when the tannery had been completed. Reed apparently was receiving funds to build the tannery from brokers, and the agreement with them soured so that Reed sued. Reed only ran the tannery for a very short time, a little less than a year between the tannery's completion in 1879 and its sale in early 1880.

Shepherd F. Smith ran the "Shanty," a boarding house for workers at the tannery; his wife, Oville, did the cooking.

McConnell and Gardner, receivers perhaps who were listed as owners, sold the tannery to Charles O. Shaw of the Shaw Bros. on January 4, 1880. That year the Census indicates the tannery was capitalized at $30,000 and employed up to thirty men with $13,000 in yearly wages. The tannery was capable of handling 30,000 hides. The hides, worth $150,000, were worth $180,000 as tanned sole leather. A quick calculation shows that Shaw, with a profitability figure of 9.3%, had made a bad purchase for there was little room for profit.

There is no record to indicate how the tannery was retained by Charles O. Shaw, son of one of the partners in F. Shaw and Co., but he continued as owner even after the bankruptcy of the parent firm. In 1882, Charles O. Shaw was described as young (19 to 20 years old), the son of Charles Shaw of Dexter, Maine. R. G. Dun and Co. ledger reported that "we understand his father built the tannery and gave it to him, pays prompt."[47] The problems of the parent Boston firm are described in chapter VII; and the Oregon Tannery suffered the same tough times. The firm also had interests in the Wevertown Tannery about this time, and suspended operations at Wevertown in September of 1886[48], removing all their activity to Oregon.

Fire plagued the tannery. The Warrensburg News, of July 16, 1891, reported that the "Boarding House at Oregon was destroyed by fire early Monday A. M. Mr. and Mrs. A. ... not at home at the time; only the caretaker, Mrs. John Ross. She and boarders in upper stories had narrow escapes. Insured $1000 building and $800 furniture."

A note in the same paper for January 29, 1891 from Johnsburg stated, "C. O. Shaw is drawing bark with some 17 teams of his own from ten miles below Philander Baldwin's place. It is reported that he has overloaded and overworked his teams to such an extent that a complaint has been made against him before a justice. They say that his men have tired out several good, young horses so they have had to draw them in on a bark rack."

Finally, the paper for the week of March 3, 1892 reported, "The Oregon tannery owned by Shaw & Co. in the town of Johnsburg was completely destroyed by fire Saturday night. Fire caught near an engine at the east end of the building as a strong west wind was blowing at the time. It was the last tannery in this section and its loss will be severely felt by many as it was the principal industry of the place. About 50 men have been thrown out of employment. The property was valued at $50,000. It was insured for about $20,000."

The accompanying drawing of the tannery site, made from measurements of the foundations, which still stand on the bank of the East Branch of the Sacandaga River, shows that all the op-

---

[47] New York, Vol. 610, p. 401, R. G. Dun and Co.

[48] It is not know whether for certain that they closed operations at Wevertown or whether the tannery there burned in 1885. In any event, Charles O. Shaw did concentrate on the Oregon Tannery after 1886.

erations in this tannery were carried out in a single attached building, a certain invitation to destruction by fire.

The Fate of the Oregon Tannery Site

Alexander Hudnut, a chemist from New Jersey, founded the Hudnut Company, which was enlarged by his son, Richard, to include perfumes and a fashionable line of cosmetics and salons in London, Paris, and New York. His sizeable fortune enabled him to acquire several homes and furnish them to suit his artistic tastes. He began buying land around the Oregon Tannery site at the turn of the century and continued buying surrounding land for the next decade.

Immediately uphill from the tannery site, he built Fox Lair, a magnificent summer home, three stories high with a huge double staircase and a veranda across the front. Art, beauty, and the good life inspired Richard Hudnut, not the wilderness around him. He filled the house with furniture from the Continent, not with the plain, rustic Adirondack tables and chairs admired by other millionaires who fled to the north woods to lead the simple life. Forty servants staffed the house. A Japanese teahouse and a nature house were built near the river, a golf course was laid out along the valley, and many barns were constructed to house carriages and animals. Willett Randall was hired to catch and care for a pair of foxes, which were kept as symbols of the estate. The foxes' lair was visible from the house, a huge aviary graced the porch, and other rare and exotic animals were housed in the barns. Every summer afternoon at five, dancing pigeons put on a show for famous guests who came from around the world.[49]

At Hudnut's death, the estate was given to the New York City Police Athletic League for a camp, and then finally to the State itself, which tore the buildings down. The estate is now part of the Forest Preserve, but the foundations of both the house and the tannery are intact.

David Dodge - Oregon Teamster

David Dodge was unique—an Adirondack teamster who kept a diary. He was a widower, a lonely man, a man who conversed with his blank book daily. Scattered quotes from earlier years are preserved by several local historians, and his entire di-

---

[49] Conversation with Nan Hudnut Clarkson

ary from January 1887 through October of 1888 has been preserved.[50]

Dodge had a house in Warrensburg where his parents lived and where he visited regularly. He also had a farm not far from Johnsburg where he lived with his two motherless children. In warm weather he farmed, haying, picking apples, sowing peas, and working fourteen to sixteen hours a day, sometimes doing "two days work in one." In cool weather, and whenever he could, he worked as a teamster, drawing pople (sic), pegwood, coal, cordwood, and hoops.

With his friend Melvin, he was part owner of a teamster outfit, which drew hides and carboys of oil and acid from North Creek to Oregon and returned finished sides of leather to the railhead at North Creek. Occasionally, when he was free from the chores of farming and when there was more work than the "boys" with their three teams could handle, he personally drove hides and leather over the same route, most often drawing sleds in winter. Dodge sometimes referred to the boys as the Baker Tribe; Oregon was just west of Bakers Mills. At other times Dodge wrote about Dogtown, perhaps another name for the same settlement.

Melvin sold the teamster business for $600 in August of 1888. From all the entries concerning wages and expenses, it appears that Dodge was a teamster principally because it provided the income to pay off the debt on his farm.

Many entries in the diary describe how lonesome Dodge was. He read (he mentions love stories and books about distant places), visited neighbors, and squired a few young women when the opportunity arose. He employed a simple code to conceal the entries describing his contacts with these women, particularly his Jennie. (The code is remarkably simple to break; it consisted of replacing each letter with the one that precedes it in the alphabet.) The code conceals such details as the fact he received from her a "sweet kiss."

The diary is full of references to his misfortune with horses, the expense of buying new ones, and his bad luck when they died. One horse he purchased died within a month. Another cost $125. His horses were often lame, limiting his ability to make extra money.

---

50 I first saw the diary in a transcription of the original that was given me by William Waddell of North Creek. The diary was later given to the Adirondack Museum.

When he drove to the Oregon Tannery west of Bakers Mills from the railhead at North Creek, he followed Pleasant Valley Road south to the road that is now NY 8. That road was built in 1878, and the picture on page 161 of the road builders' camp clearly shows the mountain view to the north as you would see it from a point just east of the tannery site.

Dodge noted that he made a "round trip with two teams, finished heavy Texas hides and commenced on lot of Nova Scotia hides, 3800 of them" in November 27, 1885. (A note for Monday September 12, 1887, in the extant diary marks the end of the second year he had kept a diary.

Dodge began the year of 1887 drawing loads of pople (sic, poplar or aspen used for barrel staves) from Johnsburg to the mill in Warrensburgh. Shortly after, he began drawing hides and leather again, and his entries for the early part of 1887 paint a grim picture of the rigors of the job.

February 1887

Monday 7th. Hitched a load of hides Melvin had ready for me and went to Oregon and brought out a load of leather, 2680#.

Wednesday 9th. Went to Oregon and got back home three o'clock. Took Dick [a horse] and Melvins cutter and harness and drove to the Creek after Miss Curtis; she ise going to stay at Melvins a few days with Lily as [he] is in the woods draying bark, and make Bertie some clothes. ... Melvin is getting three dollars per day, fifty cents more than the other teams. Dick has got the horse distemper again, goes about with his eyes shut, and looks awful sorrowful.

Thursday 10th. Made a round trip to-day and got in before seven, took in 3520# grain for Straight and brought out only 2100 leather. Earned seven dollars and ninety-five cents. A very nice day and just as good sleighing as any body has got.

Friday 11th. Stormy again, snow and rain. Have been to the Creek and to Oregon again today, carried in the same as I did yesterday but did not bring out any leather. Thought my team had done enough without. Earned $5.95. Frank and Bertie did not bring any leather on account of the rain.

Wednesday 16th. Splendid weather. Have no hides to draw now so we had to go in empty today. Mr. Shaw was at Oregon and said we must do the freighting cheaper this summer, for one shilling [about a quarter of a dollar] each way. Did not tell him I would do it for that and may loose my job. He said there was a man wanted it for that price. Bill is sick.

Thursday 17th. Found no hides at the Creek to-day either so made up my mind to go home, got all ready to start and Kit was taken sick so had to give up going today, and when we got home Dick was taken sick and was very sick for a couple hours, but got better before bed time. Melvin came home today, there was no roads to any more bark. Melvin paid me the twenty-five dollars due me on the lot here and intrest (sic), also his next payment on the teams, not due until the first of March. Only one hundred fifty more due on the contract. I have two hundred dollars ready for my payment on the farm, in the spring. Eighty more to earn, hope I may have the luck to get it without selling anything.

Thursday 24th. Went to the Creek empty, this morning, and not knowing whether I would have a load back or not, but found three car loads of hides there. The wind blew a perfect gale at the Creek this afternoon, blew Melvin off his load and about twenty-five hides were carried several rods. Have a bottle of ink to-night.

Friday 25th. Snowed and drifted so that we had a hard time to get through to-day, did not get to the height of land until four o-clock and to Oregon at seven, had to shovel all day. Stopped and feed our teams in the road and eat our dinner, and nearly froze while doing it.

Saturday 26th. Did not get home from Oregon until two o-clock, went to bed (how foolish, but the boys would do it, I tried to get them not to) and slept an hour or two, then got up and started for the Creek. Snowed all day and the loads drawed so hard going home we left one load at Hacks and put two teams on the head load.

Sunday 27th. This is one of the days we have "earn" tell on, but never before seen. The snow flies fearful. The road will be all filled full again and more too.

Monday 28th. The last day of February and an awful rough day, the wind blows and the snow flies to beat the world. We have stayed in the house all day, have not tried to break out roads any because we knew it would drift in again nearly as fast as we could shovel the snow out. I have repaired and oiled my harnesses today, worked at it nearly all day.

March

Tuesday 1st. A nice day. We shoveled this forenoon and at noon put four teams onto two loads and started toward Oregon, did not expect to get through to-day but met several teams coming out and as we were so behind with our work concluded to go through if we were late. Got to Oregon after six, started to come back at eight. 100 hides on each load only.

Wednesday 2nd. Did not get home from Oregon until two again this morning. Had a couple hours sleep then started for the Creek, did not get in until late to-night. Very bad going, but has been a nice day again.

Saturday 5th. Another nice day, but think it will snow to-morrow, though I hope not for we have got headed for the wrong way again. Had to go to Oregon to-day, so we have got to let the leather stand here over Sunday and have four loads (12700) here and have room for only three under the sheds, but I think I have got it covered so it will not get damaged if it does storm. Got in at five o-clock to-night, seems good to get in before dark again. We met Mr. Shaw going to Oregon this afternoon.

Sunday 6th. Found it snowing when I got up this morning as I had expected. It snowed all day steady. Expect to have a hard time getting the loads through to-morrow.

Monday 7th. We got up at one this morning and at two started for the Creek and well ? we got through, but I am afraid it was wicked to draw our teams the way we did, though they all seemed willing to pull their best every time, and we shoveled the snow out on all the steep hills. Got out there at ten o-clock. Brought back all the hides we had there, and do not expect any more before the last of the week as the trains are blocked with snow again. The snow packed to-day so our loads came back very nicely this afternoon.

Tuesday 8th. ... We are drawing for one shilling per hundred each way now.

Tuesday 22nd. Has snowed all day. One year ago to-day we broke through to Oregon with wagons, though it snowed nearly all day then and we went in with sleds once or twice more after than. To-day the snow there is at least five foot and I think more through the woods. I put fifty dollars in the bank yesterday.

Wednesday 23rd. Another foot of snow and drifted bad again.

April

Friday 1st. Clear and pleasant. Melvin and I have made a round trip again to-day. Rec'd a letter from Miss ----. Melvin tipped over a load of hides.

Teamsters hauling and stacking bark at the Oregon Tannery, courtesy Lewis Waddell.

Monday 4th. Warm and this afternoon rainy. The roads are getting very soft. Took in 9300# hides. The snow is about four feet deep but settling fast.

Tuesday 5th. Went to the Creek and found lots of water in the road. Dug some drains and let the water run off and got through allright but when we came back had our horses down in the water and nearly tipped over.

Tuesday 12th. Am at Johnsburg to-night, started at half past five [returning from Warrensburgh] did not get here until three. Brought up Bill and had to come on the walk all the way, and started to come up the river road and found the water and ice about six feet deep in the road and had to go back to Warrensburgh and come up the plank. The boys started for Oregon yesterday and again this morning but the drifts were so soft they could not get through, only got as far as Doley. We borrowed a new plow and undertook to plow the road but the snow was so hard in the road we smashed the plow and gave it up.

Wednesday 13th. We started for Oregon again this morning with about ten hundred on apiece and went in all right. Put on about twenty hundred of leather apiece and did not come out "all right" cut off had our horses down, chopped, shoveled and lifted and drawed our horses until nine o-clock in the evening then left two loads in the woods beyond Andrew Wescots and put two teams on one load and thought we could take that home, but got one team down, one horse top of the other and had to work at least half an hour to get them up, then left that load (at the height of land) and came home with our horses and thought we were lucky to get them home alive. Got home at eleven.

Friday 15th. Went through to the Creek with wagons for the first time, one month later than last year lacking one day. Got through much better than I expected, only brought home twenty five hides apiece. Got home before dark.

May
Monday 2nd. Went to Oregon to-day with four teams, the roads are much better than I expected. They are not rolling any now, there is no leather dry, and they are going to build over the old furnace, besides, the smokestack to the new furnace has fallen down again. Do not think they will get to rolling again under two weeks. Have about fourteen hundred sides on hand so we will not be out of work very long.

Friday 6th. ... Got my pay for last month to-day only $187.00, but as much as I expected.

Dodge spent the summer farming, occasionally drawing wood and hoops, but no hides. The following winter it snowed a foot in mid-December, so they could begin sleighing and Dodge began drawing hides again. The entries in the diary vary little—illnesses, visits to friends, reading out loud to the boys, and letters from friends and relatives liven the otherwise difficult work. The diary is almost the same as the year before, except for March—and the blizzard.

February 1888

*Monday 13th. Had over 400 sides to-day. Received our pay for last months freighting today. $184.35. Mr Shaw says he wants me to stay and do the freighting this summer, would not hear to my leaving at all, had thought of going to ***** this summer.*

March
Sunday 11th. Has snowed nearly all day, but has not amounted to much yet. Went down and had Mrs. Scribner cut my hair this morning and this morning went to Mothers and carried the children, drove Mage side of Dick and I went up to see Elijah Brown, Cousin Eliza Maxim is at Mothers. Have been down to johns this evening. I intended to go to church to the Village but it stormed to hard.

Monday 12th. Has snowed all day the heaviest snow storm we have had this winter. Wanted to send a letter to town but there has not been a team through today. Bertie and I have been sawing wood in the shed.

Tuesday 13th. Has snowed all day again, do not think there was ever such a snow storm in this country before. Tom Galbraith says there has fell three feet, but it has drifted here so I cannot tell. Think we will have a big time breaking roads when it stops snowing. I took a terrible cold yesterday.

Wednesday 14th. Morning clear and pleasant. It is lucky for us poor mortals that the snow did not come until near spring, now we know it must soon began to melt, anyway. Evening; Have been breaking road this afternoon, drove my horses down to Johns and back (without sleds) and up to Everts and back, then hitched onto one sled and drove down to the end of the bet and came back and put on the plow and plowed through to Charles Browns and back.

Thursday 22nd. Went to town to-day to hear from Baker (rec'd a letter with $36.00 in it last months freighting) that I need not come up at all as they would finish the leather this week and that there would be no more until about the first of May and that he would send Dick back Sunday.

XI

Saratoga County

One of the most fascinating of the early Colonial tanneries was the Eli Beecher Tannery, built in Beecher's Hollow in the Town of Edinburgh. The allure stems from the tannery's location in a cluster of industries tightly strung out along Beechers Creek, a small tributary of the Sacandaga. The industries depict the industrial revolution in microcosm. Beechers Creek tumbles precipitously from the mountains north of the river, falling several hundred feet in half a mile. There were at least a half dozen dams on the creek, running such diverse enterprises as a rake factory, a casket factory, a sawmill, carding mills, and so on. The upper dam, with a small pond, served the Ellithorpe distillery, which became the Beecher Tannery in 1802. This became the Lyons and Prindle Tannery in 1825. Apparently this tannery was listed as belonging to Crowe and Kyner in the 1850 Census. After 1855, it was run by George F. Cameron.[1] Throughout, the tannery produced upper-leather, only 500 sides in 1850, 1200 in 1860, even less in the two succeeding census years.

With a few exceptions, this very small, Colonial scale tannery, was typical of those in Saratoga County. Too much of the land in the southern and eastern part of the county had been cleared for farming to permit the harvest of hemlock bark for large scale tanning.

Corinth had a small tannery in 1818, and another on the Kayaderosseras in 1855.[2]

Ballston Spa's tanneries were typically small, with three tanneries listed in 1850, one of which also produced boots and shoes. The tanneries listed in succeeding years produced calf skins (1860) and sheepskins (1870).

The number of small tanneries in the more accessible towns, Greenfield, Providence, Wilton, and Galway, was seven in 1850 and again in 1860, although only one had the same propri-

---

1 Dunn, *Saratoga County Heritage*, p. 339

2 Dunn, ibid, p. 289 and p. 291

etor. Thereafter, the number of tanneries throughout the entire county declined to seven in 1870 and five in 1880.

The exceptions to this small scale were located either north of the Sacandaga River or in the Town of Wilton. The huge upper leather tannery, owned by Samuel Haight, was established late in the tanning era, shortly before 1880, in Wilton. It reported producing 100,000 sides of upper leather in 1880. This huge tannery was a branch of Hall, Haight and Company of New York and Boston, which was incorporated into the American Hide and Leather Company in 1895.[3]

The Sacandaga River provided a different means of transporting bark to one of the county's two larger sole-leather tanneries. Saratoga County bark was drawn from mountains to the north of the river near Edinburgh in winter and piled on the banks where it could be loaded in scows in warm weather for the trip to the tannery at Conklingville (then Osborne's Bridge) in the Town of Hadley. Poor and Company ran two woodburning, side-wheeler steamers as far upriver as Batchellerville. One of the steamers blew up, the other, the Whipporwill, was in service until 1883.[4]

A tannery was built in Hadley in 1848 by Col. Gordon Conklin, founder of Conklingville[5]. Different owners were listed in the 1850 and 1860 Census, and in 1863[6] it was acquired and run by Henry Poor and Son, leather merchants from New York. In 1850, 30,000 sides were tanned; 40,000 were tanned in 1860 when William Gates, the manager of record, appears to have had a very profitable year. Henry Poor and Son produced fewer sides (34,000) in 1870, but they were extraordinarily high in value ($207,000). That year, Henry Poor and Son opened a second tannery upriver in Day with the capacity to produce 40,000 sides of sole leather. The first year, 32,000 sides worth $109,000 were tanned.

There is no census record for the Poor Tannery in Hadley in 1880; it may have closed. Their tannery in Day continued to produce 40,000 sides in 1880, but with the price of leather so low that year, it is questionable whether they made any profit at all.

---

[3] Norcross, ibid, p. 189

[4] This information was in a letter from Ira Gray, whose mother worked in a large boarding house near the tannery; also Dunn, ibid, p. 314.

[5] Dunn, ibid, pp. 323-324

[6] Dunn, ibid, p. 314

For all the economies of hauling bark by river steamer, Henry Poor and Son paid $5.00 a cord for 2,500 cords of bark at its Day tannery in 1870, $6.00 a cord for the 4,000 cords needed downriver at the Hadley tannery.

A second tannery, owned by H. R. Kathan, was active in Day in 1880, but with a small production and no more than four workers. Equally small was the tannery of Krigg and Son to the east on the Kayaderosseras Creek in Corinth. It is not known whether this was a successor to a small tannery noted in the 1850 Census, but not in the intervening years.

Given the relatively small scale of all but the Poor tanneries, and the high cost of bark that even they encountered, it is hard to understand how Samuel Haight could be confident enough in the bark supply to invest $120,000 in his Wilton tannery in 1880. Although only upper leather was tanned, hemlock bark, 5,000 cords of it, were needed in 1880, and as the Census noted, that bark had to be hauled from as far away as Warren County.

XII

Essex County

Essex County's location and rich, tillable lands adjacent to Lake Champlain invited farmers to settle soon after the Revolution. Scattered among them were several who served as Colonial tanners. The County Census indicates a production of a fair number of cattle to supply these tanneries. In 1839, there were sixteen tanneries, all quite small, and twelve of them were near Lake Champlain.

Larger sole-leather tanneries were constructed almost as early as in Warren County and in many ways, the growth of Essex County's tanning industry was very closely tied to Warren County's expansion. The same men who invested in Warren County tanneries built operations in Essex County.

One Warren County tanner, Milton Sawyer, with interests in five tanneries there, built or owned part of at least four more in Essex County. Family records indicate he was involved in eight or nine tanneries, but it has been difficult to confirm that number from other records. It is only with the help of the R. G. Dun ledgers that this has been possible.[1]

In Essex County, Sawyer, who owned the Schroon Lake and Hoffman tanneries, expanded in 1869 to a tannery on The Branch. For this distant move, he either picked the wrong year or the wrong place, because his profits, as noted below, were very thin for the year 1870. Before the end of that decade, Sawyer was in bankruptcy. Sawyer may also have invested in the Excelsior Tannery, a fourth tannery in the northern Schroon Lake area, which has been difficult to document.

Edgar W. Burhans, brother of Col. B. P. Burhans of Warrensburg Tannery, built the North Hudson Tannery, but it appears that the family's tanneries were independent operations. This, too, was a short lived operation, for the 1880 Census indicates no hides were being tanned there.

---

[1] See references this chapter and in the Warren County chapter.

Curiously, the wave of tanning expansion did not come west and inland from Lake Champlain with its railroads and barge travel: the principal growth sprang from the same links that thrust tanneries into the wilds of Warren County, the plank roads that were tied to Warrensburg through North Creek or the roads along the valley of the Schroon River. We can speculate that this was because the necessary quantities of hemlock bark had been stripped from the Champlain Valley as that valley became farmland. If Sawyer and Burhans, with their tanneries in the upper Schroon Valley, were lured there by their search for bark, they must have been disappointed: 1870 saw costs of $5.00 a cord.[2] This cost, combined with the high costs of hides and the great distances of hauling them to their remote locations, was financially devastating to Sawyer and caused the closing of Burhans' Essex County tannery.

It really is difficult to understand why the cost of bark should have been so high in Essex County. The hillsides east of the site of the North Hudson Tannery are today covered with a maturing hemlock forest, richer and more luxurious than almost any stand that has been cut. The revegetated areas along the trail to Bass Pond and around that pond and east to Berrymill Pond are covered today with trees that indicate these northern slopes were a perfect place to grow hemlock. Stands with such a rich monoculture would have been prized indeed.

This speculation on the forests leads to the conclusion that something else was a factor in the demise of these tanneries–distance from good transportation, aspects of the economic climate, or hidden or unknown elements.

Essex County Bark

From the 1870s on, there are scattered references in the Census and in local histories to the fact that some of Warren County's bark came from Essex County, all, of course, shipped by team. Truman Hayes, whose story enlivens the account of the Horicon Tannery, also dictated a story about working on a bark crew, the only record we have of how a crew worked together.

---

[2] 1870 Census, Essex County

The events, when he was sixteen, occurred about 1880. Hayes, who died in 1969 at the age of 94 dictated this to A. Tripp, a relative by marriage. The account begins with a description of a trip through Essex County when he was thirteen to begin work as a lumber jack.

Perhaps you might be interested in knowing ..... that we peeled the bark from the hemlock trees. After the bark was peeled, the logs were cut up into 13 1/2 foot long. .... Bark peeling usually commenced about the first of May and would last about six weeks. The bark was used for tanning leather. Sometimes a jobber with twenty five or more men peeling bark will divide them up into what is called crews, four men to a crew. One man chops the trees down, one man trims the tree, one man cuts through the bark clear around the tree every four feet, and then he slits, or splits the bark on top of the tree. Then the spudder, as he is called, peeled the bark. He does it with a tool called a spud, and it is shaped something like a chisel, only larger, weighing about six or seven pounds. It has a handle about 18 or 20 inches long. The sharp end of the spud was stuck into the slit on top of the tree and then worked down between the bark and the wood, and then with a quick pull of the spud toward the spudder the bark was all peeled from the side of the tree next to him. Then the same operation was used on the other side of the tree. ....

The spring I was 16 I was working in the barkwoods for Mr. Ross. As I remember it there were twenty men, five crews, four men to a crew. Each crew had to keep count of the trees he peeled during the day. There was one always more or less racing to see which crew peeled the most trees. From sixty to one hundred trees was a good day's work. ... There was one crew that was supposed to be the best crew in the woods. They were big, husky men and the man who chopped the trees down was a man by the name of Ed Coward, a great chopper. There was no other crew expected to be able to peel as many trees as his crew could. But --- they overlooked the Hayes crew. The crew I was in was made up of all Hayes: Ed Hayes chopped down the trees. (He was a cousin of mine ...) I chopped the limbs off the trees, and next to me was my cousin, Eugene Hayes, who fixed the bark for the spudder. My brother Charlie spudded the bark .... They were all good men but with a boy of 16 along to do the trimming, which was a man's job, we weren't supposed to have a ghost of a show. Mr. Ross would come around three or four times a week and count the trees to see if the right account had been given in the night before, so every crew was careful to give in the right count. When the bark peeling was over (about six weeks) Mr. Ross reckoned up the number of trees each crew had peeled, and to the surprise of all the men it was found that the Hayes crew had peeled 30 more trees than the great Ed Coward crew. WHOOPS! Didn't the Hayes crew do some yelling!! Mr. Ross gave us all five dollars a piece, and he placed his hand on my shoulder and said "Truman, you are a boy in years, but you surely did a big man's work."

So I will tell you a little about it [peeling bark]. We usually commenced work about 6:30 in the morning and got through about 6 at night. We usually carried our dinner and it consisted of bread, meat, beans and molasses and sometimes cookies or fried cakes. Never butter. The plague of the bark peelers is flies: big flies, little flies and all kind of flies except peaceful and gentle flies. There were the mosquitoes constantly yelling 'Coming, coming,' and they were by the thousands and millions and each one trying to stick his bill into you first, and deepest. And then there were the billions of black flies who never told you they were 'coming' but commenced work at once. They would crawl into your eyes, ears, nose, and mouth, in fact any opening they could find. And then there was another small fly, so tiny you could hardly see him. We called him 'All jaws.' After a few billion had bit you your flesh would smart as if it had been burned. No, we didn't have anything to put on our faces to keep them away as they do now. ... About noon we were ready for dinner. We uncovered our dinner pail, and sometimes a few hundred ants as well. They were always ahead of us, but these we could drive off, and they were the least of our troubles, but the flies never were so happy or mean as they were when we were trying to eat our dinner. They would light on our head, on our meat, by the hundreds. They got stuck in the molasses after you had put it on the bread. We just didn't have time to drive them away... so many a fly met an untimely death.... the days work done we went back to the shanty and after supper went out doors trying to get some rest, and the four small fires out of wet, rotten wood to make plenty of smoke. ... in that way we could beat those flies, but don't think they gave up. When 9 o'clock came and we were ready for bed we found the flies still up and ready for business. We were ready for bed but the flies weren't. So, we built smudges in the chambers to kill or drive out the insects and the room would be so blue with smoke it would kill nearly anything.. there was a small window in each end of the room so the smoke got out finally --- and after a while we went to sleep and then nothing short of a panther could have awakened any of us.

Port Henry

In 1839, a clothing factory in Port Henry was enlarged and converted into a tannery, which remained in operation until about 1860. It was styled variously as the A. B. and C. W. Huntley Co. and the John B. Huntley Co., the latter according to the 1850 Census, which indicates its total production was valued at only $1,260. With only one worker, this tannery is obviously comparable to the early Colonial operations. The 1860 Census lists Abraham B. and Clark W. Huntley as owners of a slightly larger tannery in Moriah.

Essex - South Census District

Several other Colonial tanners were located in the southern part of Essex County; among them four persisted until after 1850 and were recorded in that early Census, though all were very small, one- or two-man operations. Ransom Noble produced 600 sides in 1850; C. Kidder, 400; Edmund Hoffingle (sp.), 100 with some skins; O. Ivey (sp.), of Crown Point, 200 hides. All used hand tools. Only one in Crown Point was still producing leather in 1860, the tannery owned by Julius C. Brevort. A tanner with a similar name was working in Willsborough in 1870, both tanning and currying a small amount of leather. It is possible that this operation was continued under a different name in 1880 at the same location on the Bouquet River. Two other small tanneries are noted in the 1870 Census in the region close to Lake Champlain.

In 1850 there were no tanneries in the Northern or Schroon Census District of Essex County, as the interior western portion was designated.

Elizabethtown

The Elizabethtown Tannery began similarly as a very small operation. Started in 1820 by Henry Noble, it also manufactured shoes and harnesses.[3] Henry was joined by his son Charles H. Noble, and the firm of C. W. and H. Noble continued until 1885, a remarkable span. However, as the sequence of Census reports indicates, it was never a large operation. The one worker listed in the 1850 Census produced sides worth but $800. In 1860, two workers produced only 320 sides of sole leather. With a third worker in 1870, production was up to 1,400 sides worth $5,000, while 100 cords of bark at $5.00 a cord was used in the process. In 1880, the production was reduced to 900 sides, worth a mere $2,000. The 1880 Census notes that Charles H. Noble also produced boots and shoes. This fact, plus the small size, undoubtedly accounts for the longevity of the operation.

Minerva

The tannery at Minerva is a prime example of the county's relation to and dependence on neighboring Warren County to the south and east. Minerva's Alpine Tannery was one of the very early larger operations. Land (525 acres) for the tannery on Minerva Creek was bought by Levi Olmsted in 1847 from Ed Talbot and Th. Leonard. The expense of building the tannery apparently bankrupted Levi in 1848, for he was bought out by Sanford Olmsted that year. The tannery changed hands again in 1855, when Aaron Olmsted bought in, but this arrangement was short-lived.[4]

In 1856, Alpine Tannery was sold to E. A., H. A. Fenn, and W. F. Fenn and David S. Munger, owners of the Pottersville Tannery. Bankruptcy stalked the Alpine Tannery again in 1858, when it was sold to or taken over by Fraser, Major and Company, of New York City, chief creditors, who also took over Warren County's Pottersville Tannery at the same time. Alpine Tannery burned in 1867, having produced sole leather for a brief twenty years, though the owners continued to draw bark to the Pottersville Tannery for a few more years.

In those twenty years, the tannery brought considerable growth and some prosperity to the town. The growth of Minerva

---

[3] Watson, *History of Essex County*

[4] Watson, ibid, p. 476, Minerva Historical Society, *History of Minerva*, pp. 59-61

Corners was so great that a nearby center was established, Olmstedville, named for the original owners of the tannery. Typical of the way such tannery towns grew, representatives of the tannery met boats in New York City and enticed men to work in the tannery and women to work in the boarding houses, of which Olmstedville and Minerva had two. (A story related by a woman whose grandmother had been so hired told how a young son of the family drowned in a tannery vat.) Of the town's eight tanners listed in the 1860 Census, one was a Scot; but the rest were Irish, and of those, O'Neil, Waldron, Lindsay, McCluskey, and Ryan were born in Ireland.[5]

The community around the tannery grew to 1,082 residents in 1865. The Census for 1860 gives $9,000 as the value of the tannery's real property. That year it produced 23,000 sides of sole leather, worth $78,000. With 29 employees, these statistics rank it smaller than the Warren County tanneries in operation that year. Still, it was pulling from 3,000 to 5,000 cords of bark from surrounding forests, forests that in later years also had to supply the North Creek Tannery. It is significant that at a time when North Creek and Oregon tanneries to the south were flourishing, all the land and buildings, including the company store, attached to the Alpine Tannery were sold in 1871 for $3,750.

Milton Sawyer

Schroon Lake Tannery

A mid-sized tannery was erected by Lorenzo Hall in 1852 at a site about 2 miles from Schroon Lake, on the north side of the road running west from the State highway at the south end of the village (today's Hoffman Road). The source of water power was a stream, today known as Rogers Brook, which drained Little Roger Pond (now North Pond), Big Roger Pond (now Big Pond) and Bullet Pond. Before 1860, the tannery was acquired by Milton Sawyer of Glens Falls, one of the tanning en-

[5] Minerva, ibid

trepreneurs from Warren County who expanded into Essex County.[6]

(In 1957, Milton's granddaughter, Marjorie, wrote of being taken to the site of the tannery by Ray Connell, a native of Schroon and grandson of Herman Noxon, who was foreman at the tannery. At the time of her visit, a large barn, the former boarding house, and several workers' houses were still standing.)[7]

Sawyer produced 300 tons of sole leather worth $120,000 in 1860 at the Schroon Lake Tannery, which employed 25 workers and used 3,750 cords of bark. It appears to have been a very profitable operation in 1860, but not so in 1870 when the real property value was given as $100,000. That year's expenses (hides, $98,560; wages, $5,600 for fourteen workers; bark, $9,000 for 1,800 cords; and wood) totaled $113,160, almost as much as the value of the sides produced, $120,000. This translates into a profitability figure of 5.7%, well below what was needed to sustain the operation. This lack of profitability in 1870 is strange, because almost all other Adirondack tanneries did very well, according to computations based on the Census record for that year. Things got no better, for in a letter dated September 13, 1879, his son Joseph wrote, "*I hope tannery will be sold. Father is talking about running it himself. He got Russell and Crandall to hold on til Nov. 1 to give him a chance to redeem it. ... Of course, he can't raise the money, I guess R. would not wait long if he had a chance to sell. Father thinks the folks can live at Glens Falls and he go up and take care of the tannery. I am hoping Bloomingdale will buy before long.*" In a letter the next month, Joseph Sawyer wrote, "*I think B. will buy tannery inside of two weeks if father does not - Cosgrove has told Charles [another Sawyer son] that they have about made up their minds they have got to buy it in order to get their money out of their bark. They have engaged Noxon to come in and run it if they do buy. I don't expect father to do anything.*"

The Branch

Essex County Historian William Watson noted that a tannery is "now [1869] being built by Milton Sawyer."[8] This tannery,

---

6 Watson, ibid, p. 474
7 Letter from Janet Appleyard
8 Watson, ibid, p. 474

also known as Sawyer and Mead, was on the West Branch of the Schroon, three miles from the State Road. It principal building measured 263 by 60 feet, and it consumed 3,000 cords of bark a year. There is no Census record for 1870, perhaps because production was just beginning, but this tannery was also sold, for in 1880, J. S. Woodward and Co. are listed as the owners of the tannery on The Branch, which produced 20,000 sides worth $60,000, a sum barely exceeding costs. Several owners are reported in 1881, A. C. Emerson and Co., which also had interests in the Horicon Tannery, Essex County Tanning Co., and finally in 1882 the Woodward brothers.[9] However, these reorganizations did not manage to revive the tannery, and nothing was produced there in 1881 and the business was closed in 1882.

Hoffman Tannery

Milton Sawyer was involved in a third tannery, the Hoffman Tannery, located 6 miles west of Sawyer's Schroon Lake Tannery. According to Watson, it was built in 1856 by Bracket and Boyle and bought by Sawyer in 1869.[10] This was a modest tannery, producing 16,000 sides in 1870 and consuming 900 cords of bark.

Schroon or Excelsior Tannery

Essex County Historian Watson says there was a small tannery, owned by Benjamin Wickham, on the east side of Schroon Lake, opposite the Schroon Lake Tannery. Another reference describes a Schroon Tannery erected in 1861 by William Potter and Daniel Wyman, which at the time produced only upper leather.

The 1870 Census lists an Excelsior Tannery in the Town of Schroon, with a production of 16,000 sides, but so far this information has not been positively associated with any other records. The Census lists expenses of $2,500 for wages, $4,500 for bark, and $47,780 for hides. With a production valued at only $60,000 this gives a profitability figure of 5.4%, low enough to explain why the tannery disappeared without a trace.

---

[9] New York, Vol. 94, p. 384, R. G Dun and Co.
[10] Watson, ibid, p. 474

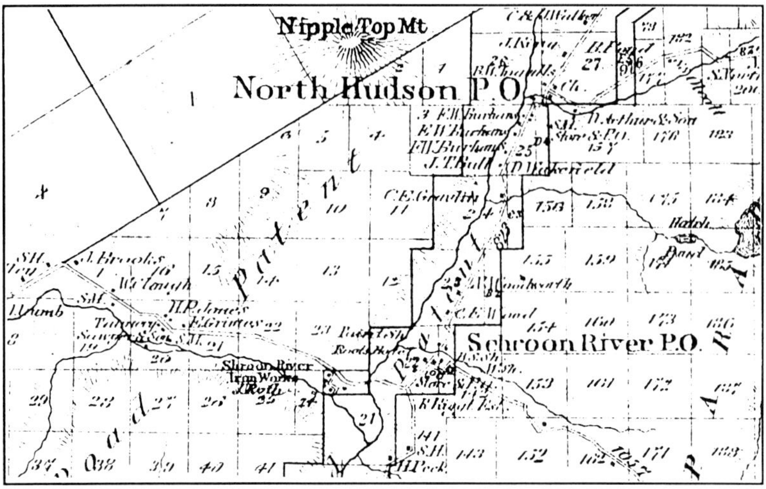

Essex County map locates the Sawyer Tannery on the Branch and the Burhans Tannery at North Hudson, courtest of the Adirondack Museum.

This is one of the more problematic identifications, but it is quite likely that the Schroon tanneries mentioned in Watson and the Excelsior Tannery were one and the same. There is one other brief reference in 1872 to Milton Sawyer's four Essex County holdings: "two active tanneries, the North Hudson Tannery [The Branch], and one that burned last winter."[11] It is quite likely the tannery "that burned" refers to the Excelsior Tannery and, if so, these four tanneries in Essex County and the five in Warren County add up to the nine that family records indicate Sawyer owned in whole or in part.[12]

Edgar W. Burhans

North Hudson

The North Hudson Tannery of Edgar W. Burhans, brother of Col. Burhans of Warrensburg, was slightly more suc-

---

[11] New York, Vol. 93, p. 223, R. G. Dun and Co.

[12] Letter from Janet Appleyard, great-grandaughter of Milton Sawyer.

cessful than the contemporaneous ones owned by Milton Sawyer, perhaps because Burhans' expansion into Essex County began earlier than Sawyer's. The tannery on a branch of the Schroon River (now called Black Brook) was built by Erastus B. Potter and sold in 1859 to Edgar Burhans.[13] The 1860 Census lists the owners as Burhans and Osborne and states that the tannery was not yet completed. In 1861, the new tannery was reported as being "somewhat in debt and depressed by reason of the times."[14] Osborne sold out in 1864.

In 1870, the North Hudson Tannery, under the style E. W. Burhans & Sons, produced 14,000 sides of sole leather, worth $76,000. The 1,500 cords of bark cost more than $5.00 a cord to bring to the tannery. In 1880, a nephew, Frank Burhans, was said to be running a tannery in North Hudson, but there is no other record of it, except the statement that it was located on Clear Brook, a name which is no longer used for any brook in the area. The Census gives no production figures for it. The demise of this tannery may have stemmed from the cost of bark and hides, but certainly the fact that it took a team four days to make the round trip from the railhead at Glens Falls must have hastened its last days.

Tanning Ends in Essex County

Two small local tanners and Woodward's Branch Tannery were all that were left in Essex County in 1880. Tanning had all but ended there, well before it ended in Warren County to the south where tanneries were still importing bark from Essex County. Certainly Essex County's bark supplies were not exhausted. The conclusion that the tanneries had been built too far from railheads may be the only explanation for the end of tanning in Essex County.

13 Watson, ibid, p. 474

14 New York, Vol. 93, p. 169, R. G. Dun and Co.

XIII

Clinton County

Clinton County had twenty-nine Colonial tanners listed in the 1850 Census as serving the surrounding farming communities, though at least one of these one-man operations expanded in future years into a large sole-leather tannery.

None of those listed in 1860 can even be considered large, compared with those establishments being built to the south. In fact, nine were so small they had but one or two workers: the Alstona Tannery in Altona (600 sides upper leather); the Aaron Barker Tannery, Chazy (200 sides leather, 20 horse); the Francis Gilbert Tannery, Chazy (350 sides plus 250 skins); Fish and Co., Schuyler Falls (600 sides and 300 skins); Geo. Featherstone Tannery, Black Brook (1800 sides plus calf skins); P. M. Shaw, Black Brook (600 sides plus calf skins; H. Martin, Peru (2400 sides plus skins); Albert Kennon, Plattsburgh (500 sides); Carter and Son, Village of Plattsburgh (800 sides plus skins). These establishments were all small enough that they probably functioned as Colonial tanneries, drawing most of their raw hides from the surrounding countryside.

J. S. Goodnow & Co. of Keeseville, W. and E. Sawyer of Ellenburgh, and Solomon Clears & Co. of Black Brook were only slightly larger. A. M. and P. D. Moore had the only two substantially larger tanneries in the County: Saranac (5,000 sides and six workers) and the Village of Plattsburgh (8,000 sides and eight workers).

Charting trends in Clinton County is almost impossible because the entire United States Census record for Clinton County for 1870 is missing, not only from the accessible microfilms, but from the original ledger, a huge volume, two by three feet and six inches thick, housed in the New York State Archives Library in Albany.

By 1880 the Census indicates there were but two small tanners left: Hawkins & Co. of Mooers and Harris Post of Chazy. The Ellenburgh Tannery owned by the Sawyers continued to operate and was considerably bigger than two decades earlier, producing $57,000 worth of hides in 1880. This sole-leather tannery was converted to produce only upper leather, and is described in a contemporary newspaper account below.

There were two larger tanneries in 1880 in Altona: The Robertson Tannery, which produced $84,000 worth of hides and Clark & Co., which produced $45,000 worth of hides, were still relatively small when compared with Warren and Essex counties.

Moore & Co. continued to produce sole leather in Plattsburgh in 1880 as it had in the previous two decades, $36,000 worth in that year. Two newspaper accounts, 1869 and 1875 below, describing the Moores' Redford Tannery and the 1878 article on the Sawyer Tannery in Ellenburgh both mention the growing shortages of bark and the distances over which it had to be hauled. The Moore and Sawyer enterprises are the only two "larger" tanneries, and none of these establishments had capacity and number of employees equalling tanneries in counties to the south.

Perhaps because so much of Clinton County's land was already being farmed, the hemlock tanning boom never expanded on a large scale in Clinton County. There was one tanner (Isaac Pinckney, name and records partly illegible in the Census), who noted that part of his 250 cords of bark came from Canada.

The Moore Tanneries

The Moore brothers, Alanson W., Allen M., and Perley D., were substantial businessmen. Perley, under the style of P. D. Moore and Co. of Boston, lived in Boston and apparently handled the importing of green hides and sale of leather for the family's Clinton County tanneries. In 1868, A. M. and P. D. were in business with William "Forest" Graham, a lumberman from Altona said to be worth a half million.[1] In 1869, the Moores were said to have been in the tannery business for over twenty years and to be worth upwards of $200,000. R. G. Dun lists three Clinton County locations for their tanneries: Redford, Saranac, and Plattsburgh, but it is unclear whether the reference is to Redford in Saranac township, implying they had only two tanneries. In

[1] New York, Vol. 52, p. 206, R. G. Dun and Co.

addition to these tanneries, P. D. Moore had one in Franklin County that was opened around 1880.[2] The last of their Clinton County tanneries was sold in 1883. All were variously listed under the style of one or more of the brothers, but it appears their finances were interlocked.

Contemporary newspaper accounts do bring the Moore enterprises to life. The **Plattsburgh Republican** of July 23, 1869, reported on the "Forest" tannery, located west of Mooers Junction on the Ogdensburg and Lake Champlain Railroad.

> The tannery in its present form was started about January 1867 by Wm. Graham of Altona and Messrs A. M. and P. D. Moore of Plattsburgh. The main building is 250 feet by 50 feet and two and a half stories high. The building housing the steam boiler and leaches is of the same height. There is a 35 horsepower engine and the only fuel used for heating the boiler is wet tan-bark, taken directly from the vats. This is a newly patented process. ... There are 100 square vats 7 feet by 9 feet and 5 feet deep, capable of tanning about 30,000 sides of leather per year. The leather is of the best quality from Spanish hides. They use from 2,000 to 2,500 cords of bark per year, using up 6 cords each working day. The liquor is extracted from bark by a patented steam process.
>
> The entire establishment is under the supervision of Norman Pearl and about 25 men are constantly employed, making altogether quite a village.
>
> During the bark-peeling season in June the company employs 50 to 60 men in the woods at that business alone. The timber they dispose of for saw logs.
>
> P. D. Moore & Co. have a leather store in Boston, No. 195 Congress Street, at which most of the leather manufactured here at the Plattsburgh and Redford tanneries is disposed.

The **Plattsburgh Republican** of March 27, 1875, featured:

A. Moore & Company
Sole Leather Manufactory at Redford, N. Y.

> One of the most conspicuous structures on the Saranac River is the tanning establishment of A. Moore & Co., at Redford, a large, low flat-roofed building standing on the west bank of the river just below the lower bridge, surrounded by huge piles of hemlock bark, and surmounted by a tall pipe

[2] 1880 Census, Franklin County

which sends forth a cloud of steam continuously and is visible for a long distance up or down the river. This site was purchased by Messrs. A. M., P. D., and A. Moore, of the late Leander Cadwell, in September 1857, and included a grist mill already erected, and one-half of the water power at this point together with about sixteen acres of land; the object being the erection of a sole leather tanning establishment which should utilize the immense quantities of hemlock bark that for years had been wasted by lumbermen on the river and its tributaries both above and below. Work was immediately commenced and about one year from that time the establishment was completed. The dimension of the first building were 100 feet by 45 with two wings for a Bark Mill, Boiler Room, &c.

But it was soon found the capacity of the establishment was far less than what the business required and two years later an addition of 105 x 45 feet was erected, making the whole building 205 x 45 feet exclusive of the wings. This building contained 140 vats, 9 feet by 4 1/2 and 4 1/2 feet deep with 7 leaches each 24 feet by 12 and 4 1/2 feet deep. From that time the business was carried on continuously until the spring of 1862, when a freshet swept away the dam, and nearly the whole season was occupied in rebuilding it, the work having been accomplished in from eight to seventeen feet of water. Very little interruption to the business was occasioned by this, however, for a steam engine was soon procured and attached to the boiler, (which is ordinarily used only for heating water, sweating &c.,) thus affording a good substitute for the water power.

In 1868 extensive repairs and improvements were made, among which were Allen & Warren's patent leaches.

FIRE

On the 28th day of April 1871 while everything was running in fine order, the tannery being well stocked, the whole establishment was consumed by fire together with nearly all the stock with the exception of the leather in the vats—which was of course safe if not suffered to remain too long—including 600 cords of bark. Hardly a vestige of the concern remained, and the prospect was sufficient to dishearten any but thorough, energetic business men, which the members of this firm, however, proved themselves to be by commencing the work of putting things in shape for the rebuilding as soon as the heat subsided sufficiently to allow them to do so. There was not a stick of timber left to commence with, but they lost no time, sending men immediately to the woods to get out timber for the frame, while others were set to collecting other necessary material, machinery, &c., and within four months from the time of the fire the present building, which is of the same dimensions as the one burned, was completed, and its machinery, including all the modern improvements, in running order. Seldom in the history of Clinton County have such extraordinary obstacles been overcome in so short a time.

The article went on to describe the steps in the process of tanning, and some of the machinery:

BARK MILL a small upright cylinder some two and a half feet in diameter having a perpendicular shaft running through the entire of it to which is attached, near the top of the cylinder large iron teeth which break the bark up as it is thrown in by the workmen, while below this the particles are found quite fine.
THE LEACHES. These leaches, which as stated before are constructed under Allen & Warren's Patent are each 16 feet in diameter and 6 feet deep, and hold about 10 cords each. The tannic acid is extracted from the bark by leaching with hot water, and the water is distributed evenly over the upper surface of the bark by means of an arm reaching from the center of the vat to the outside and revolving horizontally upon a pivot at the center. ... There are two of these leaches, and while one is being filled, the bark in the other is undergoing the above process. This is a great improvement over the old method. It takes from 20 to 24 hours to extract the tannic acid from the bark, after which the latter is shoveled out into the
PATENT OVENS, where it is used for fuel to make steam with. This process is also a patented one, and is of great practical value, saving, as it does, an immense amount of fuel. These ovens are kept running night and day through the year, for if the fire is suffered to go out great expense is incurred in kindling it again. The refuse bark is shoveled in wet, just as it comes from the leaches, and so perfect is the construction of the kilns, that in a few moments the moisture is completely evaporated from it, when it burns readily. From the leaches the liquor, strongly impregnated with tannic acid, is drawn off into the vats, of which there are 140, ranged along side of each other in four tiers, 9 by 4 1/2 feet and 4 1/2 feet deep. The strength of the liquor in these vats is graduated according to position, this being determined by a "barkometer," which shows the specific gravity of the liquid, this of course being the test of its strength. We now come to the process of
PREPARING THE HIDES The leather manufactured here is almost exclusively the produce of hides which are imported from South America - mostly from Buenos Ayres. They are dry and hard when they come to the tannery, being nearly as

stiff and unyielding as sheet iron, and are first softened by immersing in warm water, after which they are put into the HIDE MILLS in each of which are three wooden hammers—having blunt iron pins upon their beveled faces—big enough to test the strength of GOG MAGOG, GOLIATH, or any other giant. Here they are mauled, pounded, and squashed in a most ignominious manner for two hours, or until properly softened—sometimes when they are very hard and refractory, it being necessary to continue the process a much longer time—after which they are taken out and each divided into two halves lengthwise with a sharp knife.

The next process is SWEATING which is performed in dark, tight, villainous smelling cells. This has for its object, just a near enough approach to decomposition to enable the hair to be removed easily. About one hundred hides are hung in each of these "sweat pits" and subjected to a heat of 65 or 70 degrees from two to five days, when they are taken out. The foreman of this tannery, Mr. John Fortune, has recently introduced an improvement in these pits, consisting of a double floor, by means of which a much more uniform temperature is produced at the top and bottom of the pit. The next operation is

BEAMING The hide is here laid upon a convex inclined table called the "tanners' beam," where the hair and flesh are scraped off and the stray hairs shaved off with long savage looking knives, leaving the hide clean and white, ready for the vats. They are then immersed in a coloring bath, and afterwards in a weak solution of sulphuric acid, with which one of the vats is filled, where they are suffered to remain a short time. In this solution, a remarkable change takes place. The hide, which was before, comparatively thin, has now increased in thickness perceptively, and has a pulpy appearance. The object of this is to open the pores for the reception of the tannic acid, which has a remarkable affinity for the gluten, of which the hide is almost exclusively composed, the two united forming the leather. Now the hides are placed, first in a very weak solution of the tannic acid, remaining, however, only a short time before being taken out and being immersed in a little stronger solution, and so on—thus going the round during which they are changed twenty or thirty times until finally they reach the last in which the strongest solution used. The time occupied in this process averages about four months. This same liquor is used over and over and as it becomes too weak to be of service, is pumped up, where it is heated by steam and again leached through fresh tan-bark. In these vats, the hides are thoroughly saturated with tannin and undergo a complete change in which they gain about 75 per cent over their original weight when they first came from market. They are now taken to the LEATHER WASHER which consists of two large wooden cylinders, armed with splint brooms extending their whole length. These cylinders revolve in opposite direction in a tank of water, the brooms in one cylinder nearly touching those in the other. They are enclosed by a wooden cover having a false top, between which and the true top a flood of water is forced from each side by a pump; a slit parallel to the cylinders and between them allows the hides to be lowered down, one at a time, between the cylinders, where they are thoroughly washed, after which they are taken to the loft and oiled lightly and hung up to dry. After being partially dried they are taken to

THE ROLLER where they undergo the last important process. The roller is of brass about 8 inches long and 5 inches in diameter at the ends, being a little larger in the middle, having thus a slightly convex surface. This is attached to a pendulum, which is worked back and forth about two feet over a large platform, there being a smooth wooden track directly underneath the roller. The workman takes the side of leather upon this platform, and by dexterously shifting its position, as may be necessary, at the same time bringing the roller down by means of an ingenious device worked by foot power, rolls every part of the leather, thus thoroughly compressing it as well as giving it a fine polish. After this, the leather is thoroughly dried, when it is again rolled and stamped, this being the last process before sending it to market.

All the machinery in the establishment is driven by water power of which there is an abundance, the only use to which the steam is applied being for heating the water, drying, sweating, warming the rooms, &c.

The entire tanning department has been under the supervision of Mr. John Fortune for the last fourteen years, and the fact that the quality of the leather produced here is unexcelled by any in the market, furnishes the best evidence that he is a thorough master of the business. The rolling department has for fourteen years been under the charge of John Anderson, who is one of the most reliable men about the establishment, and many others of the other employees have worked continuously for the Company from six to fifteen years. This is a most significant fact, and speaks volumes in favor of both employers and employees. At the time the tannery was built, the Company also erected a store, which they placed under the charge of John Davidson, who had formerly been one of the most skillful workmen in the glass factory and he has also remained with them ever since in the same capacity. His sterling integrity is recognized by the whole community as well as his courteous and kind treatment to all, both high and low, and it is generally understood that whoever deals with John Davidson, even to the smallest child, is sure of getting full weight and measure.

The present members of the firm are A. M. Moore, of Plattsburgh, Perley D. Moore, of Boston, where most of the leather is sold, A. Moore, of Plattsburgh, who was a resident of Redford and had the charge of the entire manufacturing establishment from the time it was started until 1871, and Ely B. Allen, who was at that time admitted as a partner, and is now chief manager of the business at the manufactory.

About 18 hands are employed in the tannery, and the establishment has contributed and is yet contributing much to the material prosperity of the whole vicinity. During the last year, 17,000 sides of leather were tanned here and it is expected that the number this year will reach 20,000. About 1,800 cords of bark are used on an average each year and over 2,500 have been brought in during the past winter.

This bark has been hauled from 6 to 11 miles and from 20 to 30 teams have been employed all winter in getting it in. An average of about five trees are required to each cord of bark, so that from 12,000 to 13,000 trees were cut to get in the stock of bark now on hand.

The amount of this useful and rapidly decreasing material which has been wasted on the Saranac river in times past has been enormous, but its value is now so well understood that it will probably be carefully saved hereafter. The attempt to extract the acid from the bark and condense it so as to make its transportation any great distance practicable and profitable has not heretofore met with sufficient success to warrant its introduction to any considerable extent and the plan of bringing the hides to the bark will not probably be superseded for a long time to come. Although hemlock bark is becoming scarce in Clinton Co., there are yet large forests of it around the base and the slopes of Mt. Lyon which will probably suffice to keep this tannery running for many years to come, thus scattering the blessing of remunerative labor far and wide in the future as it has in the past.

The Sawyer Tannery at Ellenburgh

Aaron Sawyer purchased the water power on the Chazy River in 1851 to run the immense sole-leather tannery he built. In 1868 the firm added steam power.[3] The main building, 228 by 40 feet had an attached L 40 by 40 feet and a finishing building 60 by 40 feet. The main building was two stories tall. Initially, the tannery had the capacity for 18,000 hides per year, which were supplied by a Boston firm.[4] A fire in 1877 and the subsequent rebuilding of the tannery is described in the newspaper article reprinted below. But already, by 1877, bark had to be hauled from upwards of ten miles from the tannery, which had consumed over 25,000 cords prior to 1877.[5] The firm of W. and E. (William and Edwin) Sawyer of Boston apparently financed the expansion of the Ellenburgh Tannery and ran it quite successfully until about 1880, when William Sawyer took over as sole owner. He continued, tanning leather under contract, through the end of the decade, doing well until 1890 when he closed the tannery claiming that he was losing money.[6]

Plattsburgh Republican
Home Enterprises No. 33, March 16, 1878

Ellenburgh:

W. and E. Sawyer's
Tannery at Ellenburgh

In 1840 the Ogdensburgh and Lake Champlain Railroad reached Ellenburgh from the east, and this new enterprise gave a fresh impulse to business. In 1845, the population of Ellenburgh was 902, 1849 it was 1,504, and from that time it was steadily increased, the Census of 1875 showing a population of 3,186. The opening of this road through an undeveloped region so rich in natural resources, attracted many enterprising businessmen from New England, among whom was

MR. A. SAWYER, A TANNER who came to Ellenburgh Corners in 1852 and purchased the water power below the bridge, where he built an immense tannery for sole leather. At

---

3 Hurd, *History of Clinton and Franklin County*, p. 321

4 Ibid, p. 321

5 Ibid, p. 321

6 New York, Vol. 52, p. 60 and Vol. 53, pp. 427, 523, and 606, R. G. Dun and Co.

first, the works were run by water, but in 1868 a steam mill was added. These works consisted of a main building, 228 x 40 feet, with an L 40 x 40 feet, a finishing room 60 x 40 feet, and many other smaller buildings. The main buildings were two stories high and furnished with vats, machinery, and all the appliances of a first-class sole leather tannery, with a capacity of 18,000 hides per year. This immense business was carried on nearly, if not quite, continuously for 25-years, or up to the 17th of last June, the hundred and second anniversary of the Battle of Bunker Hill, when about 3 P. M., a spark of

FIRE caught from the engines as is supposed and in less than two hours, the whole establishment was in ashes. The work of destruction was complete with the exception of the hides in the vats, and even these were greatly damaged. In just one week, as soon as the insurance was adjusted, the work of

REBUILDING was begun, and about the first of last December the new works commenced running. The present buildings consist of a Dry House, 30 x 80 feet, a Yard Building 96 x 40 feet containing 76 vats, each 4 x 8 feet and 5 1/2 feet deep, the Beam House Room 70 x 80 feet—an irregularly shaped building containing machinery, beams, vats, &c. Formerly, sole leather was tanned and finished here, but now only upper leather is tanned, the process of tanning and finishing being entirely distinct.

THE PROCESS OF TANNING is as follows: First the hides are put into what is called the "hide wheel" —a large wooden cylinder which turns on a horizontal axis, the ends of which are closed up some two or three feet from the periphery towards the center. The hides are thrown inside this wheel, where there is plenty of water circulating, and as it revolves, they are tumbled about until they become thoroughly softened. Then they are taken to the "Beam" which consists of a beam some ten feet long with a convex upper surface with one end lower than the other. On this the hide is fastened with the hair side down, and "fleshed" -before the flesh being thoroughly scraped from it. Next the hides go to the lime vats where they remain about eight days, then they are taken to the beam again, and the hair is removed, after which they go again to the hide wheel and are washed thoroughly. Then they are subjected to what is known as the "graining process," being placed in a vat with a liquid, in which the wings of a horizontal wheel work them over thoroughly many times, the object being to take the lime out completely, by a combination of mechanical and chemical means; then they go back to the wheel and are washed once more and then to the beam again where they are "short haired" with a long knife, i.e. thoroughly cleaned; then they go to another set of graining vats, where the last vestige of lime is taken out; then once more to the hide wheel for a final washing; thence to the coloring vats where the color is "set" and then they are ready for the handling vats where they are "handled" daily for twelve days, or changed in vats containing tanning liquor of graduated strength, and finally, are placed in the tan vats, where they remain about sixty days from which they are taken out and dried and are ready for the market.

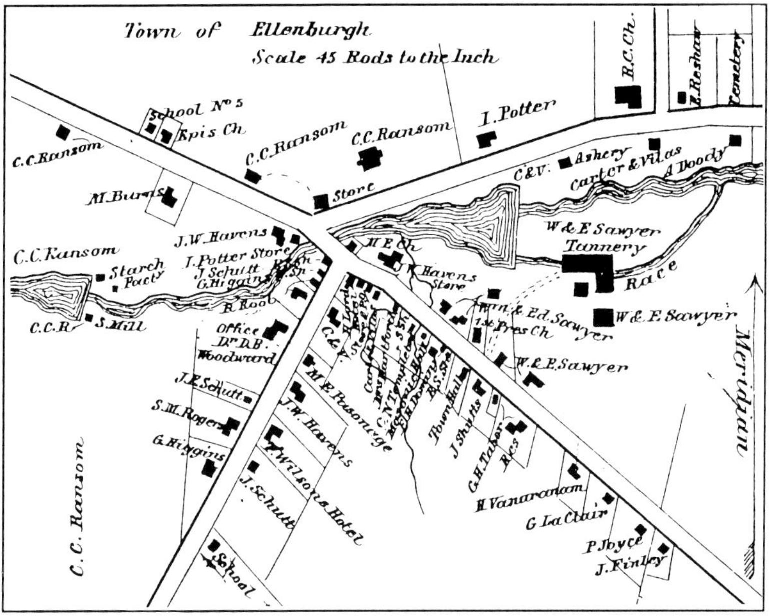

From the 1869 Atlas, Courtesy of the Adirondack Museum

THE MACHINERY of the establishment consists of an ordinary bark mill, in which the hemlock bark is ground, the hide wheel, the tank, where the liquor is heated, and the pump. This last article is one of the most important appliances of a tannery. The liquor or extract of tannin, which is obtained by boiling the tan bark, must undergo an almost continual circulation through the different vats, and in order to accomplish this, the force of gravity is utilized. The liquor running down a gentle incline through the wooden pipes, to its destination and so around the circuit, being thus used over and over. But it finally gets to the foot of the hill and here is where the pump comes into play, to raise it up to the highest point again, where it once more starts of its own accord. Now the liquor has more or less sediment in it, and the consequence is that an ordinary pump is apt to get out of order. This is a common trouble among tanners, but the elder Sawyer when he built these works shrewdly determined to avoid this trouble and, abandoning all modern pumping devices, went back about twenty-one hundred years and borrowed an idea from the old Sicilian (sic) philosopher Archimedes—the Archimedean Screw, which was invented and used for irrigating and draining purposes. The pump here is an exact duplicate in principle of the old Archimedean Screw, consisting of a wooden cylinder 27 feet long and 28 inches in diameter, having a screw blade turn spirally around the solid axis, like a big auger enclosed inside of a cylinder. The tube is inclined at an angle of 45 degrees. The lower end is immersed in a tank of the liquor, and by means of cog wheels it revolves slowly about on its axis, and this raises the liquor and discharges it at the upper end; from here it goes to the tank, where it is heated, and then runs in underground tubes back to the vats and so on, a constant circulation being kept up. There are but few of these pumps in operation in this country, but Mr. E. Sawyer, managing proprietor of the works, assured us that he would use no other style of pump, as he considered this superior to all others for his purpose.

THE CAPACITY of the present works is about 12,000 hides per year, affording steady employment for about twelve hands, each workman being capable of turning off on an average 1,000 hides per year. This amount of work requires from 8,000 to 10,000 cords of bark annually. The former works having consumed from 20,000 to 25,000 cords. The greatest distance from which bark is hauled is about ten miles. The bark is mostly purchased of lumbermen, who usually peel it and pile it up, and the company haul it themselves in the winter. Bark is becoming somewhat scarce, but there is believed to be sufficient within an available distance to run many years yet. The present proprietors of this tannery are E. Sawyer, of Boston, and W. Sawyer, of Malone, sons of the original owner. The establishment has been one of the most important ones on this stream during the past twenty-five years—adding in no small degree to the prosperity of the town—and it bids fair to continue so for many years to come.

XIV

Fulton County

The north country's earliest tanneries

Fulton County's participation in the tannery business is unique in the north country: Tanning began here before any other northern county and the industry proliferated into many different kinds of tanning. Among the few hemlock tanneries that processed shoe leather, two were among the Adirondacks largest; one was the best documented of any in the north country. Tanning of specialty leathers from imported skins, a process that does not use hemlock bark, and the manufacture of gloves were the basis for the county's economy from the early nineteenth century until today. Both glove and shoe leather tanning continues in the county today, albeit on the fringe of the Blue Line and with chemicals substituting for vegetable tanning materials.

Sir William Johnson, one of the county's first settlers, was agent for King George III and Representative to the Indian Nations in the decades preceding his death in 1774. He was a General in the French and Indian War and acquired large tracts of land in the Mohawk Valley, gifts from the Mohawk Indians later confirmed by Royal Grant.

In 1862 he built a large home north of the valley and proceeded to lay out a settlement nearby on the lines of an English village, complete with streets in a 3-block by 3-block array, with schoolhouse, a church, and homes for those he induced to settle in the village. Throughout the 1760s, he referred to his little village, the future Johnstown, named for his son, in letters to his friends, which described in detail his attempts to plan the village and bring to it settlers who would enhance its economy. Among the tradesmen and craftsmen he encouraged to emigrate from Scotland were two tanners who were engaged to bring the art of tanning to the north country.

While the supply of cows for hides was always limited to the number raised to support the small community, another source of skins quickly developed. Trade with the Indians brought deer skins through Johnstown. Local legend has it that a group of tinsmiths settled in Kingsboro, a crossing north of Johnstown. The skins they received in trade for their tinwares began a new industry, skins, not for boots and shoes, but skins for clothing, gloves, and mittens. At the same time as the tanning of deer skins developed, many small glove and mitten manufacturers sprang up. These, like the tanneries, where small, initially cottage industries.

The number of deerskin tanners quickly grew and one family, the Heacocks, specialized in tanning deerskins from the early 1800s through the present. Among their prized possessions is a license to manufacture leather dated 1815. The tanning of deerskins was accomplished by many different methods. Some used the brains of deer, a technique learned from the Indians. Some used salt, eggs, or alum.

A precise history of the early tanners has not been collected[1], but with the aid of the United States Census of Manufactures, the story picks up at mid-century.

In the Town of Johnstown in 1850, there was but one hemlock tanner, Eli Pierson. His was a relatively small establishment, producing $3,000 worth of leather in 1850 and $5,000 worth of cow hide leather and $1,200 worth of calf skins in 1860, when Pierson had two or three workers and a "one horse bark mill." John Peck, however, had a larger establishment with eight workers, and in 1860, he produced 1,400 sides of sole leather.

By 1870, there were no hemlock tanners in the Town, but there were fourteen tanners who dealt in specialty leathers, many of these in conjunction with glove and mitten manufacturing. Most of these mills, which specialized in oil finishing leather, became known as skin mills, to differentiate them from the tanners of cow hides. Three skin mills specialized in the finishing of kid skins, two were small, with annual production valued at $5,000 each, but one, L. Dodge and Son, was large with a yearly output worth $57,000. With one exception, Kenney and Freeman, with a production of $5,000 worth of deer and sheep skins annually, all the other tanneries were fairly substantial.

---

[1] A second volume on tanning, this one on the tanning of specialty leathers in Fulton County, is contemplated. It will differ from this history from the tanning of sole leather, and will involve an analysis not only of the early tanners but of tariffs and unions and the industry in the early twentieth century.

The largest of the ten remaining, Chester and Miller, employed nineteen men and produced $150,000 worth of finished deer and sheep skins. The Heacock firm produced $88,000 worth of deer skins. The average number of employees of the ten larger skin mills was 13.7 and their average production was valued at $96,633. In the township as a whole, specialty leathers valued at $1,038,330 were produced. For the first time, the Census of 1870 mentions the source of foreign skins which were becoming the basis of the local industry. Tanning of skins and glove manufacturing were making Johnstown a very wealthy town.

Tanning in Other Townships

At the same time, hemlock tanning for sole leather became a substantial enterprise in the county's northern towns, Bleecker and Caroga, in areas that are now part of the Adirondack Park. In southern townships, hemlock bark tanning continued from early in the century into the 1880s, with the hemlock shipped from northern townships in later years.

The reasons that Fulton County was so successful in this business are obvious. The region was close to the wooded wilds necessary for large supplies of hemlock bark and at the same time it was close to the railheads at Fonda and Amsterdam, which were also ports on the Erie Canal. A good plank road was built from Fonda, north to Johnstown and on to Newkirks in 1849.

According to Frothingham's "History of Fulton County," the village of Oppenheim had a tannery run by Peter Cline and his son, Knapthalee, which opened in 1805 and closed in 1836 when "the stream failed."[2]

Nicholas Gray was the owner of Ephratah's first tannery.[3] On the eastern part of Ephratah village at the site of an old grist mill built by Sir William Johnson, Mortimer Wade had a tannery. It produced both tanned "slaughter hides" and tanned "deacons and kips," different kinds of calf skins. Its production valued at about $13,600 in 1860 expanded to a value of $18,900 in 1870, but shrank again by 1880 to but $6,600 worth of hides and skins

[2] Frothingham, *History of Fulton County*, pp. 544-545
[3] Frothingham, ibid, p. 531

in an operation that was quite seasonal, lasting but four months of the year.[4]

Ephratah had three other very small tanners in 1850 and one, S. Brooks & Co., large enough to tan 12,000 sides using 1,100 cords of bark. In 1860, H. D. H. Snyder[5], a tanner with origins in the Swamp who later became very important as a Lewis County tanner, had a fairly large establishment with 136 vats, a steam engine, a bark mill, and two hide mills with eight leaches. He produced 28,000 sides of sole leather using 2,800 cords of bark. Before the decade was out, he had moved his operations to Lewis County.

That same year, the Census indicates that the tannery of Peter Simmons tanned cow hides, calf skins, and horse skins. He also made shoes and boots and gloves and mittens. Though his was a modest establishment, it persisted through the 1880 Census, never growing significantly and using, all the while, the water power of the Caroga Creek.

The Town of Perth is listed as having one small tannery and that also persisted from 1860 through 1880, tanning skins and a few hides with modest amounts of bark.

In the Town of Broadalbin, Cornell and Northrup had a small hemlock hide tannery in 1850. All the later tanneries, five in 1860 and one in 1870, specialized in skins for gloves and mittens and several of those produced the finished gloves and mittens as well.

Frothingham calls Flevel Bartlett the "father of tanning industry in Mayfield."[6] In 1850, both Hiram Gates and the firm of Wait and Simmons produced leather, with only the latter using hemlock bark (a modest 80 cords) to tan cowhides. Hiram Gates' operation continued on a very small scale through the 1860s, when he was joined in that town by John Brown, who also produced a small amount of finished leather.

The 1860 Census for Mayfield records three hemlock tanneries that tanned hides, one with but three workers, using 300

---

[4] Census, 1860, 1870, 1880, Fulton County

[5] It is not clear whether the owner of this tannery was H. D. H Sr. or Jr. It may be that the capital alone came from the father's New York firm. It may also be that the son ran the tannery for his father. What is certain is that the son did move to Lewis County, where with the help of his father's money, he established himself as a local entrepreneur.

[6] Frothingham, ibid, p. 513

cords of bark and producing $15,680 worth of sides. The second, with 10 workers was capitalized at $40,000 and consumed 1,600 cords of bark to produce $64,000 worth of leather. The third was a one-man operation. There is no record of these mills in the 1870s when an apparently new mill, run by Norman Gifford, used 1,400 cords to produce $84,000 worth of leather. Three other tanners dealt in both hides and skins in modest establishments. The Mayfield firm of Kasson and Johnson, which started in 1859 and had a sequence of five different owners, produced specialty leathers as well as some upper leather in 1870. That year, George Allen is also listed as running a skin mill finishing sheep, boar, and calf skins.

By the 1880s, all but one of the Mayfield Town tanners were mostly dealing with specialty leathers. Two skin mills were using the power of the Kenyotto (sic, now Kennyetto) and Cranberry creeks, at sites later drowned by the Sacandaga Reservoir, to produce finished skins and a few sides. Lewis Brownell, using a stream in Jackson Summit (the West Stony Creek) had a hemlock bark tannery producing $22,000 worth of sole leather and consuming 800 cords of bark. At the same time, the Brownell family had other, larger establishments in Hamilton County.

Northampton, in 1850, had two one-man tanneries and two that were larger. One employed nine workers and produced 11,000 sides in 1850 and a slightly smaller amount in 1860. The second, with twenty workers, produced 22,000 sides worth $49,500 in 1850.

In 1860, J. and G. LeFevre had a larger Northampton tannery, capable of producing 16,000 sides of leather worth $64,000. The tannery was built in 1848 and stood about three-fourths of a mile from Northville. In 1858, the owners were reported as having lost money in common with other traders.[7] Apparently they bought hides when their price was high, and lost when the price of leather fell. They managed to survive during the Civil War, but went out of business in Fulton County in 1865.[8] The tannery burned in 1867 and was rebuilt, only to burn again in 1874. It is not clear if the LeFevre family still owned the tannery in these later years. Some of the LeFevres shortly moved to Lewis County, where the family had built a

---

7 Frothingham, ibid, p. 462

8 New York, Vol. 99, p. 53, R. G. Dun and Co.

tannery in 1852. Members of the family were still running the tannery at Beaver Falls in Lewis County when it closed in 1894.[9]

It is possible that William Wright succeeded as owner of the LeFevre Fulton County tannery shortly after it burned. The Census for 1870 credits the Wright firm with producing 17,000 sides of sole leather worth $85,000 with twenty employees. The tannery consumed 1,500 cords of bark $5.00 a cord. The costs for bark, $7,500, approached the total annual pay roll, $8,400.

Joseph Helterline of Stratford started with a quite small establishment, but in 1860 he imported 4,000 Buonos [sic] Ayers and Oronoche [sic] hides. His fifteen employees turned them into $20,500 worth of leather. His 1870 output, 9900 sides, only 1,900 more than a decade earlier, was worth double the value of his 1860 production.

There was a second sole-leather tanner in Stratford in 1870, Hyde Dutton and Company, whose production was slightly larger than Helterline's. The two other tanneries listed in 1860, owned by William H. Kibbe and William M. Smith, handled mostly skins, as did the Carryl and Company in 1870.

It is obvious that these few hide tanneries in the southern part of the county were probably all that could be supported from land that had already been effectively converted to farmlands. A very different story existed in the northern townships that are now within the Blue Line of the Adirondack Park.

Here hemlock tanneries producing sole leather on a large scale were appearing on a scale exceeding those in the Hudson River towns of Warren County.

Newkirks Tannery

The first large tannery was built in the Town of Caroga in 1843 by Garrett Newkirk and John Littlejohn.[10] This tannery, on a small dammed pond on Caroga Creek, was producing leather valued at $48,000 in 1845. According to the 1850 Census, the tannery's production was valued at $62,500 and 2,600 cords of hemlock valued at $6,500 were consumed.

---

[9] Letters from Lewis VanArnum

[10] Frothingham, ibid, p. 220

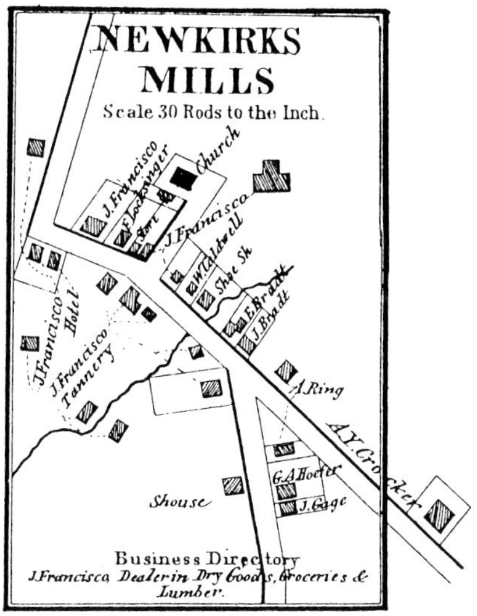

Newkirk also ran a sawmill with an output valued at $18,000 and two other smaller sawmills were active in the town. In 1855, two years before the tannery was discontinued, the value of its 22,000-side output was $72,000. The settlement at Newkirks, the largest in the Town of Caroga in 1846, did not begin with the tannery. Garrett A. Newkirk had settled there in the 1830s and by 1840 he was running a sawmill on the bank of the pond created by his dam.

By 1846, there were enough craftsmen and workmen to create a small village of twenty buildings. At that time, the community, which was the home of the famed "trapper" Nicholas Stoner, merited a comment from Stoner's biographer, Jeptha R. Simms. "At the present time, the old trapper resides in the town of Caroga, Fulton County; at a settlement which has recently sprung up, called Newkirks Mills. He owns a comfortable dwelling in which he lives, draws a pension from the federal government, and from keeping several boarders who work in the mills, which the industry of a smart wife enables him to do, he passes down the evening of his life very comfortably. Garet (sic) Newkirk, the proprietor here, has an extensive tannery, and a saw mill in which two saws are almost constantly rending asunder the trunks of the surrounding forest. The place has some fifteen or twenty dwellings, a schoolhouse, a post-office, called Newkirks Mills & Co., and is situated pleasantly on the outlet of the Caroga Lakes, two crystal sheets of water several miles in circuit, located some twelve to fifteen miles to the westward of Johnstown. Since the above was written, a public house has opened at this place, several new dwellings erected, and a plank-road constructed from thence to Fonda, sixteen miles distant."[11]

Newkirk served as supervisor of the Town of Bleecker, which at that time included the future Town of Caroga, and after

[11] Simms, *Trappers of New York*, p. 161

the towns separated, he hosted Caroga's first town meeting at his home. He served in the State Assembly for a year in 1844. His home was an imposing Greek revival mansion with a two-story-high central portion with pillars to the porch roof, which was the full two stories high. One-story wings flanked the central portion of the home. The mansion burned long after Newkirk sold it. Newkirk's had a church, too, whose neoclassical facade resembled the mansion.

Newkirk was instrumental in having the new plank road from Fonda completed to his settlement in 1849, and the road was such an improvement over the rutted dirt road it replaced that the Fourth of July celebration of its opening was duly noted by a newspaper account. "No less than six hundred vehicles of every description joined to celebrate the opening of the road. ... Our carriage wheels called out [from Fonda] on a smooth plank floor; and without a jolt or jar, we rolled along thru ravines, up the valleys, over the hills, thru the woods and swamps until the fold of the star spangled banner across the land announced the terminus of the magic ride."

Newkirks' tannery business ended precipitously with the financial panic of 1857 and was assigned to receivers; Newkirk was bankrupt and shortly moved to St. Louis.[12] The land was sold to John Francisco, who lived in the Newkirk mansion and continued to log in the area.

Bleecker

The Town of Bleecker stretched from the settlement of Gloversville north to the Hamilton County border. Its forests enticed the building of a number of tanneries, whose total production appears to exceed the neighboring Town of Caroga. However, while Caroga's tanneries are extremely well documented, only sketchy outlines describe those in Bleecker.

Frothingham states that Wm. I Bellinger had the first tannery in the town. In 1850, George Deming tanned a small number of hides.[13] F. D. Wasson was listed as a tannery in 1855.[14]

[12] New York, Vol. 99, p. 16, R. G. Dun and Co.

[13] Census, 1850 Fulton County, the name is unclear and may be Dunning

Bleecker Tannery

In the south end of the township, the Richards Company, or Richards & Hamlin, or Bleecker Tannery, was established about 1846 or 47. It was located on the outlet of Tannery Pond, which is now called Vandenburgh Pond. In 1850, it produced 20,000 sides of leather valued at $41,000 and consumed 2,500 cords of bark valued at $6,250.

The firm was reorganized as I. A. and A. J Hamlin in 1853 and as Hamlin and Ford in 1855.[15] The panic of 1857 must have affected the firm, because the partnership was dissolved in 1859 with Ford moving to Massachusetts and Hamlin "doing little, has been sued, don't pay promptly."[16] His fortunes quickly turned around because the Census for 1860, which was based on 1859 totals, reported that he tanned $64,000 worth of leather.

The Bleecker Tannery still employed a dozen workers a decade later, but its output was much reduced; only 2,000 sides of "foreign" hides were tanned that year. It is possible that this tannery was owned by John Peck in 1870, when 4,000 hides were tanned. By 1880, the tannery under new ownership again was devoted exclusively to skins. The 1868 County Atlas shows a large second tannery, a fairly large complex, also near the outlet of Tannery Pond, owned by Wooster and Vandenburgh. It is not clear whether there were two tanneries in the area and no Census data confirm that ownership.

Pinnacle Tannery

A much larger tannery complex, the Smith and Deming Tannery,[17] was in operation much longer than the giant tannery at nearby Wheelerville in Caroga township. It was located in the northeastern part of the Town of Bleecker, and the Pinnacle Post Office was built nearby on Barlow (Ballou) Road to serve it. Its principal buildings were on the West Stony Creek and seem to have been run by a sequence of partnerships and possibly a few mergers. The 1868 Atlas shows a pond on West Stony Creek, just upstream from the tannery, but the dam that created the pond has disappeared.

---

[14] Frothingham, ibid, p. 562

[15] Hildebrandt, *Hides and Hemlock*, pp. 15-16

[16] New York, Vol. 99, P. 12, R. G. Dun and Co.

[17] Frothingham, ibid, p. 563

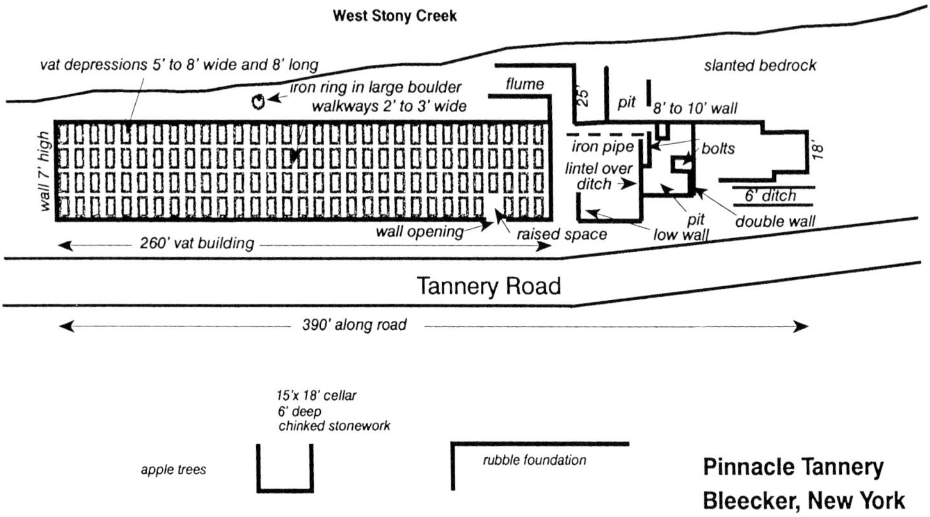

The tannery was listed as the firm of Smith and Hanley in June of 1855[18] with a capital investment of $6,000 and 1,000 cords of bark. By 1860, under the name B. Smith and Company, Fulton County Tannery, it was importing 7,000 "foreign" hides to produce $50,000 worth of sole leather. Sixteen workers earned an aggregate average monthly wage of $320.[19] In 1865, the firm of Smith and Hanley[20] became the firm of Smith and Young,[21] apparently through merger with the firm of James H. Young, whose "Forest Tannery" is described in the 1860 Census as employing fifteen workers and having the capacity to tan 9,000 foreign hides worth $50,000. The Forest Tannery stood on the outlet of Vandenburgh Pond, closer to East Lake, which later became a part of Peck's Lake. It may have ceased operation with the merger.

---

[18] New York State Census

[19] U. S. Census, 1860

[20] This firm was also doing business in Hamilton County at the same time.

[21] Frothingham, ibid,p. 563

By 1870, the firm, with no increase in capital investment, is listed in the Census as being owned by W. Smith. Smith was joined by a Jonathan Young in 1869 and the firm became insolvent and failed "badly." Smith died without a will and his mother, Hezekiah, continued as owner.[22] Hiram Deming joined as partner in 1875 and the tannery's output increased steadily. In 1880, Smith and Deming employed as many as thirty workers with a total annual wage of $6,444 and a production of 50,000 sides worth $250,000. The Census contains the note that 2,700 cords of bark were "hauled from woods north for a distance."[23] The tannery burned on November 28, 1882 with a loss of $10,000, only half of which was covered by insurance. Deming, who had an interest in at least one other Fulton County tannery, was still in the tannery business in 1884, and apparently the tannery was rebuilt.[24]

Foundations for the 390 by 44-foot building are remarkably intact, showing an unusual type of construction, which reveals the walls of individual vats. Other tanneries have longitudinal depressions indicating sluiceways between the rows of vats. Pinnacle's vats and the walkways between the rows of vats appear to have been built up from earth and rubble. (Colton had a long mound through the middle of the vat building, the only other tannery found with such a raised earthen division.)

The tannery was built right beside the West Stony Creek, so close that one foundation wall forms a bank of the creek. The outline of trenches and flumes indicates how water was flushed through the building, although no channel remains to indicate how water was diverted into the building.

The tannery closed about one hundred years ago—long enough for not only pioneering trees, but huge hemlock and yellow birch to fill the vat building. Floyd Chappel of Caroga remembered helping his father dismantle the tannery buildings some sixty years ago. The vat building yielded planks 2 feet wide and 36 to 48 feet long. He remembered a stone building, built into the side of the hill near the tannery, that was used for chemical storage and "all tanneries had such a building," he recalled.[25]

---

[22] New York, Vol. 100, pp. 18, 222, R. G. Dun and Co.

[23] 1880 Census, Fulton County

[24] ibid

[25] Conversations with the author

Old Pine Tannery

Among the strange problems I have encountered while tracing the history of particular tanneries is the fact that certain tanneries, located deep in the wilds, often near county borders, either have records in counties other than their location, or no records at all. One such mystery tannery, whose story was largely fleshed out by the present owner of the site, was the Old Pine Tannery or Sornberger (sometimes Sornburgh) Tannery on the North Branch of West Stony Creek, near the Hamilton County border. Oddly enough the name Sornberger does not appear on any of the deeds for the property, which have a gap for the years between 1859 and 1891.

The 1870 Census credits this tannery with a real property value of $30,000 and a capacity for tanning 16,000 sides, which that year were worth $75,000. Foundations, 40 by 210 feet, for the tannery are still visible on the west side of the creek, which in high water washes the tannery foundation. There was a blacksmith shop and steam boiler building. Piers on either side of the creek were intended for a bridge that apparently was never built. In 1869, Sornberger appealed to the County Judge the determination of the Commissioner of Highways to refuse to lay out a highway to the tannery. The judge appointed a committee, which reversed the decision. On January 18, 1870, the town highway committee met to "let out a job on a new piece of road laid out by referees"[26]; but there were no bidders and none appeared at the next meeting on the 31st. Finally, on February 8, 1870, the town voted to raise $1,100 to build a bridge over the creek and dam at the Sornberger Tannery and to extend the road to the Hamilton County line. Sornberger, who was also Justice of the Peace, moved away in 1871; for the town board met on April 17, 1871, to appoint a new Justice of the Peace. Sornberger's "removal from the county" may have been caused by the failure to build the bridge and the lack of road may explain the tannery's very short existence.

---

[26] The current property owner, Charles P. Brown, researched town and county records to produce the background and quoted information on the Sornberger Tannery.

Wheelerville

From tannery to the north country's first planned resort
An example of absentee ownership
Detail of community life and the economics of tannery workers

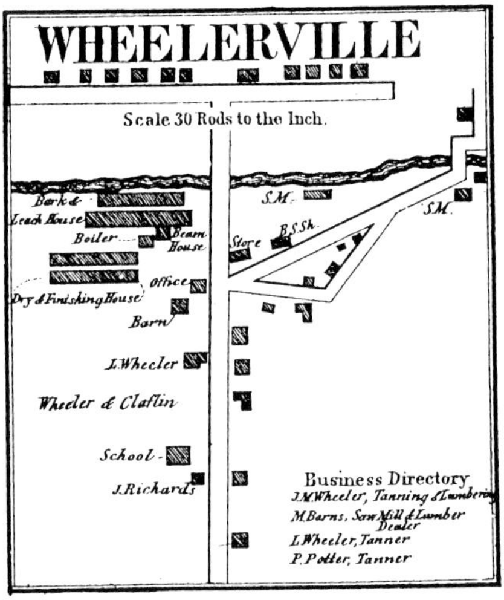

A second tannery (Newkirk's was the first) in the Town of Caroga was built in 1865. Not only was this tannery in the settlement later named Wheelerville one of the north's country's best documented, but it serves as a good example of the tanneries that were financed by moneys from Massachusetts' shoemakers. Further, the enterprise documents a new phase in Adirondack development, the appearance of a planned resort community.

The Claflin connection is fascinating. Lee Claflin was an orphan from Milford, Massachusetts, who amassed a significant fortune as a shoe manufacturer. His son, William, was born in 1818 and educated at the Milford Academy. He entered his father's business and extended it to a wholesale boot and shoe business in St. Louis in 1838. By 1845 he was back east and joined his father's firm, Lee Claflin Company. "He was the founder and for many years president of the Hide and Leather Regional Bank of Boston and an organizer of two other banks."[27]

During the hectic years that his company was expanding into the tannery business in the Adirondacks, the decades immediately after the Civil War, William Claflin's principal interests seem to have been politics. From 1866 through 1869, he was Lieutenant Governor of Massachusetts and, from 1869 through 1871, he served as Governor. He was active in the anti-slavery movement, using his own funds to buy and free Missouri slaves. He fought for legal suffrage for women, and during his term as

[27] Obituary, copy in the files of the Caroga Historical Society

governor, bills were enacted "extending the rights of women, bettering the condition of criminals, establishing a bureau of statistics for labor, protecting destitute children, and regulating divorce."[28] He was President of the Board of Trustees of Boston College and a trustee of Wellesley and Mount Holyoke colleges and the New England Conservatory. He served as a representative in the Forty-fifth and Forty-sixth Congresses.

This man, whose name, along with his wife's, appears on deeds acquiring over 20,000 acres in the Town of Caroga alone, nearly two-thirds of the town's total acreage, had a phenomenal impact on the southern Adirondacks. His vision for developing the land created one of the region's first planned resorts. Yet, he rarely, perhaps only once, visited the area, and left the day-to-day managing of this phase of his interests to others.

Claflin had a tannery in partnership with Jonathan W. Wheeler of North Becket County in the Berkshires, Massachusetts. (It may be that Claflin represented the financial investment in this firm, while Wheeler was the practical tanner; this was the arrangement at Caroga.) In 1865, also in partnership with Wheeler, Claflin was able to purchase most of the 20,000-acre parcel for less than $4.00 an acre. Compare this with the salaries of the tannery workers, which ranged from just under a dollar to two dollars a day.

Claflin's interest in the area had an inflating effect on nearby land prices, for that same year he had to pay a Francis Fry $800 for a 35-acre Tract adjacent to the future mill site. Claflin continued buying land, adding small parcels from tax sales from the State of New York in 1866 at remarkable prices: 160 acres for $16.16; 150 acres for $23.72; 160 acres for $12.65; and a third 160-acre parcel for $12.63. Some of these lots were in nearby Benson, and further acreage in the Benson Tract was purchased from individuals at an average of just over a dollar an acre. In 1868 he purchased large lots in the Town of Arietta, Hamilton County, for a second tannery, paying $4.30 for lots 23 and 24 in the Lawrence Patent, land running to the Sacandaga River and Good Luck Lake and part of lot #90 in Benson. His holdings in both Fulton and Hamilton counties, eventually comprised 30,000 acres. This much land was needed to supply the 6,000 cords or more of bark his two tanneries consumed annu

---

[28] ibid

Wheelerville Tannery store and bark sheds surround the main tannery buildings (photo appears to have been printed in reverse), courtesy Bruce Busch.

ally in their twenty years span of operation. Claflin held these lots until 1882, when all were sold to Fayette Shaw and others.

How did William Claflin change the way of life in the town? His land purchases were just the beginning, because his capital investments were listed in the 1870 Census as being $150,000. A newspaper account in the **Gloversville Intelligencer** in March 1868 states that "Messrs. Wheeler and Claflin have invested several hundred thousand dollars in land, saw mills, and tanneries. We have it from good authority that they have one of the largest and best tanneries in the State." A complex of unattached buildings was erected along the outlet stream of Irving pond (the inlet of Canada Lake) near the site of an abandoned saw mill.

The buildings that housed the different operations were as widely spread out as any Adirondack tannery. Huge vat and leaching sheds, measuring 426 and 350 feet long, were constructed near the stream. There were two drying sheds, each about 350 feet long. A tremendous barn for the company's horses and oxen was constructed a hundred yards away, built into the side of a hill near the road. In it the company kept oxen on the first floor, horses on the second (which was on the level of the upper slope of the hill) and hay on the third floor. Across the main road from the barn stood the company store; a spur from the main road divided the store, so that merchandise could be unloaded under cover.

Photographs show piles of bark and wood, the beam house, and company houses dotting the nearby hillside. The Little Red House on the Hill was the company boarding house.[29]

All that construction took place in the span of a year, 1865, and sparked a building boom nearby. In 1866, a tavern was constructed at the five corners intersection south of the tannery.

The Plank Road

The plank road from Fonda through Newkirks Mills was extended to Wheelerville and north to the Claflin sawmill at Pine Lake and on to Arietta, where the Claflin's Hamilton County tannery was built. The road was built of 8-foot planks over solid ground and 12-foot planks through swamps and wet ground at a cost of $7.00 a rod[30] ($2,240 a mile), a substantial figure in light of the distances, over fifteen miles to be covered, and in comparison with the cost of land. The planks were cut at the Pine Lake sawmill from hemlock logs. That mill was owned by the Wheeler-Claflin enterprises jointly with Milton Barnes, who ran it.

Needless to say, this road was an important part of the tanning operation. The reasonably good roads from Johnstown north were one of the reasons that the tannery could exist at all. But the roads alone were not sufficient, for an article in the March 11, 1868, **Gloversville Intelligencer** reports that Messrs. Wheeler and Claflin "were in favor of a railroad." A letter, on the letterhead of Lee Claflin & Son, Boston, U. S. A., signed Lee Claflin & Son, dated March 5, 1887, and addressed to Mr. J. M. Dudley, asks, "How about that R. R. Co which is being organized to run from Fort Plain. Has it backing enough to go through? We have offered to give $5000 as soon as trains are running from Wheelerville to Fort Plain."[31]

Several letters deal with the fact that the Town of Caroga chose not to maintain Claflin's plank road, claiming that they were private roads. Finally, on May 10, 1890, Lee Claflin & Son

---

29 The horse and oxen barn survives as the Nick Stoner Inn, a handsome building located on the Nick Stoner Golf Course, whose greens and fairways were carved from the vacant fields left by the tannery. The company store is now the town offices for Caroga. The red house and several other company houses survive as homes or summer residences.

30 Copy of letter in the author's collection, written by Claflin.

31 Letters in the collection of the Caroga Historical Society

wrote, "We are willing the plank road through the woods should be made public. We have a few plank which have been in use on a bridge, some 3000 feet in good condition, which we will contribute toward fixing up the road, should Mr. Northrup [purchaser of several of the Claflin lots on Canada Lake] and friends repair the same."

From 1868 through 1870, the regular stage ran from Fonda north to Wheelerville. In 1870, a reporter for the same Gloversville newspaper described the tannery as well as the ride to it.

The Tannery

At Wheelerville we noted quite a few items of interest - how sole leather was made so firm, smooth, and giving had always been a mystery to me, but upon entering one of the buildings after another it was made plain at once.

A hose was attached to the steam boiler. The miller pressed the hides by moving the steam rapidly back and forth over the surface of the hides which were held by the workmen. By pressing upon a lever with his foot, as much pressure is applied to the leather as he judges necessary to make it a substantial and durable article. It seems the most dangerous work for brains or hands of any we have seen for a long time.

The next step too far forward would bring the workman's skull against a shaft that moves back and forth with the power of forty sledge hammers; too close a movement with the hands would bring them under a roller that would destroy bone and muscle in a twinkling.

We enter the "Vat-building," four hundred and twenty-six feet long - containing two hundred vats, one hundred on a side; the great length of the building, four hundred and twenty-six feet, causes men at the other end to look small. Hides to be properly dressed, the workmen tell us, should lay in the liquor about six months; one hundred and twenty-five are placed in a vat—these multiplied by two hundred, the number of vats will show the number of hides which may be in process at a time.

The vats are connected by pipes, so that the liquor can be changed from one to the other by simply removing the faucets. A steam force-pump is also so arranged that the fluid can be carried into a building adjoining, and again leached through the ground tan bark; then heated up by steam pipes, and returned to the "vat building," as we named it.

Wheelerville Tannery; horse barn on right with red boarding house beyond, courtesy Bruce Busch.

> Between 6,000 and 7,000 cords of hemlock bark are used every year; it is ground up in machines that look very much like the "corn crackers" used in gristmills; from the grinding machines, an augur-like apparatus carries it into the upper story and to such leaches as may be desired. After being leached out, a passage is opened at the bottom of the leach, and water turned in from conveniently arranged conductors, and the then valueless bark run out into the water flowing under the building; the buildings are all put up in a substantial manner, as we looked at them we heard Mr. Levi Wheeler describe the varied use and conveniences of the steam engines, steam-pipes, water-pipes, store-rooms, dry-rooms, &c., we purposed to give them all more than passing notice, but space will not permit, and we must content ourself with a sketch merely, though we make a few notes additional: In one of the drying rooms we were informed by Mr. Wheeler that there were 6,000 feet of steam pipe.
>
> At the Wheeler and Arietta tanneries, during the year, about 250 tons of leather are dressed; this is carried by teams to and from Fonda.

The completion of the Fonda, Johnstown, and Gloversville Railroad in November 1870 brought the railhead even closer. At the insistence of the Claflin enterprises, and reputedly with their money, a more level road was constructed in 1874 and 1875 to Caroga Lake from Gloversville via Pecks Pond, the route of the present highway NY 29A. Over this highway, many teams pulled loads of hides and finished skins, as well as the oils used to finish the skins. The planks were in such good condition that a former highway superintendent in Caroga, Emmet Stock, remembered that the planks had to be removed before the road could be covered with macadam, some time after 1910.[32]

The home built for Jonathan A. Wheeler continued to be used as the residence of the head tanner. It was the settlement's most elegant structure, boasting the only bathtub in Wheelerville.

By 1872, Claflin had bought out the Wheeler interest in the tannery, but not before the settlement was firmly named Wheelerville.

The Company Store and the Community

The tannery was the center of the settlement's life, as well as its raison d'etre. The tannery bell not only called the men to work, it roused them to emergencies. The settlement began as a frontier town, but the company store supplied everything a family needed as records of the store indicate, and if this was living on the edge of wilderness, it certainly was a well-supplied existence.

Surviving from the tannery days are several books that give the prices of commodities in the company store. Eva Peters Koetteritz, daughter of a local logger, rescued the Wheeler-Claflin store's 1884 inventory. She remembered that the store closed in 1893 or 1894. A list of sales from that store records not only the prices, but serves as a census of the settlement's inhabitants.

Coffee was 17¢ a pound, vinegar 17¢ a gallon, Japanese tea 30¢ a pound, corned beef but 8¢ a pound, dried apples 9 1/2¢ a pound, and sugar 7¢ a pound. The store also sold spring beds, $4.00; rocking chairs, $1.00; sheeting at 5 and 3/4¢ a yard; shawls for $1.00; and spittoons for 14¢.

The store's inventory for 1884 has one page covering "Flour, feed & grain," fourteen pages of "Hardware & Woodenware," everything from scissors, to gun powder, to pick handles, horse wisks, clothes ringers, teakettles, locks, pails, tin pans and coffee mills, and screws and stovepipes. The four pages of "Drugs" listed cough drops, Hurichs Plaster, Essence of Life, vanilla, castor oil, and Gel Arsenic. Among the canned goods were pineapples, pears, peaches, lobsters, clams, oysters,

---

[32] Conversations with the author

Wheelerville Tannery with workers' houses on hill behind, courtesy Bruce Busch.

salmon, and sardines. Candy and crockery were enumerated, everything from covered chambers to spittoons and flower pots, chimney lamps to boat lanterns. There were chairs and mattresses and beds. Groceries included yeast cakes, molasses, lard, cloves, beans, crackers, "Jap" tea, and oat meal. Mittens and boots, undershirts and overalls, sheeting and overcoats, shawls and even hoop skirts were stocked. All manner of yard goods by the bolt, ladies hose, corsets, hats, and caps, and woolen shirts, thread, buttons, and pins, dominoes and mouth organs, pipes and tweezers, lace collars, school books, and envelopes were there. Among the store fixtures listed in the inventory were a platform scale, a small iron safe, and a buffalo (whatever that might have been).

The Methodist Episcopals built a church, a doctor settled in Wheelerville, and the school was built in 1868, but the community's real growth lay elsewhere.

The Resort

Even more impressive than the extent of the Claflin tannery were Claflin's plans for the area. Shortly after he acquired the surrounding lands, which included title to two-and-a-half-mile-long Canada Lake (formerly Fish Lake), he began plans for a four-story hotel. The structure, 40 by 86 feet, was built about a half-mile from the tannery on the north shore of Canada Lake, near its inlet. On its completion in 1866, only one year after the tannery was built, the Canada Lake House was described as "nestled up to a miniature mountain that almost joins on to the rear of the house. Its rocks and bushes are apparently as wild as nature left them." Manager W. R. Tunicliff provided "all necessary refreshments and luxuries." The happy proprietor continued the festivities the next summer as the **Johnstown Democrat** reported in June 1869. According to the **Gloversville Intelligencer** reporter who made a spring 1870 visit to the hotel, "We enjoyed ourselves during the three day visit. ... The hotel is a five story building within a few rods of the clear water of Canada Lake. There are twelve or fifteen row boats, a sail boat, and horses and carriages, always ready for the pleasure of guests."

The establishment witnessed New Year's rides and balls, with tables "spread with everything that is tempting to the eye or appetite of the guests." And in the evening, Cromwell's Full Band will discourse music in the large sightly Hall, which commands a fine view of the lake and mountains in the vicinity. A large barn has just been completed, in which more than two hundred horses can be stabled. Mr. T has now every needed facility, outdoors and in for the public accommodation—and all who go there on "New Years" or other occasions may expect, and will enjoy a happy time." However, all these festivities were short lived. The Canada Lake House had eight managers in as many years; it closed in 1877, and did not reopen until 1883. The following year, the structure was destroyed by fire.

The year 1883 marked the second phase of Claflin's development of the lake, for it was then that his firm began in earnest the selling of lake lots on Canada Lake.[33] The tannery itself was sold in 1882.

While much lumber was cut from the surrounding forests, there is evidence that the heavily wooded slopes of Canada Lake were preserved to enhance the value of lake-shore property. Throughout the decade of the 1880s, the Claflin enterprise corresponded with potential buyers. Some of this correspondence and the birth of the summer resort is described in the book "Caroga, the Town Recalls its Past," which has a series of pictures of the resort. A letter from Lee Claflin & Son to Mr. J. M. Dudley of Johnstown, a prospective purchaser, dated March 5, 1887 stated:

---

33 *The deed for the author's camp at Canada Lake dates from 1883 and it appears that the camp was built that summer for the man who ran one of the steamers that served hotel guests.*

> *It is our intention to have the lake shore surveyed and have developed into Cottage lots, in such a way that it will be an agreeable place for summer residents and tourists. How we shall dispose of the land we are not yet quite decided whether it will be best to sell or lease on a long term. We think the lakes and the country about have natural attractions enough to draw summer residents and excursionists and as population increases in the valley, there is a demand for such a place to go to in the summer months.*
>
> *We shall of course wish to protect the land from any improper uses and in which ever way we decide to dispose of it shall want to make some conditions. We are disposed to co-operate with responsible parties in some plan of development if it can be made mutually satisfactory. Please inform us what you think might be done and how many there are in your town who would be likely to join us or who could want land for building purposes.*

The huge Pine Lake Sawmill, built by the Claflin enterprise at the same time as the tannery and run by Milton Barnes, continued into the 1880s. It not only turned out hemlock planks, but large quantities of lath, one of the few other things for which hemlock was useful. A first hand newspaper account of its operations, written by the same reporter who described the tannery, is also quoted in the **Caroga** history.

The Tannery Workers

The tannery payrolls, given in the "Pay Roll Leger (sic)" now in private hands, establish the number of employees for the years 1873 through 1877 more accurately than any Census report. The workers ranged from a low of fourteen men in the tannery itself, to nearly a hundred, presumably including those employed to cut hemlock and peel its bark.

The men worked ten hours a day, winter and summer, averaging about twenty-five days a month, and quite a few worked twenty-seven and one even worked thirty-one. The number of workers averaged 48.5 in 1874, 35.6 in 1875, 52 in 1876, and 79 for the first nine months of 1877 (the extent of the payroll record). In 1874, the average daily wage was $1.70. In 1877, the minimum salary was $.83 a day. Most men received $1.25 a day, while some received $1.50 a day, and six men received $2.00 a day.

Wheelerville Tannery workers, courtesy Bruce Busch.

The bookkeeper must have had quite a time with the records, however, for daily wages were given in fractions, 1.331/3, 1.381/2, 1.662/3, 1.921/3, as well as such round figures as 1.54, and 1.25. Most amazing is the variety of pay scales, for at most a handful of workers earned each rate.

The workers' payroll for the year 1876 totaled $18,997.96, showing substantial agreement with the estimates given for other tanneries of the period in the Census of Manufactures.

From 1876 through the early 1880s, the number of employees was fairly stable at about eighty. Some of the workers settled in the Town of Caroga, for their names survive. Many were Irish, presumably itinerants.

Several family groups stand out among the workers. Valentine Frank was listed in the December 1873 roll as a worker at 1.54 a day. Gradually, more Franks were added to the rolls, until in May of 1877 all but one of the males in the family were employed: Valentine at 1.25 a day, Pat at .831/3, Paul at 1.25, James at 1.25, John at 1.25, J. at 1.25, and A. at 1.162/3. One more son, Frank, was added to the payroll in September. Thomas Lynch appears to have been joined by his three sons; there were four Conroys, three Garners, and three Swears (variously Sweers).

That tannery workers were considered to be at a low social level is demonstrated by a letter from a law clerk to Judge J. M.

Carroll of Johnstown. The clerk visited the tannery in August 1871 to take evidence for a law suit. He wrote,

> *If you want to see a wild country, go northwest from Johnstown about 20 miles. They eat like a parcel of hogs only not quite as much ceremony, their dress are like hogs (nearly) but not quite as neat. Their education is not as good for all they know is to Swear and Drink, Fight and St--- (make it rhyme).*

Pollution

Rufus Alex Grider, an itinerant painter, who chronicled in sketches and written accounts many historic sites in the Mohawk Valley, visited Canada Lake in 1896. One of his sketch books remained in private hands through the 1970s. In it Grider complained about the pollution of the lake from the spent bark washed from the tannery. In his writing Grider takes pains to establish the fact that fishing was excellent in the years before 1866:

> *Fishing before the year 1866 is still recollected and spoken of by those who visited the Lake ere the lumbering & tanning began. Mr. Isaac M. Davis, Merchant at Fonda N. Y., visited the Lake in 1860. In later years, he says that the Statements that fish were abundant is true. That he caught speckled Trout at many places, - at Sand Point, in West Lake - in Black Hole, in the Outlet, also in the stream above the land and below the Stone dam, also around the Island.*
>
> *At Sand Point was a breeding place. He says the water was pure & clear, through 20 feet of water I could see the white sand and bottom distinctly.*
>
> *My guide Avery told me that one night when gliding along quietly with lighted torch he saw the white bottom covered with Lake Trout, could spar as many as he desired.*
>
> *Avery also told me that one cold spring morning the sun shone brightly, when rowing quietly along the North shore of the Lake, below Stony Point, he saw hundreds, perhaps thousands of white projections on the glassy surface, it proved to be a large school of Lake Trout with their Dorsal fins above the surface of the water, they were enjoying a sun-bath, as soon as the waves, or the noise of the approaching boat reached, all disappeared caused commotion in the water as did the ascending air bubbles of every fish which descended.*

Lake Trout weighing over 22 pounds & speckled trout weighing 2 to 7 pounds were caught there before the Saw-dust - Tan-bark and liquor from the tanning vats were emptied into this charming fish producing Reservoir, the bottom of the Lake became coated with brownish deposit which destroyed the food upon which the young fish live, the floating sharp sawdust entered into the gills of the fish and interfered with their breathing and killed them.

The Sawdust and Bark should have been burnt & the lake left unpolluted as they found it.

The guide Avery before 1860, it is said, introduced that freshwater Shark the Pickerel, later Mr. Tunicliff of the first Hotel planted the Otsego Lake Bass, here called Perch, also a voracious fish eater, the two varieties soon cleared the lake of the "speckled beauties" not one remains.

Whether the fishing was destroyed directly by the pollution or whether it deteriorated because of the introduction of the two warm water species is uncertain. What is certain is that the tannery undoubtedly was responsible for both, for around the lake it was always acknowledged that the perch and pickerel were introduced so that the tannery workers would have summer fishing—the trout are most easily caught in spring, because as the water warms, they would dwell in the cooler depths of the lake. The lake's depth, 152 feet just west of the Island is more than adequate for lake trout.

Arietta Tannery

A footnote to the Hamilton County tanneries is a small chapter in the Claflin story. Here, the Census again gives most of the details.

The Claflin enterprises erected another fairly large tannery in 1868 on the shore of the West Branch of the Sacandaga River, at the site of an old, small sawmill. The 1870 Census lists three owners for the Claflin tannery in Arietta: Wm. Claflin, W. F. Claflin, and a H. A. Wooson. The tannery was built shortly after the one in Wheelerville. The plank road leading to it was constructed of planks sawn at the Pine Lake Mill; the road was completed in 1868 or 1869.

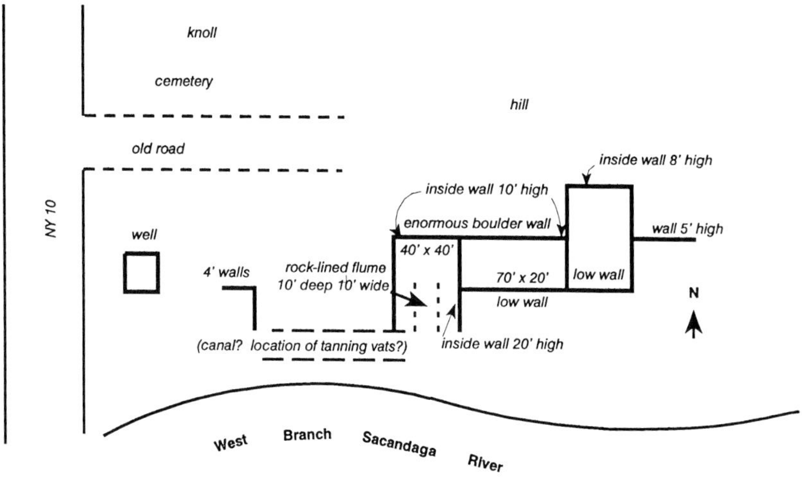

Sketch of Arietta Tannery foundations

For reasons not known, the Arietta Tannery had closed before 1880. It is possible that it was not economical, but the Census seems to refute that possibility. One local resident, Lyman Avery, whose family has lived in the vicinity since the time of the tannery, recalled hearing that everyone at the tannery died within a short period of time. He attributed the deaths to "trichina" - from tainted meat, presumably pork. There is no question that waves of diphtheria swept the countryside in those and later years. Whatever the cause, there is a little pine-covered knoll behind the tannery site, where there are many unmarked graves or graves with only a small stone for identification.

The tannery was sold in 1882, along with the one at Wheelerville, to Charles W. Clement and three Shaws, Fayette of Newton, Blackly of Montreal, and William of Boston.[34] However, there is no evidence that any hides were tanned at Arietta after 1880.

The Wilderness

While the tannery interests of Lee Claflin and Son live on in Wheelerville, in memorabilia and in buildings, the Arietta site became so quickly overgrown that fishermen who walked beside

[34] Aber and King, *History of Hamilton County*, p. 319

the creek in the 1920s and 1930s did not even know of the foundation ruins. I walked the area many times before I accidently stumbled on them. Wandering from the fisherman's path that leads beside the river through tall weeds, I was tripped by an unseen object that turned out to be a bent iron pipe. I fell into a trench six feet deep - to look up dazed at a wall two and a half stories tall. Many times since I have explored the site; others have measured it. We have discovered bits of pots and pipe among the ruins. But the ruins are perplexing, for in order to incorporate the space to tan and handle 50,000 hides a year, the tannery had to be a multi-story building, quite different in layout from the sprawling complexes of buildings at Wheelerville.

If today you walk along the riverside path, you will most likely notice nothing, even if you try to study the space between the river and the hillside as closely as possible. Walk through the field along the river, then head back west. You have to push through the brush and climb the hillside; notice "an odd array of small spruce trees roughly in a line." They grow on an earth covered stone wall. Next toward the west, invisible until you are almost upon it, you should discover a two-foot-thick stone wall. It outlines a 40 by 40 foot room. The highest part of the walls is about six feet high, but tumbled piles of moss-covered rocks show they must have been taller. Inside is a tangled mass of second-growth beech, three dead pines, and many bushes and weeds. Litter from the tannery operation is everywhere, concealed in the dense growth. There are old bricks, rusty iron straps and flat plates. In the southwest corner is a 15-foot I-beam.

Continuing back to the west, you can pace off two 70-foot walls. One is low, nearly invisible, and but a foot high and equally wide. Twenty feet north, against the hillside, a second wall, constructed of enormous boulders, rises eight feet. These walls lead to a more spectacular ruin. Here, a second 40 by 40 foot room is constructed of smaller, more rectangular stones, with obviously more care taken to face the wall. In the northwest corner, the wall is 20 feet high and on its top grows a tall birch. There is a door-like opening blocked by a large mound of fallen rocks and at the upper side of this door is a five foot inner wall, an alcove, perhaps, or an opening for a water conduit.

Running part way through the center of the room is a six-foot deep and about six-foot wide flume. Rocks peeping out from moss show it is lined with stone. Its north end stops at an immense flat stone block. The western wall of the room is obviously constructed in two levels, the first about 8 feet tall, the upper terrace about 3 feet. An east-west running ditch can be discerned running from the flume. More walls, low ones are totally concealed by interlocking aspens between the last room and the road. Pine and hemlock, birch and aspen, brambles, goldenrod and asters, all conceal these ruins. If our knowledge of the Claflin company's Arietta Tannery operation rested only on these ruins,[35] reconstruction of the tannery's past would be slight indeed. Even with some of the records of its past, it remains one of the more mysterious sites in the Adirondacks.

Economics of the Claflin Enterprises in Caroga

The 1870 census lists the firm's capital investment at the Arietta Tannery as $50,000, significantly smaller than the $150,000 given for the Wheelerville site, although that year both tanneries list the same number of workers, an average of 25, with $12,000 annual wages each.

The Wheelerville Tannery consumed some 5,000 cords of bark, the Arietta tannery 3,000. The latter was valued at $18,000, or a dollar a cord more than the Wheelerville bark. Is it possible that the costs where higher because of the distances of hauling bark through a roadless wilderness?

The Arietta Tannery had a 20 horsepower source, while the Wheelerville one listed a 30 horsepower source from the inlet of Canada Lake. Wheelerville also had a 10 horsepower steam and "1 French machine and 2 engines." Another possible explanation of the differences in costs between the two tanneries may be due to the fact that the Wheelerville Tannery finished leather by currying it, or applying $1,500 worth of oil. Because no finishing was done at Arietta, it appears that their tanned sides were sent to Wheelerville for this last step.[36]

The 1870 Census shows that, at Arietta, 25,000 hides cost $100,000. Wages, wood, and 800 cords of bark brought the costs to a total of $132,400, yielding a profit of $17,600 when the 50,000 sides were sold for $150,000. The Wheelerville Tannery that year spent $105,000 for 20,000 hides and, with wages and raw materials, that tannery's costs were $143,400. Compare this

---

[35] Drawing and description of the tannery site courtesy of F. B. and Ruth Rosevear.

[36] Wheelerville originally tanned sole leather but changed to uppers. Pieces of scrap upper leather have been recovered from the site of the drying shed.

with the value of sole leather, 40,000 sides brought $160,000, or a margin of only $16,500 and a profitability figure of 11.3%.

Within the decade of the 70s, at these rates, capital investments might be recovered and a small real profit realized even though the parent company suffered heavy losses in 1879.[37] Certainly profit remained possible though slim at Wheelerville. In 1880, the value of the capital investment was reported as diminished (amortized?) according to the census to $50,000, and the annual payroll totaled $24,026. The operation used 1650 cords of bark and 9,490 gallons of oil. In tanning 18,000 hides worth $96,000, 36,000 sides worth $119,000 were produced for what appears to be a net loss. However, by switching methods and producing curried leather to raise the value of the leather to $157,720, a potential profit of $28,800 was produced.

Although the Claflin Company continued to obtain land as late as 1881 through mortgage foreclosures, the company ceased paying taxes on much of their holdings that same year. Because of New York State's instant foreclosure rule for out-of-state residents, there was a tax sale in 1885 and the bulk of the Claflin lands became part of the newly created Adirondack Forest Preserve. The Claflins retained only the land around Canada Lake that was to become the resort.

The local tannery interests of Lee Claflin and Son were sold in 1882, the same year the parent company's shoe factor in Hopkinton, Mass. was destroyed by fire.[38] It was sold to the Shaw Brothers firm of Boston, which was wildly acquiring scattered tanneries throughout the Adirondacks, all of them showing little profit or verging on bankruptcy (see Chapter VII). The Shaws' financial problems meant that the tannery's days were over. The company ran the tannery for a awhile longer, but by October 1888, all the machinery was removed from the tannery buildings, reportedly to Olean, New York, in the Southern Tier.

There is no written record to indicate why Lee Claflin & Co. sold when it did, for the operation, though not particularly profitable, was at least as profitable as contemporary Adirondack tanneries. The fact they ceased to pay taxes on their land may have been an indication that hemlock was scarce or that the company was experiencing difficulties elsewhere. But with the tannery business souring everywhere in the Adirondacks, per-

---

[37] Mass. Vol. 69, pp. 599 A/10, R. G. Dun and Co.

[38] ibid.

haps Claflin was just a better businessman, who cleverly sold before things got too bad and wisely turned to exploiting the land for a resort.

XV

Hamilton County

Hamilton county's participation in the hemlock bark tanning boom began before the 1850s and lasted at least until 1892 when four large tanneries were still active in the county. Tanneries at Griffin, Wells, Piseco, and Hope were as long-lived as any hemlock tanneries in the Adirondacks, possibly because there was never a tremendous amount of tanning in the county and bark supplies may just have lasted longer, possibly because these sites were more profitable than the Adirondack average. The large sole-leather tanneries were in the southern and middle parts of the county; there were none in the far north of the county, which was too remote from any railroad. Further there is no record that the county's northern forests were ever harvested for hemlock bark.

When early settlers moved north from Northville along the Sacandaga River and the East Stony Creek, Wells and Hope Falls gradually grew into thriving communities. Settlers were attracted to the Sacandaga Valley in the early 1790s and arrived in such numbers that the Town of Wells was formed in 1805. The road connection with the south and Northville was expanded northward that same year along the Sacandaga Valley from Wells toward Lake Pleasant. Another road pushed north in 1812 from Northville over "the Hardscrabble" toward Hope Falls. By 1818, a more level connector from the Sacandaga Valley along the East Stony Creek also led to Hope Falls.

Both Wells and Hope Falls grew into typical southern Adirondack farming and logging communities, with 300 residents in the Town of Wells, which encompassed both communities. The separation between the two communities was small but the poor roads connecting them made even the ten miles between them too great a journey to travel for town meetings. Hence by 1818, the southern part of the town split off into the Town of Hope Falls.

Hope and Hope Falls

After 1818, Hope Falls grew quickly, with over 600 residents by 1822, twice the size of Wells to the north. Around 1846, Smith and Company opened a tannery and a saw mill on the west side of the East Stony Creek. In 1848, the tannery was known as Smith, Slocum & Co.[1] In 1849 the company purchased over a thousand acres to the north and east of the tannery. One of the original principals, according to Aber and King in the **Hamilton County History**, was a Squire Lawton who withdrew the same year, selling out his interest for $2,200 to a trio who reorganized the company as Smith and Ressiguie.[2] The trio, consisting of John Ressiguie, William A. Smith, and Patrick N. Crowe, capitalized the firm at $12,000. According to the 1850 Census, they employed twenty-one workers, whose total monthly wage was $420. Theirs was a water-powered operation with one bark mill, one hide mill, three heaters, and six leaches. The tannery shed, with ninety-one vats, was reasonably large for the day. Its size permitted the annual production of 14,000 sides of sole leather valued at $35,840.

It is difficult to imagine the sleepy settlement of Hope Falls and the rest of the Town of Hope supporting thirteen saw mills and a grinding mill, but transportation made the difference. There were excellent—for the day—roads from the Mohawk Valley from both Fonda and Amsterdam, north to Broadalbin and Mayfield, where level roads along the Sacandaga Valley led to Northville and along the Sacandaga River and the East Stony Creek. Connectors were not as short as those to Warren County communities near the Hudson River, but short enough to make tanning economical.

A comparison between logging and tanning can be derived from the 1850 Census. The value of the production of the thirteen saw mills was $25,955, nearly $10,000 less than the value of the sole leather. But, if you subtract the wages, $5040, and the cost of raw materials, $2975 for bark and $17,640 for hides, the profit of over $10,000 is quite comparable to the profit derived from the mills.

---

[1] Aber and King, *History of Hamilton County*, p. 153
[2] Aber and King, ibid, p. 409

In 1856, the firm of Smith and Ressigue acquired more land and a sawmill site from William Wright.[3] Sometime in the 1850s, the tannery was significantly enlarged, for by the end of that decade, the capital investment was given as $35,000. Inflation could account for only a very small portion of that figure, for the thirty workers earned an average monthly wage of $680. Bark consumption escalated to 3,000 cords a year, but its price tripled to a value of $9,000.

Significantly, the company in 1860 turned out 30,000 sides of leather, valued at $120,000. The price of sole leather had jumped from about $2.50 a side to $4.00; a large portion of that jump was reflected in the cost of the raw materials, for hides cost $5.00 (or $2.50 for a raw side). Even with that jump, the company's economic picture remained bright, with a profit after costs of $26,840, an enormous sum even when compared with the increased investment.

In 1859, Patrick N. Crowe, who had opened a short-lived bank in Hope Falls in 1851, sold his interest for $20,000 and left to start his own business in Wells. Smith and Ressiguie was dissolved in 1868, and the firm continued as Wm. A. Smith and Co.[4]

The **Hamilton County History** lists many of the tannery workers who were employed there and in the other businesses in the town. With names like McGinnis and Hanley predominating, it is easy to see that the tannery workers were mainly Irish, but the rest of the residents appeared to have much wider origins.

Smith was joined by his sons, for the firm of W. A. Smith and Sons listed W.A., C.A., and W.D. Smith as proprietors in the 1870 Census. In 1872, the tannery was said to be the largest in Hamilton County.[5] The power source was no longer water, but steam. The real property was valued at $40,000 and the firm was operating for a full twelve months of the year with thirty-five male and two female employees. The $1,500 payroll represents nearly a doubling in the average worker's monthly wage. And, although the value of the firm's production exceeded that of the previous decade by $10,000, totalling $130,000, the company only tanned 26,000 sides of leather. Profits looked good, $47,000, but costs were rising. Hides were still $5.00 a piece, but the 2,800 cords of bark consumed $16,000, or $5.70 a cord,

---

[3] Aber and King, ibid, p. 399
[4] New York, Vol. 110, p. 465, R. G. Dun and Co.
[5] Aber and King, ibid, pp. 125, 153-4, 399-400

nearly triple that of twenty years before. How far did the barking crews range to find adequate stocks of bark and how much of the increased cost was teamsters' pay? With 24% profitability, the firm was purchased by Hope Falls' second tannery, Lewis Brownell and Bros., whose profitability was only 11% in 1870.

The Brownell firm had its origins in the 1840s, when Orra Brownell had a tannery in Fulton County and later acquired a mill lot also on the East Stony Creek. There is no record that he ran a tannery on the site in 1850, but in 1855, the firm was known as Orra Brownell and Sons "with Robert 28, Orra Jr. 25, John 23, and Ira 21 listed as participants."[6] In 1856, Orra was reported to have sold his sons "equal undivided four-fifths of Lot 4, Patent 11 in Bergen's Purchase for $5,000. The money was to be used to pay four-fifths of a mortgage on the premises given by Orra Brownell to Brown and Sherwood, hide and leather merchants of New York City, and other mortgages.

The investment must have been successful, for in 1860, the firm was able to produce $84,000 worth of sole leather. Their expenses were $5,400 for 1,800 cords of bark, the same rate as Smith and Ressiguie, but their capital investment was listed as only $12,000, compared with $40,000 for Smith and Ressiguie. Significantly, the Brownells managed to pay $1 less per hide for raw materials. Even with the reduced profits for sides, $3.50 a side, the company's profits totaled $25,580.

The 1870 Census lists four brothers as proprietors of Brownell and Bros. Tannery with a capital investment of $36,500. The firm employed eighteen men and three children[7] with an annual payroll of $10,000. That year, the brothers paid $50,000 for 9,000 hides, more than a dollar more per hide than W. A. Smith and Sons. The Brownells spent $6.00 a cord for the 2,000 cords they consumed and their costs exceeded the value of the sole leather they produced by $2,500, mostly because they received but $4.50 a side for their product, $.50 less than the Smith Tannery.

A fifth son, Lewis took over the firm in 1875 and it became known as Lewis Brownell and Bros. The next year the brothers purchased W. A. Smith and Sons. In 1880, the Brownells had

---

6 Aber and King, ibid, pp. 140-141

7 The United States Census of Manufactures lists both men, women, and children as workers in the tanneries. There were very few women, but many tanneries, especially in the 50s and 60s, reported one or a few children as workers.

two listings in the Census of Manufactures as well as the tannery in Mayfield in Fulton County; the Hamilton County firms combined production of 49,000 sides was worth $230,240 at a profit of about $49,000.

No small reason for this profitability must be due to the fact that in November, 1875, the Fonda, Johnstown and Gloversville Railroad (F J & G) reached all the way to Northville, shortening the one-way distance over which hides had to be hauled by nearly thirty miles.

Apparently the firm was able to remain in business into the 1890s, for both John and S. M. Brownell were listed as resident tanners. But they were the only tanners, and soon the company produced only planed lumber. With the demise of the lumber and tanning business, the Town of Hope began to shrink precipitously, so that, by 1905, only 300 residents remained.

Wells

The settlement of Wells on the Sacandaga River began earlier than the one at Hope Falls. William Wells opened a small grist and saw mill north of the present village at the mouth of Mill Creek in September 1792. That creek was also known as Tanworks Creek in the early 1800s and the county's first tannery was started there by Isaiah Whitman, Jr. Before 1820, Isaiah sold the tannery, complete with pond, tanhouse, auxiliary buildings and equipment, to his brother Platt, according to the **History of Hamilton County**. This small, Colonial scale tannery, was sold to Truman Brown in 1841.[8]

The settlement was so distant from the railroad in Amsterdam, over forty miles, that it took William Petit's team four days to make the round trip.[9] Thus, it is difficult to understand why sole-leather tanneries, which were so dependent on transportation, ever became established in Wells. In spite of all the apparent hardships, two large tanneries were built there.

---

8 Aber and King, ibid, pp. 152-4. Note that specific information in that history's introductory chapters is often inconsistent with information in chapters describing the various towns.

9 Aber and King, ibid, p. 69, p. 155

However, confusion in the names of owners, the failure of these names to match other historical records, and the illegibility of the Census reports does make precise definition of Wells' two major tanneries difficult. Whether there were actually two tanneries on Mill Creek or whether cloudy records just confuse the issue is a puzzle. However, it is known with certainty that a tannery was operated by Wm. R Weld in 1850 in Wells. It is likely that a succession of owners preceded Mr. Weld, whose capital investment of $6,000 was relatively small. The monthly payroll of two to four workers and the tannery's yearly consumption of seventy-five cords of hemlock bark was equally small. The Census notes that he produced only upper, not sole, leather.

Wells Upper Tannery

In 1866, Patrick Hanley, whose tannery in the southern part of town had burned, joined forces with Albert J. Smith to form the firm of Smith and Hanley.[10] The firm grew slowly, reaching a capital investment of $11,000, with fourteen workers, a monthly payroll of about $584 and a production of sides valued at $64,000 by 1870. The **Hamilton County History** is the only source of later information: William W. Burnham became receiver for the company in 1874. However, the firm continued with Hanley, joined by his father-in-law, Edward Hayden. With the death of Hayden, Hanley and Hayden became Hanley and Son as Thomas joined his father. The firm experienced difficulties in the later 1870s but was reorganized and continued until 1900. The history states that "Irish born Patrick Hanley died March 27, 1910, at the age of ninety of influenza and is buried in Wells."[11] He survived the tannery by a decade.

During the last year for which records are available (1880), Hanley and Son remained a marginally profitable business, capitalized at $20,000 and using both water power (10 horsepower from Mill Creek) and steam from two boilers (32 horsepower). The Hanleys were caught in a squeeze of rising prices, with 8,000 hides costing $45,000, or $5,000 more than a decade earlier, and the 16,000 sides the mill was capable of producing yielding $59,840, or over $5,000 less than a decade earlier.[12]

---

[10] Prior to this time, the firm of Smith and Hanley had been established in Bleecker, Aber and King, ibid, pp. 69, 155.

[11] Aber and King, ibid, pp. 973-974

[12] Census, Hamilton County, 1870 and 1880

The workers of Wells undoubtedly bore the brunt of these reverses in the market, for an average of twenty workers earned $1,000 less in annual wages than did the fourteen workers in the prosperous year of 1860.

Wells Lower Tannery

Numbers tell a different story for Wells' Lower Tannery, the one on the bank of the Sacandaga River that became known as the Wells Tannery. The firm originated with land purchased in 1850 by John Reed[13] of Gilboa and James Cunningham and William J. Powell of Schenectady. They organized the William J. Powell & Company and began a tannery business. Again, according to the **Hamilton County History**, Cunningham was replaced by Henry N. Vedder in 1855, and he in turn was replaced in 1857 by Joseph H. Horsfall.[14] Piecing the chain of owners tenuously, it seems that the tannery was owned by Hanley and Smith in the next few years. Possibly the panic of 1857 caused this undocumented shift of ownership.

The tannery was considered larger than its rival in the north of the village. Already, by 1860, its production of 212 tons of sole leather was valued at $108,800.[15] However, in this case, the 212 tons reported represented 34,000 sides, which calculates out to a sale of $3.20 per side, somewhat less than contemporary sales from Brownell's in Hope Falls, and considerably less than the $4.00 a side earned by the firm of Smith and Ressiguie. Perhaps it was the vision that the Wells Tannery had a greater potential, for in 1859 Patrick N. Crowe sold his interest in the Hope Falls Tannery and joined Hanley and Smith. The tannery burned in 1866 and, as noted above, Hanley withdrew to the Upper Tannery. Crowe rebuilt, naming his business at this time the Wells Tannery.[16]

By 1869, Crowe had sold his interests in the tannery, the buildings, land, tenements[17], dam, water power, and all for

---

[13] It is tempting to think that this John Reed was the same man who later ran the North Creek Tannery and went on to build the tannery at Oregon.

[14] Aber and King, ibid, pp. 915, 969

[15] In the 1880 Census, some reports give the amount of leather produced in pounds rather than sides as in earlier decades. This makes precise comparison with earlier years difficult.

[16] Aber and King, ibid, p. 970

[17] The name given workers' housing in the Census records.

$21,150. The buyer, Edward Spaulding[18] of Massachusetts valued his real property in the next year's census at $45,000. By the next year, Spaulding and Sons had opened two of the north country's largest and last-to-be-built tanneries: The St. Regis Tannery in Franklin County and the St. Lawrence Tannery near Colton on the Raquette. (The parallel fate of those tanneries is discussed in the respective county chapters.)

The figures for the 1870 Census indicate that the business was successful, at least initially, for it realized a profit of $45,500 a year. This was in spite of the fact that the 3,000 cords of bark consumed cost $18,000, the payroll for 30 workers totaled $14,000 annually, and the raw hides cost $75,000. Altogether, 1870 was a very good year–the tanned sides were worth $140,000.[19]

It is amazing that a business whose yearly production as of 1869 was valued at $140,000 could undergo so many reverses in the next decade. Business transfers certainly indicate that this may have been the case. Spaulding took a partner in 1872, then sold the business for $27,000 to a local Wells resident four years later. Perhaps it was a mortgage foreclosure that allowed Spaulding to reclaim the business a year later. After failing again in 1877, either he finally managed to sell it to William E. Plummer of Newton, Massachusetts, of Plummer took over as receiver for the property. Whatever the case, by 1879 was listed as owner.[20]

Plummer listed his real holdings at $100,000 in 1880. He employed an average of thirty-four men and had a payroll of $10,000. Daily wages of $.80 to $1.00 were quite low, however. The increased production required 4,500 cords of bark–a staggering amount. Assuming bark was piled beside the Sacandaga in the traditional sheds 12 feet wide and 8 feet high, that much bark would cover 6,000 running feet, more than a mile! Still, it appears that in 1879, it ought to be profitable to tan, with a yearly production of 60,000 sides bringing in $150,000. At that time, the Wells Tannery was powered by the Sacandaga River (60 horsepower) and three boilers, which produced another 70 horsepower.

---

[18] Aber and King, ibid, p. 970

[19] 1870 Census, Hamilton County

[20] New York, Vol. 110, p. 487, R. G. Dun and Co.

Was it falling profits or lack of investment cash that induced Plummer to sell out within eighteen months to the Shaw Brothers? According to the **Hamilton County History**, the Shaw Brothers continued to operate profitably,[21] despite the Boston firm's bankruptcy (see Shaw in Part I).

The property the Shaw Brothers acquired was described as covering thirty acres, with a blacksmith shop and mill pond in addition to the tannery proper. Even the disastrous fire of 1886 did not still the tannery, for Charles W. Clement, the receiver for the Shaw firm, which was just emerging from bankruptcy, built a third tannery on the site.[22] Tanning in Wells must have been considered profitable and there must not have been any question about the bark supply.

The firm, F. Shaw and Co. or Shaw Brothers is the same one that purchased marginal operations all over the Adirondacks in the early 1880s and experienced such a spectacular bankruptcy in 1883. The fire may have saved their investment in Wells. The third tannery on the site continued until 1894, when it was leased to the Philadelphia Warehouse Company.[23]

In spite of the fact that, conservatively, 216,000 cords of bark had been removed from the surrounding countryside on the Sacandaga River and East Stony Creek valleys, production did go on until the mid 1890s. Without production records for the late 1880s and the early 1890s, it is difficult to estimate the amount of bark consumed. But, marvel at the fact that over the years, through 1880, bark stacks 288,000 feet in length–fifty-four miles of sheds–were consumed in these valleys alone!

Since slow-growing hemlock would not regenerate during these decades to harvestable size, this means that hemlock was stripped from at least 54,000 acres, eighty-four square miles. Little wonder that an important note in the sale to the Shaw Brothers included an old bark yard in the valley and a new bark yard on the hill.

The tannery, by the way, survived as a veneer mill, until it, too, was destroyed by another fire.

---

[21] Aber and King, ibid, pp. 69, 155

[22] Aber and King, ibid, p. 970

[23] ibid

Hamilton County's Northern Tanneries

The lack of corroborating Census records[24] affects the histories of Hamilton County's four northern tanneries, making it impossible to compare their outputs with other tanneries. For two of the tanneries no first-hand descriptions exist; they are recorded only in deeds and the **Hamilton County History**.

Of the two with little information, one was a small family affair, run by the brothers Henry and Theodore Lamker of Morehouseville continuously from 1854 to 1895. Morehouseville was a small settlement to the west of Piseco, with but 219 residents in the late 1860s. In 1870 the total value of the brothers' tanned products was only $1,060. Apparently they tanned only deerskins, with a "secret formula" of alum and salt that rendered the skins white.[25]

Rubbing from the stamp used to mark Silver Lake Tannery sides.

Silver Lake Tannery, Rudeston or Piseco Tannery

Extraordinary distance from railheads and poor access roads placed this tannery on lot 157 near Oxbow Lake outlet at Piseco at a great disadvantage compared with other Hamilton County tanneries. The main access was north from Wells to Speculator via Gilmantown Road, then along the south shore of Lake Pleasant and west-southwest to the tannery, adding at least twenty-four miles of poor roads to an already long haul. I have discovered no certain record of its existence before 1881 when it was sold by George M. Voorhees of Amsterdam to the Shaw Brothers, the same firm that was acquiring so many failing Adirondack tanneries (see Chapter VII). The tannery waned with the Shaw Brothers' problems and they either defaulted or sold it, because by 1896 the site was owned by a John P. Weber

---

[24] A critical page is missing from the ledger that contains the 1880 Hamilton County record. Both the microfilm and the original were checked in an effort to obtain this missing information.

[25] Aber and King, ibid, p. 867

of Boston. It was sold again to George E. VanArnum in 1900.[26] It is not known when the tannery closed, but tanning had essentially stopped in 1897. In 1910, George B. Howland rented the tannery boarding house at Piseco and became proprietor of a hotel and boarding house, the Howland House, which featured Friday evening dancing.

A brass stamp, used to mark finished sides, is in the Piseco Historical Museum, but there are no ruins to show where the tannery buildings stood. It is known that the tannery occupied the site of a saw mill and shingle making mill, run by Amos Dunning, Ephraim Phillips, and Henry Scidmore. As testimony to the wilds, a report, if true, in the **Hamilton County History**, identifies twelve saloons between the settlements of Piseco and Lake Pleasant, along the teamsters' route to the tannery, in a distance of fewer miles than there were saloons.

The demise of this tannery did not occur before it too witnessed a "tannery death" by drowning. A great many tanneries have tales of similar catastrophes, though they do not have the romantic overtones of the logging industry's loss of river drivers with the dangerous searches for bodies. All we know is that at Piseco, on September 2, 1893, a John Burns of Rudeston was drowned in a vat from which he was removing sides.

Ted Aber, Hamilton County Historian, discovered the names of men who were peeling bark, Owen Fraser and Leroy Brownell; hauling it, Dennis Donohoe and George Grinnell; and grinding it, Judy DeGroff. W. N. Courtney, a local man with a reputation as a great fisherman, also worked in the tannery.

A third Hamilton County tannery, the one at **Arietta**, is discussed in the chapter on Wheelerville in Fulton County, for the two tanneries were related by roads and ownership. When the Arietta Tannery closed around 1882, its bark was shipped north to the Silver Lake Tannery, which not only tanned leather but made and shipped extract.[27] It seems almost impossible that barrels of extract were shipped from this remote site over rough roads to Wells or further south to Northville and there are no records to indicate just how much extract was shipped and over what period.

---

26 Aber and King, ibid, pp. 320, 355

27 Aber and King, ibid, p. 324

Griffin

A picture made more complete by memories and archaeology

Griffin became the site of one of the larger Adirondack tanneries, though later residents' claim that it was one of the two largest is as unfounded as all other such claims. This one undoubtedly persisted because the tannery lasted into the 1890s and because there were so many who remembered it and a few who actually documented stories from its heyday.

Griffin is different for other reasons. A small, but thriving community preceded the tannery, which was built rather late in the tannery era, almost at the time others were folding and moving on; and although its community survived into this century, it disappeared as completely as any tannery settlement. But, for some reason, the stone foundations and the artifacts at this site are better preserved than at many other sites, so Griffin has provided a key to exploring more fragmented ruins.

The lack of Census information is most unfortunate in that its absence deprives us of an economic comparison with the tanneries in southern Hamilton County, but with views of the ruins to spur the imagination and with the vivid accounts of one of its residents, the Griffin Tannery appears as real as any in the Adirondacks.

The Town of Wells planned road districts and laid out roads north from the village along the Sacandaga River in 1838 and 1839.[28] They headed north, continuing toward Lake Pleasant, with a branch east along the East Branch of the Sacandaga toward the gorge at Griffin.

Before delving into Griffin's history, first walk with me to the deserted settlement. Drive along the highway that winds northeast beside the East Branch in the northern part of the Town of Wells, Hamilton County. About two miles from the confluence of the East Branch and the Main Branch, a small, dirt road forks north. Park and walk along it as it winds around a hemlock covered knoll–remarkably tall, mature specimens cover the steep slopes. The road reaches the East Branch at the "modern," 1903 iron bridge.

Stop at the bridge and enjoy the views. Downstream the deep gorge of the East Branch funnels spring floods between

---

[28] Aber and King, ibid, p. 927

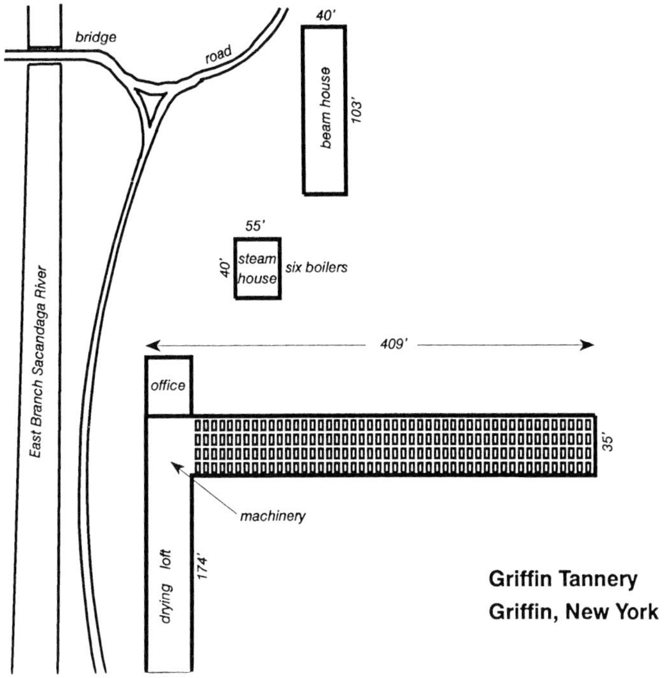

Adapted from drawings by Frank Girard

walls made deeper and darker by shrouds of hemlock. Upstream, the rapids end in two hundred yards or so and the water becomes smooth and deep. I will be your guide for this modern visit, but for a view of the past, Frank Girard will be your guide. Frank's father, Henry J., moved to Griffin in 1883 and later ran a hotel there. Frank's papers and his talks with old-timers in the valley are the source of most of what is known of Griffin. A copy of these papers was given to me, along with other notes on life in the settlement, by Frank's younger sister, Ouida, who has written about her family in **Griffin: Ghost Town in the Adirondacks and Other Tales.**

A walk through the deserted settlement would yield scant information without Frank Girard's notes. Across the bridge, a road turns right along the river. Instead of taking it, duck into the woods at about a forty-five degree angle with the road. In just a few feet, you cross the remains of a rock wall. Follow along it, discovering that it is 103 feet long. A second wall, which butts up against a natural rock ledge, parallels the first, making a rectangle 40 feet wide. Only gradually can you discern the fact that these walls outline the foundations of a building, for the space is filled in with balsam and popple whose trunks are a foot and a half in diameter and more. You are standing in the building where once hides were sweated and soaked to remove the hair. And, what happened to the hair? Ouida Girard remembered that it was flushed into the river; she recalled swimming near the dam and touching the bottom–where dense mats of slimy, squishy, decaying hair had settled. She described how a lot of the "hair got caught in the 'Big Eddy' and settled to the bottom and when we swam there, we noticed how 'spongy' the bottom was and that there were no stones at all."[29]

Walk east from the southeast corner of the sweating building to discover another foundation, this one of a two-story building whose entire lower floor was of stone. Cut-stone arches top the lower windows. Pieces of metal and fire brick are scattered about. Chains and gears are visible outside the northern corners of this building, which once housed six boilers. The building measured 40 feet by 55 feet and the steam produced here supplied the sweating building and made power for grinding bark.

Continue east; the going is very rough. Brambles and small shrubs fill a wet, swampy area, the east side of which is bordered by a ditch. Just beyond, you will encounter another low rock wall. You can see thirty-five feet beyond the wall to the far side of this foundation, which backs up against a low hillside formed by another rock outcrop. This building too is filled with balsam and popple, with spruce, hemlock, and swamp maple. It is so long and so overgrown that you will have trouble even imagining the extent of the ruins of the vast building you are standing in. According to Frank Girard's papers, and he measured the buildings many years ago before they were so overgrown, this shed that housed the vats was 409 feet long.

With difficulty we remeasured the shed. We were tempted to dig among the roots and trees to discover the extent of vats that once filled the tannery shed. At times the outline of a sunken channel–the sluice-way for flushing water through the shed–makes a faint depression in the detritus. The accumulated duff and root masses exceed a foot in thickness, making digging almost impossible. Fortuitously, on each of several visits to the

[29] Letter to the author.

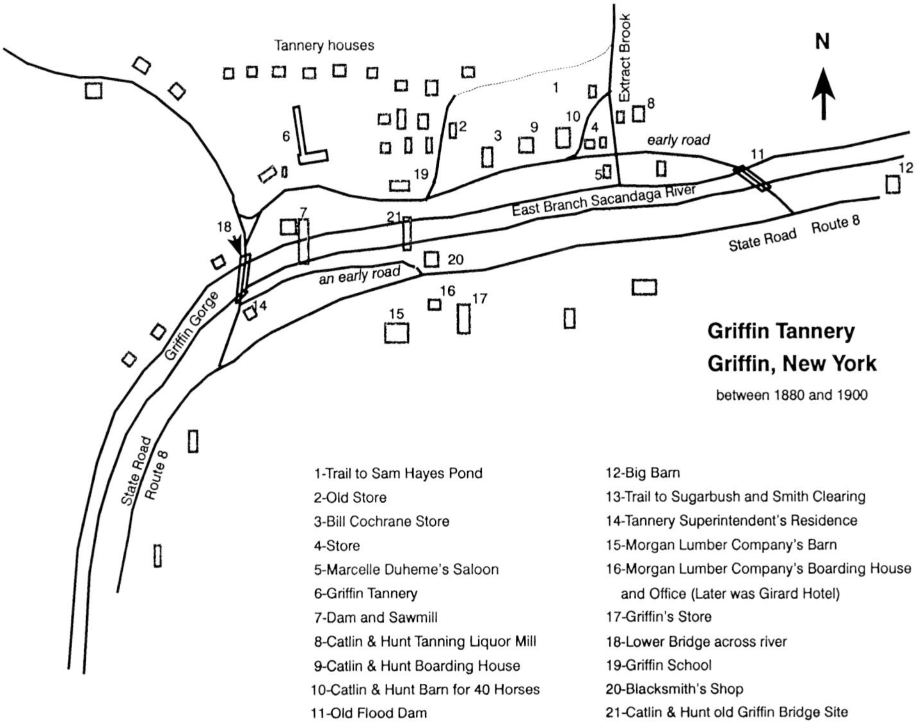

Adapted from drawings by Frank Girard

ruins, freshly fallen balsams have toppled, upending shallow root masses from the soil below. One upturned root mass about eight feet in diameter exposed well preserved planks and iron spikes that clearly outlined the walls of a vat. The vats were lined with a yellowish clay. This clay made them watertight, and it was certainly not a local clay. I have never found a description of a vat shed that implied that such a clay was used for any purpose in the Adirondacks, but one treatise on tanning recommended, in 1902, that clay be used to prevent the loss of leachate from the wooden vats.

Each rectangle was almost 6 feet wide and about 8 feet across in the direction of the long axis of the shed. In the center between the double rows of vats, the depression, the obvious sluiceway, is filled with the reddish shreds of hemlock bark.

Another time, the root mass of a second smaller fallen tree appeared smooth, as if a rock covered with dense mosses had been pulled up with by the roots. Closer inspection revealed that it was a side of leather, perfectly tanned; it had been sitting in the acid soil that accumulated on the tannery floor for over a hundred years.[30]

At the north end of the building, a rise in the ground falls off again to a depression filled with alders. This appears to be a holding pond for water for the tannery, and Ouida Girard wrote of seeing a long and sinuous chain of wooden pipes that brought water from Tower Brook to the east. She remembered that Tower Brook was dammed so that its water could be carried about a half a mile through the nine or ten inch timbers that had been hollowed to a diameter of four or five inches. These wooden pipes were held together by iron bands. Most of the way on the slight downgrade, the pipe was placed on the ground, though where it crossed depressions, the ground was piled up for support.

Follow the long vat room toward the river. Typically, water was flushed through such a building to exit in the river. I asked Ouida if the spent bark was also flushed into the river as it was at Canada Lake. She remembered that most of it was used, dried for burning or to pack ice houses. Beyond the southern end of the tannery vat building, a pile of spent bark is concealed in a bramble thicket. On one expedition, we kicked at the soft pile and exposed another piece of thick cow-hide, well tanned.

Perpendicular to the tannery vat room was a long, 174-foot, building, which was about as wide as the vat building. This held the drying loft to the east of the vat building and an office to the west.

Walk east along the road. In a small opening in the dense growth, not twenty feet from the road, a large piece of fluted cast iron hides in the grass. It suggests a giant coffee grinder; it was a part of a bark mill.

Uphill to the northeast on the knoll behind the building with the leaches, rectangles of boulders are the piers on which the workers' homes stood. None of these company houses had cellars, but a few had large flat stone stoops. Downslope to the east is a beautiful rock-lined well. Traces of an old roadway circle the knoll. Heading toward posted lands along the road beside the river, you pass a private house—once the old schoolhouse at Griffin. As the road curves north, continue east on a narrower

---

[30] This piece of leather has been given to the Adirondack Museum.

Griffin Tannery Settlement, courtesy Ouida Girard

track. The depressions of huge cellar excavations lie to the north of the old road. To the south are the foundations of the saloon, Bill Cochran's store, and the Catlin and Hunt Boarding House—a rough structure built to house workers, which later became the first Girard's Hotel. Nearby are the foundations of the Catlin and Hunt barn—a large, 40- by 100-foot structure for forty horses, the twenty teams that brought bark from surrounding hills and transported hides and sides to the railheads. The teams used a bridge across the Sacandaga at the head of the rapids west of the present bridge.

The surviving pictures of the Griffin Tannery are blurred with age as proud descendents have shown them many times. They depict the ghostly shape of the tannery buildings, a bare hillside—with not one tree—behind a settlement that straggles along the river. Pictures show the old dam, which backed up the East Branch of the Sacandaga River for nearly half a mile. They show tannery workers, wives and girl friends, loaded on a wagon of bark. Town records tell us who were the proprietors of the many support businesses, who were the school teachers, who were some of the tanners. Pictures show a remarkably large settlement, now a true ghost town; it is difficult to reconcile the visual image of these pictures with the bits and scraps that are concealed in the dense forests that now cover the hillside of the valley. The casual visitor might never know there was anything more to this lovely gorge beneath the bridge than the beautiful waterfall.

The Historical Record

Frank Girard interviewed many old-timers and searched town records to prepare a paper for the Hamilton County Historical Society in 1954. At that time, he was able to talk to descendents of the original settlers, Ben and Jim Wadsworth, who lived in Warrensburg, and Frank's uncle, Peter T. Girard of Wells. Some of the old tannery records had been preserved by John E. Hosley, and these too were incorporated into his paper. My account of Griffin is taken from that talk, with the permission of Ouida Girard, Frank's younger sister, with new information supplied by the R. G. Dun Ledgers and deeds for the site.

According to Frank Girard's research, there were four families on the East Branch of the Sacandaga River near Griffin, each arriving in the decade between 1835 and 1845. Josiah and Phil Wadsworth, Billy Wells, and Charles Martin settled on opposite sides of the river at the head of the rapids (the future sites of the tannery and Girard's Hotel). The settlements stretched two miles to the east near the "big bend" in the river, where Daniel Wadsworth also built a sawmill.

These settlers were the first to clear the virgin forests and the first to harvest the majestic pines. They farmed and logged; gradually a settlement accumulated around the head of the rapids, where by 1855 Charles Martin had erected a saw mill. According to the **History of Hamilton County**, that mill was sold several times, first to J. C. McDonald & Co. The Wadsworth mill went from that family to the Abrams, then to John Russell of Glens Falls and Henry Tefft of Sandy Hill to become part of the firm of Tefft and Russell of Fort Edward. By 1865, the latter firm had acquired all the Philip Wadsworth land nearby. James Moon, agent for Tefft and Russell, also took over the operation of the Charles Martin mill at the head of the rapids and for a short time in the late 1860s and early 1870s, the settlement became known as Moon's Mills.[31] The mill dam on the Sacandaga at the head of the rapids backed up a half-mile-long pond to supply water to float logs to Wells and beyond.

In 1872, the firm of Catlin and Hunt of Wells purchased the Daniel Wadsworth lands. What follows is an anomaly, and the intriguing details are tantalizingly incomplete. That firm

---

[31] Aber and King, ibid, p. 928

Ghostly old photo of Griffin Tannery and smokestack, courtesy John Teachout.

built an "extract mill" on the west side of the brook that flows into the Sacandaga just to the east of Griffin. That brook was given its present name "Extract," a name which briefly was used by the settlement. The mill, about a quarter of a mile up the brook, used a water wheel to grind bark and "had three vats where they boiled and stored liquor."[32] Lore has it that the hemlock liquor from these vats was shipped in huge wooden barrels through Wells to the railhead at Amsterdam. If so, this was an extraordinary undertaking. Very few Adirondack sites shipped extract: Chases Lake in Lewis County, perhaps Silver Lake Tannery. The distance over which the heavy barrels would have to be hauled from Griffin to the railhead at Northville or to Amsterdam and the quantities of tanning liquor needed stagger the imagination. What was happening elsewhere to make this kind of shipment economical? Before 1895, a few other sites shipped bark, but usually to other mills nearby, and rarely those at a distance, and usually only after the tannery closed or was destroyed by fire and owners were trying to recoup their losses by disposing of existing stocks of bark. The whole reason for building tanneries in the wilds of the Adirondacks was that the transport of hides and oils and chemicals to such sites and the shipment of leather sides from such sites were economically more favorable

---

[32] Aber and King, ibid, p. 829; I have seen depressions that might indicate the three vats and associated buildings, but could not find them again in recent years.

than the shipment of liquor or bark anywhere. In the next two decades, shipment of bark and liquor became more prevalent. Was the extract mill at Griffin a sign of the future? Or were shipments like this designed to briefly prolong the life of tanneries to the south, which had exhausted their bark supplies?

Barking operations existed at the same time as James Moon was logging surrounding hills. At Griffin, the settlement grew around the two mills, the saw mill and the extract mill, and only after the community was established did the tannery appear.

Catlin and Hunt, who came to Griffin from New York City in 1872 to log the area, failed within two years. Their property was found to have been previously mortgaged for more than its value. No property could be leased so creditors could not realize a "single cent on their claims."[33] Catlin and Hunt did built the huge horse barn[34], whose foundations are still visible at the site.

In 1873 both Catlin and Hunt and Tefft and Russell were active in the future Griffin area; the settlement had over a hundred workers. That year, the settlement's namesake acquired buildings and a mortgage on lands held by Tefft and Russell. Through a default in bonds dated September 3, 1873, Stephen A. Griffin, 2nd, acquired lands in the northeast corner of Township 29 of the Totten and Crossfield Patent in Hamilton and Warren counties, 10,000 acres as described in Book 24 of Hamilton County deeds. For these tracts he paid $7,010.37. What happened to Catlin and Hunt is not clear; nor is it clear just when the tannery was built on the site or who built it, but it must have started tanning hides in the late 1870s.

Book 15 of Hamilton County's deeds records that Griffin increased his holdings in 1882 by acquiring more lands in the northeast part of Township 10, the Morehouse Tract: lot 13, lands which Tefft and Russell had sold to Catlin and Hunt in 1872, lot 14 in the 3rd allotment of Townships 10 and 29; lot 15, which lies partly in Hamilton and Warren County, 5,120 more acres in the northwest corner of Township 29; and assorted other acreages.[35] All these were adjacent either to the Griffin

---

33 New York, Vol. 110, p. 474, R. G. Dun and Co.

34 Aber and King, ibid, p. 929

35 It is interesting to note that for some time, Town of Johnsburg Historian Lewis Waddell (of Wevertown) was convinced that Griffin held no lands in Warren County because there were no such records in Warren County. It is equally perplexing to

area or to the Oregon Tannery, which was less than 10 miles northeast along the East Branch of the Sacandaga, near the point where that river makes a sharp bend to the north.

Whether or not Griffin ever owned or managed the tannery, he certainly was active in barking operations. Griffin contracted to sell George McConnell and Walter L. Gregory of Boston all of the hemlock bark on the trees on part of his 43,000-acre holding on May 5, 1877. It was stipulated that "if the bark on the trees of this land did not amount to 50,000 cords, the deficiency could be overcome by peeling and taking bark from the adjoining lands most convenient to the tannery now being built by McConnell and Gardner at Smith's Place, so-called."[36] Note that the contingency in this contract implies that not much more than one cord of bark per acre was likely to be harvested!

Griffin may have run his namesake tannery in the interim or he may have had nothing more to do with it than supplying bark. R. G. Dun and Co. described him as a lumberman and owner of a large store in Griffin, but does not mention him as an owner of a tannery.[37] All that is known for certain is that Rice, Emery & Company took over the operation of the tannery at Griffin and that a contract to operate it was signed between Nehemiah W. Rice, Frederic W. Emery, and Edward L. Pickard of Massachusetts in March, 1880.[38] Rice, Emery and Company owned a sawmill in Wells in 1880 according to the Census, but there is no listing for a tannery under that name. The parent Boston firm, under the style, N. W. Rice and Company, also had a tannery at Fine in St. Lawrence County, and was reported to have a first class credit rating in the late 70s and early 1880s. Emery became a partner in 1883 and in spite of some losses, the Boston firm was reputed to be worth upwards of $600,000 that year, though it shrank considerably toward the end of the decade.[39] See the St. Lawrence County chapter and Part I for more on its activities in the Adirondacks.

---

discover that those lands in Johnsburg, Warren County, were registered with the deeds of Wells, Hamilton County. These deeds account for more than 31,000 acres of the 43,000 that the *History of Hamilton County* claims Griffin acquired in the area.

36 Aber and King, ibid, p. 929; the Smith's place referred to here is where the Oregon Tannery was built.

37 New York, Vol. 110, p. 492, R. G. Dun and Co.

38 Aber and King, ibid, p. 930

39 Mass. Vol. 77, pp. 416, 445, R. G. Dun and Co.

Griffin Tannery workers, courtesy Ouida Girard

Time has concealed details of Stephen Griffin's activities as completely as the forest has concealed the tannery site. According to Smith's History of "Warren County," Stephen Griffin, 2nd, sold all his interests in Warren and Hamilton counties in 1882 and retired to Warrensburg.

By 1880, the arrival of the tannery created a boom in the town, which now bore Griffin's name in spite of his tenuous connection to the tannery. Forty-five men were employed in the tannery and twenty-two houses were built for them (rent 50¢ a week). A cord of wood for heat was but 75¢. A post office was established on October 4, 1880, with James B. Wilson as postmaster. Charles Griffin, Stephen's nephew, held the post five years later and ran a company store for Morgan & Co[40]. which had on June 21, 1882, acquired lands and lumber interests from Stephen Griffin.[41] In 1882, a school was built with Henry J. Girard as trustee. With the addition of the Morgan & Co. boarding house, built in 1883, the settlement boasted two "hotels," a telegraph office, and a saloon. A store, with a strict prohibition against the sale of intoxicating liquors, changed hands several times in the next few years.

---

[40] Morgan and Company lands were later incorporated into International Paper Company.

[41] Aber and King, ibid, p. 930

Load of Bark at Griffin Tannery with Nellie McCarthy Girard, Frank Girard, Minnie McCarthy, Julia McCarthy, Pat and Frances Girard, courtesy Ouida Girard

Here we pick up Griffin's story as remembered and recorded by its inhabitants. The Joseph Girard family settled in Canada from France, then emigrated from Canada, first to Vermont in 1827. Their movement was typical of many French-Canadian families and the first Girard, Joseph (father of nineteen children, most of whom remained in Canada) had a son, Francois, who moved to Sandy Hill (Hudson Falls) where there was a large French-Canadian settlement. With his wife, also a French-Canadian, he bought a 140-acre farm near Wevertown, where he had nine children, the three oldest of whom were boys, soon able to work on the farm. With the death of the oldest son, the next two, Henry and Eleazer, moved in 1882 to Griffin to find work in the new tannery. With their sister to keep house, they settled in one of the company houses, and by 1883, the rest of the family had moved from the hard farm life to the new boom town.

For a time, the sister, Myra, kept school. Henry, whose job was that of night watchman in the boiler room, fell asleep on the job one night and was promptly fired. He fled to the gold fields of Colorado from which he returned six months later. He and his brother, Eleazer, bought the Rice, Emery & Co. boarding house and turned it into a "hotel," covering the tar paper with clapboards and facing the building with a two-story veranda. A large sign, Griffin House, was added along with a ballroom made by pushing out the walls of two smaller rooms. Henry was named trustee of the newly-formed school and was instrumental in hiring the new school teacher, whom he married a few years later. His wife was Nellie McCarthy, daughter of Irish immigrants. Her father had worked in the Wevertown Tannery and when that closed, he, with other employees, was paid in land; and thus he too became a farmer in Wevertown.

This joining of French-Canadian and Irish immigrants was symbolic of tannery town settlers throughout the Adirondacks—all the pay rosters list a majority of French or Irish names. But, the Girards were not quite typical, for when the tannery closed down, they elected to stay, moving in 1895 to the Henry Morgan Co. boarding house and lands on the south side of the river. There they farmed and raised a family, which included Frank, on whose tannery history notes this account is so dependent, and Ouida, whose book **Griffin: Ghost Town of the Adirondacks** contains so many details of farm life in an isolated Adirondack community at the turn of the century.

The schoolhouse, which was built in 1882 (possibly 1868), persisted until 1919. Frank Girard remembered that most of the tannery and sawmill buildings had disappeared during the decade 1900 to 1910. Lumber was taken from many of the company houses to build houses in Wells. Gradually, over the years, even the people who continued to live in the other tannery houses abandoned them. The Girards remained, not selling their farm until the 1970s.

Returning to the history of the Griffin Tannery, operations there ceased about 1891 and in 1893, Rice, Emery, & Co.'s interest in it was incorporated into the United States Leather Company, which in turn sold its "entire holdings for $700 to John G. Hosley of Wells in 1896. With the land went the Extract Lot and other property owned by the company. The company would be allowed five years to dispose of its "tannery buildings and appliances, including those on said lands, such tannery buildings consisting of the Dry House, Loading Room, Rolling Loft, Office, handlers and Yard, the Leach House, Beam House, and Engine House, Sweat Pits and Bark Mill."[42] If all the build-

---

[42] Aber and King, ibid, p. 934

ings were not removed by 1901, the remaining buildings were to become the buyer's property.

The community at Griffin lasted for four or five decades; the tannery for only about a decade and a half. If anyone needs to be convinced of the complete disappearance of the tannery settlement, let him walk among the ruins and foundations and see how completely the forest has reclaimed this settlement of 300 individuals in just nine decades.

XVI

The Western Adirondacks

In many ways, the spread of tanneries into the western Adirondacks paralleled developments in the east. The major difference was that, except for Herkimer County, the west lagged behind the east. Herkimer County, which touches the Mohawk Valley, had many early Colonial tanners and only a few hemlock bark, sole-leather tanneries. These were clustered in the southern part of the county and by the second half of the century had switched to the tanning of specialty leathers as in Johnstown in Fulton County. It is extraordinary, but no large tanneries appear to have been built in the wild lands of the northern part of the Herkimer County and only one in the remote interior of the county's mid-section, undoubtedly because of distances from railroads and the shortage of good roads. Herkimer's northern hemlock stands, if harvested at all, were shipped west to the Black River Valley or southwest to the lower West Canada Creek Valley.

Oneida County, too, participated in tanning early on as a part of its expansion into the Mohawk Valley. The one exception was a group of tanneries in the northeastern corner of the county, a small part of which lies within today's Blue Line.

Farming, with its attendant Colonial tanneries, spread north along the West Canada Creek Valley and on beside the Black River during the first half of the nineteenth century. The real advance of tanning into the western Adirondacks occurred after the completion of the Black River Canal in 1855. The Black River and Utica Railroad was extended through that valley to Boonville in 1855, to Lowville in 1867, Carthage in 1871, and Clayton in 1873. As proximate as that railroad was to the western Adirondacks, most of the region's tanneries were built close to the Black River Valley. Only a few were built in the western Adirondack foothills away from transportation, even though most of the bark used was hauled from those foothills. This situation is unlike the eastern Adirondacks, where many tanneries were built far from railroads and canals. Around 1870, as the railroad grew, those supplies of bark sparked the building of several of the largest tanneries in the north country in the sparsely settled northwestern corner of what is now the Park.

The next to last rail lines to penetrate the western Adirondacks, the Carthage and Adirondack and the Cranberry Lake railroads, completed in the late 1880s, served the last great wave of logging in the Park. They also served two of the larger tanneries built very late in the era in the Oswegatchie Valley.

The Adirondack Division of the New York Central Railroad did not penetrate the heart of the western Adirondacks until 1891, so late that it, too, only served a very few tanneries, for only a handful remained active in the mountains and no new ones were constructed there after that date.

Straddling the Black River and touching a forested region that remained unharvested up to the 1870s, Lewis County was poised to join the expansion of tanneries into the Adirondacks in a big way. Here, in the foothills of the western Adirondacks, was a wave of tannery building that overshadowed the expansion in the east in Warren County. The expansion in the west began almost two decades later because of the late development of transportation. Here, the largest tanneries in the Adirondacks were erected, frequently by men with connections and financial roots in the Swamp. Most of the largest tanneries were erected fairly late, after 1870, and even they began closing down in the 80s, reportedly for want of bark. This western impetus to build the means to destroy the hemlock forests was greater, briefer, and ultimately much less well documented that in the east. But, even though Lewis County's story is briefer, it has one high point—the revelation, given in that county's chapter, of which Adirondack tannery was the largest based on building size and the largest based on output.

A few tanneries in Lewis, Jefferson, and Franklin counties survived past 1890 when the companies that controlled them became incorporators in the United States Leather Company. As individual tanneries were absorbed into that great conglomerate and quickly dismantled, the western Adirondacks witnessed the closing of the era in which sole leather was tanned with hemlock bark.

XVII

Herkimer County

Two small rivers flow from the Adirondacks south through Herkimer County to the Mohawk River: the West Canada Creek traces a portion of the county's western boundary, the East Canada Creek separates southern Herkimer County from Fulton County. Tanning in lower Herkimer County was initially closely related to the settlement of the Mohawk Valley, then it continued north along the two Canada Creeks.

Among the county's early tanners were Henry Ellison of Herkimer who had a tannery on the West Canada Creek shortly after 1800. The East Canada Creek "affords a large supply of water at most seasons of the year, and being intersected with many falls has been used to some extent for manufacturing."[1] A tannery was located at Ingham's Mills on that creek and another was built at Brockett's Bridge (Wintonville, later Dolgeville) before 1830. The Winton Tannery was bought out and became one of the area's largest sole-leather manufacturers, see below.

Histories record a number of tanneries in valley towns at the end of the eighteenth and beginning of the nineteenth century.[2] A dozen of these Colonial or small tanners were still in operation in Mohawk Valley towns according to the 1850 Census; that number had shrunk to seven by 1860, three by 1870. They tanned both soles and upper leather; a mixture that included mostly local hides. Little Falls had a considerably larger tannery in the 1870s and 1880s, but it tanned mostly skins. It did use 1200 cords of bark, costing nearly $7 a cord in 1870, and in 1880, the Census reported that it used over 3,000 cords, supple-

---

[1] Benton, *History of Herkimer County*, p. 437

[2] Hardin's *History of Herkimer County* records tanneries in German Flats, Mohawk Village, two in the Town of Little Falls, Middleville, Salisbury, Devereaux, Salisbury Corners, Dolgeville, Danube, Van Hornesville, Starkville, Smith's Corners, Warren, Cedarville, Elizabethtown, Spinnerville, West Winfield, Crane's Corners, Grant, Gravesville, and Frankfort, and the towns of Schuyler, Newport, Norway, Russia and Ohio.

mented by oak bark from St. Lawrence County. Three other skin mills were located in the southern part of the county in 1880.

In the central part of the county, a cluster of tanneries was built along Spruce Creek in Salisbury Center; others were located a few miles to the west at Salisbury Corners (now Salisbury) or to the east toward Emmonsburg. Salisbury is mid-way between the Mohawk Valley and the northern forests that are now part of the Adirondack Park.

The first tannery in Salisbury Center was built in 1806 by Nathaniel Peck. Local histories note a small tannery near the Union Church. John Dietz had a tannery near the lower covered bridge; it was still operating in 1880 when Charles Dietz reported tanning mostly skins. Isaac Kibbies' Upper Leather Tannery produced a small amount of leather and was owned by George Wagner in 1869. A tannery built in 1825 by Sherrill Reed was said to fail at that early date due to lack of bark, as did the tannery erected about 1826 by Aaron Bartlett.

The first tannery in Salisbury Corners was built by Amos Griswold in 1802. All in all, there were eight tanneries within a radius of seven miles, a remarkable number even given that they were all Colonial or small establishments.

This chapter focuses on the tanneries north along the East Canada Creek or to the west toward the valley of the West Canada Creek, where it separates Herkimer and Oneida counties. It is in these parts of Herkimer County that the larger tanneries that specialized in sole leather were found.

The first tannery on the upper reaches of the East Canada Creek was established by Daniel Cross in 1812 in Stratford. A few miles to the south, on the banks of the creek, a tannery was built by John C. Pitt, which, according to the 1850 Census, averaged eighteen workers and produced over $50,000 worth of sole leather from dry imported hides. Sometime in the next decade it appears this tannery was enlarged and renamed the Emmonsburg Tannery after a settlement by that name across the creek in Fulton County, although the tannery was located on the Herkimer County side of the creek. In 1870, the Census reported the Emmonsburg Tannery had a capital investment of $140,000 and produced 34,000 sides of sole leather worth $134,000. It consumed 3,000 cords of bark or more annually throughout the 70s. In 1880, the tannery produced 25,000 sides worth $125,000.

The Manheim Tannery

The largest sole–leather manufacturer in the eastern part of the county was built south of Salisbury in Dolgeville on the East Canada Creek in the town of Manheim. It was erected in 1830 by Major D. B. Winton and acquired before 1850 by a firm from the Swamp. This immense tannery, with real property valued at $125,000 in 1850, had been enlarged and financed by the Swamp trading company, Thorne, Watson, Corse and Company.

Watson was a brother-in-law of Gideon Lee. Thorne, Watson, Corse and Company was formed in 1843 and dominated tanning in New York City until 1852 when it broke up; but Thorne, Watson and Company continued in various forms until the death of Jonathan Thorne in 1884. Thorne supplied green hides to tanneries in Warren and Lewis counties. He became a very wealthy man from tanning, and later raised and developed strains of cattle at a very fancy farm in Dutchess County.

The Manheim Tannery had 50 workers in 1850, making it among the largest sole-leather manufacturer on the fringe of the Adirondacks, even larger than those being built in Warren County. In 1850, 24,500 hides were tanned to produce $135,150 worth of leather, consuming in the process 5,500 cords of bark at $3 a cord. The number of employees and the production was lower in the 1860 Census, though the 20,000 hides tanned were worth $160,000. The 6,000 cords of bark cost $3.50 a cord. Apparently the tannery burned in the next few years.[3] Oliver LaDue managed the tannery from about 1857 to 1861 and the tannery is depicted under his name in an 1857 map of the county.

A second tannery in Manheim in 1860 was owned by Erastus Ingham, but its production was a sixteenth the size of the Thorne establishment.

---

[3] Hardin, ibid, p. 335 indicates that the tannery "ceased entirely in 1872" and that the property was purchased by Alfred Dolge. There is no Census record for the tannery for 1870, so it may have ceased operating before 1869. Hardin also states that the closing was due to the failure of the bark supply and that it was one of the largest in the United States. He says it burned in 1845 and was rebuilt shortly after. A closing due to a shortage of bark in this middle-southern part of the county is a real possibility.

Tanneries Adjacent to the West Canada Valley

At the same time that tanneries were being built in the eastern part of the county, others were constructed in towns of the West Canada Valley: Henry Waterman had a small tannery in Newport spanning the decade 1850 to 1860. It and an enlarged successor tannery that survived until 1880, tanned mostly skins.

The Town of Russia had four sole-leather tanneries in 1860, the largest, on Cold Brook, owned by Peter Countryman, having been built before 1850. The Countryman Tannery continued as a substantial establishment until after 1880[4], but in the later years mostly skins were tanned.

A second sole-leather tannery was built on Elk Creek in the Town of Russia in the late 1870s and the 1880 Census reported a production of 12,000 sides.

The Middleville Tannery

The Town of Fairfield, just to the west of Salisbury, had a very large sole-leather tannery that was owned in the latter part of the nineteenth century by George M. Thomas. The operation of this tannery actually spanned 144 years, though for most of the time it produced upper leather and tanned a variety of skins.

The tannery, in Middleville, started as a small operation on Maltanner Creek about 1814. This establishment burned and was rebuilt on the banks of the West Canada Creek. In 1850 it produced 28,000 sides worth $48,000, and enlarged again, but by 1880, its production, valued at over $100,000 was mostly skins.

The owner of the tannery "was a strong advocate of, and very influential in, the establishment of a branch line of the Buffalo-Albany railroad from Herkimer northward through the West Canada Valley. It is said that he was extremely proud of his efforts in this regard. This seems to be supported by the fact that an observation platform was built into the tannery, facing the

---

[4] Hardin, ibid, p. 437 states that the tannery closed in 1878, but there is an 1880 Census record for it, indicating the tannery was operating in 1879, the year the 1880 Census record was compiled.

railroad tracks so that he could point out to visitors the results of his endeavors."[5]

Early tannery workers in Middleville were Germans, supplanted in the 1850s by Irish immigrants, and later by Polish immigrants. The firm became Thomas and Burns, with Burns taking over as resident manager. The second tannery burned about 1903 when the combination of the burning building and the fires in the piles of bark threatened most of the village.[6] The tannery was again rebuilt and about this time, chrome replaced bark as a tanning agent, so the old tannery pits were filled in and covered. That might end this book's interest in the tannery, except for the remarkable fact of the tannery's longevity. The firm was sold after World War I to a Boston company, resold to A. C. Lawrence Company a division of the Swift Packing Company in 1920, and closed in 1931. That year, it was reopened as the Middleville Leather Corporation by William Haight of the American Hide and Leather Company with money raised from local investors. It closed briefly during World War II and was again reorganized again under the direction of William Haight and continued until he liquidated the business in 1960.

The LaDue Tannery

The Role of the Company Store

In 1853 Oliver Harvey and William LaDue built a large tannery at Gray[7] on Black Creek in the Town of Ohio. The tannery's address is sometimes given as Wilmurt, and the Census placed it in the Town of Norway.[8] The 1860 Census gives it a real property value of $100,000; that year it employed fifty workers and produced 32,000 sides worth $170,000. Four ledgers from the company store associated with this remote tan-

[5] Tumminello, *The History of the Middleville Tannery*, paper in the files of the Herkimer County Historical Society. This paper contains a detailed history of the tannery written by the daughter of one of the tannery workers.
[6] ibid, p. 3
[7] variously Grayville or Graysville
[8] Black Creek divides the towns of Norway and Ohio

nery and a volume detailing tannery wages and expenses from 1858 to 1866 are in the collection of the Herkimer County Historical Society. The elegant script titles of the account book call this the La Dew Tannery. These books and the Census give the spelling both ways, but it almost appears as if a typographical error in the printing of the ledger had induced the change from LaDue to La Dew.

Many stories of northern tanneries indicate the role of the company stores and the fact that most financial transactions were carried out by the stores. It was often said that tanners were in debt to the stores and served almost as indentured workers. Without the La Dew ledgers, this aspect of tannery life would have remained just a rumor.

The ledgers assigned the store's customers an account number. All transactions and purchases were recorded under both the name and the account number. On separate pages of the 1859 ledger, tannery workers' wages were tallied under the heading "Labor applied to Sundries." Workers averaged less than twenty-four days a month, and wages were all under a dollar, many under half a dollar a day. In contrast, under the headings "Bark to Sundries," in September and October of that year, a few accounts were credited with sizeable sums: of the more than forty workers who supplied bark, most received under $100, but two received $768.89 and $589.82. Under the heading of "Team applied to Sundries," eleven teamsters were credited with a total of $179. Sundries were billed to the Boarding House as well as to the workers. A few accounts record amounts in cash paid to suppliers of the store, but there are no records of workers receiving cash. It may be that there were separate records now lost, but the most obvious conclusion is that all of a worker's money went to the company store or the boarding house.

In 1879, the LaDue Tannery was acquired by Thomas E. Proctor of Boston. At that time it was the largest tannery in the area and was officially called the Graysville Tannery. Proctor later became the first President of the United States Leather Company (see Part I and the Oneida and Jefferson County chapters for more on Proctor's tanneries.) In 1880, the Graysville Tannery employed thirty men and tanned 20,000 sides, worth $100,000. The tannery closed in 1887.[9]

[9] Hardin, ibid

Logic dictated that most of these Herkimer County tanneries be located close to transportation available from the Mohawk River and the East and West Canada valleys. There is no question but that the tanneries in the West Canada Valley pulled enormous amounts of hemlock from Herkimer County forests to the northeast. However, with the exception of the tannery at Gray, no large tanneries were located in the interior upland and northern portion of Herkimer County. There were few roads and those that led into the northern part of the county approached from the east and Lewis and Oneida counties. Whatever bark was harvested from the northern reaches of the county went to tanneries outside the county, and in spite of later claims of bark shortages, much of Herkimer County's bark was never harvested.[10]

[10] The Adirondack League Club reported an unwanted preponderance of hemlock at the end of the nineteenth century.

XVIII

Oneida County

Oneida County straddles the Mohawk Valley and the pattern of development of the part of the county close to the Mohawk River occurred at the same time as the shores of the Hudson were being developed. Early in the nineteenth century it was transformed from an agricultural county to one with many small manufacturers, including tanneries and the county was heavily engaged in tanning after 1845. According to the 1865 Census of the State of New York, 242 men were employed in twenty-nine tanneries most located in towns close to the Mohawk Valley.

Only a small part of Oneida County lies in what is now the Adirondack Park. That part is the apex of the county's northeast corner, which is a triangle bounded on the southwest by the Black River. Several of the county's larger sole-leather tanneries were in that northeastern region and all certainly drew bark from the low mountain region to the east in Lewis and Herkimer counties, which does lie within the Park.

Closest to the Adirondack region were the tanneries in Boonville, Remsen, and Forestport. Samuel Johnson had a sole-leather tannery in Boonville which spanned all the decades of the Census. It tanned $11,157 worth of sides and skins in 1850; it produced $78,500 worth of sides in 1860; its reduced output in 1870 included mostly skins; and in 1880, it produced only $32,000 worth of leather.

Two tanneries were located in the southern part of the triangle. The John B. Griffith Company started quite small in 1850 and continued small as the J. and W. Griffith Company in 1860. By 1880, there were two Griffith tanneries: Charles Griffith produced $8,900 worth of leather in Remsen and William Griffith and Son produced $40,598 at a tannery on the West Canada Creek. The Census notes that the latter drew bark from land owned by A. Thorne, a Lewis County tanner.

R. R. Thomas and Son had a small tannery in Remsen in 1860; it produced $13,000 worth of sides and skins in 1870, $16,000 worth in 1880.

At Hawkinsville on Cummings Creek where it flows into the Black River below Forestport, the Eureka Tannery was built by the sons of William Anderson in 1852.[1] The tannery building 316 by 40 feet housed 152 vats, a bark mill, and a leach house. Recorded under the Boonville Census in 1870, the Anderson and Sons Tannery produced $24,000 worth of sides and $15,900 worth of skins. Still owned by the Anderson family in 1880, the G. B. Anderson Company produced 22,000 sides worth $88,000. Col. George Robertson, who had started in the tanning business with Zadock Pratt, was said to have an interest in this Forestport tannery along with three other tanneries in the Catskills.

The Proctor and Hill Tannery of Forestport

The tannery located closest to today's Adirondack Park and the largest of Oneida County's sole-leather manufacturers was in Forestport. A Civil War veteran, Brig. Gen. Jonathan A. Hill, and Thomas E. Proctor, purchased a tannery about 1867 on Big Woodhull Creek, just below the confluence of Big and Little Woodhull creeks, and just above Big Woodhull Creek's confluence with the Black River.[2] The tannery had built by Robertson and Pitcher in 1854 and the new owners enlarged it to include 240 vats.[3] It could use five to six thousand cords of bark a year. The Census indicates that the tannery consumed 4,000 cords of bark in 1870 at a cost of $5.50 a cord.

An indication that the business was just underway in 1870 comes from the Census report: 19,000 hides worth $90,000 were tanned but only 26,000 sides worth $200,000 were produced.[4]

---

[1] Thomas, *Black River in the North Country*, p. 74

[2] Beers, *Atlas of Oneida County, 1874*

[3] The **Boonville Herald** of June 18, 1888 gives the number of vats as 200.

[4] Every other entry for tanneries gives the number of sides produced as precisely twice the number of raw hides to be tanned. From these numbers it can be inferred that the tannery was just starting up.

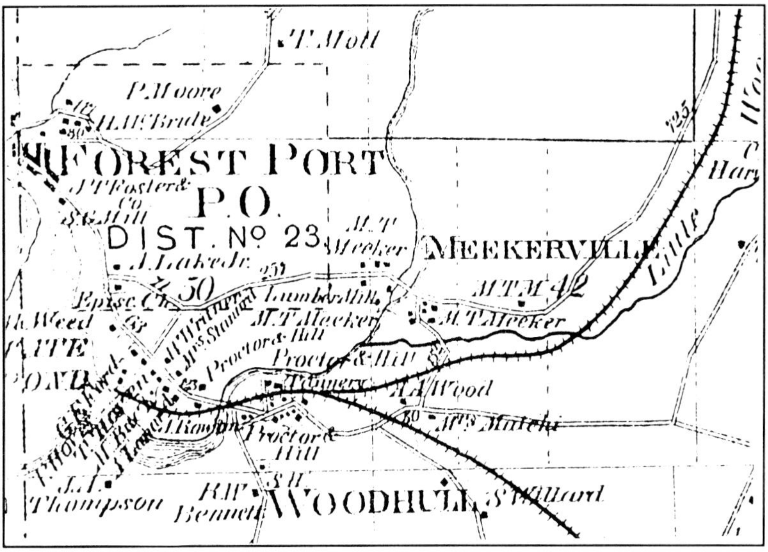

From the 1874 Atlas, courtesy of the Adirondack Museum

Proctor, from Boston, was the financier of the company.[5] General Hill, as he was always called, a tall, bearded gentleman, who had lost an arm in the Civil War,[6] managed the practical part of the business and understood tanning from beginning to end. Proctor, the future president of the United States Leather Company, also had tanneries in Herkimer and Jefferson counties in New York State, two tanneries in Pennsylvania, and one each in Maine and Massachusetts. The men entered a side of sole leather from the Woodhull (Forestport) Tannery at the Centennial Exposition in Philadelphia in 1876 and it won a first prize.[7]

Still known as Proctor and Hill in 1880, the company produced 50,000 sides worth $320,000. Proctor seemed to survive on high volume, for his gain at this Oneida County tannery was but 21%, with a very low profitability percentage of 8.3. His operation in Jefferson County at Wilna was even more marginal, 20% gain, 8% profitability. Not enough data are given in the 1880 Census to compute gain for the firm's other tanneries, but

---

5 Thomas, ibid, p. 75
6 ibid
7 **The Lumber Camp News**, pp. 11, 15

it is easy to surmise that making money with such slim margins was risky enough to induce Proctor to later become an incorporator of the United States Leather Company.

In contrast to the threatening financial problems, the **Boonville Herald** of June 1888 in a detailed description of the tannery, indicated that it was a thriving enterprise, with capital investment of $225,000, which included 30,000 acres of land, all but 2,000 of which were in adjacent Herkimer County, and a 300-acre farm capable of producing 200 tons of hay and 1,500 bushels of oats for the tannery's fifty horses and 400 bushels of potatoes for the workers, who lived in the company's twenty-two tenement houses. The tannery, said to be 860 feet long and 60 feet wide (a possible exaggeration), employed sixty men year round with wages totalling $2,500 a month and another hundred men at $40 per month plus board in bark peeling season from the end of May until October. The operation appears to have been efficiently designed, with machines to grind eighteen cords of bark daily, steam-fed leaches, and boilers that consumed the spent bark both to heat the liquor and the tannery.

All this must have come to a precipitous halt in the next year or so, for only Proctor's Wilna Tannery of the three he had in New York State survived into the 1890s to become part of the conglomerate operation, along with his tanneries in Pennsylvania. Proctor closed the Forestport Tannery so hastily that he abandoned huge piles of hemlock bark, which could still be seen on the banks of Big Woodhull Creek years later.[8] Proctor always functioned as the outside partner; Hill lived in Forestport and also ran the Blue Eagle Boarding House. When the tannery closed, Hill moved to Pennsylvania to continue in the tanning business.

The seven tanneries listed in 1880, all lying in the small triangular region of Oneida County just outside the Park, represented a remarkable concentration of tanneries in a small area. Their ability to sustain bark tanning seems even more remarkable when we consider the huge tanneries to the north in adjacent Lewis County and those to the east in Herkimer County, tanneries that undoubtedly hauled bark from some of the same sources.

[8] Thomas, ibid, p. 91

XIX

Lewis County

Only a small part of the western Adirondacks encompasses any of Lewis County but Adirondack forests supplied bark for a number of large tanneries that were located in that county both inside and outside the current Park boundaries. Lewis County straddles the Black River Valley and its commerce grew with the building of the Black River Canal, which was completed in 1855, and later with the parallel railroad through the valley. The canal was designed to provide additional water to the Erie Canal and to transport lumber and agricultural products, but as a bonus the canal made tanning possible in Lewis County.

There were a few of the smaller tanneries associated with farming before mid-century. One or two tanneries were built just after the canal was completed, but the height of tannery building occurred about the time the Black River and Utica Railroad was completed as far as Lowville (1867). Associated with the railroad was a hide house erected in Glenfield near the railroad tracks to accommodate the tanning industry. The hide house stored green hides awaiting teams to draw them to the tanneries and leather awaiting shipment on the railroad.[1]

It is not clear whether the late wave of tannery building occurred because of the improved transportation, or because there were untouched quantities of bark in this region, while supplies in other places were declining. Or, perhaps, we can surmise from the sheer size of the expansion of tanneries, both causes were equally important. As elsewhere failure of the bark supply is mentioned as the cause for the industry's demise.

The value of the sides produced in Lewis County in 1880 exceeded one and a half million dollars. This figure is quite substantial when compared with counties to the east. Lewis County also differed from those counties in the way its tannery era was

[1] Bowen, *History of Herkimer County*, p. 407

abbreviated. Not only did large-scale, sole-leather tanning begin later in Lewis County than in the eastern Adirondacks, the peak of the tanning era lasted little more than a decade.

The western Adirondacks is blessed with a number of streams flowing west from the foothills. Woodhull, Crystalline, and Cummings creeks and the Beaver, Otter, Oswegatchie, and Moose rivers, in addition to the Black River, all had tanneries. The adjacent low mountain regions farther to the east were covered in dense forest that was not heavily logged until the arrival of the railroads after 1891, at the end of the tanning era.

Several of Lewis County's largest tanneries played an important role in Adirondack history. With a few exceptions, they were all built or expanded around 1870, many with financial backing of men or firms from the Swamp; all suffered reduced profits in 1880 and financial difficulties around 1883; and almost all closed in the decade of the 80s.

The terms "largest" and "mammoth" were applied to several, and statistical comparison certainly gives credence to those claims. It is strange, given all the previously untapped forests not far to the east, that the shortage of bark, or perhaps the high costs of hauling it to the tannery sites, was still said to account for the demise of tanning in Lewis County in the 1880s. The tanning era was undoubtedly compressed because of the huge size of Lewis County's tanneries and their voracious appetite for bark, but as elsewhere turmoil in the sole-leather industry took its toll.

The tannery towns nearest the Black River Valley survive, especially those with commerce and other industries; while those to the east are now small hamlets if they still exist at all.

Chase's Lake Extract Mill

One of the very few north country extract operations was located in Lewis County. According to Hough's "History of Lewis County,"[2] "the extract mill was erected on the outlet of Chase's Lake in 1871. Since the fall of 1875, it has been owned and run by the firm of Lewis, Crawford, and Co. It has a capacity for

[2] Hough, *History of Lewis County*, p. 547

working 4,000 cords of hemlock bark a year, and of making about 3,500 barrels of extract. It is run day and night (Sundays excepted) and employs about 10 men in the woods. The process consists of grinding, leaching, and boiling in vacuum pans to the consistency of a syrup, weighing ten pounds to the gallon. In warm weather, carbolic acid is sometimes added to prevent fermentation. The company have a tram-road about five miles long and two sawmills for cutting the peeled logs into lumber."

Port Leyden Tannery

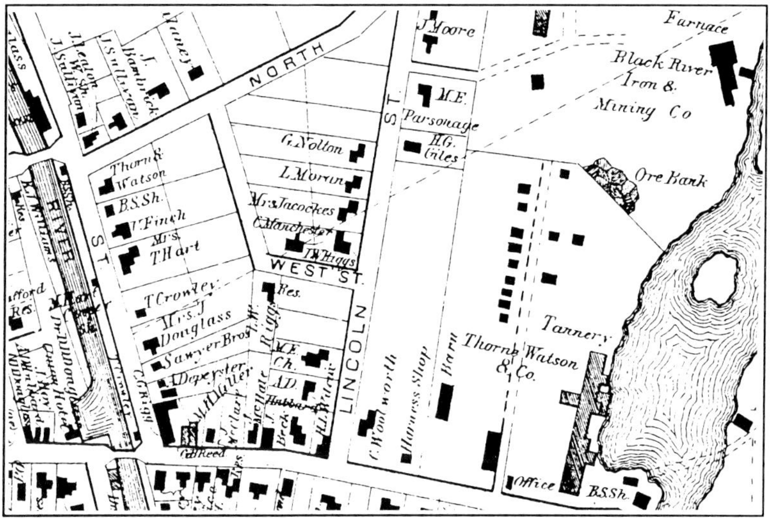

From the 1875 Atlas, courtesy of the Adirondack Museum

Port Leyden was called Kelsey's Mills until 1832. The Black River Canal reached Port Leyden in 1850. Its first small tannery was built by Cornwall Woolworth on Black River in 1842; it was capable of producing 3,000 to 4,000 sides a year, and by 1855 was producing 12,000 to 16,000 sides a year.

H. D. H. Snyder, Jr. and his brother Augustus (much more about the Snyder brothers below) bought this tannery in 1855. H. D. H. Snyder, Sr. had a large tannery in Ephratah, Fulton

County, in 1860. He had started tanning in Green County and was originally a partner with William Creighton Lee, youngest son of Gideon Lee. That partnership was dissolved in 1871. (Lee's sons continued in business until they sold to the United States Leather Company in 1893.)[3]

Undoubtedly money from the senior Snyder financed the purchase of the Port Leyden Tannery, and a $12,800 loan to his son in 1863 permitted his namesake to assume the brother's interest.[4] Snyder was a member of the State Assembly and Port Leyden's leading industrialist, building its two iron smelters and a magnificent home on a bluff overlooking the town.

The Snyders enlarged the Port Leyden Tannery in 1858; the 1860 Census reports a production of 32,000 sides valued at $120,000. The tannery was enlarged again in 1864 to include a vat building 450 by 40 feet[5], increasing the total capacity to 65 to 70,000 sides a year. The Black River Flood, which occurred in 1869 when the dam at North Lake was washed out, flooded the tannery, causing $50,000 worth of damage. The tannery was rebuilt and continued at a high level of production; it employed eighty men with wages of $38,000 a year and consumed about 7,000 cords of bark a year, worth $38,500. In 1872, the value of the 1.3 million pounds of leather produced was said to be worth upwards of $400,000 in Boston or New York markets.[6] Five water wheels were required to run all the machinery. Snyder also had a lumber mill with a "two-story circular saw" capable of sawing 10,000 feet of lumber per day.[7]

Thorne, Watson and Company of New York City, whose huge Herkimer County tannery had burned several years earlier, took over the Port Leyden Tannery by 1875, and in April of that year, the tannery burned in a fire that also destroyed the adjacent saw mill and blacksmith shop. According to local historian Matthew J. Conway, H. J. Botchford leased the site later that year and was in the process of rebuilding the tannery when he died. The Botchford brothers' company, described below, was

---

[3] Norcross, ibid, p. 59

[4] New York, Vol. 147, p. 92 R. G. Dun and Co.

[5] Photo in Bowen, p. 361

[6] This is the highest value for any tannery in the North Country; but because there are no figures for other tanneries for 1872, we have to rely on the Census years for comparisons.

[7] *Lewis County Gazetteer*, 1872, p. 111

one of the county's largest, surviving the one brother's death. It owned and operated other tanneries, but never reopened the Port Leyden Tannery.

Moose River Tannery

Lyon and Snyder Mammoth Tannery

This "Mammoth" tannery was built at a fording place on the Moose River, which became known as Moose River Settlement, eleven miles upstream from Port Leyden and just downstream from McKeever. According to historian Joseph F. Grady, the site was "strategically located near Brown's Tract Road in the heart of an extensive hemlock forest."[8] Lyman R. Lyon purchased 95,000 acres of the John Brown's Tract in 1850 for $12,500, a fortuitous move in light of the area's future for hemlock bark tanning.[9]

Lyman R. Lyon, with his large tract, and H. D. H. Snyder, Jr., with his flair for expansion, formed a partnership to build the tannery in 1866. This tannery burned at least twice, in 1875 and 1883, though one historian says it burned three times. (At the time it burned in 1875, it was owned by the Botchfords, and when it burned in 1883, it was owned by Hersey and Company[10] of Boston.)

Both Lyman R. Lyon and H. D. H. Snyder, Jr. were entrepreneurs on a grand scale. With four other men, Snyder formed the Port Leyden Iron Company in 1864. It was capitalized at $200,000. Two furnaces were constructed on the Black River at the Hellgate Flume; the river provided water-power for the draft-blast operation. One furnace exploded within a month of its completion in 1864.[11] By December 1867, the **Boonville Herald** described the iron works as "a bottomless abyss ... in which they have poured their money ... without the slightest prospect of its return."

---

[8] Grady, *The Story of a Wilderness*, p. 116

[9] Brown, *John Brown's Tract*, p. 322

[10] This company went be various styles: Charles Hersey and Company and Low, Hersey and Company.

[11] Conway, *Port Leyden - "The Iron City,"* pp. 36-41

Lyon and Snyder Mammoth Tannery at Moose River 11 miles from Port Leyden, courtesy of the Town of Webb Historical Society, Old Forge.

This began Snyder's financial downfall, from which his Lewis County interests never recovered. Within a decade he had left Lewis County, abandoning his beautiful house on the hill in Port Leyden, and when last heard from was somewhere in South America.[12]

Lyman R. Lyon built steamers that plied the Black River Canal, owned huge tracts of land, and invested in several tanneries. Lyon's death in 1869 also had an adverse effect on Snyder's finances.[13] With the dissolution of Lyon and Snyder, the Mammoth Tannery began to have problems. While Snyder was assumed to have title to the tannery and large property that went with it, Thorne, Watson and Co. of New York was reported to have an $80,000 mortgage on his holdings.[14] Lyon's estate passed to his widow and children and they maintained an interest in the tannery and landholdings.

---

[12] Conversations with M. J. Conway

[13] New York, Vol. 147, p. 103, R. G. Dun and Co.

[14] New York, Vol. 147, P. 103, R. G. Dun and Co.

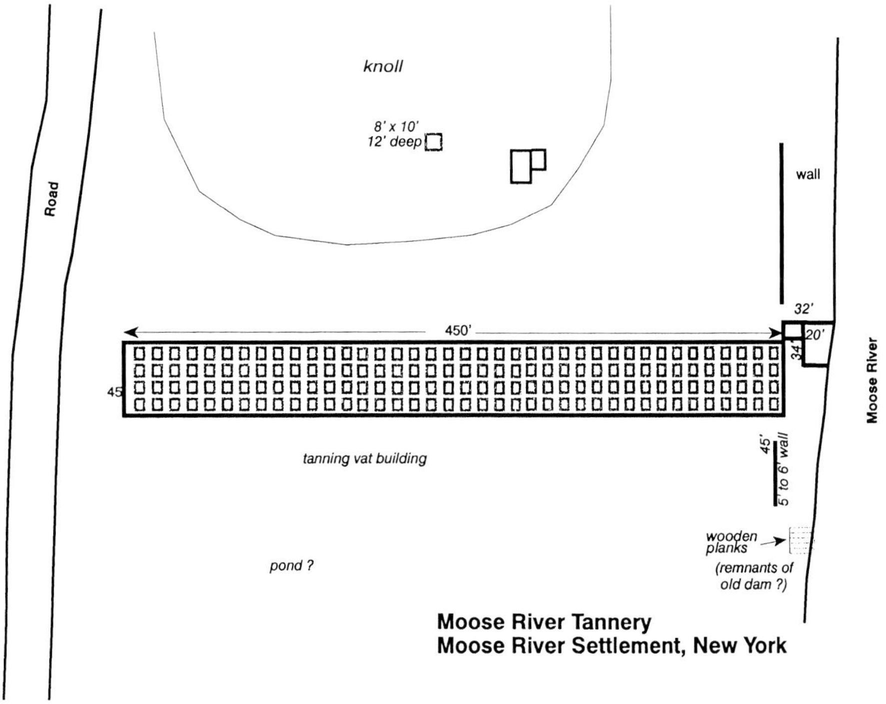

Moose River Tannery
Moose River Settlement, New York

Photos show the huge vat building, presumably with a second story devoted to drying rooms. Although later historians claimed the vat building measured 630 feet, the clear outlines of the its foundations are 450 feet long. Nevertheless, if tannery building size is the criterion, then this is indeed the largest in the Adirondacks, even if it was not as large as some claimed. With 288 vats, 45 pools and 8 leaches, it had a capacity of tanning 80,000 sides of sole leather a year. Today, depressions of almost every one of the vats lining the floor of the vat building are still visible.

Associated with the tannery were a boarding house, blacksmith shop, a sawmill producing two to eight million board feet of lumber, and a hide house. Also in the tannery settlement was a large hotel—A. W. Lawrence's Moose River House—with rooms for twenty-five guests. A number of homes for workers surrounded the tannery.

After Lyon's death, the bark from his holdings on the John Brown's Tract continued to be available to the tannery and the Lyon and Snyder Tannery kept that name for a while after Lyon's death. However, before 1872, the Moose River operation was transferred to Todd and Kennedy, and in 1874, upon Todd and Kennedy's bankruptcy, the tannery was acquired by H. J. Botchford. (See below for more on the Mammoth Tannery under Botchford's ownership.) Under the name Lyon and Botchford, the tannery continued until 1878, when it suspended business and discharged all hands.[15] This tannery and the one at Port Leyden leased by the Botchford brothers from the Lyon estate around 1872 were run by them with investments by Hersey and Company of Boston, and that firm was listed as owner of the Moose River Tannery when it burned in 1883.[16]

The Hersey Company negotiated a contract in 1884 with Nicholas Teal of Port Leyden to haul and deliver all freight to the Moose River Tannery. The contract specified the loading and unloading of "hides, leather, merchandise, grain, acid, oils or other without extra compensation," the payment of all damages to any freight such as breakage or getting wet by rain or any storm, and all road work necessary for freight to pass. All this was to be done for 9½¢ per hundred pounds.[17] A newspaper account later notes that "Due to Mr. Teal's inability to read or write, he was taken advantage of, and forced into bankruptcy."[18]

Local historian Joseph F. Grady notes that a band of St. Regis Indians was employed at the Moose River Tannery. According to David Beetle, who talked with old timers who remembered the tannery, the Moose River smelled for a considerable distance from its banks.[19]

The Census valued the 60,000 sides produced in 1870 at $294,000. That value is the second highest of any tannery in the Adirondacks in the 1870 Census. Only the Greig Tannery was larger. Hence, if production is the criterion, then Lyon and Snyder is again near the top in any contest for largest.

---

[15] New York, Vol. 147, p. 263, R. G. Dun and Co.

[16] New York, Vol. 147, p. 350, R. G. Dun and Co.

[17] Contract between Nicholas Teal and Hersey and Company

[18] Newspaper article on the Teal family believed to have been clipped from the **Boonville Herald**, in the collection of M. J. Conway.

[19] Beetle, *Up Old Forge Way*, p. 27

H. J. and G. M. Botchford & Co.

The Botchford sons, with their father David, had interests in four tanneries in Lewis County: the Mammoth Tannery described above, Moose River Number Two built in 1879, one on Otter Creek above Partridgeville, and a fourth in the Town of Diana. Actually, if you consider their brief attempt to revive the Port Leyden Tannery, they had interests in five of the county's tanneries. During the short period, little more than a decade, in which the Botchfords were active in tanning in Lewis County, it was said that the money behind their three operations was Charles Hersey and Co. of Boston.[20] Whether it was the family or the Boston company that benefited most from the Botchfords' Lewis County tanneries is unclear; what is known is that the Botchfords produced more sides in a year and had a greater value of production than any other family group or corporation in the Adirondacks.

The father, David, had been involved in Catskill tanneries at Hunter in Greene County and at Woodland in Ulster County. Henry J. was born in Ulster County, trained as a lawyer for a time, and served in the Civil War, rising from private to Captain. Henry's wife was a Woodworth, a daughter of another Ulster County tanning family. He arrived in Lewis County around 1870, built or rebuilt the Otter Lake Tannery, and became associated with the Moose River Tannery. He was a master at trade, knowledgeable about both the theory and practice of leather making. "In the National Tanners' Exchange held in Philadelphia in 1876 and in New York in 1877, he was prominent among the debaters on the art of leather tanning."[21] He ran for the State Assembly and Senate, winning a seat in the latter, from which he was disqualified because he served as postmaster of Moose River Settlement at the time.

Otter Creek, Otter Lake, Partridgeville, or Glensdale Tannery

This tannery was variously known by all four names. It was built upstream on Otter Creek, close to John Brown's Tract. The creek was dammed at the site of the tannery, hence the name "lake." The Partridge family had a sawmill at a second dam

---

[20] New York, Vol. 147, p. 310, R. G. Dun and Co.

[21] Hough, ibid, p. 279

downstream, explaining why the tannery was sometimes called the Partridgeville Tannery.

The Otter Creek Tannery was 360 by 50 feet with 124 vats and four leaches.[22] It employed upwards of fifty men and annually consumed 4,000 cords of bark to produce 30,000 sides of sole leather. According to some accounts, it was built in 1867 by H. J. and G. M. Botchford and burned in 1870, only to be rebuilt. However unclear the origins of the tannery, the Botchfords apparently joined up temporarily with Chester J. Lyon, who was an heir of his father Lyman's estate, to form Lyon and Botchford, the name by which the Otter Creek Tannery was briefly known. Chester lost heavily and in 1872 was "considered as having failed individually and will close the tannery."[23] George M. Botchford, the less well-known brother, ran the tannery from then until it closed in 1889. When it ceased operating, the shortage of bark was given as the reason for closing. As early as 1880, the tannery, located in the town of Grieg, was pulling bark from distant forests in Brantingham Township and the Brown's Tract.

Its size and capacity made it a fairly typical Adirondack tannery and associated with it were 35 tenement[24] houses. The real property was valued at $58,000 in 1880, a decrease from the 1870 value of $75,000. Also decreasing in this interval were the profits, for 36,000 sides in 1870 were worth $150,000, while 60,000 sides were worth only $140,000 a decade later. This meant that profits were shrinking: in 1870 the gain exceeded $40,000; in 1880 costs ($108,000 for leather, as much as $16,000 for 4,700 cords of bark, and wages of over $12,000) equaled and probably exceeded profits.

In 1889, Charles F. Partridge purchased the tannery, along with the store, houses, and shops, and converted it to a hardwood sawmill. However, Hersey and Company of Boston, which assumed ownership of much of the Botchford property, must have retained 400 acres of the Otter Creek Tannery's land, for there is a contract between an assignee of the Hersey Company (bankruptcy again!) for the 1895-sale of that land for a mere $300.[25]

---

22 Bowen, ibid, p. 364

23 New York, Vol. 147, p. 198, R. G. Dun and Co.

24 Worker's houses were called tenement houses in contemporary accounts.

25 Lewis County Historical Society

Beach and Dodge Tannery

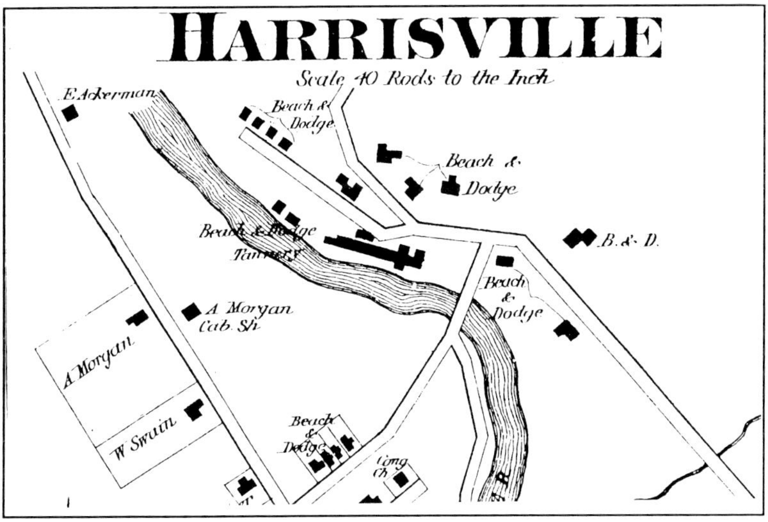

From the 1875 Atlas, courtesy of the Adirondack Museum

In 1880, Henry J. and his father purchased a tannery in Harrisville, which was located on the Oswegatchie in the Town of Diana. That year the Census valued its production at $136,000. The 3,500 cords of bark used all came from the surrounding town. This tannery was the former Beach and Dodge Tannery, which was built in 1859 and enlarged in 1866. According to the 1870 Census, it employed sixty workers and its production totaled 54,000 sides worth $275,000. It cost $22,000 to obtain the 4,000 cords of bark consumed that year, a price that indicates that the cost of bark was rising quickly in the Black River Valley.

The Diana tannery burned in 1877, and it was insured for $50,000. Associated with it was a large tract of timberland worth upwards of $40,000. Beach and Dodge planned to rebuild the tannery, but sold the property to the Botchfords.[26] The Botchfords may also have been associated in this venture with Charles W. Hersey and Co. of Boston. In 1879, it was said that David Botchford, "a practical tanner," had "a good bargain on buying

[26] New York, Vol. 148, p. 310, R. G. Dun and Co.

the tannery,"[27] and he, too, shipped his hides to Thorne Watson of New York.

Moose River Tanneries under the Botchfords

Henry J. Botchford was associated with the Moose River Tannery as early as 1870, the year after the death of Lyman R. Lyon. The Botchfords' Moose River Tannery, the one owned originally by Lyon and Snyder, was twice the size of their Otter Creek Tannery in both capacity and value of real property. In 1872, it was reported that the Botchfords intended "to start at the Moose River Tannery, which is at present occupied by Todd and Kennedy."[28] At first they tanned green hides at Moose River that were supplied by Thorne, Watson and Co. R. G. Dun ledgers reported that the tannery and adjacent lands were sold to Thorne, Watson and Co. after a foreclosure of $44,000, and the Botchford brothers were said to own only a half interest in it.[29] By 1874, Henry J. gained control of the Moose River Tannery. He experienced difficulties in 1878, although some of the problems may have had more to do with a suit with the Lyon estate than with the economic climate.

Whatever the climate, it must have changed the very next year, for Henry J. began building a tannery, known as Moose River Number Two, less than a third of a mile upriver from the Mammoth Tannery. Constructed during 1879 and 1880, this tannery had only 150 vats, compared with the 220 of the original building. The foundations of the vat building, approximately 240 by 40 feet and the parallel depression that indicates a second building of equal size lie directly behind the Lawrence Hotel site. One end of the vat building is a smooth-faced, laid-up wall over ten feet tall. The vat building has a curious ten-foot square similarly walled structure about mid-way in the structure. It is possible that rerouting of the road has cut off a few feet from the buildings, which now are about fifty feet from the river. The building was said to be 310 feet by 50 feet wide. Given the odors associated with tanneries, its location so close to the hotel is strange.

It is unlikely that the 1880 Census figures cover production at both sites, but production at Moose River was certainly

---

27 New York, Vol. 147, p. 310, Vol, 148, p. 350, R. G. Dun and Co.

28 New York, Vol. 147, p. 161, R. G. Dun and Co.

29 New York, Vol. 147, p. 161, R. G. Dun and Co.

greater than a decade earlier. In 1880, the real property was valued at $150,000. With 75,000 sides worth $300,000 produced, the tannery had the largest recorded production value for 1880. That Census indicates the Botchford Tannery consumed 3,750 cords of bark, pulled mostly from John Brown's Tract. With wages of $40,000 for an average 123 employees and raw hides worth $225,000, yielding a profitability factor of 11.7%, even this large operation must have been barely profitable in 1880.

The Botchford Fortunes

In 1881, Henry J. Botchford arranged to construct eleven miles of telegraph line from his home in Port Leyden to the tannery store at Moose River Settlement. He died in 1882 at the age of 42. The Mammoth Moose River Tannery burned in 1883. At that time, Hershey and Co. was listed as owner and the loss forced the Boston firm to make an assignment of the property. This bankruptcy clouded ownership of the property for many years.

G. M. Botchford continued to run Moose River Number Two at least through 1888. The **Boonville Herald** of January 1888 describes the operation in detail and adds the note that the bark piles were in tiers about 600 feet long, ten feet wide and thriteen feet high. It reported that well-informed employees thought the tannery would not operate after the following season - the amount of bark brought in being much less than before.

Not only did Botchford have the greatest value of production at the Moose River site for a single tannery in 1880 in the Adirondack region, the family's combined businesses dwarfed all other Lewis County giants. Untangling their business record has been difficult because there is a continuous line of financial records for only one tannery at Moose River. It is not really clear whether the Botchfords or Hershey and Co. benefited most from the Lewis County investments.

From 1874 on, R. G. Dun and Co. indicates that the Botchford firm was associated with Low Hersey and Co. of Boston.[30] The Hersey Company was said to have a controlling interest in the Moose River Tannery and held a mortgage on the Botch-

---

[30] New York, Vol. 147, p. 253, R. G. Dun and Co.

ford's Greig tannery (presumably the Otter Creek Tannery).[31] The Otter Creek Tannery continued to be profitable through this period as did the tannery at Diana. Nevertheless, Herny J.'s death in 1882 and the fire at Moose River in 1883 must have had a detrimental effect. Shortly afterwards, Hersey and Co. is listed as owner of most of the Botchford properties, all of which closed within a few years. The new tannery at Moose River Settlement apparently produced leather for only a few years, giving it one of the briefest existences of any tannery.

The family, which truly deserved claims to greatness, with the largest tannery and the highest production value in the Adirondack region, disappeared from the scene. The Botchfords for all the extent of their tanneries, were only dominant for the span of a little more than a decade.

Beaver Falls Tannery

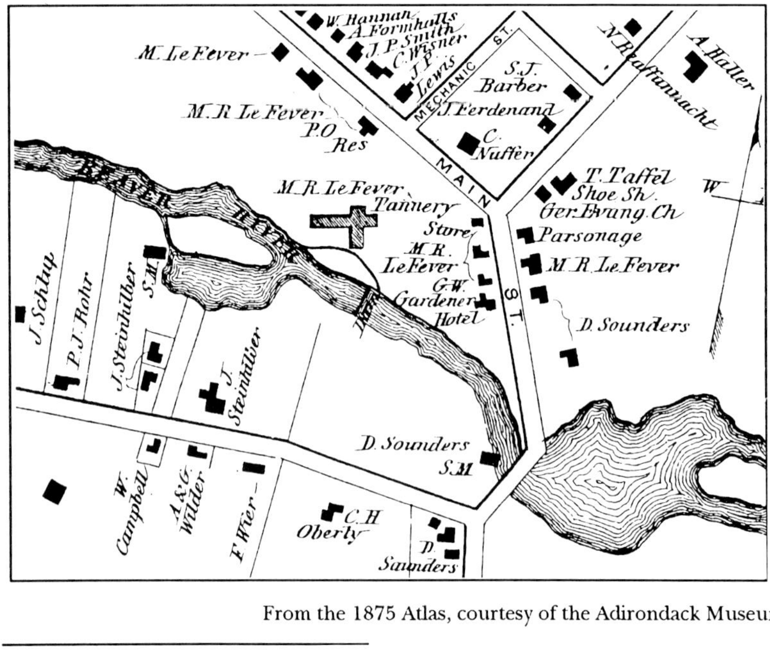

From the 1875 Atlas, courtesy of the Adirondack Museum

---

31 ibid

Beaver Falls Tannery and bark sheds, courtesy Lewis S. VanArnum

Among the oldest and longest-running of the larger tanneries in Lewis County was the Beaver Falls establishment of Martin R. LeFevre. It was opened in 1852 and closed in 1894. Hiram Lewis, the first owner, sold it to Wm. C. LeFevre in 1856 and his son, Martin R. LeFevre, took it over in 1864 after the closing (or sale) of the LeFevre Northampton, Fulton County, tannery, which he had managed. He ran the Beaver Falls Tannery continuously for almost thirty years. Even the fire of 1874 did not slow the business for it was insured for $7,500 and rebuilt "better than before."[32] The rebuilt tannery contained eighty

Barking crew, Beaver Falls, left rear Abram N. VanArnum and J. D. Lewis, courtesy Lewis S. VanArnum.

[32] New York, Vol. 147, p. 154, R. G. Dun and Co.

vats.[33] The hides were furnished by LeFevre and Smith, brokers from Albany. William LeFevre was a member of this firm, which also owned a thousand acres of timberland in Croghan.[34]

Lewis S. VanArnum, Beaver Falls historian, wrote that "My father came to Beaver Falls in 1881. He was then nine years old. His father worked for the tannery as foreman of the wood's crew. For the next thirteen years, my father was in and out of the tannery and was familiar with its operation."[35] Mr. VanArnum had a picture showing his grandfather, Abram N. (the bearded man with an account book), his father, and Martin R. LeFevre, owner of the tannery and the company store. Also shown are J. D. Lewis and his wife Julia Slocum Lewis. J. D. Lewis worked for the tannery when he first came to Beaver Falls, but left the tannery to found the Beaver Falls Pulp and Paper Company.

Compared with other Lewis County tanneries that were close to or in the Adirondack region, the LeFevre Tannery was modest in size, its production rising from 10,000 sides in 1860 to 14,000 in 1870 to 18,000 in 1880. Although it appears to have been a profitable operation even in 1880, its profits were never large, and its profit margin throughout was the smallest in Lewis County.

Bark loads waiting to be weighed, Beaver Falls Tannery, courtesy of Lewis S. VanArnum.

---

33 Hough, ibid, p. 167-168

34 New York, Vol. 147, p. 154, R. G. Dun and Co.

35 Letter to the author

Croghan Tanneries

Two tanneries were located in the Town of Croghan (variously spelled Grogan) on the Beaver River.

Rice Brothers

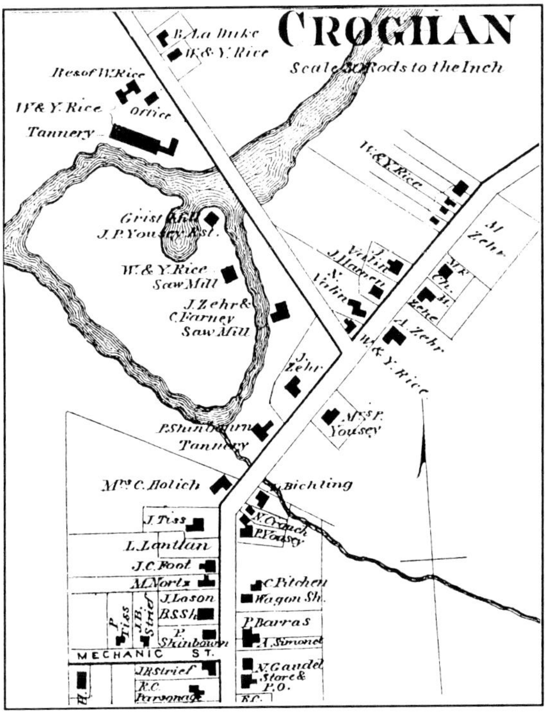

From the 1875 Atlas, courtesy of the Adirondack Museum

One of the tanneries was owned by the Rice brothers (see below for their story). Their Croghan Tannery had half the capacity of the one they built at Jerden Falls, but it was still an extensive establishment. The Croghan Tannery was built in 1857, and rebuilt after an 1865 fire.[36] It tanned 16,000 sides in 1860 and must have been enlarged when it was rebuilt, for it tanned 30,000 sides worth $120,000 in 1880. Sherward Bullard and Company bought the Croghan Tannery in 1883 and kept it open until it was incorporated into the United States Leather Company in 1893.

Belfort Tannery

The second sole-leather tannery in the Town of Croghan was upriver on the Beaver in the settlement of Belfort. It was

---

[36] Hough, ibid, pp. 167-168

built in 1865 and owned in the 1860s by Wm. H. Peer[37] and in the 1870s by James H. Morrow. In 1870, this tannery produced $100,000 worth of sides (22,000 sides), a smaller production by 5,270 sides but greater value by $10,000 than the tannery output in 1880, when it was owned by Samuel Branaugh. This tannery, with a capacity of 35,000 sides, worth just over $90,000, consumed 3,500 cords of bark a year and employed upwards of twenty-five men. It remained in operation until 1891.[38]

New Bremen Tannery

The Belfort Tannery was one of two owned by Branaugh. His New Bremen Tannery, built in 1853, experienced serious difficulties in the early 1860s[39] It passed into the hands of David Stewart in 1868. Thorne, Watson and Company held a mortgage on the New Bremen Tannery and foreclosed in 1875, selling it immediately to Hiram Gowdy.[40] In 1880, the Census lists Gowdy as owner of two tanneries: the one on Crystal Creek in New Bremen that produced 33,000 sides of sole leather worth $132,000 in 1880 and a much smaller one on Mill Creek in Lowville. The Lowville tannery was built in 1863 and employed only six or seven men. The building, 127 feet by 35 feet and two and a half stories high for a third of its length, was fairly small.[41]

Jerden Falls

Reminiscences of a Tannery Owner's Daughter

The hamlet of Jerden Falls was originally called Jordan Falls for its location near the falls on the Oswegatchie River. An itinerant preacher visited the falls on the Oswegatchie and took out his hymn book to sing "On Jordan's stormy banks I stand"

---

37 Hough, ibid, pp. 67-68; Peer is variously spelled Pier in the Census and other accounts.
38 Bowen, ibid, p. 102
39 New York, Vol. 147, p. 92, R. G. Dun and Co.
40 Hough, ibid, p. 490
41 *Lewis County Gazetteer*, p 117

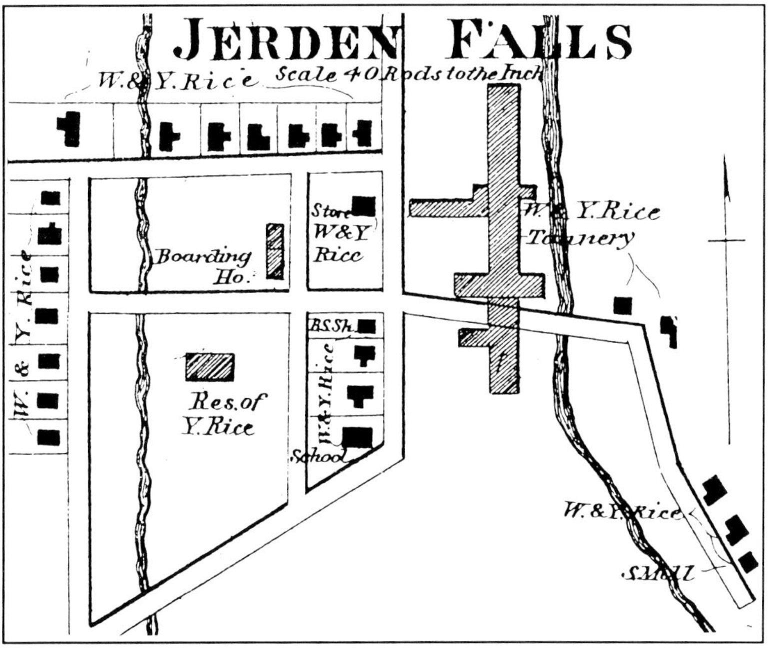

From the 1875 Atlas, courtesy of the Adirondack Museum

and the place was named Jordan Falls after that.[42] Sometime later, the name came to be spelled with two e's, though both spellings were used at the time the tannery was there.

Another of the "largest" in the area, this tannery was built in 1870 with a capacity of 70,000 sides of sole leather. It used upwards of 7,000 cords of bark and employed forty men year-round, one-hundred in bark season. The tannery was built on the West Branch of the Oswegatchie River and a considerable settlement grew up around it in the decade after it was built. A century later, the site was just the intersection of two dirt roads back in the wilderness.

The tannery, which sometimes went by the name Castorland, was owned by the Rice brothers, Wirt and Yale, who reported in the 1870 Census that they produced 60,000 sides worth $240,000, using 6,000 cords of bark. The Census for 1880

[42] Unpublished article by Marjorie Hough in the Lewis County Historical Society collection.

Jerden Falls Tannery with at least ten wagons of bark lined up in front of the ends of four bark sheds.

indicates that their operation on the Oswegatchie remained profitable, with production twice that of their Croghan Tannery.

Bark remained plentiful until the area was ravaged by forest fires in 1888, but transportation was always a problem at the Jerden Falls Tannery. Hides had to be hauled by horse and wagon first to Croghan then on to the railhead at Castorland[43], where the company shipped 1,000 tons of leather to New York City by rail annually. The first part of the trip to Croghan was over "fifteen miles of poor and sandy road, three miles of which was corduroy."

Sherwood Bullard and Company supplied hides to the tannery for many years.[44] The Jerden Falls Tannery was sold in

---

[43] There is some confusion about the name Castorland. There was a railhead by that name, some miles distant from the tannery, but the name was also applied to the tannery, and Susan Rice remembered that each side of leather shipped from Jerden Falls was stamped with the name Castorland. The name Castorland was originally applied to the lands in the western Adirondack region that were owned and briefly settled shortly after 1800 by immigrants from France.

[44] New York, Vol. 148, p. 423, R. G. Dun and Co.

1883 to Bullard and Son of the Swamp in New York City and closed right after the fires in 1888. In 1893, the Jerden Falls Tannery was incorporated into the United States Leather Company when the Bullard Company's other tanneries at Star and Belfort (Croghan) were also added to the giant corporation.[45] Shortly afterwards, all three tanneries were closed.

For a while, Erien Yousey farmed the abandoned Jerden Falls Tannery site, which was sold to the state in 1934 and reforested by the CCC shortly afterwards.

The Rice Family

The Rice family had its origins in the Catskills, learning the tannery trade there before heading for Lewis County. Three brothers were the sons of Amos Rice of Windham. Wirt Rice came to Lewis County in 1853 and apprenticed at a small tannery business in Greig owned by Cyrus Pratt. A second brother, Blair, had worked at a tannery in Broome County. In 1857, they built the tannery in Croghan. They were joined by the third brother, Yale, in 1864. Yale Rice had been a bookkeeper in his uncle Loring Andrews' wholesale leather house in New York City. The Croghan Tannery was rebuilt in 1865, after a fire destroyed part of the buildings.

The Rice brothers bought the Oswegatchie tract in 1870, quickly building not only the tannery, but a company store, a school house, and a boarding house with one hundred beds. Their father was briefly associated with them before retiring to Lowville. Blair soon left the enterprise, but his brothers remained. Wirt was the practical tanner, and Yale the businessman, traveling twice a year to New York City to "see about contracts," according to his daughter. He discussed the business with their uncle, Loring Andrews, who served as broker for their hides and leather[46] and whose brokerage house presumably provided the brothers with investment capital.

Susan, daughter of Yale Rice, remembered going to the settlement before the tannery was in operation. "We slept in a shanty on a bed of pine boughs, ate bean soup at a long table outdoors, and in the evening St. Regis Indians who worked for

---

[45] Norcross, ibid, p. 188; it is unclear what tannery he refers to as Star.
[46] Hough, unpublished article, ibid.

the firm danced on a bridge over the Oswegatchie to entertain us." Later, Susan wrote about the tannery in "Family Reminiscences," a paper quoted by Marjorie G. Hough in an article in **North Country Life**.

In 1871, the Yale Rices built a house with a steep roof inset with dormer windows and a piazza all around bordered by rustic posts. The house was on a hill overlooking the Jerden Falls settlement, and the fact the house was never painted indicates the impermanence of the settlement, of which only the schoolhouse survived a century later.

Life in the wilds was softened by the regular arrival of many magazines, newspapers, and great numbers of books. Susan Rice's reminiscences are the only extant recollections of family life at an Adirondack tannery. She portrays an amazingly primitive life, which stands in sharp contrast to the regular arrival of the **New York Tribune, Harper's Bazaar, and Scribners.**

> *Three times a week the teams came, three or four big wagons drawn by large horses, bringing hides and provisions, and the mail. We could hear the rumble of the wagons on the corduroy road long before they came in sight, and awaiting their unloading was always exciting.*
>
> *While the winters were long, with snow piled high around us, paths tunneled to the school house and store, we had fun coasting and playing in the snow, and there always seemed plenty to do. Few visitors came in the winter. A Methodist minister came once in two weeks and preached in the school house.*
>
> *What did we do in Jordan [sic] Falls for a doctor? We never thought we needed one! In pioneer fashion, our mother had no doctor to care for her even when a baby sister, Marion, was born, or later when John and Bess followed. Aunty Dekin, a practical nurse and midwife, came a few weeks before the expected event. She was a sensible, pleasant woman, and we enjoyed her visits. I think, but I am not sure, that a doctor from Croghan sometimes was sent for, but he was never in our house that I know of. When I had chicken pox very badly, and was left with a running sore throat behind my ear, Father consulted an herb doctor by the name of Carley; he prescribed a poultice of grated carrots, which might have been more beneficial, I imagine, taken internally, though I certainly did recover. Mother dosed us for small ailments with castor oil and rhubarb syrup. I remember being given picra, a dark villainous compound. For colds, we had some sickish stuff called hive syrup, and something called squills. Father*

drank boneset tea when he was out of sorts, or took rhubarb root. Mother had violent headaches, which she endured stoically. Sometimes she applied a mustard plaster to her neck, or a large horseradish leaf.

Mother thought raw foods harmful. In the spring she and Annie Crimmins made root beer, supposed to be wholesome. We were a healthy family, really, and throve on our diet of bread, potatoes, codfish and mackerel, green vegetables in the summer only, and plenty of apples in winter. Father always bought five or six barrels of apples in the fall and stored them in the cellar. The firm bought a herd of cows and milk was sold at the boarding house; we had milk, but I do not ever remember drinking it. The only cereal I remember was corn meal mush. A meat wagon came once in awhile, and we had fresh meat then. Both at our house and in the boarding house, a good deal of salt pork and milk gravy were served. When the pigs were killed, we had sausage and wheat cakes.

Buckwheat cakes we had for breakfast all winter. They were made of yeast, and of course Mother made her own yeast. The batter was mixed at night and set in a warm place to rise. Each morning part of the batter was kept over to start the next day's cakes. We used raw coffee beans which we roasted in the oven and then ground in a coffee grinder. We children were allowed to drink coffee Sunday mornings. Butter was bought by the tub, covered with brine. As I remember, Father bought it in Croghan. In the spring when the maple trees were tapped, we feasted on maple sugar. Wax [maple syrup] on snow and stirred sugar were great delicacies. The syrup would not keep until the winter, but the stirred sugar was moulded into square loaves which were cut up and melted for winter pancakes.

In the woods were wild raspberries and some blackberries. Mother had currant and gooseberry bushes in the garden. She made preserves for winter but they were only used for company; we ate applesauce or dried peaches, usually. We never saw oranges, except at Christmas. Grapefruit was unknown. Grapes could not be grown because of the short growing season.

The company store sold staple dry goods ordered from Utica. Sometimes Father went down there to select the goods. In winter we wore woolen dresses covered by long-sleeved gingham aprons to keep them clean. We wore knit hoods in winter, and woolen shawls. I never had a coat until we moved to Lowville where I was to go to school. In summer, we had shakers (a kind of straw bonnet) or fancy sunbonnets. When we went to Callicoon in summer, we wore hats, but how we got them, I don't know.

When Susan was sixteen and her sister Milly thirteen, they went to school in Lowville, renting a house near their grandfather.

Marian, John and Bess had whooping cough that winter, and for Mother it was a hard and trying time. The next winter, after a summer back in Jordan Falls, we all had mumps.

We never went back to Jordan Falls after our two winters in Lowville, for that summer the firm decided to sell the tanneries to Bullard & Co. of Boston, for $200,000. Uncle Wirt had already moved to Carthage, but he took his share and invested it in a tannery in Potosky [Petosky], Michigan, joining his brother, Blair.

Greig Tanneries

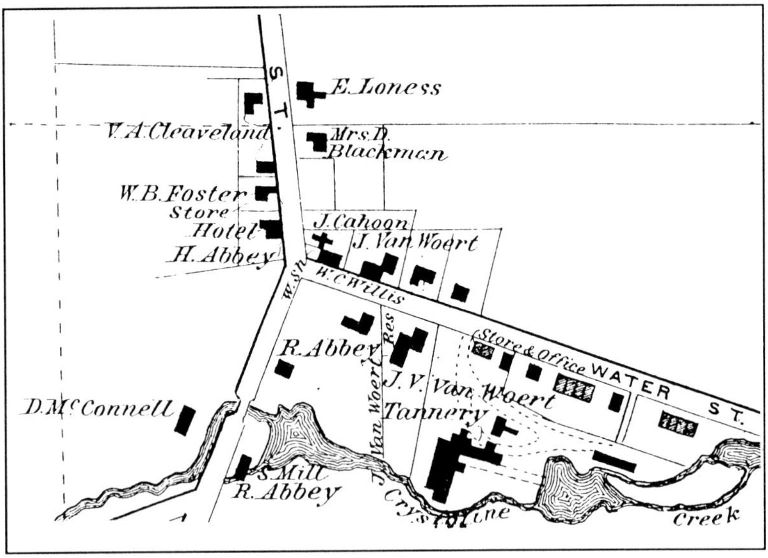

From the 1875 Atlas, courtesy of the Adironack Museum

There was a small tannery in Greig and two distinctly larger ones. Both of the larger ones were ultimately owned by Jacob VanWoert, but inconsistencies in local histories make it difficult to be certain that information on them has been properly assigned. Both of the larger tanneries were apparently built about 1850 and later enlarged.

Brantingham or Upper Greig Tannery

The smaller of the two in the Town of Greig was built on Fish Creek, a tributary of the Black River, "in the spring of 1849 by Cyrus. R. Pratt"[47]. It went by the name Brantingham or Upper[48] Greig Tannery. It had fifty-eight vats, four leaches, seven pools, and twelve handlers-vats.[49]

Sometime around 1870 it was acquired by Jacob VanWoert, the son of John V. VanWoert of the Swamp. The father had settled in New York from Massachusetts in 1829 and established a firm, which remained in business for 63 years and owned a number of tanneries in New York and Pennsylvania. The parent firm undoubtedly financed the son's tanneries.[50] In 1870 the Brantingham Tannery produced 42,000 sides of leather worth $124,000 and in 1872 it tanned 36,000 sides of sole leather, employed twenty-three men, and consumed 3,600 cords of bark.

Greig Steam Tannery or the Lower Greig Tannery

The Greig Steam Tannery was located in Grieg Village and was built about 1849 by John R. Williams of Troy. This tannery had a tremendous capacity (70,000 sides) and it is unclear whether it was built with this capacity or more likely enlarged at some later time in its existence.

Ownership of this Greig tannery has been difficult to trace. Hough says it passed through the hands of various owners and that Cyrus R. Pratt had a three-fourths interest in it. He sold part of it to Lyman R. Lyon and for a time it was run by Lyon and Snyder. According to the 1870 Census, it was at one time owned by Chester J. Lyon. The tannery would have passed to Chester Lyon on the death of his father, and this undoubtedly accounts

---

47 Hough, ibid, p. 234

48 The confusion in the Town of Grieg centers around whether this was the Upper or Lower Tannery. The 1874 Gazetteer confirms that this was the smaller of VanWoert's tanneries.

49 *Lewis County Gazetteer*, p. 96

50 Norcross, *A History of the New York Swamp*, pp. 179-180

for the fact that the tannery was listed in Chester's name in 1870. His tenure as a tanner was short-lived, for the buildings were sold to Jacob VanWoert in 1870.[51]

Capitalized in 1870 at $100,000, with fifty workers, it was capable of producing 70,000 sides annually. The value of the tannery's 1870 production, $315,000, was the greatest of any tannery listed anywhere in the Census. The tannery was said to have three wheels, four rollers, four hide mills, four turbines, three bark mills, and one elevator.

It is not known whether the figures for VanWoert's production in 1880 are for this or both tanneries, but the 1880 Census reports that 64,000 sides (worth $250,000) were tanned by him. That year, the tannery consumed 5,000 cords of bark that were hauled from the eastern part of the Town of Greig.

Other Lewis County Tanneries

The rest of the tannery records are so fragmented that it is difficult to tell precisely where they were and who owned them, but most were located to the west of the larger ones described above.

Among the tanneries recorded in 1850 was the very small establishment of F. W. Northrup, who also made shoes and boots.

West Turin had several small tanneries: John Fleishman in 1870, L. Sprague and Sons, 1870; Wm Witke, 1880. Turin had a tannery so small Horace Johnson only had one employee in 1860. Cyrus S. Bill had an equally small tannery in Turin, though it was in continuous operation for at least two decades, spanning the interval between 1850 and 1870.

Leyden had another small tannery recorded in 1870 as owned by Mills and Rasada. Early tanneries were also found in the towns of Martinsburg and Pinckney. Local histories record tanneries in 1870 in Deweyville, Dayansville, and Constableville.

Campbell J. Switzer had a small tannery on the Deer River in the 1870s. This may be the same tannery known as the Austin

---

51 Hough, ibid, p. 234

Tannery that was said to flourish in 1873 through 1877. This tannery closed in 1880 and was destroyed by flood in 1890.

The Town of Osceola in Lewis County had one modest tannery in 1870, owned variously by Wilcox and Earl, and Wm. R. Willetts.

When comparing the Census with business registers and local histories, it is difficult to sort out the proprietors' names; often there is no concurrence. The 1872 Business Directory listed eighteen tanneries, about the same number as the 1870 Census, but many of the names are different. The directory also lists thirteen tanners in Greig, twelve in Croghan, two in Diana, four in Leyden, two in Lowville, and five in New Bremen. These numbers represent the foremen and tanners, not the bulk of the tannery workers.

Tanning Ends in Lewis County

Tanbarking was a major event. An 1874 account relates that "the bark peelers of the Moose River Tannery were paid off Friday last; made the village lively in preparation for the July 4th celebration."[52] The bark supply certainly held up through the 1870s. "A large number of teams from Canada went on their way to the woods of Lewis County" in 1879.[53]

Many of the tanneries in Lewis County closed during the decade of the 1880s. Three of the largest, owned by the Rice brothers, the Botchfords, and Jacob VanWoert, were taken over by Boston firms in 1883. All had reported difficulty harvesting bark in later years. But as a footnote to the shortage of bark, it should be observed that the Frank A. Cutting Company, dealer in hemlock bark located in Boston, who owned a huge bark track on the St. Lawrence and Franklin County border, contracted with the firm of Mess. Johnston and Son of Port Leyden in 1907 for 2,000 pounds at $5.50 a cord. The contract, specified bark that was of good thickness, flat and well-saved, so it is likely the supply was a remnant of earlier years. Perhaps the Lewis County tanneries that experienced problems in the 1880s and closed

---

52 **Lowville Journal and Republican,** July 8, 1874

53 ibid, Jan. 28, 1879

precipitously in the early 1890s still had a bark supply when they ceased operations. And, perhaps, this also substantiates the conclusion that the economic upheavals of the tanning industry in 1883 were as fatal to the industry in Lewis County as was the shortage of bark.

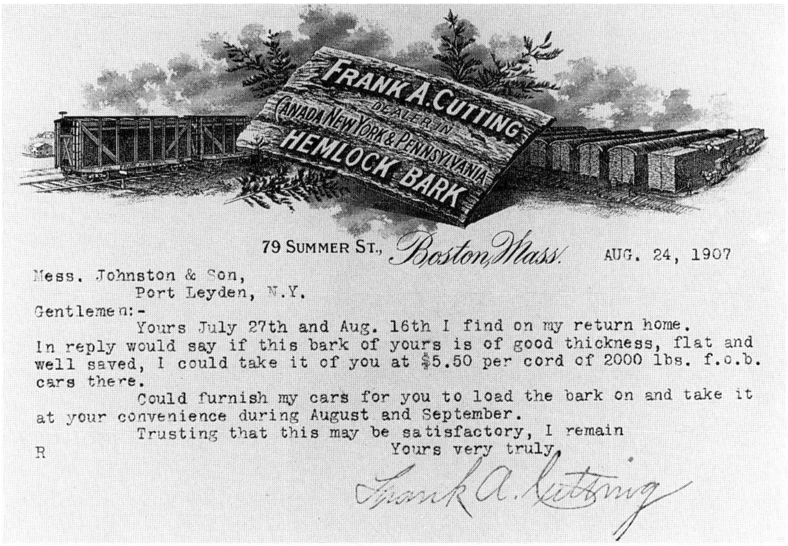

FRANK A. CUTTING
DEALER IN
CANADA NEW YORK & PENNSYLVANIA
HEMLOCK BARK

79 SUMMER ST., Boston, Mass. AUG. 24, 1907

Mess. Johnston & Son,
Port Leyden, N.Y.

Gentlemen:-

Yours July 27th and Aug. 16th I find on my return home. In reply would say if this bark of yours is of good thickness, flat and well saved, I could take it of you at $5.50 per cord of 2000 lbs. f.o.b. cars there.

Could furnish my cars for you to load the bark on and take it at your convenience during August and September.

Trusting that this may be satisfactory, I remain

R

Yours very truly,

Frank A. Cutting

Courtesy of George Cataldo

XX

St. Lawrence County

St. Lawrence County had a number of tanneries in its northern farming communities and two significant sole-leather tanneries within or close to the present Park boundary. Both of these tanneries, the St. Lawrence Tannery at Colton and the Rice, Emery Tannery at Fine, are discussed in detail below and both are remarkable for their wonderfully preserved and accessible foundations, which invite exploration. Before discussing them, here is a brief survey of the county's other nineteenth century tanneries.

Rural St. Lawrence County in 1850 consisted of several small agricultural towns on the border of what is now the Adirondack Park. In the southwestern towns closest to the Park, only four tanners were listed in that year's Census: three were small, undoubtedly farmers who also tanned (one of whom was in Hopkinton, a town now in the Park); and one, the establishment of Erastus Vilas on the Oswegatchie, was large enough to employ six workers. In the more northern towns around Canton and Potsdam, closer to the St. Lawrence River, there were six tanneries with one or two workers, five with three workers. All of the county's tanneries tanned a mixture of hides and skins and all but one were small enough to be categorized Colonial tanneries.

The number of tanneries in 1850 decreased by two in the next decade; and, although thirteen Colonial tanneries remained, by 1860 their location and size began to reflect the transitions observed elsewhere in the north country. One of the larger tanneries, in Canton Village, tanned both hides and skins and employed ten workers. There was a cluster of tanneries on the Oswegatchie: the two small ones owned by Erastus Vilas and W. F. Griffin were long-running establishments, having been noted in the 1850 Census and the 1870 Census as well. They tanned both soles and uppers and each sold $500 worth of hair as a by-product. F. N. Burt had a "Morocco" tannery, and in

1870, when his establishment spent "two months at rest," he tanned 20,000 skunk skins worth $6,000.

By 1870, the size of the tanneries both inside and outside the Park had changed significantly. While there were still eleven Colonial tanners, there were seven large tanneries: Those in Parishville, Norfolk, Gouveneur, Morristown, and Edwards produced mostly soles with some upper leather. One tannery in this class managed to produce $54,600 worth of leather even though it had only seven employees. A Potsdam establishment, owned by Duff and Foster, produced $66,000 worth of leather; one in Canton produced $69,500 worth of leather.

At least ten Colonial tanners continued in St. Lawrence County in 1880, located in farming communities on the lower Oswegatchie River, Little River, the East and West Branches of the St. Regis River, Grasse River (two), and Trout Brook. Six more small tanneries with up to nine employees were scattered outside the present Blue Line.

In 1880, in addition to S. R. Spaulding's St. Lawrence Tannery and Rice, Emery's Fine Tannery, there were two other larger tanneries, located just outside the Park, one in "Pitcairn on the Racket"[1] [sic] and the other on the Grasse; they had productions valued at $47,500 and $37,000, respectively.

The St. Lawrence Tannery

The first of the larger-sole leather tanneries, the establishment of L. Hull, was built in 1856 in the Town of Colton, to the north of the present Park boundary. The site is on the Raquette River, "midway on the great fall."[2] As is the case everywhere else, the local history dubbed it the "largest in the State."[3] It was a considerable establishment because, according to the 1860 Census, it produced $80,000 worth of sole leather

[1] 1880 Census

[2] Reed, Lorena Bullis. *Colton*, p. 14

[3] To visit the site, park beside the Colton Historical Society Museum and walk along the trail beside the Raquette. The trail follows an old road to a new footbridge built by Niagara Mohawk Power Company over the flume below the dam. The ruins are between the trail and the river and begin immediately opposite the footbridge.

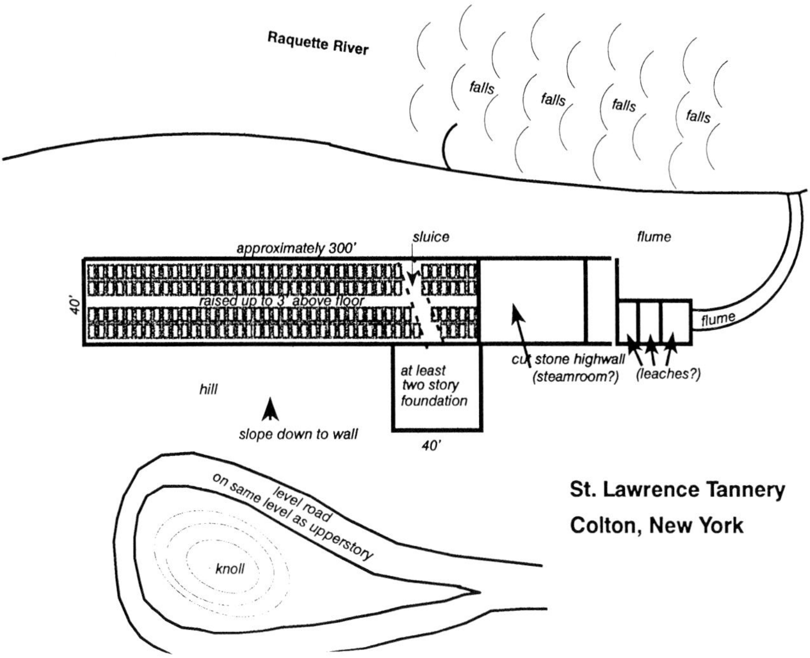

St. Lawrence Tannery
Colton, New York

tanned from American green hides and employed twenty-six workers.

The Hull Tannery was acquired by S. R. Spaulding Company in 1868. It is not clear whether the new owners enlarged the tannery or just increased production, but by 1868, well before the railroad, the tannery had grown to become the first of St. Lawrence County's truly large sole-leather tanneries. By 1870, it employed thirty-three workers and produced $200,000 worth of sole leather.[4]

"The tannery was 400 feet long and 42 feet wide with three leaches, which were eighteen feet in diameter. The leaches were eight feet deep and would hold twenty-two cords of bark. The vat building contained three hundred twenty vats and the tannery consumed five thousand cords of bark annually. One hundred teams were employed to haul in the bark from a radius of thirty miles."[5]

---

[4] 1870 Census, St. Lawrence County

[5] Reed, ibid, p. 30. The distance for hauling bark-thirty miles-is the largest quoted for any tannery in the north country. Because it exceeds the distance teams could travel in a day, the figure seems questionable.

The S. R. Spaulding Tannery was also called the St. Lawrence Tannery. S. R. Spaulding and Son was a Boston firm with tanneries also in Franklin and Hamilton counties. The senior Spaulding died in 1875. With Spaulding's death in 1875, the son, Edward G., took over the family business. The affairs of the tannery turned sour in 1876, and under the style of the son, E. G. Spaulding, it continued to decline. In 1877, there was a "serious interruption in the business," and before the end of 1878, the firm had failed. The tannery was acquired by Shaw Bros. of Boston in July of 1879.[6]

The 1880 Census notes that the tannery was located on the "Rackett [sic] River" and that its production value had dropped to $96,000 while the number of sides produced fell from 56,500 to 40,000. The Shaw Bros. firm failed in 1883 and the disposition of the Shaw tanneries is discussed in Chapter VII. The St. Lawrence Tannery was sufficiently well-located so that C. W. Clement, trustee for the failed Shaw Brothers firm, kept the business open until 1898.

A glimpse at the way the tannery was run in the years after the Shaw failure comes from recently discovered ledgers of the St. Lawrence Tannery. Like most remote tanneries, this one had a company store, and the finances of the store and the tannery and its workers are inexoribly intertwined.

The 1885 ledger names the workers, who were mostly Irish (there is an Irish Settlement Road leading west from Colton). It records pay vouchers to teamsters for hauling bark; to vendors for shipments of hay, beef, wood, honey, tallow, and oil; and to blacksmiths. Other payments were for taxes ($124.84), and for beam work ($7.36), piling (presumably bark, amounts ranging from $1.50 to $14.35 and totalling about $60.00)[7], and swamping [clearing brush], $5.00. Workers were paid for such tasks as grinding bark, rubbing spots, night work, yard work, work in handlers, and carting bark.

Regular payments were recorded to George E. VanArnum of the International Leather Company for raw hides. In the last years of the tannery's existence, the company store deducted amounts from worker's wages for merchandise, but almost every employee's account shows additional cash payments.

---

6 New York, Vol. 553, p. 579, R. G. Dun and Co.

7 Many teamsters were expected to unload and stack whatever they hauled. This is the only indication of a separate amount paid for piling bark.

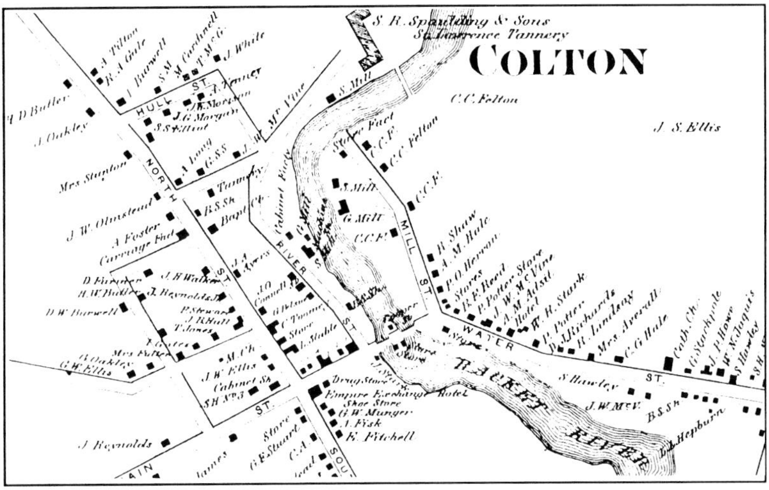

From the 1865 Atlas, courtesy of the Adirondack Museum

George B. Wilson, who managed the tannery in its later years, received $66.67 a month in 1897. Ledger entries report funds under such headings as "tan labor to sundries," "tan labor to cash," "tan trucking (31815 # @.09, $28.63 and 22710# plus 2 bbl oil 800 lbs, $19.97 and .82.)" Monies were constantly sent to the trustee or received from him for wages. As an indication of troubles to come, a check for $1,200 from the trustee C. W. Clement was "protested" in February of 1897, entailing a fee of $2.02, which had to be paid by the tannery.

Seasonally, the number of workers varied greatly, from fourteen laborers in December of 1896 to forty-nine laborers working in March of 1897, some of them hauling bark and some of them in the tannery. However up to 1898, there was no significant change in the number of workers, which might fortell the closing of the tannery. For all the transactions recorded in the ledgers, there is no real indication of failing profits—these were in the records of the parent company in Boston.

Rice, Emery and Company

St. Lawrence County's largest tannery was owned by Rice, Emery and Company of Boston. That firm, successor to N. W. Rice and Co. in 1883 with the addition of Rice's brother-in-law, experienced troubles along with other tanners in 1878 and 1883 and had shrunk considerably by 1886.[8] They had a tannery at Edwards and acquired the tannery at Griffin in Hamilton County in 1880, but their largest was at Fine in St. Lawrence County and was said to be the "best in the state."[9]

Earliest records of this tannery date to 1869[10] and it presumably began operation in late 1869 or early 1870, too late to be tallied in the 1870 Census. This was one of the last of the large tanneries built in the Adirondacks. It was located on the Oswegatchie[11] and in 1880 employed twenty-seven men and produced $200,000 of sides (54,000) from $145,000 worth of hides. When it was constructed, the nearest railroad station was DeKalb Junction on the Black River Railroad and R. J. Fairbanks of Hermon had the contract to transport hides and leather with his two- and four-horse teams.[12] It is amazing that this tannery could survive under these conditions.

The tannery, later called the Scriba Tannery in local histories, was located immediately south of the village of Fine, close enough for villagers to hear the mill whistle, which blew three loud blasts at 5:30 in the morning to awaken employees, again at 6:30 to signal time to start for the mill, and at 7:00 to indicate when workmen were supposed to start their day's work.[13]

Rice, Emery and Company had a tannery at Edwards, a few miles outside the present Blue Line. It remains something of an enigma; there are no Census records for this tannery so it is difficult to discover just how large it was. The tannery was

---

[8] Mass. Vol. 77, p. 416, R. G. Dun and Co.

[9] New York, Vol. 554, p. 938, R. G. Dun and Co.

[10] Brownell, *The Old Tannery at Fine*, **The Quarterly**, publication of the St. Lawrence County Historical Association, p. 7, says the construction of the tannery began in 1870 and that the tannery opened in 1872. Hough, p. 220 gives the date it started as 1870.

[11] The tannery is on the east side of Route 58, immediately north of the bridge over the Oswegatchie and north of Route 3 at Fine. A path leads into the woods at the north end of the guard rail and the tannery ruins begin within a hundred feet. They lie between the path and the river.

[12] Brownell, ibid

[13] Brownell, ibid

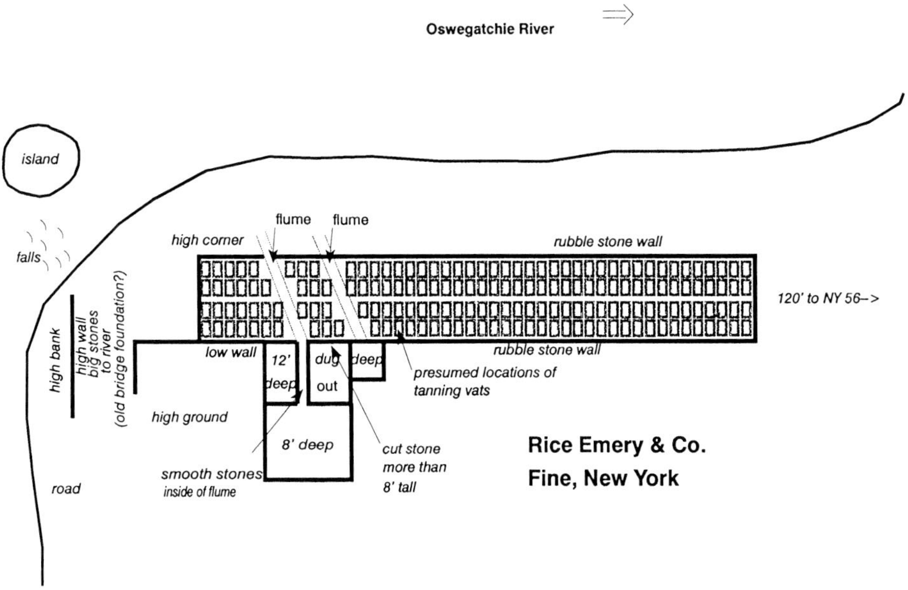

established in the late 1860s. It was owned by Gilbert and Co. in 1869 when that firm was dissolved, explaining why there is no 1870 Census record for the tannery. Rice, Emery and Company bought the tannery in 1872. It was said to be worth $100,000 in 1874.[14] No information has been found to indicate why the tannery closed in the next few years, but the lack of 1880 Census records indicates it was not operating in 1879. Perhaps economic problems of 1878 brought about the closing.

The arrival of the Carthage & Adirondack and Cranberry Lake railroads by the end of the 80s only briefly aided Rice, Emery and Company's large establishment at Fine. With other Rice, Emery and Company holdings, it was incorporated into the United States Leather Company in 1893, which only ran it for two more years, before dismantling it.

Because the Census no longer kept records on tanneries in 1890, there is little more hard information on the last few years of this tannery's existence and no indication of how profitable it was or how close it came to exhausting the local bark supply.

---

[14] New York, Vol. 553, p. 456 and Vol. 554, p. 708, R. G. Dun and Co.; these records from the ledgers are the only information on the Edwards Tannery, other than a brief mention in Hough.

The Four Large Northwestern Tanneries

One other St. Lawrence County tannery has an intriguing and incomplete record: Hough says that a tannery was built just across the county line from Harrisville in 1861 by Dr. Pearly Johnson. This tannery was owned in 1883 by Thomas E. Proctor and may have gone by the name Oswegatchie.[15]

Hough noted that four of the large tanneries in this northwestern corner of the Park–two in Harrisville (the Botchford tannery in the Town of Diana, Lewis County, and the one just across the line in St. Lawrence County owned in 1883 by Proctor), the Rice, Emery and Company Tannery at Fine in St. Lawrence County, and the Lewis County tannery at Jordan (Jerden) Falls–had a capacity to tan 300,000 sides a year, consuming 30,000 cords of bark, and clearing 7,000 acres of woodland a year.[16] The fact that these tanneries survived to become part of the United States Leather Company meant that hemlock was stripped from at least 100,000 acres of this corner of the north country in the closing years of the Adirondack hemlock bark tanning era.

---

[15] It is unclear which Census records refer to this tannery, but it is known that when Proctor joined the United States Leather Company, the only tanneries he owned that were still operating in the north country were on the Oswegatchie and at Wilna. His other tanneries were at Greenwood, Lycoming, Ralston, Penfield, Summit, Falls Creek, and Athens. Norcross, ibid, p. 186.

[16] Hough, *History of Lewis County*, p. 220

XXI

Jefferson County

Jefferson County's tannery record[1] only barely touches the Adirondack region; in the mid 1800s, it was largely a farming region, similar to St. Lawrence County. There is some indication that its tanneries depended on Adirondack bark; more likely their bark was supplied locally or by the Tug Hill region to the south. Jefferson County's tanneries are included here only to complete the north country record; to demonstrate the similarity between the evolution of tanneries in this county and in the Adirondack region; and to complete the ownership record of Thomas E. Proctor, one of the western Adirondacks' tanning giants.

In 1850 there was a total of twenty-one tanneries: nineteen with fewer than four workers, and two in the Watertown area with seven and nine workers and $18,000 and $20,000 production in sides, respectively.

Two more tanneries were added to the county Census in 1860; eleven were quite small (of which two have indecipherable Census records), three with about $10,000 in production and one slightly larger in Champion with five workers that used a couple hundred cords of bark. The production of the four tanneries in the Watertown area ranged in size from $17,500 to $68,000 with up to sixteen employees. A fairly large tannery in Rutland employed fourteen workers and produced $45,000 worth of sides.

The Town of Wilna, however, had three tanneries, with five, twenty, and ten workers, production worth $28,800, $39,600, and $52,500 and consumption of bark listed at one, three, and two thousand cords, respectively.[2]

---

1 This county report is produced solely from Census records and is therefore slim.

2 Unfortunately the Census does not explain why the tannery with the most employees and bark consumed had the smaller production. The information could have been erroneously entered in the Census ledger or the tannery could have been just starting

The number of tanneries had decreased to thirteen by 1870. The seven Colonial tanneries and two of the small tanneries, located in Rutland and Wilna, tanned both hides and skins, and one, Hiram Herring of Rodman, a tanner of upper leather, noted in the 1870 Census that "he lost money, paid too much for his kid!" The two small tanneries each had eight employees and produced about $60,000 worth of leather.

The third Wilna tannery was new, capitalized just prior to 1870 at $150,000 by Thomas E. Proctor. It employed twenty workers and produced $150,000 in output. More of Proctor's fortunes are discussed below.

The year 1880 saw two fewer tanneries, three very small ones, five mid-sized ones (with $25,000 to $35,000 production), and three giants. All but two tanned skins and upper leather.

Two tanneries in Carthage on the Black River drew bark from Wilna and Croghan and regions to the east in what is now the Adirondack Park. These employed twenty-three and twenty-eight workers and produced $180,000 and $88,000 worth of hides respectively. The process consumed 3,600 and 3,000 cords of bark at the two establishments.

The one remaining tannery in Wilna in 1880, still owned by Thomas E. Proctor, produced $100,000 worth of sides with forty workers. It consumed 3,500 cords of bark that was harvested in Lewis County to the south. As noted, Proctor's tanneries, here and in counties to the south (see Oneida and Herkimer County references)[3], were marginally profitable in 1880. This contrasts with the figures for 1870, which may be questionable because of the start-up of the tannery. Notably, in 1870, Proctor's Wilna tannery, recorded a gain of $91,500 and a profitability percentage of 48, about the highest of any computed for a north country tannery. One wonders if profits like this continued long enough to allow the company to write off the huge investment in the tannery complex before the margins began to shrink so precipitously. Proctor's experience in Jefferson County only adds to the reasons he must have had for being active in the incorporation of the United States Leather Company.

---

up. Discrepancies like this do make the Census information suspect, but, fortunately, such errors are few.

[3] There are insufficient records to compute the profitability of Proctor's St. Lawrence County tannery.

XXII

Franklin County

Two of Franklin County's tanneries, the ones at St. Regis Falls and Chateaugay, were located on the northern border of the Adirondack Park. All the others were well north of the present Blue Line, and none were further south in Franklin County, deep within the Park boundary.

There was a Colonial scale tannery in Fort Covington as early as 1818; northern Franklin County was very much an agricultural area and numerous small tanneries were scattered there. Tanning on a larger scale came into the northern part of the county via the Ogdensburg and Lake Champlain Railroad, which was completed in 1848.

The Mohawk and Malone Railroad, which finally opened up the southern part of the county, was not completed until the 1890s, just as tanning was disappearing from the region. The combination of agricultural lands in the northern part of the county and lack of railroads in the southern part explains the fact there were never more than a few of the larger sole-leather tanneries in the county before 1890. However, the northern component of the Mohawk and Malone Railroad, the Northern Adirondack Railroad Company, was extended south from Moira, a station to the west of Malone on the Ogdensburg and Lake Champlain Railroad, as far as St. Regis Falls in 1883 and to Santa Clara in 1884[1], helping to keep alive one of the Adirondack region's last tanneries. The railroad supported shipment of bark out of the region, making it an enigma why no larger tanneries were built further south along the route of the railroad as it was pushed into virgin territory in southern Franklin and St. Lawrence counties after 1890. Transportation seems to have had no effect on the failure of the tannery industry to expand.

In 1860, all the county's seven tanneries were fairly small and all but one was located in Malone and areas north of the

---

[1] Kudish, Michael. *Where Did the Tracks Go*, p. 61

present Adirondack Park. A. Lincoln tanned 2,000 sides of leather in Malone; an A. Lincoln (the same?) also had a tannery in Fort Covington; Hiram Thompson's establishment in Malone appears to be the largest Franklin County tannery.

The Chateaugay Tannery, which is not mentioned in the 1870 Census, employed four men in 1860. Owned by the Derby family from 1829 on, this tannery was leased to Enoch Miller of Malone during the Civil War. In 1876, it was purchased by William S. Douglas and considerably enlarged.

In addition to the St. Regis Tannery, described below, there were seven tanneries in Franklin County in 1870, four in Malone. Of those in Malone, the former A. Lincoln Tannery, now styled Lincoln and Miller, had nearly tripled the value of its production to almost $15,000. Sydney Gillett and Wallace Webster produced both sole and upper leather totalling $10,000 each. Enoch Miller was Malone's largest tanner, with 1870 production valued at $70,000. A. M. Lincoln's tannery in Fort Covington remained small and a new tannery was added to the county's Census for Moira, that of Jonas Clay.

In addition to St. Regis and a revived tannery at Chateaugay, there were seven other tanneries in the county listed in the 1880 Census. Lincoln & Miller on the Salmon River in Malone appears to have had a smaller output than the precedessor company of a decade earlier. Also on the Salmon in Malone was the R. L. Webster Tannery, but if it was a successor to the earlier Wallace Webster tannery, it certainly was enlarged during the decade of the 70s. By 1880 it produced 50,000 sides (probably upper leather) worth $180,000, and currying increased that value to $225,000. It employed upwards of one hundred men.

Two of Malone's tanneries burned on October 20, 1879, just as the 1880 Census was being completed. The fire started at the Webster Tannery and "instead of giving the alarm promptly, the (watch)man ran nearly a quarter of a mile to notify the foreman privately. By the time that the alarm was sounded, the entire structure was wrapped in flames, and with but a scant water supply, nothing could be done to save the establishment, nor much to protect adjacent property. The heat was so fierce that the Lincoln & Miller Tannery on the west side of the river was soon burning, and was destroyed."[2] The Webster Tannery

[2] Seaver, Frederick J. *Historical Sketches of Franklin County*, p. 466.

was rebuilt and "burned for the sixth and final time in 1893. ... It had not been operated for some time, and contained little stock. An offer of $15,000 for it had been made a short time previously, and refused as ridiculously inadequate."[3]

Webster Bros. had a second, smaller tannery in Moira capable of producing 30,000 sides a year, with fifteen employees. Moira's only other tanner, S. W. Lawrence employed no more than three men. Fort Covington's tannery, owned in 1880 by James Blansfield, was also small, with but four employees.

The tannery in Chateaugay, restyled as H. & A. Douglas & Co. by 1880, had been considerably expanded after William Douglas and his son Hiram bought it in 1872. The Census gives its 1880 production as nearly 22,000 sides worth $85,000, hardly enough to justify the claims of a local historian who said this "mammoth" tannery employed over one hundred men.[4] In 1891, "market conditions were ... unfavorable, and the concern lost money. It was burned in 1891."[5] The loss to its owners was said to be $65,000, but the loss to the village of an industry whose daily payroll was said to be $500. was devastating.

St. Regis Tannery

The county's largest sole-leather tannery, on the St. Regis River in the Town of Dickinson, on the northern border of the Adirondack Park, was built in 1865. Located just downstream from the bridge over the St. Regis in the settlement of St. Regis Falls, it was built by S. R. Spaulding & Company, which built the St. Lawrence Tannery on the Raquette about the same time. That company also acquired a large tannery in Wells in Hamilton County in 1869.

Title for the site of the St. Regis Tannery was obtained by Solomon R., Edward, and Francis Spaulding of Boston and James H. Young, who supervised the building of the tannery and became its first superintendent. When it failed for the first time in 1878, it was operating under the style of Spaulding and

[3] ibid, p. 467
[4] ibid, p. 256
[5] ibid, p. 256

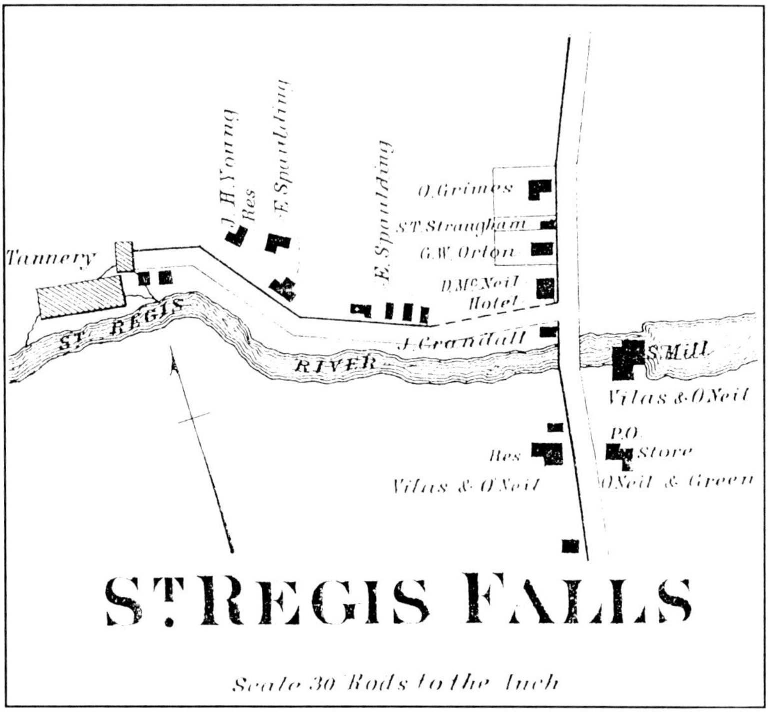

From the 1865 Atlas, courtesy of the Adirondack Museum

Bumstead. Perly D. Moore and Co. leased the tannery for a year or two around 1877 or 1878. The Moore Co. also had a large establishment on the Salmon River in Malone in 1880 and Moore's brothers were both tanners in nearby Clinton County. The St. Regis Tannery was acquired by the Shaw Brothers firm of Boston in 1879 and converted into an upper-leather tannery.[6] In 1880, Moore appears to have had as small a profit margin at his Salmon River Tannery as the Shaw company had at St. Regis; and neither were very profitable.

In 1870, under the name S. R. Spaulding & Son Tannery, the St. Regis firm tanned 28,800 sides of sole leather, worth $115,200. With the death of the senior Spaulding, the son's successor company, E. G. Spaulding and Co., experienced the same problems as the company's tannery at Fine. When the St. Regis Tannery was purchased by Shaw Bros. of Boston, the firm

6 Seaver, Frederick J., ibid, pp. 549-550

kept J. H. Young as agent instead of installing their agent, Lubbie. The first year they were reported to be stocking up heavily with hides and bark. It is interesting that the R. G. Dun ledger for Franklin County reports that nothing was known of the Shaw firm locally.[7]

Beer's Atlas for 1876 shows the tannery with one large building and a much smaller detatched structure. It also shows the residences of both J. H. Young and E. Spaulding, indicating the latter had moved to St. Regis Falls from Boston.

In 1880 the real property value of the St. Regis Tannery was given as $100,000. The Shaw company, which figured in so many north country tanneries, appears to have acquired another losing operation, whose worth the company overvalued. Under the Shaws, the company tanned almost twice the number of sides in 1880 as the predecessor company had in 1870 (48,000 versus 28,800), but the value of the production fell to $108,000. With $6,447 in wages, $90,000 in raw hides, and $4,560 for bark, their costs, exclusive of taxes and interest on the tannery, were almost as big as their income.[8] Local histories note that they employed upwards of a hundred and fifty men if teamsters and bark-peelers are counted.

In 1881, the tannery was rated as financially safe beyond question. Young retired in 1882 after seventeen years with the tannery. Even the advent of the railroad in 1883 did not affect the Shaw's bankruptcy, but it may have made it possible for others to continue the operation in St. Regis Falls. By 1884, after the failure of the Shaw firm, C. L. Clement, the trustee of Shaw Bros. and Co., had taken over management of the tannery. The tannery was said to have resumed in January 1886, but went out of business again under the direction of Clements by June of that year.[9]

The tannery was reorganized and renamed the St. Regis Leather Co. and converted to the production of upper leather sometime in 1887. Typically, the **Adirondack News** of March 12, 1887, in recording the change, called the St. Regis Leather Co. "one of the largest tanneries in Northern New York," employing upwards of fifty men, "but when running to full capacity doubtless double that amount will be employed."

---

[7] New York, Vol. 97, p. 373, R. G. Dun and Co.

[8] 1880 Census, Franklin County

[9] New York, Vol. 97, p. 373, R. G. Dun and Co.

The Shaw Brothers firm, which owned the St. Regis Tannery in the early 80s, figured in many bankruptcies and reorganizations of north country tanneries. Fayette Shaw began as a leather merchant in Boston in 1867, and the firm of Fayette Shaw and Bros. had several different locations in Boston in the years before 1879. Their Adirondack holdings and the firms' bankruptcy in 1883 are described in Chapter VII.

However, their bankruptcy was predictable as early as 1880, at locations other than in Franklin County. At Oregon the Census indicates costs ($150,000 in raw hides, $13,000 in wages, $15,000 in bark) were almost equal to the value of his finished leather, $180,000, this on top of a $30,000 capital investment. (While statistics from the Census for individual years are not precise indicators of profit or loss, the shrinking difference between costs and the value of the finished leather is an all too obvious trend in the 1880s, and not just for the Shaws.) Members of the Shaw firm apparently survived the company's bankruptcy, for they continued in business in Michigan, but never again in the Adirondacks.[10]

Most of the other Shaw tanneries in northern New York were dismantled shortly after the bankruptcy, but the St. Regis Leather Co. resumed operation around 1892 under the ownership of the George H. Maddox Company of Boston until 1895 and continued under the ownership of Arey, Maddock[11] & Locke until it failed for the last time in 1901. After that the tannery was converted into a chair factory.[12]

How much bark the northern tanneries drew from the mountains to the south is unclear; certainly the tanneries in Malone and Chateaugay would have hauled bark from regions now lying within the Park and it is known for certain that one of those two tanneries close to the Park was forced to haul bark from great distances. In 1895, the St. Regis Tannery or Leather Co., as a part of the George H. Maddox Company of Boston, received bark shipped via rail from the Santa Clara Lumber

---

10 Watson, *Economics of Cattlehide Tanning*, p. 29

11 The name Maddox is variously spelled Maddocks in different accounts. Maddox is believed to be correct only because it was used in the Meigs' account and in the R. G. Dun Ledgers. It is likely that the firm of George H. Maddox was reorganized as Arey, Maddox, & Locke, so ownership in the last decade of the company's existence was continuous.

12 Seaver, ibid.

Company to the south. Santa Clara employed weight as a method of determining the amount of bark, a method recorded at only one or two other sites (specifically Beaver Falls). Titus B. Meigs, who chronicled the Santa Clara Lumber Company, described a disagreement between St. Regis's local superintendent and Meigs' father over how much ice and snow figured in the weight of the bark.[13] Meigs credited his father's diplomacy with straightening out the dispute in the lumber company's favor.

Maddox and Meigs, proprietors of the two largest industries in the area, the tannery and the sawmill, figured in one of the most unusual events to befall an Adirondack tannery. When Maddox was considering reopening the tannery in 1892, his Boston firm wrote the town fathers that "if the rum traffic could be abated," the firm would move their finishing works from Lowell, Massachusetts to the St. Regis Falls Tannery. An Excise Commissioner was elected with the pledge that, "if elected, he would stand true to the cause of temperance," so the company began moving equipment into the tannery. The Commissioner "turned colors" and that same year three licenses were granted to sell rum. "According to the paper of the day, 'dozens of employees were found drunk and away from their posts of duty.' Mr. Meigs, of the Santa Clara Lumber Co., and Mr. Maddox were extremely unhappy and warned that 'something had better be done.' Something was done! A new slate of candidates was selected to redeem the pledge. Ministers from St. Regis Falls and Dickinson held evangelical services and all voters were written letters to support the anti-license cause."[14] That fall "No license" candidates were elected The company bosses were so elated the noonday whistles were sounded for half an hour, Mr. Maddox promised the townspeople that he would build a clubhouse for the young men of the town, and Mr. Meigs promised to give $100 annually to the Young Men's Christian Association.

---

[13] Meigs, Titus B. *The Santa Clara Lumber Company*, 1888-1938, p. 51

[14] Wever, Judy R. Taken from an article written by her for the **St. Regis Falls Bicentennial Newsletter** and adopted for the **Malone Evening Telegram**. Her article was based on an article in the **Adirondack News**.

The Cutting Tract

Franklin County offers a footnote to the Adirondack hemlock bark, sole-leather tanning industry, one more indication that Adirondack bark was not exhausted. In 1892, Frank A. Cutting of Boston, a hemlock bark dealer, acquired 10,000 acres around Lake Ozonia in the Town of Hopkinton, St. Lawrence County, and in adjacent Franklin County. He purchased the tract "solely for bark" and sold off the pine and spruce. The railroad was extended to the Cutting Tract west from the vicinity of McCavanaugh Pond along Stony Creek to permit the harvest of hardwoods, softwoods, and bark. Cutting built one-hundred special railroad cars to carry bark, which was shipped out of the Adirondacks up to the time the track was purchased by the Gould Paper Company in 1926.[15] The railroad cars form part of Cutting's letterhead, reproduced on page 296. Cutting apparently dealt with bark from all around the northwestern Adirondack region as well as from Canada and Maine. Incongruously, shipment of bark by railroad to the sole-leather tanneries proved to be a smaller part of the economic equation that governed the location of tanneries at the end of the nineteenth century than it had earlier. Cutting shipped bark right up to the very year that tanners solved the problems of using chrome to tan sole leather.

[15] Trimm, Paula. *Looking Back Upstream, St. Regis Falls and its Past*, pp. 94, 102.

XXIII

Epilogue

The sum of these Adirondack county stories, which tell of building roads—dirt tracks as well as plank roads—into the wilderness and constructing huge tannery buildings and the concomitant saloons, hotels, houses, stores, churches, and schools, adds up to a picture that explains the development of the Adirondacks. Tanning was the industry that settled much of the Adirondacks.

The reports of fires, the records of company stores, the memoirs of the workers, the tales of long drives by teamsters, and the cries of "the bark is gone" all breathe life into conditions a century and more ago. The ubiquitous notes on business failures, bankruptcies, and absentee owners tell a tale of a troubled industry. All this comes from reading the individual accounts.

Compare this with the knowledge that the tanning industry survived, albeit elsewhere. Note that the forests were not all gone. It is significant that none of the county chapters really explains the industry's demise or failure to expand further in the Adirondacks. These explanations lie elsewhere—in the development of big business in America. The reader is invited to return again to Part I to understand how Adirondack tanneries related to the national scene and how the industry was controlled by forces outside the mountains. Few people in the Adirondacks ever understood the industry's role in the Park. The brief introduction to what was happening nationally is necessary to understanding the dénouement of the Adirondack story; for the fate of the industry in the Adirondacks was determined by men and events in Boston, New York City, and centers in the west.

Appendix

Letter from Hon. Zadock Pratt to Campbell Morfit[1]

In his 1852 work, *The Arts of Tanning, Currying, and Leather-dressing,* Campbell Morfitt states that "the Hon. Zadock Pratt is the most experienced manufacturer of leather in the United States. He has kindly furnished me with the following particulars of his tanneries at Prattsville, N. Y., wherein it is used to the extent of 6000 cords annually." His statement is so full and comprehensive, that we give it in the original language. Pratt's account is not only the fullest description of tanning in the Catskills, it is the best description of the art as it was known at the beginning of the Adirondack hemlock bark tanning era. For that reason, most of the letter is reproduced in an appendix.

My tannery is an immense wooden building, 530 feet in length, 43 feet in breadth, and two stories and a half high. Adjoining the centre of the tannery, are two bark sheds, 125 feet long by 24 feet wide; and, near the east end of the tannery, a store-house 40 by 60. On the same level; 100 feet from the tannery, are some dozen houses, built in a line parallel with the tannery, for the convenience of the workmen. The main road through the village is about twelve rods distant, and parallel with the tannery. Within the area of the tannery are contained 300 vats, tanning over 60,000 sides a year, with conductors to draw the liquor to the pump, affording about 46,000 cubic feet of room for tanning purposes, and 7640 in the beam-house. A largewing, 40 by 80 feet, extending over the stream, contains twelve leaches, each of them furnished with copper heaters, containing about 13,000 cubic feet, and also the back loft, through which, in the course of the year, passes more than 6000 cords of bark. The mills through which it is ground are capable of grinding over a cord of bark per hour; and it has connected with it a pump of sufficient capacity to deliver 1000 feet of 'ooze,' or water charged with tannin, in 30 minutes. The beam-house contains 30 vats, equivalent to 7640 cubic feet. It has connected with it three hide mills, for softening the dry Spanish hides, and two rolling machines, capable of rolling 500 sides of leather per day. Outside of the building, but connected with the beam-house by an underground communication, are eight stonesweat-pits, with pointed arches and flues. The pins [sic] are of the most approved size, being in area 10 feet by 14, and in depth 8 feet, with a spring of water at one corner.

Since I first commenced business, the gain of weight in converting hides into leather, has been increased nearly 50 per cent.

[1] Morfit, *The Arts of Tanning, Currying, and Leather-dressing*, pp. 320-335.

That is, that from a quarter to a third more leather can now be obtained from a given quantity of hides, than at the time when I learned my trade at my father's tannery, conducted in the old-fashioned way, some 40 years ago.

The great improvement in weight seems to have been gained by the judicious use of strong liquors, or ooze," obtained from finely-ground bark, and by skillful tanning.

The loss and wastage upon hides, from hair, flesh, &c., may be estimated at from 12 to 15 per cent. In order to produce heavy weights, the hides should not be reduced too low in the beam-house, and should be tanned quickly and with good strong liquors, particularly in the latter stage of the operation. To green hides, particularly, nothing can be more injurious than to suffer them to remain too long in weak 'ooze.' They become too much reduced, grow soft, flat, and flabby, lose a portion of their gelatine, and refuse to 'plump up.'

On the other hand, however, the effects of an early application of 'ooze,' that is too strong and too warm to green hides, is very injurious. It contracts the surface fibres of the skin, tanning at once the external layers so 'dead,' as it is termed, as to shut up the pores, and prevent the tannin from penetrating the interior. This renders the leather harsh and brittle. It will from this be seen that, in the question of the proper strength of liquor alone, there is room for the exercise of the greatest judgment and the most extensive experience. In the impossibility of adapting fixed rules to the innumerable variety of cases, nothing can be depended upon but the judgment of the practical tanner.

In softening hides, and preparing them for the process of tanning, a great deal also depends upon the judgment of the person superintending the operation, inasmuch as the diversities in the qualities and characteristics of hides render it impossible to subject them to anything more than a general mode of treatment.

In 'sweating,' the character of the hides and the temperature, are essential, but every-varing [sic] considerations. As a general rule, however, the milder the process of preparing the hides for the bark, the better. Unnecessarily severe or prolonged treatment inevitably attended with a loss of gelatine, and a consequent loss of weight and strength in the leather. Too high a temperature is particularly to be avoided. In almost every lot of hides, particularly Oronocos, however, there are generally some that prove very intractable - resisting all the ordinary modes of softening. For such, a solution of ashes, potash, or even common salt, will be found to be beneficial, and pecularly so in hot weather. As I have said, no precise rule can be given as to the length of time required for the preliminary process of soaking and 'sweating,' so much depending upon the qualities of the hides, and the temperature at which these operations are conducted.

The following table may, however, be found useful in conveying an approximation to a definite idea of the practice in my tannery.

	Temperature			
Soaking days	40° days	50° days	60° days	70°
Buenos Ayres hides	10 to 12	8 to 12	6 to 8	3 to 6
Cartagena and Laguaira	8 to 12	7 to 9	5 to 7	2 to 3
Sweating				
Buenos Ayres hides	15 to 20	12 to 16	8 to 12	2 to 3
Cartegena and Laguaira	15 to 20	10 to 15	6 to 8	2 to 3

I would here remark that I changed the process from soaking to sweathing, for the sole leather, in 1836—the only change in tanning I have made for twenty years; and for heavy sole leather, it has been proved to be quite as good as liming if not better, and, somewhat cheaper; besides yielding a greater gain of weight, and when well earned, making leather more impervious to water. Liming and 'bating,' however, for upper and light leather, is preferable; and, if the same improvements had been adopted with the lime process, of strong liquor and quick tanning, it is not yet certain that the same results would have been attained.

Salted hides do not require more than two-thirds the time to soak; but generally rather longer to sweat. After the hides are prepared for tanning, the next process is what is commonly called 'handling,' which should be performed two or three times a day in a weak 'ooze,' until the grain is colored. New liquors, or a mixture of new and old, are preferable for Spanish or dry hides—old liquor for slaughter. They are then, after a fortnight, laid away in bark, and changed once in two or four weeks, until tanned. Much care and judgment are necessary in proportioning the continually increasing strength of the liquors to the requirements of the leather in the different stages of this process.

The liquors should also be kept as cool as possible within certain limits, but ought never to exceed a temperature of eighty degrees; in fact, a much lower temperature is the maximum point, if the liquor is very strong; too high a heat, with a liquor too strongly charged with the tanning principle, being invariably injurious to the life and color of the leather. From this it would seem, that time is an essential element in the process of tanning, and that we cannot make up for the want of it by increasing the strength of liquor, or raising the temperature at which the process is conducted any more than we can fatten an ox or horse by giving him more than he can eat.

I have mentioned the injurious effects resulting from too strong a solution of the active principle of the bark; on the other hand, the use of too weak solutions is to be avoided. Hides that are treated with liquor below the proper strength become much relaxed in their texture and lose a portion of their gelatine. The leather necessarily loses in weight and compactness, and is much more porous and pervious to water. The warmer the weak solutions are applied, the greater is the loss of gelatine. To ascertain whether a portion of weak liquor contains any gelatine in solution, it is only necessary to strain a little of it into a glass, and then add a small quantity of a stronger liquor. The excess of tanning in the strong seizing upon the dissolved gelatine in the weak liquor, will combine with it, and be precipitated in flakes, of a dark curdled appearance, to the bottom. At the Prattsville Tannery, the greatest strength of liquor used for handling, as indicated by Pike's barkometer, is sixteen degrees; of that employed in laying away, the greatest strength varies from thirty to forty-five degrees.

After the leather has been thoroughly tanned and rinsed, or scrubbed by a brush machine or broom, it will tend very much to improve its color and pliability to stack it up in piles, and allow it to sweat until it becomes a little slippery from a kind of mucus that collects upon its surface. A little oil added to this stage of the process or just before rolling, is found to be very useful.

Great caution is necessary in the admission of air in drying when first hung up to dry. No more air than is sufficient to keep the sides from moulding, should be allowed. Too much air, or, in other words, if dried too rapidly in a current of air, will injure the color, giving a darker hue, and rendering the leather harsh and brittle. To insure that the thick parts, or butts, shall roll smooth and even with the rest of the piece; it is necessary that the leather should be partially dried before wetting down for rolling, and that, when wet down, it should lay long enough for every side to become equally damp throughout.

The following table, condensed from the tanning records of 200,000 hides exhibits the time required to tan the various descriptions of hides at my establishment, during period of four years. It will be seen that the same descriptions of hides required different times in different years. This is owing mainly to the difference in the temperature and weather of the several seasons, and the quantity of sides and strength of liquor in the vats, and lastly to the different conditions and qualities of the different lots of the same description of hides.

(Chart shows times ranging from 4 months 20 days to 7 months 10 days. Sides were from San Juan, Orinoco, Laguaira, Matamoras, Montevideo, Honduras, Buenos Ayres, Chagres, Rio Grande, California, and Buffalo.)

From the above table, it will be seen that the average time of tanning in 1842 was five months and seventeen days; of 1843, five months and twenty-two days; of 1844, six months; and of 1845, six months and eleven days. Average of the whole time, five months and twenty-seven days. The average weight of the leather was over eighteen and one-half pounds per side. This, according to the best authorities we have at hand, is considerably below the time employed in England. There, it is not uncommon thing for eight and ten months to be employed in tanning a stock of leather, and some of the heaviest leather, it is said, takes even fourteen and eighteen months. Such deliberation undoubtedly insures a fine quality of leather, but it may be questioned whether there is not a great loss of weight—a loss of interest on capital, and in consequence an unnecessary enhancement of price, which does not suit the American market.

In order to show the amount of business done, I have carefully collected and tabularized, from my books, the following statistics of the 'Prattsville Tannery' for twenty years, in tanning about 1,000,000 sides of sole leather.

3,666 acres of bark land—10 square miles,	
18 cords to the acre—120,000; at $3 per cord	360,000
No. of days work peeling and piling ditto	118,875
4 trees to the cord	475,500
120,000 loads, or cords—264,000,000 lbs	132,000
1,444 acres of wood land—	
32,000 loads, or cords, worth	32,000
oats	41,000
hay	2,500
313,000 days' work in tannery-	
1,000 years labor at $14 per month	162,000
Board at $1.50 per week	78,000
500,000 hides weighing 10,000,000 lbs.	1,750,000

And in justice to my workmen, I ought to say, without the use of ardent spirits, or ever having a side of leather stolen.

A glance at this table will at once convince any one that the advantages of such an establishment are not confined to the amount of value produced.

Bibliography

Primary Sources

United States Census of Manufactures, 1850, 1860, 1870, and 1880. All information on tanneries for the 12 counties that intersect or comprise the Adirondack Park.

Census of the State of New York, 1855, 1865, 1875

R. G. Dun and Co. Collection: County ledgers in the collection for Boston, Mass., New York City, and Warren, Essex, Clinton, Fulton, Oneida, Lewis, Franklin, and St. Lawrence Counties were consulted. These ledgers, whose volume and page citations are referenced, contain information on businesses and businessmen from the late 1840s through the 1880s. The ledgers are in the Manuscript and Archive Department, Baker Library, Harvard University Graduate School of Business Administration.

Unpublished Articles

Broutty, Linda and Joan Schlier. *History of Jerden Falls*. Crogan, New York.

Girard, Frank B. *The History of Griffin*. Paper delivered to the Hamilton County Historical Society.

Meigs, Titus B. *The Santa Clara Lumber Company*, 1888-1938, Collection of the Adirondack Museum.

Murphy, James A. *The Wevertown Tannery*, talk prepared with the help of Lewis Waddell, Town Historian, and given to the Historical Society.

Hough, Marjorie G., *A Tannery at Jordan Falls*, Lewis County, paper in the Lewis County Historical Society.

Letters and Original Documents

Lee Claflin & Son, numerous letters concerning the Wheelerville tannery

Osborne, Myron, Assignee: "Valuable Property for Sale"

Hayes, James Truman: Letter dictated to Albro Tripp, 1969, concerning tanbarking in Essex County. Collection of Warder Cadbury

Deeds, Hamilton County, Books 10, 15, and 24

Dodge, David. *Diary*, January 1887 through October 1889. Copy of the Diary was given me by William Waddell of North Creek. A copy is now in the Adirondack Museum.

Girard, Frank B. *History of Griffin*, with maps of the tannery site, private papers of family reminiscences.

Grider, Rufus A. *Souvenir of Canada Lake, New York 1896*. Notebook of watercolor sketches and interviews with local people. In private hands.

Indenture and Deed between Jonathan Thorne and Burnam & Gray, Warrensburg, January 15, 1838.

La Dew Ledgers, 1857-1865; four volumes relating to the (Ladue) La Dew Tannery and the company store, collection of the Herkimer County Historical Society.

St. Lawrence County Tannery Ledgers, 1885, 1896, 1897, in the collection of the Colton Historical Society Museum

Tumminello, Joan Dromgoole. *A History of the Middleville Tannery*. September 1987, Paper in the Herkimer County Historical Society.

Wheeler Claflin Company Store, Inventory, 1883, gift of the Peters Family to the Caroga Museum.

Wheeler Claflin Payroll, 1870-1879. In private hands.

Published Primary Sources

Child, Hamilton. *Gazetteer and Business Directory of Lewis County, 1872-1873*. Syracuse: Journal Office, 1872.

Dictionary of Terms Used in the Hides, Skins and Leather Trade. United States Department of Agriculture, Handbook No. 465, April, 1974.

Dutton, John. *My Last Pilgrimage, Ch. V,* privately printed

Atlases

Atlas of Clinton County. New York: F. W. Beers, A. D. Ellis and G. G. Soule, 1869.

Atlas of Franklin County New York. Philadelphia: D. G. Beers and Co. 1876

Atlas of Herkimer County New York. New York: Beach Nichols, 1868.

Atlas of Lewis County. Philadelphia: Pomeroy and Whitman, 1875

Atlas of Montgomery and Fulton Counties, New York. New York: J. J. Stranahan and Beach Nichols, 1868.

Atlas of Oneida County New York. New York: D. G. Beers and Co., 1874.

New Topographical Atlas of Essex County. Philadephia: O. W. Gray and Son, 1876.

New Topographical Atlas of St. Lawrence County New York. Philadelphia, Stone and Stewart, 1865

Warren County New York. New York: F. W. Beers and Co., 1876

Interviews with and letters from descendents of tannery owners and workers

Farrar Family: Stewart Farrar, Warrensburg

Girard Family: Ouida Girard, Lake Pleasant

Sawyer Family: Janet Appleyard, Glens Falls

Bowman Tannery: Ira Gray, Saratoga County

Letters or interviews with bits and pieces

David G. Bailey, Research Leader, Hides and Leather Laboratory, USDA, Philadelphia, PA

Warder Cadbury, Albany

George Cataldo, Glenfield

Bruce Cole, Crandall Library, Glens Falls

Isabell Cornell, Warrensburg

Ira Gray, Saratoga County

Cynthia Hennessy and Chris Murphy, Colton

Randall Huta, Piseco
Tim Fitzgerald, Boonville
Paul Jamieson, Canton
Richard Nason, Facts compiled from Finch, Pruyn and Co. records
Peter O'Shea, Fine
Jack Parsall, Beaver Falls
George Philips, Chestertown
Philip G. Terrie, Bowling Green University
William Waddell, North Creek
Judy Wever, St. Regis Falls
Janice Whipple, Stony Creek Historical Society

Correspondence and Papers from Town and County Historians

Ted Aber, Hamilton County Historian
Jim Bailey, Plattsburgh Historian
Matthew J. Conway, Forestport
Shirley Dietch, Town of Morehouse
Caroline Fish, Town Historian Chestertown
Marion Holmes, Town of Webb Historical Society
Dorothea Ives, Town of Salisbury Historian: items from town files and personal letters
Diane Jones, Assistant, St. Lawrence County Historical Society
Mabel Jones, Town of Minerva Historian
Molly Lowell, Essex County Historical Society
Dorothy O'Brien, Lyonsdale Historian
Susan R. Perkins,
Helen Persons, Town Historian Horicon
Jane Spellman, Director, Herkimer County Historical Society
Mabel Tucker, Town of Warrensburg Historian
Pamela Vogel, Warren County Historian
Lewis Waddell, Town of Johnsburgh Historian
Marion Webb, Town of Webb Historical Association, Old Forge

Secondary Sources

Published

Aber, Ted and Stella King. *History of Hamilton County*. Lake Pleasant, New York: Great Wilderness Books, 1965.

Beetle, David K. *Up Old Forge Way and the West Canada Creek.* Old Forge, New York: North County Books, 1972.

Benton, Nathaniel S. *History of Herkimer County*. Albany: J. Munsell, 1856

Bowen, G. Byron. *History of Lewis County*, 1880-1965. Lewis County, New York: Board of Supervisors, 1970.

Brown, William H., Editor. *A History of Warren County, New York.* Glens Falls: Glens Falls Publishing Company, 1963.

Campbell, Morfit. *The Arts of Tanning, Currying, and Leather Dressing*. Philadelphia, Henry Carey Baird & Co., 1852.

Coffin, Nathaniel Wheeler. *The Forest Arcadia of Northern New York.* Boston: T. O. H. P. Burnham, 1864.

Contributors to **Hide and Leather**. *Modern American Tanning*. Compiled from articles printed in **Hide and Leather** and written by well-known Tannery Foremen, Superintendents, and Chemists. Chicago: Jacobsen Publishing Co. 1902.

Conway, Matthew J. *Port Leyden "The Iron City"*. Woodgate, New York: Tug Hill Books, 1898.

Davis, Charles Thomas. *The Manufacture of Leather*, first edition 1885, second edition 1897. Philadelphia: Henry Carey Baird & Co., 1897

Dunn, Violet B. Editor-in-chief. *Saratoga County Heritage*, Saratoga, New York: Saratoga County Historical Society, 1974.

Fels, Rendig. *American Business Cycles, 1865 - 1897,* Chapel Hill: University of North Carolina Press, 1959.

Forest Commission of the State of New York. *First Annual Report to the Legislature, 1885,* #103 Assembly. Albany, New York: The Argus Press, 1889.

Fox, William F. *The Adirondack Black Spruce; From the First Annual Report of the Forest Commission for 1894.* Albany: James B. Lyon and Co. 1864.

Fox, William F. *History of the Lumber Industry in the State of New York.* 6th Annual Report of the New York Fish and Game Commission, 1901. Reprinted: Harrison, New York: Harbor Hills Books, 1976.

French, J. H. *Gazateer of the State of New York,* Port Washington, New York: Ira J. Friedman, Inc., 1860

Garraty, John A. *The New Commonwealth, 1877-1890.* New York: Harper and Row, Publishers, 1968.

Grady, Joseph F. *The Adirondacks: Fulton Chain - Big Moose Region.* Old Forge, New York: North Country Books, 1933; Second Edition, 1966.

Hardin, George Anson and Willard, Frank Hallett. *History of Herkimer County, New York.* Syracuse, N. Y. D. Mason & Co., 1893

Haring, H. A. *Our Catskills,* Chapter V, The Hemlocks and Tanbark Peeling, New York: G. P. Putnam's Sons, 1931.

Hazard, Blanch Evans. *The Origin of Boot and Shoe Industry In Massachusetts Before 1875.* Harvard Economic Studies. Volume XXIII. Cambridge: Harvard University Press, 1921.

Hillebrandt, William. *Hides and Hemlock - A Short History of Bleeker,* privately printed by the author in Bleeker, 1976.

History of Montgomery and Fulton Counties. New York: F. W. Beers & Co. 1878

Hough, Franklin B. *A History of Lewis County.* Syracuse, N. Y.: D. Mason & Co. 1883.

Hurd, Duane Hamilton. *History of Clinton and Franklin Counties.* Philadelphia, J. W. Lewis Company, reprint 1979.

Lamb, Wallace E. *The Lake Champlain and Lake George Valleys, Vol II.* New York: The American Historical Co., Inc., 1940

Landon, Harry F. *A History Embracing Jefferson, St. Lawrence, Oswego, Lewis, and Franklin Counties, New York,* Three Volumes. Indianapolis, Indiana: Historical Publishing Company, 1932.

Lee, Hon. Gideon. *Two Lectures on Tanning.* New York: The Eclectic Fraternity, 1838

Kudish, Michael. *Where Did the Railroads Go?* Saranac Lake, New York: The Chauncey Press, 1985.
Mason, Howard C. *Backward Glances*. Volume I, II, III. Glens Falls, New York: Webster Mimeoprint Services, 1965
McMartin, Barbara. *Caroga - The Town Recalls its Past.* Caroga, New York: The Town of Caroga, 1976.
Minerva Historical Society. *Minerva 1817-1967, a History of a Town in Essex County.* Minerva, New York: Minerva Historical Society, 1968
New England Tanners Club. *Leather Facts*. Peabody, Mass.: New England Tanners Club, 1965, eighth printing 1977.
Norcross, Frank W. *A History of the New York Swamp*. New York: Published for the Author by the Chiswick Press, 1901.
Norris, James D. *R. G. Dun & Co. 1841-1900. The Development of Credit Reporting in the Nineteenth Century*. Bridgeport, Conn.: Greenwood Press, 1978.
Reed, Lorena Bullis. *Colton Story of a Town*. Colton, NY: Colton Historical Society, 1976
Seaver, Frederick J. *Historical Sketches of Franklin County*. Albany: J. B. Lyon, 1918
Simms, Jeptha R. *Trappers of New York, A Biography of Nicholas Stoner and Nathaniel Foster*. Albany: J. Munsell and Co. 1857
Smith, H. P. *A History of Warren County*, Syracuse: D. Mason and Co., 1885.
Thomas, Howard. *Black River in the North Country*. Prospect, New York: Prospect Books, 1978; first printing 1963.
Thomas, Lester St. John. *Timber Tannery and Tourists*. Lake Luzerne, New York: Committee on Publication of Local History, 1979.
Three G Fire Department. *History of Glenfield, Glendale, Grieg, Brantingham*, privately printed 1971
Trimm, Paula. *Looking Back Upstream: St. Regis Falls and Its Past. St.* Regis Falls, New York:
VanArnum, Lewis S. *Beaver Falls Cavalcade, 1794-1979*. Beaver Falls, New York, Lewis S. VanArnum, 1979.
VanWagenen, Jared, Jr. *The Golden Age of Homespun*. New York. Hill and Wang, published for the New York State Historical Society, American Century Series, 1953.
Warren County Board of Supervisors. *Warren County, a History and Guide*. Glens Falls, New York: American Guide Company, 1942.
Watson, Merrill A., D.C.S. *Economics of Cattlehide Leather Tanning*. Chicago, Illinois: The Rumpf Publishing Company, 1940.
Watson, Winslow C. *The Military and Civil History of the County of Essex, New York*. Albany, New York: J. Munsell, 1869.
Whipple, Janice M. *Stony Creek Then & Now*. Stony Creek, New York: Stony Creek Historical Society, 1980.

Periodicals

Gloversville Intelligencer, Gloversville, New York, Numerous articles, dates cited in text.
Industry and the Saranac, **Plattsburgh Republican**, March 27, 1875
W. and E Sawyer's Tannery at Ellenburgh, **Plattsburgh Republican,** March 16, 1878.

Old Days at Horicon, James Truman Hayes of North Argyle recollections, **Glens Falls Star**, 1941.
Plattsburgh Sentinel, July 23, 1869; October 10, 1890
Warrensburg News. Numerous articles, dates cited in text.

Magazines

Brownell, Catherine J. *The Old Tannery at Fine,* **The Quarterly**, Official Publication of the St. Lawrence County Historical Society, October 1963, p. 7
Farrar, Stewart. *Tanneries in Warren County.* **Adirondack Life,** June 27, 1968
Hastings, John T. *Hemlock and Hides,* **Adirondack Bits and Pieces**, Volume No. 3, Spring-Summer 1984.
Hough, Marjorie G. *Tannery Days at Jorden Falls, A Tanner's Daughter's Recollections.* **North Country Life**, Volume 6, No. 1, Winter 1952.
Macbride, David. *An Improved Method of Tanning Leather,* 1771, with an Introduction by Peter C. Welsh. **The Smithsonian Journal of History**, Volume 2, Number 4, Winter 1967-1968
Harper's Weekly, Volume XXXIV, No. 1727, pp. 171-172, *A Day in a Tannery,* sketches
Welsh, Peter C. *A Craft That Resisted Change: American Tanning Practices to 1850.* **Technology and Culture**, Vol IV, No. 3, Summer 1963.
The Lumber Camp News. December 1942. Short article, no author or title.

Unpublished Secondary Sources

Ellsworth, Lucius Fuller. *Craft to National Industry in the Nineteenth Century: A Case Study of the Transformation of the New York State Tanning Industry.* PhD Thesis for the University of Delaware, 1971; University Microfilms.
Hastings, John T. *Hemlock and Hides: The Tanning Industry in Warren County,* Paper completed for History 275, Adirondack Community College.

Photographs

The Adirondack Museum, Blue Mountain Lake
John Teachout, Griffin, New York
Bruce and Millie Busch, Caroga
Caroga Historical Association and the Town of Caroga
Stephen Farrar, Warrensburg
Lester St. John Thomas, Luzerne
Stony Creek Historical Association
Town of Webb Historical Association
Lewis S. VanArnum, Beaver Falls

Index